TAKING SIDES

Clashing Views on Controversial

Issues in Mass Media and Society

SEVENTH EDITION

TAKING SIDES

Clashing Views on Controversial

Issues in Mass Media and Society

SEVENTH EDITION

Selected, Edited, and with Introductions by

Alison Alexander
University of Georgia

and

Jarice Hanson
Quinnipiac University

McGraw-Hill/Dushkin
A Division of The McGraw-Hill Companies

Photo Acknowledgment
Cover image: © 2003 by PhotoDisc, Inc.

Cover Art Acknowledgment
Charles Vitelli

Library of Congress Cataloging-in-Publication Data
Main entry under title:
Taking sides: clashing views on controversial issues in mass media and society/selected, edited,
and with introductions by Alison Alexander and Jarice Hanson.—7th ed.
Includes bibliographical references and index.
1. Mass media. 2. Information services. I. Alexander, Alison, *comp.* II. Hanson, Jarice, *comp.*
302.23
0-07-282819-6
94-31766

Printed on Recycled Paper

Preface

Comprehension without critical evaluation is impossible.

— Friedrich Hegel (1770–1831)
German philosopher

Mass communication is one of the most popular college majors in the country, which perhaps reflects a belief in the importance of communications systems as well as a desire to work within the communications industry. This book, which contains 36 selections presented in a pro and con format, addresses 18 different controversial issues in mass communications and society. The purpose of this volume, and indeed of any course that deals with the social impact of media, is to create a literate consumer of media—someone who can walk the fine line between a naive acceptance of all media and a cynical disregard for any positive benefits that they may offer.

The media today reflect the evolution of a nation that has increasingly seized on the need and desire for more leisure time. Technological developments have increased our range of choices—from the number of broadcast or cable channels we can select to the publications we can read that cater specifically to our individual interests and needs. New and improving technologies allow us to choose when and where to see a film (through the magic of the VCR), to create our preferred acoustical environment (by stereo, CD, or portable headphones), and to communicate over distances instantly (by means of computers and electronic mail). Because these many forms of media extend our capacities to consume media content, the study of mass media and society is the investigation of some of our most common daily activities. Since many of the issues in this volume are often in the news (or even *are* the news!), you may already have opinions on them. We encourage you to read the selections and discuss the issues with an open mind. Even if you do not initially agree with a position or do not even understand how it is possible to make the opposing argument, give it a try. We believe that thinking seriously about mass media is an important goal.

Plan of the book This book is primarily designed for students in an introductory course in mass communication (sometimes called introduction to mass media or introduction to mass media and society). The issues are such that they can be easily incorporated into any media course regardless of how it is organized—thematically, chronologically, or by medium. The 36 selections have been taken from a variety of sources and were chosen because of their usefulness in defending a position and for their accessibility to students.

Each issue in this volume has an issue *introduction,* which sets the stage for the debate as it is argued in the YES and NO selections. Each issue concludes with a *postscript* that makes some final observations about the selections, points the way to other questions related to the issue, and offers suggestions for further reading on the issue. The introductions and postscripts do not preempt what is the reader's own task: to achieve a critical and informed view of the issues at stake. In reading an issue and forming your own opinion you should not feel confined to adopt one or the other of the positions presented. Some readers may see important points on both sides of an issue and may construct for themselves a new and creative approach. Such an approach might incorporate the best of both sides, or it might provide an entirely new vantage point for understanding. Relevant Internet site addresses (URLs) that may prove useful as starting points for further research are provided on the *On the Internet* page that accompanies each part opener. At the back of the book is a listing of all the *contributors to this volume,* which will give you additional information on the communication scholars, practitioners, policymakers, and media critics whose views are debated here.

Changes to this edition   This seventh edition represents a considerable revision. There are 6 completely new issues: *Do African American Stereotypes Still Dominate Entertainment Television?* (Issue 4); *Do the Mass Media Undermine Openness and Accountability in Democracy?* (Issue 8); *Do the Media Have a Liberal Bias?* (Issue 10); *Have the Direction and Power of the FCC Changed?* (Issue 13); *Is Civic Journalism Good Journalism?* (Issue 15); *Have the News Media Improved Since 9/11?* (Issue 16). In addition, for Issue 1, *Are American Values Shaped by the Mass Media?* the issue question has been retained but the Yes-side selection has been replaced to bring a fresh perspective to the debate. For Issue 14, *Media Monopolies: Does Concentration of Ownership Jeopardize Media Content?* the issue question has also been retained but both the Yes- and No-side selections have been replaced. Issue 18, *Will Technology Change Social Interaction?* contains a new issue question and a new Yes-side selection. In all, there are 16 new readings.

A word to the instructor   An *Instructor's Manual With Test Questions* (multiple-choice and essay) is available through the publisher for the instructor using *Taking Sides* in the classroom. And a general guidebook, *Using Taking Sides in the Classroom,* which discusses methods and techniques for integrating the pro-con approach into any classroom setting, is also available. An online version of *Using Taking Sides in the Classroom* and a correspondence service for *Taking Sides* adopters can be found at http://www.dushkin.com/usingts/.

   Taking Sides: Clashing Views on Controversial Issues in Mass Media and Society is only one title in the Taking Sides series. If you are interested in seeing the table of contents for any of the other titles, please visit the Taking Sides Web site at http://www.dushkin.com/takingsides.

Acknowledgments   We wish to acknowledge the encouragement, support, and detail given to this project. We are particularly grateful to Theodore Knight, list manager for the Taking Sides series. We are extremely thankful for the care given to the project by all of the staff at McGraw-Hill/Dushkin, and in particular Rose Gleich, administrative assistant, and Juliana Gribbins, developmental editor.

We would also like to thank Cheryl Christopher at the University of Georgia for her valuable assistance. Finally, we would like to thank our families and friends (Frank, James, Katie, James Jr., Torie, and Fatime Chahou) for their patience and understanding during the period in which we prepared this book.

Alison Alexander
University of Georgia

Jarice Hanson
Quinnipiac University

Contents In Brief

Contents

Professor of journalism and sociology Todd Gitlin addresses how hegemony works in entertainment television. How, he asks, do the formal and familiar devices of entertainment work to relay and reproduce ideology? His answer is that ideology is embedded in format, genre, setting and character types, slant, and solution. Professors of communication Horace Newcomb and Paul M. Hirsch counter that television serves as a site of negotiation for cultural issues, images, and ideas. Viewer selection from among institutional choices is a negotiation process as viewers select from a wide set of approaches to issues and ideas.

W. James Potter, a professor of communication, examines existing research in the area of children and television violence. Such research is extensive and covers a variety of theoretical and methodological areas. He examines the nature of the impact of television on children and concludes that strong evidence exists for harmful effects. Jib Fowles, a professor of communication, finds the research on children and television violence less convincing. Despite the number of studies, he believes that the overall conclusions are unwarranted. Fowles finds that the influence is small, lab results are artificial, and fieldwork is inconclusive. In short, he finds television violence research flawed and unable to prove a linkage between violent images and harm to children.

Marketing professors Mary C. Martin and James W. Gentry address the literature dealing with advertising images and the formation of body identity for preadolescent and adolescent females. They report a study to explore how social comparison theory influences young women. *Washington Monthly* editor Michelle Cottle takes the perspective that females are not the only ones influenced by media image. She cites polls and magazine advertising that indicate that males are exposed to images of idealized body type as well, and she argues that these images also have an impact on the male psyche.

Professor and author Donald Bogle offers a comprehensive analysis of African Americans on network series. He traces their role on prime time from the negative stereotypes of the 1950s to the current more subtle stereotypes of the 1990s. Bogle tackles the shows of the 1990s, particularly the popular and controversial *Martin*. Professor and author John McWhorter counters that stereotypes are diminishing in America. In his review of Bogle's book, McWhorter asserts that Bogle has donned an ideological straitjacket, which blinds him to the strides that African Americans have made in prime time. He concludes that the continued search for stereotypes prevents us from seeing the very real changes that have taken place in the media.

PART 2 MEDIA ETHICS 99

President of NBC News Michael Gartner argues that identifying accusers in rape cases will destroy many of society's wrongly held impressions and stereotypes about the crime of rape. Katha Pollitt, journalist and social critic, argues that the decision to reveal victims' identities without their consent cannot be justified.

Doctor Joseph R. DiFranza and his colleagues report a national study that examines the possibility of children being tempted to smoke because of the tobacco industry's use of images that appeal to and are remembered by children. Because of the profound health risks, DiFranza et al. call for restrictions on tobacco ads. Attorney George J. Annas agrees that the tobacco industry has marketed products to children, but he maintains that efforts to restrict advertising are inappropriate, perhaps even illegal. He argues that some of the restrictions that have been placed on tobacco advertisements violate the First Amendment.

John E. Calfee, a former U.S. Trade Commission economist, takes the position that advertising is very useful to people and that the information that advertising imparts helps consumers make better decisions. He maintains that the benefits of advertising far outweigh the negative criticisms. Author Russ Baker focuses on the way in which advertisers seek to control magazine content and, thus, go beyond persuasion and information into the realm of influencing the content of other media.

Yale Law School professor J. M. Balkin argues that without media, openness and accountability are impossible in contemporary democracies. However, he also states that television tends to convert political coverage into entertainment. Current focus on the "horse race" aspects of campaigns and personal scandal is detrimental to media's central mission of communicating information, holding officials accountable, and uncovering secrets. University of London legal theory professor Roger Cotterrell suggests that Balkin's argument implicitly assumes that there is a political reality or "truth," which he argues is illusory. He contends that transparency in media coverage should emphasize breach of trust as the justification for publicizing personal conduct and treat scandal as the public revelation of these breaches of trust.

Larry J. Sabato, professor of government, Mark Stencel, politics editor for
Washingtonpost.com, and S. Robert Lichter, president of the Center for
Media and Public Affairs, assert that the line dividing public life and private
life is more blurred than ever. The authors state that this is creating an age
of scandal. They conclude that this focus on politics-by-scandal results in
disaffected voters, discouraged political candidates, and news devoid of
analysis of policy issues and substantive debate. William G. Mayer, assistant professor of political science, defends negative campaigning as a
necessity in political decision making. He argues that society must provide the public with the substantive information needed to make informed
decisions at the polls and insists that this must occur during political campaigns. Therefore negative campaigns are needed so that citizens can
make intelligent choices concerning their leaders.

Journalist Bernard Goldberg looks at the common phrase, "the media elite
have a liberal bias," and gives examples of the way coverage becomes
slanted, depending upon the reporter's or anchor's perception of the subject's political stance. Journalist James Wolcott examines the impact of
Fox television network's conservative approach, as evidenced by the news
programs that feature right-wing pundits and pro-Republican views. He
contends that Fox's news and public affairs coverage attained the highest
ratings when appealing to the "angry white male."

Author Michael A. Banks explains that as more people turn to libraries
for Internet access, libraries and communities have been forced to come
to grips with the conflict between freedom of speech and objectional material on the World Wide Web and in Usenet newsgroups. He adds that
software filters are tools that help librarians keep inappropriate materials
out of the library. The American Civil Liberties Union (ACLU) concludes

that mandatory blocking software in libraries is both inappropriate and unconstitutional. Blocking censors valuable speech and gives librarians, educators, and parents a false sense of security when providing minors with Internet access, argues the ACLU.

Senators Paul Simon, Sam Brownback, and Joseph Lieberman speak up on why cleaning up television is important to the nation. They detail the frustrating experiences that caused them to support legislation to clean up television. Marjorie Heins, founding director of the American Civil Liberties Union's Arts Censorship Project, poses three questions about television ratings: First, what is the ratings system meant to accomplish? Second, who will rate programming, and how? Third, what are the likely political and artistic effects of the ratings scheme? The V-chip and television ratings will do nothing, she argues, to solve the problems of American youth and society.

Since the passage of the Telecommunications Act of 1996, the Federal Communications Commission (FCC) has undergone several revisions of its mission. Professor Robert W. McChesney and author John Nichols discuss the "media reform movement" and outline the purpose of several interest groups to deal with the FCC's changes. In particular, they critique the current role of the FCC with Commissioner Michael Powell with regard to whether or not the FCC can still claim to operate in the "public interest." Author Brendan I. Koerner sees any changes under Powell's FCC leadership as more of the same pandering to industry ties that characterized past commissions. While he feels that the direction of the FCC has been driven for some time by the promise of digital technology, he speculates that technology is now leading regulation. In this case, the power of the FCC can be seen to encourage mergers that will ultimately result in greater involvement and control by multimedia corporations.

Ben H. Bagdikian, a Pulitzer Prize–winning journalist, argues that the public must be aware of the control that international conglomerates have over the media. He contends that despite hopes that new technologies would control giant corporations, these corporations have wrested control of the production and distribution of most of the media content in the world. Conglomerate domination remains, concludes Bagdikian. Professor Michael Curtin questions whether or not concentration of media ownership leads to a conservative, homogenous flow of popular imagery. For example, television contexts around the world are increasingly featuring female characters who resist conventional gender roles. This happens because media firms benefit from transnational circulation of multiple and alternative representations of feminine desire.

Issue 15. Is Civic Journalism Good Journalism? 322

Chuck Clark, government editor of the *Charlotte Observer,* defends the use of civic journalism by the *Observer* in covering election campaigns in North Carolina. He describes the publication's goal: to provide the readers of the newspaper with enough relevant information to make decisions concerning the elections. William E. Jackson, Jr., professor and U.S. House candidate in 1996, criticizes the use of civic journalism. He charges that coverage was narrowly focused on only a few issues, evolving issues were ignored, and important other races were not covered. According to Jackson, political coverage and the people of North Carolina suffered because of this experiment in civic journalism.

Issue 16. Have the News Media Improved Since 9/11? 344

Media critic Ken Auletta discusses how the events of September 11, 2001, refocused news journalism toward foreign news and an explanation of world events. He discusses the industry's decisions about news, and the motivation of journalists who want to cover issues in greater depth. Michael Parks, director of the School of Journalism at the University of Southern California, warns that as the terrorist events recede in our memories, print and broadcast journalists will return to the same tactics they used prior to September 11th. These include less of an interest in foreign news, primarily because of the financial costs borne by the media industries.

PART 6 THE INFORMATION SOCIETY 359

Journalist Simson Garfinkel discusses how today's technology has the potential to destroy our privacy. He makes the case that the government and individuals could take steps to protect themselves against privacy abuse, particularly by returning to the groundwork set by the government in the 1970s and by educating people on how to avoid privacy traps. *Forbes* reporter Adam L. Penenberg discusses his own experiences with an Internet detective agency, and he explains how easy it is for companies to get unauthorized access to personal information. He specifically describes how much, and where, personal information is kept and the lack of safeguards in our current system.

Author Matt Goldberg discusses the way in which the estimated 150 million people around the world are changing their social interaction habits and expectations, thanks to the ability to use instant messaging (IM). By focusing on this one particular application of technology, he offers specific behavioral changes and attitudes observed in some of the IM users and then speculates as to what the eventual outcome will be as more people use IM for a broader range of purposes. Professor Peter F. Drucker, a noted expert on technological change, outlines a history of social organization in relation to technology in order to put the "information revolution" into perspective. He compares the changes in our present and future lives to the introduction of the Industrial Revolution and reminds us that while social change often takes much longer than the term *revolution* suggests, the real impact of social change is often accompanied by more subtle shifts in our institutions.

Introduction

Ways of Thinking About Mass Media and Society

Alison Alexander

Jarice Hanson

The media are often scapegoats for the problems of society. Sometimes the relationships between social issues and media seem too obvious *not* to have some connection. For example, violence in the media may be a reflection of society, or, as some critics claim, violence in the media makes it seem that violence in society is the norm. But, in reality, one important reason that the media are so often blamed for social problems is that the media are so pervasive. Their very ubiquity makes them seem more influential than they actually are. If one were to look at the statistics on violence in the United States, one would see that there are fewer violent acts performed today than in recent history—but the presence of this violence in the media, through reportage or fictional representation, makes it appear more prevalent.

There are many approaches to investigating the relationships that are suggested by media and society. From an organizational perspective, the producers of media must find content and distribution forms that will be profitable. They therefore have a unique outlook on the audience as consumers. From the perspective of the creative artist, the profit motive may be important, but the exploration of the unique communicative power of the media may be paramount. The audience, too, has different use patterns and desires for information or entertainment, and consumers demonstrate a variety of choices in content offered to them as well as what they take from the media. Whether the media reflect society or shape society has a lot to do with the dynamic interaction of many of these different components.

To complicate matters, the "mass" media have changed in recent years. Not long ago, "mass" media referred to messages that were created by large organizations for broad, heterogeneous audiences. This concept no longer suffices for contemporary media environments. While the "mass" media still exist in the forms of radio, television, film, and general interest newspapers and magazines, many media forms today are hybrids of "mass" and "personal" media technologies that open a new realm of understanding about how audiences process the meaning of the messages. Digital technologies and distribution forms have created many opportunities for merging (or converging) media. The Internet, for example, has the capacity to transmit traditional voice, mail, text, and image-based content in a unique form of instant communication while the senders of the messages may be, or appear to be, anonymous. Time-shifting, memory, storage of information, and truth all play important roles in the use of Internet communication, and call our attention to aspects of the communicative process that need fresh examination.

Still, most of the new services and forms of media rely, in part, on the major mass media distribution forms and technologies of television, radio, film, and print. The challenge, then, is to understand how individuals in society use media in a variety of formats and contexts and how they make sense of the messages they take from the content of those media forms.

Historically, almost every form of media in the United States was first subject to some type of regulation by the government or by the media industry itself. This has changed over the years; there is now a virtually unregulated media environment in which the responsibility for the content of media no longer rests with higher authorities. We, as consumers, are asked to be critical of the media that we consume. This requires that we be educated consumers, rather than rely on standards and practices of industry or on government intervention into situations involving questionable content. Although this may not seem like a big problem for most adults, the questions become more difficult when we consider how children use the media to form judgments or seek information.

The growing media landscape is changing our habits. The average American still spends over three hours a day viewing television, which is on in the average home for over seven hours a day. Politics and political processes have changed, in part, due to the way politicians use the media to reach voters. A proliferation of television channels has resulted from the popularity of cable, but does cable offer anything different from broadcast television? Videocassettes deliver feature-length films to the home, changing the traditional practices of viewing films in a public place and video distribution via the Internet is now a practical option for anyone who has transmission lines with the capacity to download large files. The recording industry is still reeling over the impact of MP3 and free software that allows consumers to sample, buy, or download music online. Communications is now a multibillion-dollar industry and the third fastest-growing industry in America. One can see that the media have changed American society, but our understanding of how and why remains incomplete.

Dynamics of Interaction

In recent years, the proliferation of new forms of media has changed on a global scale. In the United States, 98 percent of homes have at least one telephone, though there are places in the world where phone lines may be limited or where telephones do not exist at all. Over 98 percent of the United States population has access to at least one television set, but in some parts of the world televisions are still viewed communally, or viewed only at certain hours of the day. The use of home computers and the Internet grows annually in the United States by leaps and bounds, but still, only one third of the world has access to the Web. These figures demonstrate that the global media environment is still far from equitable, and they suggest that different cultures may use the media in different ways.

But apart from questions of access and availability, many fundamental questions about the power of media in any society remain the same. How do audiences use the media available to them? How do message senders produce meaning? How much of the meaning of any message is produced by the audience? Increasingly important is, how do additional uses of media change our interpersonal environments and human interactions?

Within the same framework for discussion, we must examine the power and potential of any media organization to merge and control more of what is seen and heard through the media. Once, there were more than 20 major competing media companies in the United States spanning from print to television broadcasting. Now, as one of the selection authors in this volume suggests, there are only nine companies worldwide that produce the greatest amount of media content and utilize all forms of distribution. What then, is the impact of this type of control over content?

As we begin a new century with new forms of communication, many of the institutions we have come to depend upon are undergoing massive changes. The recording industry is perhaps one of the most rapidly changing fields, with microradio and webstreaming offering different alternatives for message distribution. It is not surprising that the CD industry recently lowered prices in order to save sales at the same time that the group Metallica entered into a lawsuit against the firm Napster.com, which allowed free downloads of music files from one personal computer to another. We can expect to continue to see threats and challenges to our traditional media systems in the future. Even the ubiquitous personal computer could become obsolete with personal desk assistant (PDAs) offering cheaper, more portable forms of computing, and, in particular, linkage to the Internet.

Progress in Media Research

Much of media research has been in search of theory. Theory is an organized, commonsense refinement of everyday thinking; it is an attempt to establish a systematic view of a phenomenon in order to better understand that phenomenon. Theory is tested against reality to establish whether or not it is a good explanation. So, for example, a researcher might notice that what is covered by news outlets is very similar to what citizens say are the important issues of the day. From such observation came agenda setting (the notion that media confers importance on the topics it covers, directing public attention to what is considered important).

Much early media research comes from the impact and effect of print media, because print has long been regarded as a permanent record of history and events. The ability of newspapers and books to shape and influence public opinion was regarded as necessary to the founding of new forms of governments—including the United States government. But the bias of the medium carried certain restrictions with it. Print media was necessarily limited to those individuals who could read. The relationships of information control and the power of these forms of communication to influence readers contributed to the belief that reporting should be objective and fair and that a multiple number of views should be available.

The principles that emerged from this relationship were addressed in an often-quoted statement attributed to Thomas Jefferson, who wrote, "Were it left to me to decide whether we should have a government without newspapers, or newspapers without a government, I should not hesitate a moment to prefer the latter." But the next sentence in Jefferson's statement is equally as important: "But I should mean that every man should receive those papers and be capable of reading them."

Today media research on the relationships of media senders, the channels of communication, and the receivers of messages is not enough. Consumers must realize that "media literacy" is an important concept. People can no longer take for granted that the media exist primarily to provide news, information, and entertainment. They must be more attuned to what media content says about them as individuals and as members of a society. By integrating these various cultural components, the public can better criticize the regulations or lack of regulation that permits media industries to function the way they do. People must realize that individuals may read media content differently.

The use of social science data to explore the effects of media on audiences strongly emphasized psychological and sociological schools of thought. It did not take long to move from the "magic bullet theory"—which proposed that media had a major direct effect on the receivers of the message and that the message intended by the senders was indeed injected into the passive receiver— to theories of limited and indirect effects.

Media research has shifted from addressing specifically effects-oriented paradigms to exploring the nature of the institutions of media production themselves as well as examining the unique characteristics of each form of media. What most researchers agree upon today, is that the best way to understand the power and impact of media is to look at context-specific situations to better understand the dynamics involved in the use of media and the importance of the content.

Still, there are many approaches to media research from a variety of interdisciplinary fields: psychology, sociology, linguistics, art, comparative literature, economics, political science, and more. What each of these avenues of inquiry have in common is that they all tend to focus attention on individuals, families or other social groups, society in general, and culture in the broad sense. All of the interpretations frame meaning and investigate their subjects within institutional frameworks that are specific to any nation and/or culture.

Today researchers question the notions of past theories and models as well as definitions of *mass* and *society* and now place much of the emphasis of media dynamics in the perspective of global information exchange. A major controversy erupted in the early 1970s when many Third World countries disagreed with principles that sought to reify the industrialized nations' media. The New World Information Order perspective advanced the importance of media in carrying out developmental tasks within nations that have not had the economic and social benefits of industrialized countries, and it noted that emerging nations had different priorities that reflected indigenous cultures, which would sometimes be at odds with Western notions of a free press. The Third World countries' concerns dealt with power as imposed upon a nation from outside, using media as a vehicle for cultural dependency and imperialism.

Many of the questions for media researchers in the twenty-first century will deal with the continued fragmentation of the audience, caused by greater choice of channels and technologies for traditional and new communication purposes. The power of some of these technologies to reach virtually any place on the globe within fractions of a second will continue to pose questions of access to media and the meaning of the messages transmitted. As individuals become more dependent upon the Internet for communication purposes, the sense of audience will further be changed as individual users choose what they want to receive, pay for, and keep. For all of these reasons, the field of media research is rich, growing, and challenging.

Questions for Consideration

In addressing the issues in this book, it is important to consider some recurring questions:

1. Are the media unifying or fragmenting? Does media content help the socialization process, or does it create anxiety or inaccurate portrayals of the world? Do people feel powerless because they have little ability to shape the messages of media?
2. How are basic institutions changing as we use media in new and different ways? Do media support or undermine our political processes? Do they change what we think of when we claim that we live in a democracy? Does media operate in the public interest, or does media serve the rich and powerful corporations' quest for profit? Can the media do both simultaneously?
3. Whose interests do the media represent? Do audiences actively work toward integrating media messages with their own experiences? How do new media technologies change our traditional ways of communicating? Are they leading us to a world in which interpersonal communication is radically altered because we rely on information systems to replace many traditional behaviors?

Summary

We live in a media-rich environment where almost everybody has access to some form of media and some choices in content. As new technologies and services are developed, are they responding to the problems that previous media researchers and the public have detected? Over time, individuals have improved their ability to unravel the complex set of interactions that ties the media and society together, but they need to continue to question past results, new practices and technologies, and their own evaluative measures. When people critically examine the world around them—a world often presented by the media—they can more fully understand and enjoy the way they relate as individuals, as members of groups, and as members of a society.

On the Internet . . .

The Center for Media Education

The Center for Media Education (CME) is a national, nonprofit organization dedicated to improving the quality of electronic media, especially on the behalf of children and families. This site discusses such topics as the effect of television violence, online advertising, media images, and new technologies.

http://www.cme.org

Communication Studies: General Communication Resources

An encyclopedic resource related to a host of mass communication issues, this site is maintained by the University of Iowa's Department of Communication Studies. It provides excellent links covering advertising, cultural studies, digital media, film, gender issues, and media studies.

http://www.uiowa.edu/~commstud/resources/general.html

Kaiser Family Foundation

The Kaiser Family Foundation site provides articles on a broad range of television topics, including the V-chip, sexual messages, and programs about AIDS. From the home page, go to "select a topic" and choose television.

http://www.kff.org

Writers Guild of America

The Writer's Guild of America is the union for media entertainment writers. The nonmember areas of this site offer useful information for aspiring writers. There is also an excellent links section.

http://www.wga.org

PART 1

Mass Media's Role in Society

*D*o media merely reflect the social attitudes and concerns of our times, or are they also able to construct, legitimate, and reinforce the social realities, behaviors, attitudes, and images of others? Do they operate to maintain existing power structures, or are they a pluralistic representation of diverse views? The ways media help us to shape a sense of reality are complex. Should concern be directed toward vulnerable populations such as children? If we truly have a variety of information sources and content to choose from, perhaps we can assume that distorted images are balanced with realistic ones. But is this truly the media scenario in which we live? Questions about the place of media within society—and within what many call the information age—cannot be ignored.

- Are American Values Shaped by the Mass Media?

- Is Television Harmful for Children?

- Is Emphasis on Body Image in the Media Harmful to Females Only?

- Do African American Stereotypes Still Dominate Entertainment Television?

ISSUE 1

Are American Values Shaped by the Mass Media?

YES: Todd Gitlin, from "Prime Time Ideology: The Hegemonic Process in Television Entertainment," in Horace Newcomb, ed., *Television: The Critical View*, 6th ed. (Oxford University Press, 2000)

NO: Horace Newcomb and Paul M. Hirsch, from "Television as a Cultural Forum: Implications for Research," *Quarterly Review of Film Studies* (Summer 1983)

ISSUE SUMMARY

YES: Professor of journalism and sociology Todd Gitlin addresses how hegemony works in entertainment television. How, he asks, do the formal and familiar devices of entertainment work to relay and reproduce ideology? His answer is that ideology is embedded in format, genre, setting and character types, slant, and solution.

NO: Professors of communication Horace Newcomb and Paul M. Hirsch counter that television serves as a site of negotiation for cultural issues, images, and ideas. Viewer selection from among institutional choices is a negotiation process as viewers select from a wide set of approaches to issues and ideas.

Can the media fundamentally reshape a culture? Americans are now part of a culture in which information and ideas are disseminated. Are media simply the conduit, the information channel, through which these ideas flow? Neither Todd Gitlin nor Horace Newcomb and Paul M. Hirsch would agree with that simplistic description. But the authors do disagree significantly on the influence of media on society. Currently in mass communication research, two vastly different perspectives on the impact of media on society exist. The cultural perspective is advocated by Gitlin, the pluralistic perspective by Newcomb and Hirsch.

Gitlin outlines the hegemonic strategies of prime-time entertainment television. These strategies function to reproduce the status quo and maintain existing social power structures, he says. Despite changes in technologies and practices, Gitlin argues that the ideological core remains the same. He is not alone in his concern that electronic media are negatively influencing our society. There are a number of mass communication scholars from the critical and cultural perspectives who are concerned that the power of media to shape attitude and opinions, paired with the power of media organizations to craft messages, will inevitably result in a re-creation of current power structures, which will inequitably divide social resources.

Newcomb and Hirsch offer the opposite interpretation. They assert that television operates as a cultural forum and is central to the process of public thinking. In part, the effects of mass media on American values may be explained by examining the limits and effectiveness of popular pluralism and the processes by which that pluralism is created and maintained. Communication, according to Newcomb and Hirsch, is dependent on shared meaning. Television is dependent upon pluralism more than many other forms of discourse. So one must consider how television is implicated in the creation of patterns of interpretation and the maintenance of sharing that defines pluralism as an effective cultural norm.

The media are so pervasive that it is hard to believe they do not have important effects. Alternatively, many people do not believe that the media have personally influenced them to buy products or have harmed them, nor do they believe that the media hold a place of "prime importance" in shaping their lives. In everyday experience, many people do not consider the media as having an observable impact on them or on those around them. However, to understand how the media may shape the attitudes of individuals and of society, and how they may shape culture itself, requires that the reader stand back from his or her personal experiences in order to analyze the arguments presented on each side of this debate.

In the following selection, Gitlin argues that U.S. media, through their "taken for granted" processes and messages, help structure the practices and meanings around which society takes shape. Ideology is not imposed but is systematically preferred by certain features of television, whereas other oppositional ideas are ignored or domesticated.

In the second selection, Newcomb and Hirsch advance a cultural forum model to understand the place of television in American society. Multiple meanings are key in understanding how television operates to provide a forum for the featuring of issues and ideas. Therefore, they provide a forum wherein those issues become a focus of cultural concern. Rather than concentrating on the fears of media's influence upon society, Newcomb and Hirsch push us to examine their functions.

Todd Gitlin

 **YES**

Prime Time Ideology: The Hegemonic Process in Television Entertainment

Every society works to reproduce itself—and its internal conflicts—within its cultural order, the structure of practices and meanings around which the society takes shape. So much is tautology. In this [essay] I look at contemporary mass media in the United States as one cultural system promoting that reproduction. I try to show how ideology is relayed through various features of American television, and how television programs register larger ideological structures and changes. The question here is not, What is the impact of these programs? but rather a prior one, What do these programs mean? For only after thinking through their possible meanings as cultural objects and as signs of cultural interactions among producers and audiences may we begin intelligibly to ask about their "effects."

The attempt to understand the sources and transformations of ideology in American society has been leading social theorists not only to social-psychological investigations, but to a long overdue interest in Antonio Gramsci's (1971) notion of ideological hegemony. It was Gramsci who, in the late twenties and thirties, with the rise of fascism and the failure of the Western European working-class movements, began to consider why the working class was not necessarily revolutionary; why it could, in fact, yield to fascism. Condemned to a fascist prison precisely because the insurrectionary workers' movement in Northern Italy just after World War I failed, Gramsci spent years trying to account for the defeat, resorting in large measure to the concept of hegemony: bourgeois domination of the thought, the common sense, the life-ways and everyday assumptions of the working class. Gramsci counterposed "hegemony" to "coercion"; these were two analytically distinct processes through which ruling classes secure the consent of the dominated.... Gramsci's distinction was a great advance for radical thought, for it called attention to the routine structures of everyday thought—down to "common sense" itself—which worked to sustain class domination and tyranny. That is to say, paradoxically, it took the working class seriously enough as a potential agent of revolution to hold it accountable for its failures.

From Todd Gitlin, "Prime Time Ideology: The Hegemonic Process in Television Entertainment," in Horace Newcomb, ed., *Television: The Critical View*, 6th ed. (Oxford University Press, 2000). Originally published in *Social Problems*, vol. 26, no. 3 (February 1979), pp. 251–266. Copyright © 1979 by The Society for the Study of Social Problems. Reprinted by permission of The University of California Press/Journals and the author.

Because Leninism failed abysmally throughout the West, Western Marxists and non-Marxist radicals have both been drawn back to Gramsci, hoping to address the evident fact that the Western working classes are not predestined toward socialist revolution.[1] In Europe this fact could be taken as strategic rather than normative wisdom on the part of the working class; but in America the working class is not only hostile to revolutionary *strategy*, it seems to disdain the socialist *goal* as well. At the very least, although a recent Peter Hart opinion poll showed that Americans abstractly "favor" workers' control, Americans do not seem to care enough about it to organize very widely in its behalf. While there are abundant "contradictions" throughout American society, they are played out substantially in the realm of "culture" or "ideology," which orthodox Marxism had consigned to the secondary category of "superstructure." Meanwhile, critical theory—especially in the work of T. W. Adorno and Max Horkheimer—had argued with great force that the dominant forms of commercial ("mass") culture were crystallizations of authoritarian ideology; yet despite the ingenuity and brilliance of particular feats of critical exegesis (Adorno, 1954, 1974; Adorno and Horkheimer, 1972), they seemed to be arguing that the "culture industry" was not only meretricious but wholly and statically complete. . . .

In this [essay] I wish to contribute to the process of bringing the discussion of cultural hegemony down to earth. For much of the discussion so far remains abstract, almost as if cultural hegemony were a substance with a life of its own, a sort of immutable fog that has settled over the whole public life of capitalist societies to confound the truth of the proletarian telos. Thus to the questions, "Why are radical ideas suppressed in the schools?", "Why do workers oppose socialism?" and so on, comes the single Delphic answer: hegemony. "Hegemony" becomes the magical explanation of last resort. And as such it is useful neither as explanation nor as guide to action. If "hegemony" explains everything in the sphere of culture, it explains nothing. . . .

My task in what follows is to propose some features of a lexicon for discussing the forms of hegemony in the concrete. . . . Here I wish to speak of the realm of entertainment: about television entertainment in particular—as the most pervasive and (in the living room sense) *familiar* of our cultural sites—and about movies secondarily. How do the *formal* devices of TV prime time programs encourage viewers to experience themselves as anti-political, privately accumulating individuals (also see Gitlin, 1977c)? And how do these forms express social conflict, containing and diverting the images of contrary social possibilities? I want to isolate a few of the routine devices, though of course in reality they do not operate in isolation; rather, they work in combination, where their force is often enough magnified (though they can also work in contradictory ways). And, crucially, it must be borne in mind throughout this discussion that the forms of mass-cultural production do not either spring up or operate independently of the rest of social life. Commercial culture does not *manufacture* ideology; it *relays* and *reproduces* and *processes* and *packages* and *focuses* ideology that is constantly arising both from social elites and from active social groups and movements throughout the society (as well as within media organizations and practices).

A more complete analysis of ideological process in a commercial society would look both above and below, to elites and to audiences. Above, it would take a long look at the economics and politics of broadcasting, at its relation to the FCC [Federal Communications Commission], the Congress, the President, the courts; in case studies and with a developing theory of ideology it would study media's peculiar combination and refraction of corporate, political, bureaucratic, and professional interests, giving the media a sort of limited independence—or what Marxists are calling "relative autonomy"—in the upper reaches of the political-economic system. Below, as Raymond Williams has insisted, cultural hegemony operates within a whole social life-pattern; the people who consume mass-mediated products are also the people who work, reside, compete, go to school, live in families. And there are a good many traditional and material interests at stake for audiences: the political inertia of the American population now, for example, certainly has something to do with the continuing productivity of the goods-producing and -distributing industries, not simply with the force of mass culture. Let me try to avoid misunderstanding at the outset by insisting that *I will not be arguing that the forms of hegemonic entertainment superimpose themselves automatically and finally onto the consciousness or behavior of all audiences at all times:* it remains for sociologists to generate what Dave Morley (1974)[2] has called "an ethnography of audiences," and to study what Ronald Abramson (1978) calls "the phenomenology of audiences" if we are to have anything like a satisfactory account of how audiences consciously and unconsciously process, transform, and are transformed by the contents of television. For many years the subject of media effects was severely narrowed by a behaviorist definition of the problem (see Gitlin, 1978a); more recently, the "agenda-setting function" of mass media has been usefully studied in news media, but not in entertainment. (On the other hand, the very pervasiveness of TV entertainment makes laboratory study of its "effects" almost inconceivable.) It remains to incorporate occasional sociological insights into the actual behavior of TV audiences[3] into a more general theory of the interaction—a theory which avoids both the mechanical assumptions of behaviorism and the trivialities of the "uses and gratifications" approach.

But alas, that more general theory of the interaction is not on the horizon. My more modest attempt in this extremely preliminary essay is to sketch an approach to the hegemonic thrust of some TV forms, not to address the deflection, resistance, and reinterpretation achieved by audiences. I will show that hegemonic ideology is systematically preferred by certain features of TV programs, and that at the same time alternative and oppositional values are brought into the cultural system, and domesticated into hegemonic forms at times, by the routine workings of the market. Hegemony is reasserted in different ways at different times, even by different logics; if this variety is analytically messy, the messiness corresponds to a disordered ideological order, a contradictory society. This said, I proceed to some of the forms in which ideological hegemony is embedded: *format and formula; genre; setting and character type; slant;* and *solution.* Then these particulars will suggest a somewhat more fully developed theory of hegemony.

Format and Formula

... [T]he TV schedule has been dominated by standard lengths and cadences, standardized packages of TV entertainment appearing, as the announcers used to say, "same time, same station." This week-to-weekness—or, in the case of soap operas, day-to-dayness—obstructed the development of characters; at least the primary characters had to be preserved intact for next week's show. Perry Mason was Perry Mason, once and for all; if you watched the reruns, you couldn't know from character or set whether you were watching the first or the last in the series. For commercial and production reasons which are in practice inseparable—and this is why ideological hegemony is not reducible to the economic interests of elites—the regular schedule prefers the repeatable formula: it is far easier for production companies to hire writers to write for standardized, static characters than for characters who develop. Assembly-line production works through regularity of time slot, of duration, and of character to convey images of social steadiness.... Moreover, the standard curve of narrative action—stock characters encounter new version of stock situation; the plot thickens, allowing stock characters to show their standard stuff; the plot resolves—over twenty-two or fifty minutes is itself a source of rigidity and forced regularity.

In these ways, the usual programs are performances that rehearse social fixity: they express and cement the obduracy of a social world impervious to substantial change. Yet at the same time there are signs of routine obsolescence, as hunks of last year's regular schedule drop from sight only to be supplanted by this season's attractions. Standardization and the threat of evanescence are curiously linked: they match the intertwined processes of commodity production, predictability, and obsolescence in a high-consumption society. I speculate that they help instruct audiences in the rightness and naturalness of a world that, in only apparent paradox, regularly requires an irregularity, an unreliability which it calls progress. In this way, the regular changes in TV programs, like the regular elections of public officials, seem to affirm the sovereignty of the audience while keeping deep alternatives off the agenda. Elite authority and consumer choice are affirmed at once—this is one of the central operations of the hegemonic liberal capitalist ideology....

Commercials, of course, are also major features of the regular TV format. There can be no question but that commercials have a good deal to do with shaping and maintaining markets—no advertiser dreams of cutting advertising costs as long as the competition is still on the air. But commercials also have important *indirect* consequences on the contours of consciousness overall; they get us accustomed to thinking of ourselves and behaving as a *market* rather than a *public*, as consumers rather than citizens. Public problems (like air pollution) are propounded as susceptible to private commodity solutions (like eyedrops). In the process, commercials acculturate us to interruption through the rest of our lives. Time and attention are not one's own; the established social powers have the capacity to colonize consciousness, and unconsciousness, as they see fit. By watching, the audience one by one consents. Regardless of the commercial's "effect" on our behavior, we are consenting to its domination of the public space....

TV routines have been built into the broadcast schedule since its inception. But arguably their regularity has been waning since Norman Lear's first comedy, *All in the Family*, made its network debut in 1971. Lear's contribution to TV content was obvious: where previous shows might have made passing reference to social conflict, Lear brought wrenching social issues into the very mainspring of his series, uniting his characters, as Michael Arlen once pointed out, in a harshly funny *ressentiment* peculiarly appealing to audiences of the Nixon era and its cynical, disabused sequel.[4] As I'll argue below, the hegemonic ideology is maintained in the seventies by *domesticating* divisive issues where in the fifties it would have simply *ignored* them.

Lear also let his characters develop. Edith Bunker grew less sappy and more feminist and commonsensical; Gloria and Mike moved next door, and finally to California. On the threshold of this generational rupture, Mike broke through his stereotype by expressing affection for Archie, and Archie, oh-so-reluctantly but definitely for all that, hugged back and broke through his own. And of course other Lear characters, the Jeffersons and Maude, had earlier been spun off into their own shows, as *The Mary Tyler Moore Show* had spawned *Rhoda* and *Phyllis*. These changes resulted from commercial decisions; they were built on intelligent business perceptions that an audience existed for situation comedies directly addressing racism, sexism, and the decomposition of conventional families. But there is no such thing as a strictly economic "explanation" for production choice, since the success of a show—despite market research—is not foreordained. In the context of my argument, the importance of such developments lies in their partial break with the established, static formulae of prime time television.

... In summary it is hard to say to what extent [format changes] reveal the networks' responses to the restiveness and boredom of the mass audience, or the emergence of new potential audiences. But in any case the shifts are there, and constitute a fruitful territory for any thinking about the course of popular culture.

Genre[5]

The networks try to finance and choose programs that will likely attract the largest conceivable audiences of spenders; this imperative requires that the broadcasting elites have in mind some notion of popular taste from moment to moment. Genre, in other words, is necessarily somewhat sensitive; in its rough outlines, if not in detail, it tells us something about popular moods. Indeed, since there are only three networks, there is something of an over-sensitivity to a given success; the pendulum tends to swing hard to replicate a winner. Thus *Charlie Angels* engenders *Flying High* and *American Girls*, about stewardesses and female reporters respectively, each on a long leash under male authority.

Here I suggest only a few signs of this sensitivity to shifting moods and group identities in the audience. The adult western of the middle and late fifties, with its drama of solitary righteousness and suppressed libidinousness, for example, can be seen in retrospect to have played on the quiet malaise under the surface of the complacency of the Eisenhower years, even in contradictory ways. Some lone heroes were identified with traditionally frontier-American informal and individualistic relations to authority (Paladin in *Have Gun, Will Travel*, Bart Maverick in *Maverick*), standing for sturdy individualism struggling for hedonistic values and taking law-and-order wryly. Meanwhile, other heroes were decent officials like *Gunsmoke's* Matt Dillon, affirming the decency of paternalistic law and order against the temptations of worldy pleasure. With the rise of the Camelot mystique, and the vigorous "long twilight struggle" that John F. Kennedy personified, spy stories like *Mission: Impossible* and *The Man From U.N.C.L.E.* were well suited to capitalize on the macho CIA aura.... The single-women shows following from *Mary Tyler Moore* acknowledge in their privatized ways that some sort of feminism is here to stay, and work to contain it with hilarious versions of "new life styles" for single career women. Such shows probably appeal to the market of "upscale" singles with relatively large disposable incomes, women who are disaffected from the traditional imagery of housewife and helpmeet.... The black sitcoms probably reflect the rise of a black middle class with the purchasing power to bring forth advertisers, while also appealing *as comedies*—for conflicting reasons, perhaps—to important parts of the white audience. (Serious black drama would be far more threatening to the majority audience.) ...

Televised sports too is best understood as an entertainment genre, one of the most powerful.[6] What we know as professional sports today is inseparably intertwined with the networks' development of the sports market. TV sports is rather consistently framed to reproduce dominant American values. First, although TV is ostensibly a medium for the eyes, the sound is often decisive in taking the action off the field. The audience is not trusted to come to its own conclusions. The announcers are not simply describing events ("Reggie Jackson hits a ground ball to shortstop"), but interpreting them ("World Series 1978! It's great to be here"). One may see here a process equivalent to advertising's project of taking human qualities out of the consumer and removing them to the product: sexy perfume, zesty beer.

In televised sports, the hegemonic impositions have, if anything, probably become more intense over the last twenty years. One technique for interpreting the event is to regale the audience with bits of information in the form of "stats." "A lot of people forget they won eleven out of their last twelve games...." "There was an extraordinary game in last year's World Series...." How *about* that? The announcers can't shut up; they're constantly chattering. And the stat flashed on the screen further removes the action from the field. What is one to make of all this? ...

But the trivialities have their reason: they amount to an interpretation that flatters and disdains the audience at the same time. It flatters in small ways, giving you the chance to be the one person on the block who already possessed this tidbit of fact. At the same time, symbolically, it treats you as someone who really knows what's going on in the world. Out of control of social reality, you may flatter yourself that the substitute world of sports is a corner of the world you can really grasp....

Another framing practice is the reduction of the sports experience to a sequence of individual achievements. In a fusion of populist and capitalist dogma, everyone is somehow the best. This one has "great hands," this one has "a great slam dunk," that one's "great on defense." This indiscriminate commendation raises the premium on personal competition, and at the same time undermines the meaning of personal achievement: everyone is excellent at something, as at a child's birthday party.... All in all, the network exalts statistics, personal competition, expertise. The message is: The way to understand things is by storing up statistics and tracing their trajectories. This is training in observation without comprehension....

On the other hand, the network version does not inevitably succeed in forcing itself upon our consciousness and defining our reception of the event. TV audiences don't necessarily succumb to the announcers' hype. In semi-public situations like barrooms, audiences are more likely to see through the trivialization and ignorance and—in "para-social interaction"—to tell the announcers off. But in the privacy of living rooms, the announcers' framing probably penetrates farther into the collective definition of the event. It should not be surprising that one fairly common counter-hegemonic practice is to watch the broadcast picture without the network sound, listening to the local announcer on the radio.

Setting and Character Type

Closely related to genre and its changes are setting and character type. And here again we see shifting market tolerances making for certain changes in content, while the core of hegemonic values remains virtually impervious.

In the fifties, when the TV forms were first devised, the standard TV series presented—in Herbert Gold's phrase—happy people with happy problems. In the seventies it is more complicated: there are unhappy people with happy ways of coping. But the set itself propounds a vision of consumer happiness. Living rooms and kitchens usually display the standard package of consumer goods. Even where the set is ratty, as in *Sanford and Son*, or working-class, as in *All in the Family*, the bright color of the TV tube almost always glamorizes the surroundings so that there will be no sharp break between the glorious color of the program and the glorious color of the commercial. In the more primitive fifties, by contrast, it was still possible for a series like *The Honeymooners*... to get by with one or two simple sets per show: the life of a good skit was in its accomplished *acting*. But that series, in its sympathetic treatment of working-class mores, was exceptional. Color broadcasting accomplishes the glamorous ideal willy-nilly.

Permissible character types have evolved, partly because of changes in the structure of broadcasting power. In the fifties, before the quiz show scandal, advertising agencies contracted directly with production companies to produce TV series (Barnouw, 1970). They ordered up exactly what they wanted, as if by the yard; and with some important but occasional exceptions... what they wanted was glamour and fun, a showcase for commercials....

Later in the fifties, comedies were able to represent discrepant settings, permitting viewers both to identify and to indulge their sense of superiority through comic distance: *The Honeymooners* ... which capitalized on Jackie Gleason's ... enormous personal popularity (a personality cult can always perform wonders and break rules), were able to extend dignity to working-class characters in anti-glamorous situations (see Czitrom, 1977).

Beginning in 1960, the networks took direct control of production away from advertisers. And since the networks are less provincial than particular advertisers, since they are more closely attuned to general tolerances in the population, and since they are firmly in charge of a buyer's market for advertising (as long as they produce shows that *some* corporation will sponsor), it now became possible—if by no means easy—for independent production companies to get somewhat distinct cultural forms, like Norman Lear's comedies, on the air. The near-universality of television set ownership, at the same time, creates the possibility of a wider range of audiences, including minority-group, working-class and age-segmented audiences, than existed in the fifties, and thus makes possible a wider range of fictional characters. Thus changes in the organization of TV production, as well as new market pressures ... helped to change the prevalent settings and character types on television.

But the power of corporate ideology over character types remains very strong, and sets limits on the permissible; the changes from the fifties through the sixties and seventies should be understood in the context of essential cultural features that have *not* changed. To show the quality of deliberate choice that is often operating, consider a book called *The Youth Market*, by two admen, published in 1970, counseling companies on ways to pick "the right character for your product":

> But in our opinion, if you want to create your own hardhitting spokesman to children, the most effective route is the superhero-miracle worker. He certainly can demonstrate food products, drug items, many kinds of toys, and innumerable household items.... The character should be adventurous. And he should be on the right side of the law. A child must be able to mimic his hero, whether he is James Bond, Superman or Dick Tracy; to be able to fight and shoot to kill without punishment or guilt feelings. (Helitzer and Heyel, 1970)

If this sort of thinking is resisted within the industry itself, it's not so much because of commitments to artistry in television as such, but more because there are other markets that are not "penetrated" by these hard-hitting heroes. The industry is noticing, for example, that *Roots* brought to the tube an audience who don't normally watch TV. The homes-using-television levels during the week of *Roots* were up between 6 and 12 percent over the programs of the previous year (*Broadcasting*, January 31, 1977). Untapped markets—often composed of people who have, or wish to have, somewhat alternative views of the world—can only be brought in by unusual sorts of programming. There is room in the schedule for rebellious human slaves just as there is room for hard-hitting patriotic-technological heroes. In other words—contrary to a simplistic argument against television manipulation by network elites—the receptivity of enormous parts of the population is an important limiting factor affecting what gets on television. On the other hand, network elites do not risk investing in *regular* heroes who will challenge the core values of corporate capitalist society: who are, say, explicit socialists, or union organizers, or for that matter born-again evangelists. But like the dramatic series *Playhouse 90* in the fifties, TV movies permit a somewhat wider range of choice than weekly series. It is apparently easier for producers to sell exceptional material for one-shot showings —whether sympathetic to lesbian mothers, critical of the 1950s blacklist or of Senator Joseph McCarthy. Most likely these important exceptions have prestige value for the networks.

Slant

Within the formula of a program, a specific slant often pushes through, registering a certain position on a particular public issue. When issues are politically charged, when there is overt social conflict, programs capitalize on the currency. ("Capitalize" is an interesting word, referring both to use and to profit.) In the program's brief compass, only the most stereotyped characters are deemed to "register" on the audience, and therefore, slant, embedded in character, is almost always simplistic and thin. The specific slant is sometimes mistaken for the whole of ideological tilt or "bias," as if the bias dissolves when no position is taken on a topical issue. But the week-after-week angle of the show is more basic, a hardened definition of a routine situation *within which* the specific topical slant emerges. The occasional topical slant then seems to anchor the program's general meanings.... [I]n the late sixties and seventies, police and spy dramas have commonly clucked over violent terrorists and heavily armed "anarchist" maniacs, labeled as "radicals" or "revolutionaries," giving the cops a chance to justify their heavy armament and crude machismo. But the other common variety of slant is sympathetic to forms of deviance which are either private (the lesbian mother shown to be a good mother to her children) or quietly reformist (the brief vogue for *Storefront Lawyers* and the like in the early seventies). The usual slants, then, fall into two categories: either (a) a legitimation of depoliticized forms of deviance, usually ethnic or sexual; or (b) a delegitimation of the dangerous, the violent, the out-of-bounds.

The slants that find their way into network programs, in short, are not uniform. Can we say anything systematic about them? Whereas in the fifties family dramas and sit-coms usually ignored—or indirectly sublimated—the existence of deep social problems in the world outside the set, programs of the seventies much more often domesticate them. From *Ozzie and Harriet* or *Father Knows Best* to *All in the Family* or *The Jeffersons* marks a distinct shift for formula, character, and slant: a shift, among other things, in the image of how a family copes with the world outside. Again, changes in content have in large part to be referred back to changes in social values and sensibilities, particularly the values of writers, actors, and other practitioners: there is a large audience now that prefers acknowledging and domesticating social problems directly rather than ignoring them or treating them only indirectly and in a sublimated way; there are also media practitioners who have some roots in the rebellions of the sixties. Whether hegemonic style will operate more by exclusion (fifties) than by domestication (seventies) will depend on the level of public dissensus as well as on internal factors of media organization (the fifties blacklist of TV writers probably exercised a chilling effect on subject matter and slant; so did the fact that sponsors directly developed their own shows).

Solution

Finally, cultural hegemony operates through the solutions proposed to difficult problems. However grave the problems posed, however rich the imbroglio, the episodes regularly end with the click of a solution: an arrest, a defiant smile, an I-told-you-so explanation. The characters we have been asked to care about are alive and well, ready for next week. Such a world is not so much fictional as fake. However deeply the problem is located within society, it will be solved among a few persons: the heroes must attain a solution that leaves the rest of the society untouched. The self-enclosed world of the TV drama justifies itself, and its exclusions, by "wrapping it all up." ... On the networks, *All in the Family* has been unusual in sometimes ending obliquely, softly, or ironically, refusing to pretend to solve a social problem that cannot, in fact, be solved by the actions of the Bunkers alone....

Likewise, in mid-seventies mass-market films like *Chinatown, Rollerball, Network*, and *King Kong*, we see an interesting form of closure: as befits the common cynicism and helplessness, society owns the victory. Reluctant heroes go up against vast impersonal forces, often multinational corporations like the same Gulf & Western (sent up as "Engulf & Devour" in Mel Brook's *Silent Movie*) that, through its Paramount subsidiary, produces some of these films. Driven to anger or bitterness by the evident corruption, the rebels break loose—only to bring the whole structure crashing down on them.... These popular films appeal to a kind of populism and rebelliousness, usually of a routine and vapid sort, but then close off the possibilities of effective opposition. The rich get richer and the incoherent rebels get bought and killed.

Often the sense of frustration funneled through these films is diffuse and ambiguous enough to encourage a variety of political responses. While many left-wing cultural critics raved about *Network*, for example, right-wing politicians in Southern California campaigned for Proposition 13 using the film's slogan, "I'm mad as hell and I'm not going to take it any more." Indeed, *the fact that the same film is subject to a variety of conflicting yet plausible interpretations may suggest a crisis in hegemonic ideology.* The economic system is demonstrably troubled, but the traditional liberal recourse, the State, is no longer widely enough trusted to provide reassurance. Articulate social groups do not know whom to blame; public opinion is fluid and volatile, and people at all levels in the society withdraw from public participation.[7] In this situation, commercial culture succeeds with diverse interest groups, as well as with the baffled and ambivalent, precisely by propounding ambiguous or even self-contradictory situations and solutions.

The Hegemonic Process in Liberal Capitalism

Again it bears emphasizing that, for all these tricks of the entertainment trade, the mass-cultural system is not one-dimensional. High-consumption corporate capitalism implies a certain sensitivity to audience taste, taste which is never wholly manufactured. Shows are made by guessing at audience desires and tolerances, and finding ways to speak to them that perpetuate the going system.[8] ... The cultural hegemony system that results is not a closed system. It leaks. Its very structure leaks, at the least because it remains to some extent competitive. Networks sell the audience's attention to advertisers who want what they think will be a suitably big, suitably rich audience for their products; since the show is bait, advertisers will put up with—or rather buy into—a great many possible baits, as long as they seem likely to attract a buying audience....

Outside the news, the networks have no particular interest in truth as such, but they remain sensitive to currents of interest in the population, including the yank and haul and insistence of popular movements. With few ethnical or strategic reasons not to absorb trends, they are adept at perpetuating them with new formats, new styles, tie-in commodities (dolls, posters, T-shirts, fan magazines) that fans love. In any case, it is in no small measure because of the economic drives themselves that *the hegemonic system itself amplifies legitimated forms of opposition.* In liberal capitalism, hegemonic ideology develops by domesticating opposition, absorbing it into forms compatible with the core ideological structure. Consent is managed by absorption as well as by exclusion. The hegemonic ideology changes in order to remain hegemonic; that is the peculiar nature of the dominant ideology of liberal capitalism....

One point should be clear: the hegemonic system is not cut-and-dried, not definitive. It has continually to be reproduced, continually superimposed, continually to be negotiated and managed, in order to override the alternative and, occasionally, the oppositional forms. To put it another way: major social conflicts are transported *into* the cultural system, where the hegemonic process frames them, form and content both, into compatibility with dominant systems of meaning. Alternative material is routinely *incorporated:* brought into the body of cultural production. Occasionally oppositional material may succeed in being indigestible; that material is excluded from the media discourse and returned to the cultural margins from which it came, while *elements* of it are incorporated into the dominant forms.

In these terms, *Roots* was an alternative form, representing slaves as unblinkable facts of American history, blacks as victimized humans and humans nonetheless. In the end, perhaps, the story is dominated by the chance for upward mobility; the upshot of travail is freedom. Where Alex Haley's book is subtitled "The Saga of an American Family," ABC's version carries the label—and the self-congratulation—"The *Triumph* of an American Family." It is hard to say categorically which story prevails; in any case there is a tension, a struggle, between the collective agony and the triumph of a single family. That struggle is the friction in the works of the hegemonic system.

And all the evident friction within television entertainment—as well as within the schools, the family, religion, sexuality, and the State—points back to a deeper truth about bourgeois culture. In the United States, at least, hegemonic ideology is extremely complex and absorptive; it is only by absorbing and domesticating conflicting definitions of reality and demands on it, in fact, that it remains hegemonic. In this way, the hegemonic ideology of liberal capitalism is dramatically different from the ideologies of precapitalist societies, and from the dominant ideology of authoritarian socialist or fascist regimes. What permits it to absorb and domesticate critique is not something accidental to capitalist ideology, but rather its core. *The hegemonic ideology of liberal capitalist society is deeply and essentially conflicted in a number of ways.* As Daniel Bell (1976) has argued, it urges people to work hard, but proposes that real satisfaction is to be found in leisure, which ostensibly embodies values opposed to work.[9] More profoundly, at the center of liberal capitalist ideology there is a tension between the affirmation of patriarchal authority—currently enshrined in the national security state—and the affirmation of individual worth and self-determination. Bourgeois ideology in all its incarnations has been from the first a contradiction in terms, affirming "life, liberty and the pursuit of happiness," or "liberty, equality, fraternity," as if these ideals are compatible, even mutually dependent, at all times in all places, as they were for one revolutionary group at one time in one place. But all anti-bourgeois movements wage their battles precisely in terms of liberty, equality, or fraternity (or, recently, sorority); they press on liberal capitalist ideology *in its own name.*

Thus we can understand something of the vulnerability of bourgeois ideology, as well as its persistence. In the twentieth century, the dominant ideology has shifted toward sanctifying consumer satisfaction as the premium definition of "the pursuit of happiness," in this way justifying corporate domination of the economy. What is hegemonic in consumer capitalist ideology is precisely the notion that happiness, or liberty, or equality, or fraternity can be affirmed through the existing private commodity forms, under the benign, protective eye of the national security state. This ideological core is what remains essentially unchanged and unchallenged in television entertainment, at the same time the inner tensions persist and are even magnified.

Notes

1. In my reading, the most thoughtful specific approach to this question since Gramsci, using comparative structural categories to explain the emergence or absence of socialist class consciousness, is Mann (1973). Mann's analysis takes us to structural features of American society that detract from revolutionary consciousness and organization. Although my [essay] does not discuss social-structural and historical features, I do not wish their absence to be interpreted as a belief that culture is all-determining. This [essay] discusses aspects of the hegemonic culture, and makes no claims to a more sweeping theory of American society.

2. See also, Willis (n.d.) for an excellent discussion of the limits of both ideological analysis of cultural artifacts and the social meaning system of audiences, when each is taken by itself and isolated from the other.

3. Most strikingly, see Blum's (1964) findings on black viewers putting down TV shows while watching them. See also Willis's (n.d.) program for studying the substantive meanings of particular pop music records for distinct youth subcultures; but note that it is easier to study the active uses of music than TV, since music

is more often heard publicly and because, there being so many choices, the preference for a particular set of songs or singers or beats expresses more about the mentality of the audience than is true for TV.

4. The time of the show is important to its success or failure: Lear's *All in the Family* was rejected by ABC before CBS bought it. An earlier attempt to bring problems of class, race, and poverty into the heart of television series was *East Side, West Side* of 1964, in which George C. Scott played a caring social worker consistently unable to accomplish much for his clients. As time went on, the Scott character came to the conclusion that politics might accomplish what social work could not, and changed jobs, going to work as the assistant to a liberal Congressman. It was rumored about that the hero was going to discover there, too, the limits of reformism—but the show was cancelled, presumably for low ratings. Perhaps Lear's shows, by contrast, have lasted in part *because they are comedies:* audiences will let their defenses down for some good laughs, even on themselves, at least when the characters are, like Archie Bunker himself, ambiguous normative symbols. At the same time, the comedy form allows white racists to indulge themselves in Archie's rationalizations without seeing that the joke is on them.

5. I use the term *loosely* to refer to general categories of TV entertainment, like "adult western," "cops and robbers," "black shows." Genre is not an objective feature of the cultural universe, but a conventional name for a convention, and should not be reified—as both cultural analysis and practice often do—into a cultural essence.

6. This discussion of televised sports was published in similar form (Gitlin, 1978b).

7. In another essay I will be arguing that forms of pseudo-participation (including cult movies like *Rocky Horror Picture Show* and *Animal House*, along with religious sects) are developing simultaneously to fill the vacuum left by the declining of credible radical politics, and to provide ritual forms of expression that alienated groups cannot find within the political culture.

8. See the careful, important, and unfairly neglected discussion of the tricky needs issue in Leiss (1976). Leiss cuts through the Frankfurt premise that commodity culture addresses false needs by arguing that audience needs for happiness, diversion, self-assertion, and so on are ontologically real; what commercial culture does it not to invent needs (how could it do that?) but to insist upon the possibility of meeting them through the purchase of commodities. For Leiss, all specifically human needs are social; they develop within one social form or another. From this argument—and, less rigorously but more daringly from Ewen (1976)—flow powerful political implications I cannot develop here. On the early popularity of entertainment forms which cannot possibly be laid at the door of a modern "culture industry" and media-produced needs, see Altick (1978).

9. There is considerable truth in Bell's thesis. Then why do I say "ostensibly"? Bell exaggerates his case against "adversary culture" by emphasizing changes in avant-garde culture above all (Pop Art, happenings, John Cage, etc.); if he looked at *popular* culture, he would more likely find ways in which aspects of the culture of consumption *support* key aspects of the culture of production. I offer my discussion of sports as one instance. Morris Dickstein's (1977) affirmation of the critical culture of the sixties commits the counterpart error of overemphasizing the importance of *other* selected domains of literary and avant-garde culture.

References

Abramson, Ronald (1978) Unpublished manuscript, notes on critical theory distributed at the West Coast Critical Communications Conference, Stanford University.

Adorno, Theodor W. (1954) "How to look at television." *Hollywood Quarterly of Film, Radio and Television*. Spring. Reprinted 1975: 474–88 in Bernard Rosenberg and David Manning White (eds.), *Mass Culture*. New York: Free Press.

_____. (1974) "The stars down to earth. The Los Angeles Times Astrology Column." *Telos* 19. Spring 1974 (1957): 13–90.

Adorno, Theodor W., and Max Horkheimer (1972) "The culture industry: Enlightenment as mass deception." Pp. 120–167 in Adorno and Horkheimer, *Dialectic of Enlightenment* (1944). New York: Seabury.

Altick, Richard (1978) *The Shows of London*. Cambridge: Harvard University Press.

Barnouw, Erik (1970) *The Image Empire*. New York: Oxford University Press.

Bell, Daniel (1976) *The Cultural Contradictions of Capitalism*. New York: Basic Books.

Blum, Alan F. (1964) "Lower-class Negro television spectators: The concept of pseudo-jovial scepticism." Pp. 429–435 in Arthur B. Shostak and William Gomberg (eds.), *Blue-Collar World*. Englewood Cliffs, N.J.: Prentice-Hall.

Czitrom, Danny (1977) "Bilko: A sitcom for all seasons." *Cultural Correspondence* 4: 16–19.

Dickstein, Morris (1977) *Gates of Eden*. New York: Basic Books.

Ewen, Stuart (1976) *Captains of Consciousness*. New York: McGraw-Hill.

Gitlin, Todd (1977c) "The televised professional." *Social Policy* (November/December): 94–99.

_____. (1978a) "Media sociology: The dominant paradigm." *Theory and Society* 6:205–53.

_____. (1978b) "Life as instant replay." *East Bay Voice* (November-December): 14.

Gramsci, Antonio (1971) *Selections From the Prison Notebooks*. Quintin Hoare and Geoffrey Nowell Smith (eds.) New York: International Publishers.

Helitzer, Melvin, and Carl Heyel (1970) The Youth Market: Its Dimensions, Influence and Opportunities for You. Quoted pp. 62–63 in William Melody, *Children's Television* (1973). New Haven: Yale University Press.

Leiss, William (1976) *The Limits to Satisfaction*. Toronto: University of Toronto Press.

Mann, Michael (1973) *Consciousness and Action Among the Western Working Class*. London: Macmillan.

Morley, Dave (1974) "Reconceptualizing the media audience: Towards an ethnography of audiences." Mimeograph, Centre for Contemporary Cultural Studies, University of Birmingham.

Williams, Raymond (1973) "Base and superstructure in Marxist cultural theory." *New Left Review*: 82.

_____. (1977) *Marxism and Literature*. New York: Oxford University Press.

Willis, Paul (n.d.) "Symbolism and practice: A theory for the social meaning of pop music." Mimeograph, Centre for Contemporary Cultural Studies, University of Birmingham.

Television as a Cultural Forum

Acultural basis for the analysis and criticism of television is, for us, the bridge between a concern for television as a communications medium, central to contemporary society, and television as aesthetic object, the expressive medium that, through its storytelling functions, unites and examines a culture. The shortcomings of each of these approaches taken alone are manifold.

The first is based primarily in a concern for understanding specific messages that may have specific effects, and grounds its analysis in "communication" narrowly defined. Complexities of image, style, resonance, narrativity, history, metaphor, and so on are reduced in favor of that content that can be more precisely, some say more objectively, described. The content categories are not allowed to emerge from the text, as is the case in naturalistic observation and in textual analysis. Rather they are predefined in order to be measured more easily. The incidence of certain content categories may be cited as significant, or their "effects" more clearly correlated with some behavior. This concern for measuring is, of course, the result of conceiving television in one way rather than another, as "communication" rather than as "art."

The narrowest versions of this form of analysis need not concern us here. It is to the best versions that we must look, to those that do admit to a range of aesthetic expression and something of a variety of reception. Even when we examine these closely, however, we see that they often assume a monolithic "meaning" in television content. The concern is for "dominant" messages embedded in the pleasant disguise of fictional entertainment, and the concern of the researcher is often that the control of these messages is, more than anything else, a complex sort of political control. The critique that emerges, then, is consciously or unconsciously a critique of the society that is transmitting and maintaining the dominant ideology with the assistance, again conscious or unconscious, of those who control communications technologies and businesses. (Ironically, this perspective does not depend on political perspective or persuasion. It is held by groups on the "right" who see American values being subverted, as well as by those on the "left" who see American values being imposed.)

Such a position assumes that the audience shares or "gets" the same messages and their meanings as the researcher finds. At times, like the literary critic,

From Horace Newcomb and Paul M. Hirsch, "Television as a Cultural Forum: Implications for Research," *Quarterly Review of Film Studies*, vol. 8 (Summer 1983). Copyright © 1983 by Overseas Publishers Association. Reprinted by permission of Gordon and Breach Publishers and Horace Newcomb.

the researcher assumes this on the basis of superior insight, technique, or sensibility. In a more "scientific" manner the researcher may seek to establish a correlation between the discovered messages and the understanding of the audience. Rarely, however, does the message analyst allow for the possibility that the audience, while sharing this one meaning, may create many others that have not been examined, asked about, or controlled for.

The television "critic" on the other hand, often basing his work on the analysis of literature or film, succeeds in calling attention to the distinctive qualities of the medium, to the special nature of television fiction. But this approach all too often ignores important questions of production and reception. Intent on correcting what it takes to be a skewed interest in such matters, it often avoids the "business" of television and its "technology." These critics, much like their counterparts in the social sciences, usually assume that viewers should understand programs in the way the critic does, or that the audience is incapable of properly evaluating the entertaining work and should accept the critic's superior judgment.

The differences between the two views of what television is and does rest, in part, on the now familiar distinction between transportation and ritual views of communication processes. The social scientific, or communication theory model outlined above (and we do not claim that it is an exhaustive description) rests most thoroughly on the transportation view. As articulated by James Carey, this model holds that communication is a "process of transmitting messages at a distance for the purpose of control. The archetypal case of communication then is persuasion, attitude change, behavior modification, socialization through the transmission of information, influence, or conditioning."[1]

The more "literary" or "aesthetically based" approach leans toward, but hardly comes to terms with, ritual models of communication. As put by Carey, the ritual view sees communication "not directed toward the extension of messages in space but the maintenance of society in time; not the act of imparting information but the representation of shared beliefs."[2]

Carey also cuts through the middle of these definitions with a more succinct one of his own: "Communication is a symbolic process whereby reality is produced, maintained, repaired, and transformed."[3] It is in the attempt to amplify this basic observation that we present a cultural basis for the analysis of television. We hardly suggest that such an approach is entirely new, or that others are unaware of or do not share many of our assumptions. On the contrary, we find a growing awareness in many disciplines of the nature of symbolic thought, communication, and action, and we see attempts to understand television emerging rapidly from this body of shared concerns.[4]

◆◦◉◦◆

Our own model for television is grounded in an examination of the cultural role of entertainment and parallels this with a close analysis of television program content in all its various textual levels and forms. We focus on the collective, cultural view of the social construction and negotiation of reality, on the creation of what Carey refers to as "public thought."[5] It is not difficult to see television as central to this process of public thinking. As Hirsch has pointed out,[6] it is now our national medium, replacing those media—film, radio, picture magazines, newspapers—that once served a similar function. Those who create for such media are, in the words of anthropologist Marshall Sahlins, "hucksters of the symbol."[7] They are cultural *bricoleurs,* seeking and creating new meaning in the combination of cultural elements with embedded significance. They respond to real events, changes in social structure and organization, and to shifts in attitude and value. They also respond to technological shift, the coming of cable or the use of videotape recorders. We think it is clear that the television producer should be added to Sahlins's list of "hucksters." They work in precisely the manner he describes, as do television writers and, to a lesser extent, directors and actors. So too do programmers and network executives who must make decisions about the programs they purchase, develop, and air. At each step of this complicated process they function as cultural interpreters.

Similar notions have often been outlined by scholars of popular culture focusing on the formal characteristics of popular entertainment.[8] To those insights cultural theory adds the possibility of matching formal analysis with cultural and social practice. The best theoretical explanation for this link is suggested to us in the continuing work of anthropologist Victor Turner. This work focuses on cultural ritual and reminds us that ritual must be seen as process rather than as product, a notion not often applied to the study of television, yet crucial to an adequate understanding of the medium.

Specifically we make use of one aspect of Turner's analysis, his view of the *liminal* stage of the ritual process. This is the "inbetween" stage, when one is neither totally in nor out of society. It is a stage of license, when rules may be broken or bent, when roles may be reversed, when categories may be overturned. Its essence, suggests Turner,

> is to be found in its release from normal constraints, making possible the deconstruction of the "uninteresting" constructions of common sense, the "meaningfulness of ordinary life," . . . into cultural units which may then be reconstructed in novel ways, some of them bizarre to the point of monstrosity. . . . Liminality is the domain of the "interesting" or of "uncommon sense."[9]

Turner does not limit this observation to traditional societies engaged in the *practice* of ritual. He also applies his views to postindustrial, complex societies. In doing so he finds the liminal domain in the arts—all of them.[10] "The dismemberment of ritual has . . . provided the opportunity of theatre in the high culture and carnival at the folk level. A multiplicity of desacralized performative genres have assumed, prismatically, the task of plural cultural reflexivity."[11] In short, contemporary cultures examine themselves through their arts, much as traditional societies do via the experience of ritual. Ritual and the arts offer a metalanguage, a way of understanding who and what we are, how values and attitudes are adjusted, how meaning shifts.

In contributing to this process, particularly in American society, where its role is central, television fulfills what Fiske and Hartley refer to as the "bardic function" of contemporary societies.[12] In its role as central cultural medium it presents a multiplicity of meanings rather than a monolithic dominant point of view. It often focuses on our most prevalent concerns, our deepest dilemmas. Our most traditional views, those that are repressive and reactionary, as well as those that are subversive and emancipatory, are upheld, examined, maintained, and transformed. The emphasis is on process rather than product, on discussion rather than indoctrination, on contradiction and confusion rather than coherence. It is with this view that we turn to an analysis of the texts of television that demonstrates and supports the conception of television as a cultural forum.

⚙︎

This new perspective requires that we revise some of our notions regarding television analysis, criticism, and research. The function of the creator as *bricoleur,* taken from Sahlins, is again indicated and clarified. The focus on "uncommon sense," on the freedom afforded by the idea of television as a liminal realm helps us to understand the reliance on and interest in forms, plots, and character types that are not at all familiar in our lived experience. The skewed demography of the world of television is not quite so bizarre and repressive once we admit that it is the realm in which we allow our monsters to come out and play, our dreams to be wrought into pictures, our fantasies transformed into plot structures. Cowboys, detectives, bionic men, and great green hulks; fatherly physicians, glamorous female detectives, and tightly knit families living out the pain of the Great Depression; all these become part of the dramatic logic of public thought.

Shows such as *Fantasy Island* and *Love Boat,* difficult to account for within traditional critical systems except as examples of trivia and romance, are easily understood. Islands and boats are among the most fitting liminal metaphors, as Homer, Bacon, Shakespeare, and Melville, among others, have recognized. So, too, are the worlds of the Western and the detective story. With this view we can see the "bizarre" world of situation comedy as a means of deconstructing the world of "common sense" in which all, or most, of us live and work. It also enables us to explain such strange phenomena as game shows and late night talk fests. In short, almost any version of the television text functions as a forum in which important cultural topics may be considered. We illustrate this not with a contemporary program where problems almost always appear on the surface of the show, but with an episode of *Father Knows Best* from the early 1960s. We begin by noting that *FKB* is often cited as an innocuous series, constructed around unstinting paeans to American middle-class virtues and blissfully ignorant of social conflict. In short, it is precisely the sort of television program that reproduces dominant ideology by lulling its audience into a dream world where the status quo is the only status.

In the episode in question Betty Anderson, the older daughter in the family, breaks a great many rules by deciding that she will become an engineer. Over great protest, she is given an internship with a surveying crew as part of a high school "career education" program. But the head of the surveying crew, a young college student, drives her away with taunts and insensitivity. She walks off the job on the first day. Later in the week the young man comes to the Anderson home where Jim Anderson chides him with fatherly anger. The young man apologizes and Betty, overhearing him from the other room, runs upstairs, changes clothes, and comes down. The show ends with their flirtation underway.

Traditional ideological criticism, conducted from the communications or the textual analysis perspective, would remark on the way in which social conflict is ultimately subordinated in this dramatic structure to the personal, the emotional. Commentary would focus on the way in which the questioning of the role structure is shifted away from the world of work to the domestic arena. The emphasis would be on the conclusion of the episode in which Betty's real problem of identity and sex-role, and society's problem of sex-role discrimination, is bound by a more traditional conflict and thereby defused, contained, and redirected. Such a reading is possible, indeed accurate.

We would point out, however, that our emotional sympathy is with Betty throughout this episode. Nowhere does the text instruct the viewer that her concerns are unnatural, no matter how unnaturally they may be framed by other members of the cast. Every argument that can be made for a strong feminist perspective is condensed into the brief, half-hour presentation. The concept of the cultural forum, then, offers a different interpretation. We suggest that in popular culture generally, in television specifically, the raising of questions is as important as the answering of them. That is, it is equally important that an audience be introduced to the problems surrounding sex-role discrimination as it is to conclude the episode in a traditional manner. Indeed, it would be startling to think that mainstream texts in mass society would overtly challenge dominant ideas. But this hardly prevents the oppositional ideas from appearing. Put another way, we argue that television does not present firm ideological conclusions—despite its *formal* conclusions—so much as it *comments on* ideological problems. The conflicts we see in television drama, embedded in familiar and nonthreatening frames, are conflicts ongoing in American social experience and cultural history. In a few cases we might see strong perspectives that argue for the absolute correctness of one point of view or another. But for the most part the rhetoric of television drama is a rhetoric of discussion. Shows such as *All in the Family,* or *The Defenders,* or *Gunsmoke,* which raise the forum/discussion to an intense and obvious level, often make best use of the medium and become highly successful. We see statements *about* the issues and it should be clear that ideological positions can be balanced within the forum by others from a different perspective.

We recognize, of course, that this variety works for the most part within the limits of American monopoly-capitalism and within the range of American pluralism. It is an effective pluralistic forum only insofar as American political pluralism is or can be.[13] We also note, however, that one of the primary functions of the popular culture forum, the television forum, is to monitor the limits and the effectiveness of this pluralism, perhaps the only "public" forum in which this role is performed. As content shifts and attracts the attention of groups and individuals, criticism and reform can be initiated. We will have more to say on this topic shortly.

Our intention here is hardly to argue for the richness of *Father Knows Best* as a television text or as social commentary. Indeed, in our view, any emphasis on individual episodes, series, or even genres, misses the central point of the forum concept. While each of these units can and does present its audiences with incredibly mixed ideas, it is television as a whole system that presents a mass audience with the range and variety of ideas and ideologies inherent in American culture. In order to fully understand the role of television in that culture, we must examine a variety of analytical foci and, finally, see them as parts of a greater whole.

We can, for instance, concentrate on a single episode of television content, as we have done in our example. In our view most television shows offer something of this range of complexity. Not every one of them treats social problems of such immediacy, but submerged in any episode are assumptions about who and what we are. Conflicting viewpoints of social issues are, in fact, the elements that structure most television programs.

At the series level this complexity is heightened. In spite of notions to the contrary, most television shows do change over time. Stanley Cavell has recently suggested that this serial nature of television is perhaps its defining characteristic.[14] By contrast we see that feature only as a primary aspect of the rhetoric of television, one that shifts meaning and shades ideology as series develop. Even a series such as *The Brady Bunch* dealt with ever more complex issues merely because the children, on whom the show focused, grew older. In other cases, shows such as *The Waltons* shifted in content and meaning because they represented shifts in historical time. As the series moved out of the period of the Great Depression, through World War II, and into the postwar period, its tone and emphasis shifted too. In some cases, of course, this sort of change is structured into the show from the beginning, even when the appearance is that of static, undeveloping nature. In *All in the Family* the possibility of change and Archie's resistance to it form the central dramatic problem and offer the central opportunity for dramatic richness, a richness that has developed over many years until the character we now see bears little resemblance to the one we met in the beginning. This is also true of *M*A*S*H,* although there the structured conflicts have more to do with framing than with character development. In *M*A*S*H* we are caught in an anti-war rhetoric that cannot end a war. A truly radical alternative, a desertion or an insurrection, would end the series. But it would also end the "discussion" of this issue. We remain trapped, like American culture in its historical reality, with a dream and the rhetoric of peace and with a bitter experience that denies them.

The model of the forum extends beyond the use of the series with attention to genre. One tendency of genre studies has been to focus on similarities within forms, to indicate the ways in which all Westerns, situation comedies, detective shows, and so on are alike. Clearly, however, it is in the economic interests of producers to build on audience familiarity with generic patterns and instill novelty into those generically based presentations. Truly innovative forms that use the generic base as a foundation are likely to be among the more successful shows. This also means that the shows, despite generic similarity, will carry individual rhetorical slants. As a result, while shows like *M*A*S*H, The*

Mary Tyler Moore Show, and *All in the Family* may all treat similar issues, those issues will have different meanings because of the variations in character, tone, history, style, and so on, despite a general "liberal" tone. Other shows, minus that tone, will clash in varying degrees. The notion that they are all, in some sense, "situation comedies" does not adequately explain the treatment of ideas within them.

This hardly diminishes the strength of generic variation as yet another version of differences within the forum. The rhetoric of the soap opera *pattern* is different from that of the situation comedy and that of the detective show. Thus, when similar topics are treated within different generic frames another level of "discussion" is at work.

It is for this reason that we find it important to examine strips of television programming, "flow" as Raymond Williams refers to it.[15] Within these flow strips we may find opposing ideas abutting one another. We may find opposing treatments of the same ideas. And we will certainly find a viewing behavior that is more akin to actual experience than that found when concentrating on the individual show, the series, or the genre. The forum model, then, has led us into a new exploration of the definition of the television text. We are now examining the "viewing strip" as a potential text and are discovering that in the range of options offered by any given evening's television, the forum is indeed a more accurate model of what goes on *within* television than any other that we know of. By taping entire weeks of television content, and tracing various potential strips in the body of that week, we can construct a huge range of potential "texts" that may have been seen by individual viewers.

Each level of text—the strip as text, the television week, the television day—is compounded yet again by the history of the medium. Our hypothesis is that we might track the history of America's social discussions of the past three decades by examining the multiple rhetorics of television during that period. Given the problematic state of television archiving, a careful study of that hypothesis presents an enormous difficulty. It is, nevertheless, an exciting prospect.

❧⟨☉⟩❧

Clearly, our emphasis is on the treatment of issues, on rhetoric. We recognize the validity of analytical structures that emphasize television's skewed demographic patterns, its particular social aberrations, or other "unrealistic distortions" of the world of experience. But we also recognize that in order to make sense of those structures and patterns researchers return again and again to the "meaning" of that television world, to the processes and problems of interpretation. In our view this practice is hardly limited to those of us who study television. It is also open to audiences who view it each evening and to professionals who create for the medium.

The goal of every producer is to create the difference that makes a difference, to maintain an audience with sufficient reference to the known and recognized, but to move ahead into something that distinguishes his show for the program buyer, the scheduler, and most importantly, for the mass audience.

As recent work by Newcomb and Alley shows,[16] the goal of many producers, the most successful and powerful ones, is also to include personal ideas in their work, to use television as all artists use their media, as means of personal expression. Given this goal it is possible to examine the work of individual producers as other units of analysis and to compare the work of different producers as expressions within the forum. We need only think of the work of Quinn Martin and Jack Webb, or to contrast their work with that of Norman Lear or Gary Marshall, to recognize the individuality at work within television making. Choices by producers to work in certain generic forms, to express certain political, moral, and ethical attitudes, to explore certain sociocultural topics, all affect the nature of the ultimate "flow text" of television seen by viewers and assure a range of variations within that text.

The existence of this variation is borne out by varying responses among those who view television. A degree of this variance occurs among professional television critics who like and dislike shows for different reasons. But because television critics, certainly in American journalistic situations, are more alike than different in many ways, a more important indicator of the range of responses is that found among "ordinary" viewers, or the disagreements implied by audience acceptance and enthusiasm for program material soundly disavowed by professional critics. Work by Himmleweit in England[17] and Neuman in America[18] indicates that individual viewers do function as "critics," do make important distinctions, and are able, under certain circumstances, to articulate the bases for their judgments. While this work is just beginning, it is still possible to suggest from anecdotal evidence that people agree and disagree with television for a variety of reasons. They find in television texts representations of and challenges to their own ideas, and must somehow come to terms with what is there.

If disagreements cut too deeply into the value structure of the individual, if television threatens the sense of cultural security, the individual may take steps to engage the medium at the level of personal action. Most often this occurs in the form of letters to the network or to local stations, and again, the pattern is not new to television. It has occurred with every other mass medium in modern industrial society.

Nor is it merely the formation of groups or the expression of personal points of view that indicates the working of a forum. It is the *range* of response, the directly contradictory readings of the medium, that cue us to its multiple meanings. Groups may object to the same programs, for example, for entirely opposing reasons. In *Charlie's Angels* feminists may find yet another example of sexist repression, while fundamentalist religious groups may find examples of moral decay expressed in the sexual freedom, the personal appearance, or the "unfeminine" behavior of the protagonists. Other viewers doubtless find the expression of meaningful liberation of women. At this level, the point is hardly that one group is "right" and another "wrong," much less that one is "right" while the other is "left." Individuals and groups are, for many reasons, involved in making their own meanings from the television text.

This variation in interpretive strategies can be related to suggestions made by Stuart Hall in his influential essay, "Encoding and Decoding in the Television Discourse."[19] There he suggests three basic modes of interpretation, corresponding to the interpreter's political stance within the social structure. The interpretation may be "dominant," accepting the prevailing ideological structure. It may be "oppositional," rejecting the basic aspects of the structure. Or it may be "negotiated," creating a sort of personal synthesis. As later work by some of Hall's colleagues suggests, however, it quickly becomes necessary to expand the range of possible interpretations.[20] Following these suggestions to a radical extreme it might be possible to argue that every individual interpretation of television content could, in some way, be "different." Clearly, however, communication is dependent on a greater degree of shared meanings, and expressions of popular entertainment are perhaps even more dependent on the shared level than many other forms of discourse. Our concern then is for the ways in which interpretation is negotiated in society. Special interest groups that focus, at times, on television provide us with readily available resources for the study of interpretive practices.

We see these groups as representative of metaphoric "fault lines" in American society. Television is the terrain in which the faults are expressed and worked out. In studying the groups, their rhetoric, the issues on which they focus, their tactics, their forms of organization, we hope to demonstrate that the idea of the "forum" is more than a metaphor in its own right. In forming special interest groups, or in using such groups to speak about television, citizens actually enter the forum. Television shoves them toward action, toward expression of ideas and values. At this level the model of "television as a cultural forum" enables us to examine "the sociology of interpretation."

Here much attention needs to be given to the historical aspects of this form of activity. How has the definition of issues changed over time? How has that change correlated with change in the television texts? These are important questions which, while difficult to study, are crucial to a full understanding of the role of television in culture. It is primarily through this sort of study that we will be able to define much more precisely the limits of the forum, for groups form monitoring devices that alert us to shortcomings not only in the world of television representation, but to the world of political experience as well. We know, for example, that because of heightened concern on the part of special interest groups, and responses from the creative and institutional communities of television industries, the "fictional" population of black citizens now roughly equals that of the actual population. Regardless of whether such a match is "good" or "necessary," regardless of the nature of the depiction of blacks on television, this indicates that the forum extends beyond the screen. The issue of violence, also deserving close study, is more mixed, varying from year to year. The influence of groups, of individuals, of studies, of the terrible consequences of murder and assassination, however, cannot be denied. Television does not exist in a realm of its own, cut off from the influence of citizens. Our aim is to discover, as precisely as possible, the ways in which the varied worlds interact.

Throughout this kind of analysis, then, it is necessary to cite a range of varied responses to the texts of television. Using the viewing "strip" as the appropriate text of television, and recognizing that it is filled with varied topics and approaches to those topics, we begin to think of the television viewer as a *bricoleur* who matches the creator in the making of meanings. Bringing values and attitudes, a universe of personal experiences and concerns, to the texts, the viewer selects, examines, acknowledges, and makes texts of his or her own.[21] If we conceive of special interest groups as representatives of *patterns* of cultural attitude and response, we have a potent source of study.

On the production end of this process, in addition to the work of individual producers, we must examine the role of network executives who must purchase and program television content. They, too, are cultural interpreters, intent on "reading" the culture through its relation to the "market." Executives who head and staff the internal censor agencies of each network, the offices of Broadcast Standards or Standards and Practices, are in a similar position. Perhaps as much as any individual or group they present us with a source of rich material for analysis. They are actively engaged in gauging cultural values. Their own research, the assumptions and the findings, needs to be re-analyzed for cultural implications, as does the work of the programmers. In determining who is doing what, with whom, at what times, they are interpreting social behavior in America and assigning it meaning. They are using television as a cultural litmus that can be applied in defining such problematic concepts as "childhood," "family," "maturity," and "appropriate." With the Standards and Practices offices, they interpret *and* define the permissible and the "normal." But their interpretations of behavior open to us as many questions as answers, and an appropriate overview, a new model of television is necessary in order to best understand their work and ours.

This new model of "television as a cultural forum" fits the experience of television more accurately than others we have seen applied. Our assumption is that it opens a range of new questions and calls for re-analysis of older findings from both the textual-critical approach and the mass communications research perspective. Ultimately the new model is a simple one. It recognizes the range of interpretation of television content that is now admitted even by those analysts most concerned with television's presentation and maintenance of dominant ideological messages and meanings. But it differs from those perspectives because it does not see this as surprising or unusual. For the most part, that is what central storytelling systems do in all societies. We are far more concerned with the ways in which television contributes to change than with mapping the obvious ways in which it maintains dominant viewpoints. Most research on television, most textual analysis, has assumed that the medium is thin, repetitive, similar, nearly identical in textual formation, easily defined, described, and explained. The variety of response on the part of audiences has been received, as a result of this view, as extraordinary, an astonishing "discovery."

We begin with the observation, based on careful textual analysis, that television is dense, rich, and complex rather than impoverished. Any selection, any cut, any set of questions that is extracted from that text must somehow account for that density, must account for what is *not* studied or measured, for the opposing meanings, for the answering images and symbols. Audiences appear to make meaning by selecting that which touches experience and personal history. The range of responses then should be taken as commonplace rather than as unexpected. But research and critical analysis cannot afford so personal a view. Rather, they must somehow define and describe the inventory that makes possible the multiple meanings extracted by audiences, creators, and network decision makers.

Our model is based on the assumption and observation that only so rich a text could attract a mass audience in a complex culture. The forum offers a perspective that is as complex, as contradictory and confused, as much in process as American culture is in experience. Its texture matches that of our daily experiences. If we can understand it better, then perhaps we will better understand the world we live in, the actions that we must take in order to live there.

Notes

1. James Carey, "A Cultural Approach to Communications," *Communications* 2 (December 1975).

2. Ibid.

3. James Carey, "Culture and Communications," *Communications Research* (April 1975).

4. See Roger Silverstone, *The Message of Television: Myth and Narrative in Contemporary Culture* (London: Heinemann, 1981), on structural and narrative analysis; John Fiske and John Hartley, *Reading Television* (London: Methuen, 1978), on the semiotic and cultural bases for the analysis of television; David Thorburn, *The Story Machine* (Oxford University Press: forthcoming), on the aesthetics of television; Himmleweit, Hilda et al., "The Audience as Critic: An Approach to the Study of Entertainment," in *The Entertainment Functions of Television*, ed. Percy Tannenbaum (New York: Lawrence Eribaum Associates, 1980) and W. Russel Neuman, "Television and American Culture: The Mass Medium and the Pluralist Audience," *Public Opinion Quarterly*, 46: 4 (Winter 1982), pp. 471–87, on the role of the audience as critic; Todd Gitlin, "Prime Time Ideology: The Hegemonic Process in Television Entertainment," *Social Problems* 26:3 (1979), and Douglas Kelnner, "TV, Ideology, and Emancipatory Popular Culture," *Socialist Review* 45 (May–June, 1979), on hegemony and new applications of critical theory; James T. Lull, "The Social Uses of Television," *Human Communications Research* 7:3 (1980), and "Family Communication Patterns and the Social Uses of Television," *Communications Research* 7: 3 (1979), and Tim Meyer, Paul Traudt, and James Anderson, Non-Traditional Mass Communication Research Methods: Observational Case Studies of Media Use in Natural Settings, *Communication Yearbook IV*, ed. Dan Nimmo (New Brunswick, N.J.: Transaction Books), on audience ethnography and symbolic interactionism; and, most importantly, the ongoing work of The Center for Contemporary Cultural Studies at Birmingham University, England, most recently published in *Culture, Media, Language,* ed. Stuart Hall et al. (London: Hutchinson, in association with The Center for Contemporary Cultural Studies, 1980), on the interaction of culture and textual analysis from a thoughtful political perspective.

5. Carey, 1976.

6. Paul Hirsch, "The Role of Popular Culture and Television in Contemporary Society," *Television: The Critical View,* ed. Horace Newcomb (New York: Oxford University Press, 1979, 1982).

7. Marshall Sahlins, *Culture and Practical Reason* (Chicago: University of Chicago Press, 1976), p. 217.

8. John Cawelti, *Adventure, Mystery, and Romance* (Chicago: University of Chicago Press, 1976), and David Thorburn, "Television Melodrama," *Television: The Critical View* (New York: Oxford University Press, 1979, 1982).

9. Victor Turner, "Process, System, and Symbol: A New Anthropological Synthesis," *Daedalus* (Summer 1977), p. 68.

10. In various works Turner uses both the terms "liminal" and "liminoid" to refer to works of imagination and entertainment in contemporary culture. The latter term is used to clearly mark the distinction between events that have distinct behavioral consequences and those that do not. As Turner suggests, the consequences of entertainment in contemporary culture are hardly as profound as those of the liminal stage of ritual in traditional culture. We are aware of this basic distinction but use the former term in order to avoid a fuller explanation of the neologism. See Turner, "Afterword," to *The Reversible World,* Barbara Babcock, ed. (Ithaca: Cornell University Press, 1979), and "Liminal to Liminoid, in Play, Flow, and Ritual: An Essay in Comparative Symbology," *Rice University Studies,* 60:3 (1974).

11. Turner, 1977, p. 73.

12. Fiske and Hartley, 1978, p. 85.

13. We are indebted to Prof. Mary Douglas for encouraging this observation. At the presentation of these ideas at the New York Institute for the Humanities seminar on "The Mass Production of Mythology," she checked our enthusiasm for a pluralistic model of television by stating accurately and succinctly, "there are pluralisms and pluralisms." This comment led us to consider more thoroughly the means by which the forum and responses to it function as a tool with which to monitor the quality of pluralism in American social life, including its entertainments. The observation added a much needed component to our planned historical analysis.

14. Stanley Cavell, "The Fact of Television," *Daedalus* 3: 4 (Fall 1982).

15. Raymond Williams, *Television, Technology and Cultural Form* (New York: Schocken, 1971), p. 86 ff.

16. Horace Newcomb and Robert Alley, *The Television Producer as Artist in American Commercial Television* (New York: Oxford University Press, 1983).

17. Ibid.

18. Ibid.

19. Stuart Hall, "Encoding and Decoding in the Television Discourse," *Culture, Media, Language* (London: Hutchinson, in association with The Center for Contemporary Cultural Studies, 1980).

20. See Dave Morley and Charlotte Brunsdon, *Everyday Television: "Nationwide"* (London: British Film Institute, 1978), and Morley, "Subjects, Readers, Texts," in *Culture, Media, Language.*

21. We are indebted to Louis Black and Eric Michaels of the Radio-TV-Film department of the University of Texas-Austin for calling this aspect of televiewing to Newcomb's attention. It creates a much desired balance to Sahlin's view of the creator as *bricoleur* and indicates yet another matter in which the forum model enhances our ability to account for more aspects of the television experience. See, especially, Eric Michaels, *TV Tribes,* unpublished Ph.D. dissertation, University of Texas-Austin. 1982.

POSTSCRIPT

Are American Values Shaped by the Mass Media?

Television is pervasive in American life. Yet the influence of television on society is difficult to ascertain. Although these issues are as hotly debated today as they were when these articles were written, a number of things have changed since then. Newcomb and Hirsch have noted that with the passing of the network era, the notion that television serves as a site of negotiation for cultural issues, images, and ideas has shifted. The development of multiple channels now undercuts the dominance of the "big three" network era. Now the "viewing strip" is so complex as to be almost impossible to identify. The negotiation process may be much more complex than ever, as viewers select from an ever-widening set of approaches to issues and ideas. Perhaps the cultural negotiation is now more limited because choices are more diverse. Similarly, alterations in programming strategies, particularly the creation of "niche" programming, may strain the notion of an ideological core, as advanced by Gitlin. Perhaps all this additional programming is simply "more of the same." But some argue that specialized channels and additional electronic options like the Internet open up spaces for "contested meanings" that challenge the dominant hegemonic reality.

Yet some effects of television have been dramatically illustrated. The media were instrumental in bringing together the entire nation to mourn and to respond to the events of September 11, 2001. Television's ability to bring events to millions of viewers may mean that television itself is a factor in determining the events. Television has reshaped American politics, but it may have little influence on how people actually vote. Television is now the primary source of news for most Americans. It has also altered the ways in which Americans spend their time, ranking third behind sleep and work. Yet these influences may be only a prelude to larger social changes that will emerge as technology becomes even more pervasive.

Denis McQuail, in *Mass Communication Theory: An Introduction,* 4th ed. (Sage Publications, 2000), provides an insightful review of mass communication theory, with particular emphasis on the usefulness of theories of society for understanding the influence of mass communication. Editors John Downing, Ali Mohammadi, and Annabelle Sreberny-Mohammadi, in *Questioning the Media: A Critical Introduction* (Sage Publications, 1995), provide a readable introduction to critical social issues as they relate to media, particularly media and identity.

For more from Newcomb, see his edited book *Television: The Critical View,* 6th ed. (Oxford University Press, 2000). Gitlin is the author of nine books, including *Inside Prime Time* (University of California Press, 2000) and *The Whole World Is Watching: Mass Media in the Making and Unmaking of the New Left* (University of California Press, 1980). Authors such as Neil Postman also suggest that media shape American values by changing the nature of public discourse. Postman argues in *Amusing Ourselves to Death* (Viking Penguin, 1985) that television promotes triviality by speaking in only one voice—the voice of entertainment. Thus he maintains that television is transforming American culture into show business, to the detriment of rational public discourse.

ISSUE 2

Is Television Harmful for Children?

YES: W. James Potter, from *On Media Violence* (Sage Publications, 1999)

NO: Jib Fowles, from *The Case for Television Violence* (Sage Publications, 1999)

ISSUE SUMMARY

YES: W. James Potter, a professor of communication, examines existing research in the area of children and television violence. Such research is extensive and covers a variety of theoretical and methodological areas. He examines the nature of the impact of television on children and concludes that strong evidence exists for harmful effects.

NO: Jib Fowles, a professor of communication, finds the research on children and television violence less convincing. Despite the number of studies, he believes that the overall conclusions are unwarranted. Fowles finds that the influence is small, lab results are artificial, and fieldwork is inconclusive. In short, he finds television violence research flawed and unable to prove a linkage between violent images and harm to children.

$\mathbf{Y}$ouths now have access to more violent images than at any other time in United States history, and these images are available in a diverse array of electronic sources: television, movies, video games, and music. Does such graphic, immediate, and pervasive imagery influence children's behavior and ultimately the level of violence in society? Is media a powerful force that can no longer be considered mere entertainment? Or, are Americans as a society overreacting, using media as a scapegoat for the concern over seemingly hopeless social problems?

In April 1999, after a series of similar school shootings, Columbine High School in Littleton, Colorado, was forever etched in our memory. The shootings there raised, in the most dramatic way possible, questions of how America had come to this tragedy. Did media play a role? Many would argue yes and would point to reenactments of video games, fashion choices from recent movies, imitative behaviors, and Internet discussions. Others would point to the long history of mental illness and social isolation of the perpetrators as more proximate causes.

Is media violence a threat to society? Those who would answer affirmatively might point to the content of children's viewing, arguing that it is a significant part of the socialization process and decrying the stereotypes, violence, and mindlessness of much of television fare. Others might argue that there are other negative consequences intrinsic to television viewing: the common daily fare of television themes, particularly a perception of the world as a scary place. Many would maintain that there are millions of people who watch television with no discernable negative consequences. Furthermore, they might say that there is a constellation of negative influences that seem to appear in violent individuals, a lack of proof, and an absurdity of thinking that television entertainment harms people.

Researchers began to study the impact of television on children early in television history by asking who watches, how much, and why. They analyzed what children see on television and how the content influences their cognitive development, school achievement, family interaction, social behaviors, and general attitudes and opinions. This is a large and complex social issue, so even extensive research has not provided final answers to all the questions that concerned parents and educators, professional mass communicators, and legislators have raised.

W. James Potter asserts that decades of research have led to several strong conclusions: violence is a public health problem and evidence is there to support the risks of exposure and discern the most susceptible individuals. Moreover, violent portrayals are pervasive; exposure leads to negative effects, both immediately and over the long term; and certain types of portrayals and certain types of viewers maximize the probability of negative effects. Jib Fowles disagrees. The evidence just is not that strong, he asserts, and the impact is very small when it does occur. He criticizes the methods of laboratory, field, and correlational research. Why, he asks, are such small effects considered so worthy of concern? His suspicion is that the scapegoating of media allows politicians, businesspeople, and society in general to feel they are tackling a problem without really taking any of the steps necessary to promote fundamental change.

W. James Potter

 **YES**

On Media Violence

Overview and Introduction

Violence in American society is a public health problem. Although most people have never witnessed an act of serious violence in person, we are all constantly reminded of its presence by the media. The media constantly report news about individual violent crimes. The media also use violence as a staple in telling fictional stories to entertain us. Thus, the media amplify and reconfigure the violence in real life and continuously pump these messages into our culture.

The culture is responding with a range of negative effects. Each year about 25,000 people are murdered, and more than 2 million are injured in assaults. On the highways, aggressive behavior such as tailgating, weaving through busy lanes, honking or screaming at other drivers, exchanging insults, and even engaging in gunfire is a factor in nearly 28,000 traffic deaths annually, and the problem is getting worse at a rate of 7% per year. Gun-related deaths increased more than 60% from 1968 to 1994, to about 40,000 annually, and this problem is now considered a public health epidemic by 87% of surgeons and 94% of internists across the United States. Meanwhile, the number of pistols manufactured in the United States continues to increase—up 92% from 1985 to 1992.

Teenagers are living in fear. A Harris poll of 2,000 U.S. teenagers found that most of them fear violence and crime and that this fear is affecting their everyday behavior. About 46% of respondents said they have changed their daily behavior because of a fear of crime and violence; 12% said they carry a weapon to school for protection; 12% have altered their route to school; 20% said they have avoided particular parks or playgrounds; 20% said they have changed their circle of friends; and 33% have stayed away from school at times because of fear of violence. In addition, 25% said they did not feel safe in their own neighborhood, and 33% said they fear being a victim of a drive-by shooting. Nearly twice as many teenagers reported gangs in their school in 1995 compared to 1989, and this increase is seen in all types of neighborhoods; violent crime in schools increased 23.5% during the same period.

This problem has far-reaching economic implications. The U.S. Department of Justice estimates the total cost of crime and violence (such as child abuse and domestic violence, in addition to crimes such as murder, rape, and robbery) to be $500 billion per year, or about twice the annual budget of the Defense Department. The cost includes real expenses (such as legal fees, the cost of lost time from work, the cost of police work, and the cost of running the nation's prisons and parole systems) and intangibles (such as loss of affection from murdered family members). Violent crime is responsible for 14% of injury-related medical spending and up to 20% of mental health care expenditures.

The problem of violence in our culture has many apparent causes, including poverty, breakdown of the nuclear family, shift away from traditional morality to a situational pluralism, and the mass media. The media are especially interesting as a source of the problem. Because they are so visible, the media are an easy target for blame. In addition, they keep reminding us of the problem in their news stories. But there is also a more subtle and likely more powerful reason why the media should be regarded as a major cause of this public health problem: They manufacture a steady stream of fictional messages that convey to all of us in this culture what life is about. Media stories tell us how we should deal with conflict, how we should treat other people, what is risky, and what it means to be powerful. The media need to share the blame for this serious public health problem.

How do we address the problem? The path to remedies begins with a solid knowledge base. It is the task of social scientists to generate much of this knowledge. For the past five decades, social scientists and other scholars have been studying the topic of media violence. This topic has attracted researchers from many different disciplines, especially psychology, sociology, mental health science, cultural studies, law, and public policy. This research addresses questions such as these: How much media violence is there? What are the meanings conveyed in the way violence is portrayed? and What effect does violence have on viewers as individuals, as members of particular groups, and as members of society? Estimates of the number of studies conducted to answer these questions range as high as 3,000 and even 3,500....

Effects of Exposure to Media Violence

Does exposure to violence in the media lead to effects? With each passing year, the answer is a stronger yes. The general finding from a great deal of research is that exposure to violent portrayals in the media increases the probability of an effect. The most often tested effect is referred to as *learning to behave aggressively*. This effect is also referred to as direct imitation of violence, instigation or triggering of aggressive impulses, and disinhibition of socialization against aggressive behavior. Two other negative effects—desensitization and fear—are also becoming prevalent in the literature.

Exposure to certain violent portrayals can lead to positive or prosocial effects. Intervention studies, especially with children, have shown that when a media-literate person talks through the action and asks questions of the viewer during the exposure, the viewer will be able to develop a counterreading of the violence; that is, the viewer may learn that violent actions are wrong even though those actions are shown as successful in the media portrayal.

The effects have been documented to occur immediately or over the long term. Immediate effects happen during exposure or shortly after the exposure (within about an hour). They might last only several minutes, or they might last weeks. Long-term effects do not occur after one or several exposures; they begin to show up only after an accumulation of exposures over weeks or years. Once a long-term effect eventually occurs, it usually lasts a very long period of time.

This [selection] focuses on the issues of both immediate effects and long-term effects of exposure to media violence....

From the large body of effects research, I have assembled 10 major findings. These are the findings that consistently appear in quantitative meta-analyses and narrative reviews of this literature. Because these findings are so widespread in the literature and because they are so rarely disputed by scholars, they can be regarded as empirically established laws.

Immediate Effects of Violent Content

The first six laws illuminate the major findings of research into the immediate effects of exposure to media violence. Immediate effects occur during exposure or within several hours afterward.

> *1. Exposure to violent portrayals in the media can lead to subsequent viewer aggression through disinhibition.*

This conclusion is found in most of the early reviews. For example, Stein and Friedrich closely analyzed 49 studies of the effects of antisocial and prosocial television content on people 3 to 18 years of age in the United States. They concluded that the correlational studies showed generally significant relationships ($r = .10$ to $.32$) and that the experiments generally showed an increase in aggression resulting from exposure to television violence across all age groups.

This conclusion gained major visibility in the 1972 Surgeon General's Report which stated that there was an influence, but this conclusion was softened by the industry members on the panel....

Some of the early reviewers disagreed with this conclusion....

In the two decades since this early disagreement, a great deal more empirical research has helped overcome these shortcomings, so most (but not all) of these critics have been convinced of the general finding that exposure to media violence can lead to an immediate disinhibition effect. All narrative reviews since 1980 have concluded that viewing of violence is consistently related to subsequent aggressiveness. This finding holds in surveys, laboratory experiments, and naturalistic experiments. For example, Roberts and Maccoby concluded that "the overwhelming proportion of results point to a causal relationship between exposure to mass communication portrayals of violence and an increased probability that viewers will behave violently at some subsequent time." Also, Friedrich-Cofer and Huston concluded that "the weight of the evidence from different methods of investigation supports the hypothesis that television violence affects aggression."

Meta-analytical studies that have reexamined the data quantitatively across sets of studies have also consistently concluded that viewing of aggression is likely to lead to antisocial behavior. For example, Paik and Comstock conducted a meta-analysis of 217 studies of the effects of television violence on antisocial behavior and reported finding a positive and significant correlation. They concluded that "regardless of age—whether nursery school, elementary school, college, or adult—results remain positive at a high significance level." Andison looked at 67 studies involving 30,000 participants (including 31 laboratory experiments) and found a relationship between viewing and subsequent aggression, with more than half of the studies showing a correlation (r) between .31 and .70. Hearold looked at 230 studies involving 100,000 participants to determine the effect of viewing violence on a wide range of antisocial behaviors in addition to aggression (including rule breaking, materialism, and perceiving oneself as powerless in society). Hearold concluded that for all ages and all measures, the majority of studies reported an association between exposure to violence and antisocial behavior. . . .

On balance, it is prudent to conclude that media portrayals of violence can lead to the immediate effect of aggressive behavior, that this can happen in response to as little as a single exposure, and that this effect can last up to several weeks. Furthermore, the effect is causal, with exposure leading to aggression. However, this causal link is part of a reciprocal process; that is, people with aggressive tendencies seek out violent portrayals in the media.

2. The immediate disinhibition effect is influenced by viewer demographics, viewer traits, viewer states, characteristics in the portrayals, and situational cues.

Each human is a complex being who brings to each exposure situation a unique set of motivations, traits, predispositions, exposure history, and personality factors. These characteristics work together incrementally to increase or decrease the probability of the person's being affected.

2.1 Viewer Demographics
The key characteristics of the viewer that have been found to be related to a disinhibition effect are age and gender, but social class and ethnic background have also been found to play a part.

Demographics of age and gender.   Boys and younger children are more affected. Part of the reason is that boys pay more attention to violence. Moreover, younger children have more trouble following story plots, so they are more likely to be drawn into high-action episodes without considering motives or consequences. Age by itself is not as good an explanation as is ability for cognitive processing.

Socioeconomic status.   Lower-class youth watch more television and therefore more violence.

Ethnicity.   Children from minority and immigrant groups are vulnerable because they are heavy viewers of television.

2.2 Viewer Traits

The key characteristics of viewer traits are socialization against aggression, . . . cognitive processing, and personality type.

Socialization against aggression.   Family life is an important contributing factor. Children in households with strong norms against violence are not likely to experience enough disinhibition to exhibit aggressive behavior. The disinhibition effect is stronger in children living in households in which . . . children are abused by parents, watch more violence, and identify more with violent heroes; and in families that have high-stress environments.

Peer and adult role models have a strong effect in this socialization process. Male peers have the most immediate influence in shaping children's aggressive behaviors in the short term; adult males have the most lasting effect 6 months later. . . .

Cognitive processing.   Viewers' reactions depend on their individual interpretations of the aggression. Rule and Ferguson (1986) said that viewers first must form a representation or cognitive structure consisting of general social knowledge about the positive value that can be attached to aggression. The process of developing such a structure requires that viewers attend to the material (depending on the salience and complexity of the program). Then viewers make attributions and form moral evaluations in the comprehension stage. Then they store their comprehension in memory.

Cognitive processing is related to age. Developmental psychologists have shown that children's minds mature cognitively and that in some early stages they are unable to process certain types of television content well. . . .[U]ntil age 5, they are especially attracted to and influenced by vivid production features, such as rapid movement of characters, rapid changes of scenes, and unexpected sights and sounds. Children seek out and pay attention to cartoon violence, not because of the violence, but because of the vivid production features. By ages 6 to 11, children have developed the ability to lengthen their attention spans and make sense of continuous plots. . . .

Personality type.   The more aggressive the person is, the more influence viewing of violence will have on that person's subsequent aggressive behavior (Comstock et al., 1978; Stein & Friedrich, 1972). And children who are emotionally disturbed are more susceptible to a disinhibition effect (Sprafkin et al., 1992). . . .

2.3. Viewer States
The degrees of physiological arousal, anger, and frustration have all been found to increase the probability of a negative effect.

Aroused state.   Portrayals (even if they are not violent) that leave viewers in an aroused state are more likely to lead to aggressive behavior (Berkowitz & Geen, 1966; Donnerstein & Berkowitz, 1981; Tannenbaum, 1972; Zillman, 1971).

Emotional reaction.   Viewers who are upset by the media exposure (negative hedonic value stimuli) are more likely to aggress (Rule & Ferguson, 1986; Zill-mann et al., 1981). Such aggression is especially likely when people are left in a state of unresolved excitement (Comstock, 1985).... In his meta-analysis of 1,043 effects of television on social behavior, Hearold (1986) concluded that frustration... is not a necessary condition, but rather a contributory condition....

Degree of identity.   It has been well established that the more a person, especially a child, identifies with a character, the more likely the person will be influenced by that character's behavior.

Identity seems to be a multifaceted construct composed of similarity, attractiveness, and hero status. If the perpetrator of violence is perceived as *similar* to the viewer, the likelihood of learning to behave aggressively increases (Lieberman Research, 1975; Rosekrans & Hartup, 1967). When violence is performed by an *attractive* character, the probability of aggression increases (Comstock et al., 1978; Hearold, 1986). Attractiveness of a villain is also an important consideration (Health et al., 1989)....

2.4 Characteristics in the Portrayals
Reviews of the literature are clear on the point that people interpret the meaning of violent portrayals and use contextual information to construct that meaning.

In the media effects literature, there appear to be five notable contextual variables: rewards and punishments, consequences, justification, realism, and production techniques....

Rewards and punishments.   Rewards and punishments to perpetrators of violence provide important information to viewers about which actions are acceptable. However, there is reason to believe that the effect does not work with children younger than 10, who usually have difficulty linking violence presented early in a program with its punishment rendered later (Collins, 1973).

In repeated experiments, viewers who watch a model rewarded for performing violently in the media are more likely to experience a disinhibition effect and behave in a similar manner. But when violence is punished in the media portrayal, the aggressiveness of viewers is likely to be inhibited (Comstock et al., 1978). In addition, when nonaggressive characters are rewarded, viewers' levels of aggression can be reduced.

The absence of punishment also leads to disinhibition. That is, the perpetrators need not be rewarded in order for the disinhibition effect to occur....

Consequences.   The way in which the consequences of violence are portrayed influences the disinhibition effect.... For example, Goranson showed people a film of a prize fight in which either there were no consequences or the loser of the fight received a bad beating and later died. The participants who did not see the negative consequences were more likely to behave aggressively after the viewing.

A key element in the consequences is whether the victim shows pain, because pain cues inhibit subsequent aggression. Moreover, Swart and Berkowitz (1976) showed that viewers could generalize pain cues to characters other than the victims.

Justification.   Reviews of the effects research conclude that justification of violent acts leads to higher aggression. For example, Bryan and Schwartz observed that "aggressive behavior in the service of morally commendable ends appears condoned. Apparently, the assumption is made that moral goals temper immoral actions.... Thus, both the imitation and interpersonal attraction of the transgressing model may be determined more by outcomes than by moral principles."

Several experiments offer support for these arguments. First, Berkowitz and Rawlings (1963) found that justification of filmed aggression lowers viewers' inhibitions to aggress in real life.

Justification is keyed to motives. Brown and Tedeschi (1976) found that offensive violence was regarded as more violent even when the actions themselves were not as violent. For example, a verbal threat that is made offensively is perceived as more violent than a punch that is delivered defensively.

The one motive that has been found to lead to the strongest disinhibition is vengeance. For example, Berkowitz and Alioto introduced a film of a sporting event (boxing and football) by saying that the participants were acting either as professionals wanting to win or as motivated by vengeance and wanting to hurt the other. They found that the vengeance film led to more shocks and longer duration of shocks in a subsequent test of participants. When violence was portrayed as vengeance, disinhibition was stronger than when violence was portrayed as self-defense or as a means of achieving altruistic goals.

Young children have difficulty understanding motives. For example, Collins (1973) ran an experiment on children aged 8 to 15 to see if a time lag from portrayal of motivation to portrayal of aggression changed participants' behaviors or interpretations. Participants were shown either a 30-minute film in which federal agents confronted some criminals or a control film of a travelogue. In the treatment film, the criminals hit and shot the federal agents, displaying negative motivation (desire to escape justice) and negative consequences (a criminal fell to his death while trying to escape). Some participants saw the sequence uninterrupted; others saw the motivation, followed by a 4-minute interruption of commercials, then the aggression. Both 18 days before the experiment and then again right after the viewing, participants were asked their responses to a wide range of hypothetical interpersonal conflict situations. There was a difference by age. Third graders displayed more aggressive choices on the postviewing measure when they had experienced the separation condition; sixth and 10th graders did not exhibit this effect. The author concluded that among younger children, temporal separation of story elements obscures the message that aggression was negatively motivated and punished....

Realism.   When viewers believe that the aggression is portrayed in a realistic manner, they are more likely to try it in real life.

Production techniques.   Certain production techniques can capture and hold attention, potentially leading to differences in the way the action is perceived. Attention is increased when graphic and explicit acts are used to increase the dramatic nature of the narrative, to increase positive dispositions toward the characters using violence, and to increase levels of arousal, which is more likely to result in aggressive behavior....

   3. Exposure to violence in the media can lead to fear effects.

   The best available review is by Cantor (1994), who defines fear effect as an immediate physiological effect of arousal, along with an emotional reaction of anxiety and distress.

   4. An immediate fear effect is influenced by a set of key factors about viewers and the portrayals.

4.1 Viewer Factors

Identification with the target.   The degree of identification with the target is associated with a fear effect. For example, characters who are attractive, who are heroic, or who are perceived as similar to the viewer evoke viewer empathy. When a character with whom viewers empathize is then the target of violence, viewers experience an increased feeling of fear.
   The identification with characters can lead to an enjoyment effect. For example, Tannenbaum and Gaer (1965) found that participants who identified more with the hero felt more stress and benefited more from a happy ending in which their stress was reduced. However, a sad or indeterminate ending increased participants' stress.

Prior real-life experience.   Prior experience with fearful events in real life leads viewers, especially children, to identify more strongly with the characters and events and thereby to involve them more emotionally.

Belief that the depicted violent action could happen to the viewer.   When viewers think there is a good chance that the violence they see could happen to them in real life, they are more likely to experience an immediate fear effect.

Motivations for exposure.   People expose themselves to media violence for many different reasons. Certain reasons for exposure can reduce a fear effect. If people's motivation to view violence is entertainment, they can employ a discounting procedure to lessen the effects of fear.

Level of arousal.   Higher levels of arousal lead to higher feelings of fear.

Ability to use coping strategies.   When people are able to remind themselves that the violence in the media cannot hurt them, they are less likely to experience a fear effect.

Developmental differences.   Children at lower levels of cognitive development are unable to follow plot lines well, so they are more influenced by individual violent episodes, which seem to appear randomly and without motivation.

Ability to perceive the reality of the portrayals.   Children are less able than older viewers to understand the fantasy nature of certain violent portrayals.

4.2 Portrayal Factors

Type of stimulus.   Cantor (1994) says that the fright effect is triggered by three categories of stimuli that usually are found in combination with many portrayals of violence in the media. First is the category of dangers and injuries, stimuli that depict events that threaten great harm. Included in this category are natural disasters, attacks by vicious animals, large-scale accidents, and violent encounters at levels ranging from interpersonal to intergalactic. Second is the category of distortions of natural forms. This category includes familiar organisms that are shown as deformed or unnatural through mutilation, accidents of birth, or conditioning. And third is the category of experience of endangerment and fear by others. This type of stimulus evokes empathy for particular characters, and the viewer then feels the fear that the characters in the narrative are portraying.

Unjustified violence.   When violence is portrayed as unjustified, viewers become more fearful.

Graphicness.   Higher levels of explicitness and graphicness increase viewer fear.

Rewards.   When violence goes unpunished, viewers become more fearful.

Realism.   Live-action violence provokes more intense fear than cartoon violence does. For example, Lazarus et al. found that showing gory accidents to adults aroused them physiologically less when the participants were told that the accidents were fake. This effect has also been found with children. In addition, fear is enhanced when elements in a portrayal resemble characteristics in a person's own life.

5. Exposure to violence in the media can lead to desensitization.

In the short term, viewers of repeated violence can show a lack of arousal and emotional response through habituation to the stimuli.

6. An immediate desensitization effect is influenced by a set of key factors about viewers and the portrayals.

Children and adults can become desensitized to violence upon multiple exposures through temporary habituation. But the habituation appears to be relatively short-term.

6.1 Viewer Factors
People who are exposed to larger amounts of television violence are usually found to be more susceptible to immediate desensitization.

6.2 Portrayal Factors
There appear to be two contextual variables that increase the likelihood of a desensitization effect: graphicness and humor.

Graphicness. Graphicness of violence can lead to immediate desensitization. In experiments in which participants are exposed to graphic violence, initially they have strong physiological responses, but these responses steadily decline during the exposure. This effect has also been shown with children, especially among the heaviest viewers of TV violence.

Humor. Humor contributes to the desensitization effect.

Long-Term Effects of Violent Content

Long-term effects of exposure to media violence are more difficult to measure than are immediate effects. The primary reason is that long-term effects occur so gradually that by the time an effect is clearly indicated, it is very difficult to trace that effect back to media exposures. It is not possible to argue that any single exposure triggers the effect. Instead, we must argue that the long-term pattern of exposure leads to the effect. A good analogy is the way in which an orthodontist straightens teeth. Orthodontists do not produce an immediate effect by yanking teeth into line in one appointment. Instead, they apply braces that exert very little pressure, but that weak pressure is constant. A person who begins wearing braces might experience sore gums initially, but even then there is no observable change to the alignment of the teeth. This change in alignment cannot be observed even after a week or a month. Only after many months is the change observable.

It is exceedingly difficult for social scientists to make a strong case that the media are responsible for long-term effects. The public, policymakers, and especially critics of social science research want to be persuaded that there is a causal connection. But with a matter of this complexity that requires the long-term evolution of often conflicting influences in the naturalistic environment of viewers' everyday lives, the case for causation cannot be made in any manner stronger than a tentative probabilistic one. Even then, a critic could point to a "third variable" as a potential alternative explanation.

7. Long-term exposure to media violence is related to aggression in a person's life.

Evidence suggests that this effect is causative and cumulative (Eron, 1982). This effect is also reciprocal: Exposure to violence leads to increased aggression, and people with higher levels of aggression usually seek out higher levels of exposure to aggression.

Huesmann, Eron, Guerra, and Crawshaw (1994) conclude from their longitudinal research that viewing violence as a child has a causal effect on patterns of higher aggressive behavior in adults. This finding has appeared in studies in the United States, Australia, Finland, Israel, Poland, the Netherlands, and South Africa. While recognizing that exposure to violence on TV is not the only cause of aggression in viewers, Huesmann et al. conclude that the research suggests that the effect of viewing television violence on aggression "is relatively independent of other likely influences and of a magnitude great enough to account for socially important differences."

The long-term disinhibition effect is influenced by "a variety of environmental, cultural, familial, and cognitive" factors. A major influence on this effect is the degree to which viewers identify with characters who behave violently. For example, Eron found that the learning effect is enhanced when children identify closely with aggressive TV characters. He argued that aggression is a learned behavior, that the continued viewing of television violence is a very likely cause of aggressive behavior, and that this is a long-lasting effect on children.

Once children reach adolescence, their behavioral dispositions and inhibitory controls have become crystallized to the extent that their aggressive habits are very difficult to change, and achievement have been found to be related to this effect. Huesmann et al. concluded that low IQ makes the learning of aggressive responses more likely at an early age, and this aggressive behavior makes continued intellectual development more difficult into adulthood.

Evidence also suggests that the effect is contingent on the type of family life. In Japan, for example, Kashiwagi and Munakata (1985) found no correlation between exposure to TV violence and aggressiveness of viewers in real life for children in general. But an effect was observed among young children living in families in which the parents did not get along well.

8. Media violence is related to subsequent violence in society.

When television is introduced into a country, the violence and crime rates in that country, especially crimes of theft, increase. Within a country, the amount of exposure to violence that a demographic group typically experiences in the media is related to the crime rate in neighborhoods where those demographic groups are concentrated. Finally, some evidence suggests that when a high-profile violent act is depicted in the news or in fictional programming, the incidents of criminal aggression increase subsequent to that coverage.

All these findings are subject to the criticism that the researchers have only demonstrated co-occurrence of media violence and real-life aggression. Researchers are asked to identify possible "third variables" that might be alternative explanations for the apparent relationship, and then to show that the relationship exists even after the effects of these third variables are controlled. Although researchers have been testing control variables, critics are still concerned that one or more important variables that have yet to be controlled may account for a possible alternative explanation of the effect.

9. People exposed to many violent portrayals over a long time will come to exaggerate their chances of being victimized.

This generalized fear effect has a great deal of empirical support in the survey literature. But this relationship is generally weak in magnitude, and it is sensitive to third variables in the form of controls and contingencies. The magnitude of the correlation coefficients (r) is usually low, typically in the range of .10 to .30, which means that exposure is able to explain only less than 10% of the variation in the responses of cultivation indicators. . . .

The magnitude of the cultivation effect is relatively weak even by social science standards. Cultivation theorists have defended their findings by saying that even though the effect is small, it is persistent. . . .

This cultivation effect is also remarkably robust. In the relatively large literature on cultivation, almost all the coefficients fall within a consistently narrow band. Not only is this effect remarkable in its consistency, but this consistency becomes truly startling when one realizes the wide variety of measures (of both television exposure and cultivation indicators) that are used in the computations of these coefficients.

10. People exposed to many violent portrayals over a long time will come to be more accepting of violence.

This effect is the gradual desensitizing of viewers to the plight of victims, as well as to violence in general. After repeated exposure to media violence over a long period of time, viewers lose a sense of sympathy with the victims of violence. Viewers also learn that violence is a "normal" part of society, that violence can be used successfully, and that violence is frequently rewarded.

The probability of this long-term effect is increased when people are continually exposed to graphic portrayals of violence. For example, Linz, Donnerstein, and Penrod (1988a) exposed male participants to five slasher movies during a 2-week period. After each film, the male participants exhibited decreasing perceptions that the films were violent or that they were degrading to women.

Conclusion

After more than five decades of research on the effects of exposure to media violence, we can be certain that there are both immediate and long-term effects. The strongest supported immediate effect is the following: Exposure to violent portrayals in the media increases subsequent viewer aggression. We also know that there are other positive and negative immediate effects, such as fear and desensitization. As for long-term effects, we can conclude that exposure to violence in the media is linked with long-term negative effects of trait aggression, fearful worldview, and desensitization to violence. The effects process is highly complex and is influenced by many factors about the viewers, situational cues, and contextual characteristics of the violent portrayals.

Violence Viewing and Science

Examining the Research

For the moment, it is prudent not to question the forces that gave rise to the violence effects literature and have sustained it for five decades nor to tease out the unarticulated assumptions enmeshed in it. Let us begin by taking this extensive literature entirely on its own terms. What will become clear is that although the majority of the published studies on the topic do report antisocial findings, the average extent of the findings is slight—often so much so that the findings are open to several interpretations....

Those who pore over the violence effects literature agree that the case against televised fantasy viciousness is most broadly and clearly made in the large number of laboratory studies, such as those done by Bandura. Overall, these studies offer support for the imitative hypothesis—that younger viewers will exhibit a tendency to act out the aggression seen on the screen. In this group of studies, many find the issue reduced to a pristine clarity, parsed of all needless complexity and obscurity, and answered with sufficient experimental evidence. What is found in this literature can be rightfully generalized to the real world, some believe, to spark a host of inferences and even policies. However, the laboratory is not the real world, and may be so unreal as to discredit the results.

The unnaturalness of laboratory studies is frequently commented on by those who have reservations regarding this research (Buckingham, 1993, p. 11; Gunter & McAteer, 1990, p. 13; Noble, 1975, p. 125), but the extent of the artificiality is rarely defined, leaving those who are unfamiliar with these settings or the nature of these experiments with little sense of what is meant by "unnatural." ...

[In a behavioral laboratory setting] in a room with other unmet children, the child may be unexpectedly frustrated or angered by the experimenters—shown toys but not allowed to touch them, perhaps, or spoken to brusquely. The child is then instructed to look at a video monitor. It would be highly unlikely for the young subject to sense that this experience in any way resembled television viewing as done at home.... Most signally, at home television viewing is an entirely voluntary activity: The child is in front of the set because the child has elected to do so and in most instances has elected the content, and he or she will elect other content if the current material does not satisfy. In the behavioral laboratory, the child is compelled to watch and, worse, compelled to watch material not of the child's choosing and probably not of the child's liking. The essential element of the domestic television-viewing experience, that of pleasure, has been methodically stripped away.

Furthermore, what the child views in a typical laboratory experiment will bear little resemblance to what the child views at home. The footage will comprise only a segment of a program and will feature only aggressive actions. The intermittent relief of commercials or changed channels is missing, as are television stories' routine endings bringing dramatic closure in which everything is set right, with the correct values ascendant.

The child then may be led to another room that resembles the one in the video segment and encouraged to play while being observed. This is the room that, in Bandura et al.'s (1963) famous experiment, contained the Bobo doll identical to the one shown on the screen. Is it any wonder that uneasy children, jockeying for notice and position in a newly convened peer group, having seen a videotaped adult strike the doll without repercussions, and being tacitly encouraged by hovering experimenters who do not seem to disapprove of such action, would also hit the doll? As Noble (1975) wryly asked, "What else can one do to a self-righting bobo doll except hit it?" (p. 133). There are typically only a limited number of options, all behavioral, for the young subjects. Certainly, no researcher is asking them about the meanings they may have taken from the screened violence.

In summary, laboratory experiments on violence viewing are concocted schemes that violate all the essential stipulations of actual viewing in the real world (Cook, Kendzierski, & Thomas, 1983, p. 180) and in doing so have nothing to teach about the television experience (although they may say much about the experimenters). Viewing in the laboratory setting is involuntary, public, choiceless, intense, uncomfortable, and single-minded, whereas actual viewing is voluntary, private, selective, nonchalant, comfortable, and in the context of competing activities. Laboratory research has taken the viewing experience and turned it inside out so that the viewer is no longer in charge. In this manner, experimenters have made a mockery out of the everyday act of television viewing. Distorted to this extent, laboratory viewing can be said to simulate household viewing only if one is determined to believe so....

The inadequacies of laboratory research on television violence effects are apparent in the small body of research on the matter of desensitization or, as Slaby (1994) called it, "the bystander effect." The few attempts to replicate the finding of the four Drabman and Thomas experiments (Drabman & Thomas 1974a, 1974b, 1976; Thomas & Drabman, 1975)—that children exposed to violent footage would take longer to call for the intercession of an adult supervisor —have produced inconsistent results. Horton and Santogrossi (1978) failed to replicate in that the scores for the control group did not differ from the scores for the experimental groups. In addition, Woodfield (1988) did not find statistically significant differences between children exposed to violent content and children exposed to nonviolent content....

A third attempt to replicate by Molitor and Hirsch (1994) did duplicate the original findings, apparently showing that children are more likely to tolerate aggression in others if they are first shown violent footage. An examination of their results, however, does give rise to questions about the rigor of the research. This experiment was set up with the active collaboration of the original researchers and may be less of an attempt to relicate (or not) than an attempt to vindicate. Forty-two Catholic school fourth- and fifth-grade children were assigned to two treatment groups (there was no control group). As for all laboratory experiments, the viewing conditions were so thoroughly alien that results may have been induced by subtle clues from the adult laboratory personnel, especially for obedient children from a parochial school setting. Children shown violent content (a segment from *Karate Kid*) waited longer on average before requesting adult intervention than did children shown nonviolent content (footage from the 1984 Olympic games). Again, this finding could be interpreted as evidence of catharsis: The violent content might have lowered levels of arousal and induced a momentary lassitude. The findings could also have resulted from a sense of ennui: Postexperiment interviews revealed that all the children shown *Karate Kid* had seen the movie before, some as many as 10 times (p. 201). By comparison, the Olympic contests might have seemed more exciting and stimulated swifter reactions to the videotaped misbehavior. The first author was one of the laboratory experimenters; therefore, the specter of expectancy bias cannot be dismissed.

Even if desensitization were to exist as a replicable laboratory finding, the pressing question is whether or not the effect generalizes to the real world. Are there any data in support of the notion that exposure to television violence makes people callous to hostility in everyday life? The evidence on this is scarce and in the negative. Studying many British youngsters, Belson (1978) could find no correlation between levels of television violence viewing and callousness to real violence or inconsiderateness to others (pp. 471–475, 511–516). Research by Hagell and Newburn (1994) can answer the question of whether some youngsters who view heightened hours of television become "desensitized" to violence and embark on criminal lives; unexpectedly, teenage criminals view on average less television, and less violent content, than their law-abiding peers.

Reviewers of the small desensitization literature conclude there is no empirical evidence that anything like the bystander effect actually exists in real life (Gauntlett, 1995, p. 39; Van der Voort, 1986, p. 327; Zillmann, 1991, p. 124). Even George Comstock (1989), normally sympathetic to the violence effects literature, concedes about desensitization studies that "what the research does not demonstrate is any likelihood that media portrayals would affect the response to injury, suffering, or violent death experienced firsthand" (p. 275).

I now turn from the contrivances of laboratory research to the more promising methodology of field experiments, in which typically children in circumstances familiar to them are rated on aggressiveness through the observation of their behavior, exposed to either violent or nonviolent footage, and then unobtrusively rated again. Although this literature holds out the hope of conclusive findings in natural settings, the actual results display a disquietingly

wide range of outcomes. Some of the data gathered indicate, instead of an elevation in aggressive behaviors, a diminishment in aggressive behaviors following
several weeks of high-violence viewing. Feshbach and Singer (1971) were able to
control the viewing diets of approximately 400 boys in three private boarding
schools and four homes for wayward boys. For 6 weeks, half the boys were randomly assigned to a viewing menu high in violent content, whereas the other
half made their selections from nonaggressive shows. Aggression levels were
determined by trained observers in the weeks before and after the controlled
viewing period. No behavioral differences were reported for the adolescents in
the private schools, but among the poorer, semidelinquent youths, those who
had been watching the more violent shows were calmer than their peers on the
blander viewing diet. The authors concluded that "exposure to aggressive content on television seems to reduce or control the expression of aggression in
aggressive boys from relatively low socioeconomic backgrounds" (p. 145).

Although Wood et al. (1991) report that the eight field experiments they
reviewed did, overall, demonstrate an imitative effect from watching televised
violence, other reviewers of this literature do not concur (Cumberbatch &
Howitt, 1989, p. 41; Freedman, 1988, p. 151). McGuire (1986) comments dis-
missively on "effects that range from the statistically trivial to practically
insubstantial" (p. 213). Most decisively, Gadow and Sprafkin (1989), themselves
contributors to the field experiment research, concluded their thorough review of the 20 studies they located by stating that "the findings from the field
experiments offer little support for the media aggression hypothesis" (p. 404).

In the aftermath of the thoroughgoing artificiality of the laboratory studies, and the equivocation of the field experiment results, the burden of proof
must fall on the third methodology, that of correlational studies. In the search
for statistical correlations (or not) between violence viewing and aggressive or
criminal behavior, this literature contains several studies impressive for their
naturalness and their size. Not all these studies uncover a parallel between,
on the one hand, increased levels of violence viewing and, on the other hand,
increased rates of misbehavior, by whatever measure. For example, for a sample of 2,000 11- to 16-year-olds, Lynn, Hampson, and Agahi (1989) found no
correlation between levels of violence viewing and levels of aggression. Nevertheless, many studies do report a positive correlation. It should be noted that
the magnitude of this co-occurrence is usually quite small, typically producing
a low correlation coefficient of 10 to 20 (Freedman, 1988, p. 153). Using these
correlations (small as they are), the question becomes one of the direction(s)
of possible causality. Does violence viewing lead to subsequent aggression as
is commonly assumed? Could more aggressive children prefer violent content,
perhaps as a vicarious outlet for their hostility? . . . Could any of a host of other
factors give rise to both elevated variables?

Following his substantial correlational study of 1,500 London adolescents,
Belson (1978) highlighted one of his findings—that boys with high levels of exposure to television violence commit 49% more acts of serious violence than
do those who view less—and on this basis issued a call for a reduction in video
carnage (p. 526). Closer examination of his data (pp. 380–382), however, reveals
that the relationship between the two variables is far more irregular than he

suggests in his text. Low viewers of television violence are more aggressive than moderate viewers, whereas very high violence viewers are less aggressive than those in the moderate to high range. Moreover, "acts of serious violence" constituted only one of Belson's four measures of real-life aggression; the other three were "total number of acts of violence," "total number of acts of violence weighted by degree of severity of the act," and "total number of violent acts excluding minor ones." Findings for these three variables cannot be said to substantiate Belson's conclusion. That is, for these measures, the linking of violence viewing to subsequent aggression was negated by reverse correlations —that aggressive youngsters sought out violent content (pp. 389–392). Three of his measures refuted his argument, but Belson chose to emphasize a fourth, itself a demonstrably inconsistent measure....

For the total television effects literature, whatever the methodology, the reviews...by Andison (1977), Hearold (1986), and Paik and Comstock (1994) are not the only ones that have been compiled. Other overviews reach very different summary judgments about this body of studies in its entirety. A review published contemporaneously with that of Andison considered the same research projects and derived a different conclusion (Kaplan & Singer, 1976). Kaplan and Singer examined whether the extant literature could support an activation view (that watching televised fantasy violence leads to aggression), a catharsis view (that such viewing leads to a decrease in aggression), or a null view, and they determined that the null position was the most judicious. They wrote, "Our review of the literature strongly suggests that the activating effects of television fantasy violence are marginal at best. The scientific data do not consistently link violent television fantasy programming to violent behavior" (p. 62).

In the same volume in which Susan Hearold's (1986) meta-analysis of violence studies appeared, there was also published a literature review by William McGuire (1986). In contrast to Hearold, it was McGuire's judgment that the evidence of untoward effects from violence viewing was not compelling. Throughout the 1980s, an assured critique of the violence effects literature [was] issued from Jonathan Freedman (1984, 1986, 1988). Freedman cautiously examined the major studies within each of the methodological categories.... Regarding correlational studies, he noted that "not one study produced strong consistent results, and most produced a substantial number of negative findings" (1988, p. 158). Freedman's general conclusion is that "considering all of the research —laboratory, field experiments, and correlational studies—the evidence does not support the idea that viewing television violence causes aggression" (1988, p. 158).

Freedman's dismissal of the violence effects literature is echoed in other literature reviews from British scholars, who may enjoy an objective distance on this largely American research agenda. Cumberbatch and Howitt (1989) discussed the shortcomings of most of the major studies and stated that the research data "are insufficiently robust to allow a firm conclusion about television violence as studied" (p. 51). David Gauntlett (1995)... analyzed at length most of the consequential studies. He believes that "the work of effects researchers is done" (p. 1). "The search for direct 'effects' of television on behavior is over: Every effort has been made, and they simply cannot be found" (p. 120). Ian Vine (1997) concurs: "Turning now to the systemic evidence from hundreds of published studies of the relationship between viewing violence and subsequent problematic behaviors, the most certain conclusion is that there is *no* genuine consensus of findings" (p. 138)....

Discourse Within Discourse

Opened up for inspection, the sizable violence effects literature turns out to be an uneven discourse—inconsistent, flawed, pocked. This literature proves nothing conclusively, or equivalently, this literature proves everything in that support for any position can be drawn from its corpus. The upshot is that, no matter what some reformers affirm, the campaign against television violence is bereft of any strong, consensual scientific core. Flaws extend through to the very premises of the literature—flaws so total that they may crowd out alternative viewpoints and produce in some a mind-numbed acquiescence. Specifically, the literature's two main subjects—television and the viewer—are assumed to be what they are not.

Viewers are conceived of as feckless and vacuous, like jellyfish in video tides. Viewers have no intentions, no discretion, and no powers of interpretation. Into their minds can be stuffed all matter of content. Most often, the viewer postulated in the effects literature is young, epitomizing immaturity and malleability. This literature, wrote Carmen Luke (1990), "had constructed a set of scientifically validated truths about the child viewer as a behavioral response mechanism, as passive and devoid of cognitive abilities. The possibility that viewers bring anything other than demographic variables to the screen was conceptually excluded" (p. 281). Although there is ample evidence that the young are highly active, selective, and discriminating viewers (Buckingham, 1993; Clifford, Gunter, & McAleer, 1995; Durkin, 1985; Gunter & McAteer, 1990; Hawkins & Pingree, 1986; Hodge & Tripp, 1986; Noble, 1975), this is never the version in the violence effects literature.

Television, on the other hand, is seen as powerful, coercive, and sinister. The medium is not a servant but a tyrant. It rules rather than pleases. It is omnipotent; it cannot be regulated, switched, modulated, interpreted, belittled, welcomed, or ignored. All the things that television is in the real world it is not within the violence effects literature.

The relationship between television content and viewers, as implied in this research, is one way only, as television pounds its insidious message into a hapless audience; there is no conception of a return flow of information by which viewers via ratings indicate preferences for certain content rather than other content. The only result allowable from the viewing experience is that of direct and noxious effects. Other possibilities—of pleasures, relaxation, reinterpretations, therapy, and so on—are not to be considered. The television viewing experience, twisted beyond recognition, is conceived of in pathological terms; in fact, a large amount of the research throughout the past decades has been funded by national mental health budgets.

All these preconceptions apply before a bit of research is actually conducted. The surprising result is not that there have been worrisome findings reported but that, given these presuppositions, the negative findings were not much grander still. . . .

The war on television violence, the larger discourse, has united many allies with otherwise weak ties—prominent authorities and grassroots organizations, liberals and conservatives, and the religious and the secular. We must ask why they put aside their differences, lift their voices together, and join in this particular cause. This implausible alliance constitutes a force field that waxes and wanes throughout the decades, losing strength at one point and gaining it at another; it would seem to have a rhythm all its own. What can account for the regular reoccurrence of this public discourse denouncing television violence?

POSTSCRIPT

Is Television Harmful for Children?

Much of what we know about the effects of television comes from the study of children enjoying traditional television, but this knowledge is being challenged by the impact of emerging telecommunications technology. The Internet, cable television programming, video games, and VCRs have changed the face of television within the home. Indeed, VCRs have greatly increased the control that parents have over the material to which children are exposed at young ages and have greatly increased the diversity of content that children can be exposed to as they get older. The Internet, a 500-channel world, increasing international programming ventures, and regulatory changes will alter the way children interact with electronic media. What influence that will have is very hard to predict.

One conclusion is inescapable. There is now much more diversity of media content available, and there are many more choices for parents and children. One of the clearest findings of research on the impact of violence on child aggression is that parents, through their behavior and their positive and negative comments, can have a major influence on whether or not children behave aggressively subsequent to exposure. With choices come hard decisions for parents. The promise of television and other media can now be better fulfilled, with more choices than ever before. Alternatively, a diet of violence and mindlessness is easily found.

Although this issue concerns children, there are important developmental and social differences due to age. Young children, particularly preschoolers, are most likely to be controlled by their parents, are most likely to have difficulty understanding some of the narratives and conventions of media fare, and are arguably the most vulnerable to learning from the messages of the media to which they are exposed. The "tween" years are a transition to more adult programs and themes and are a time of great transition socially. Poised between the worlds of adulthood and childhood, the tween partakes of both, sometimes with difficult consequences. Tweens are not even considered by the media to be part of the "child" audience. Their viewing patterns are much more like those of adults, and like adults they are presumed to be cognitively able to protect themselves from the effects of violence or even advertising. So they proudly proclaim that the media have no effect on them.

The National Television Violence Study, 3 vols. (Sage Publications, 1996–1998), conducted by a consortium of professors from several universities, offers a commentary on the state of violence on American television for viewers, policymakers, industry leaders, and scholars. Robert Liebert and Joyce Sprafkin's *The Early Window: Effects of Television on Children and Youth,* 3rd ed. (Pergamon Press, 1988) is an excellent introduction to the history and issues of media effects. Judith Van Evra offers a view of existing research in *Television and Child Development,* 2d ed. (Lawrence Erlbaum, 1998). School violence has revived the debate on media violence and children, according to Paige Albiniak in "Media: Littleton's Latest Suspect," *Broadcasting & Cable* (May 3, 1999). Not only television but video games come under attack. Lieutenant Colonel Dave Grossman, a former Army ranger and paratrooper, writes about video games that teach children to kill by using the same warfare tactics used to train the military, in the *Saturday Evening Post* (July/August and September/October 1999). Many articles were written after the Columbine tragedy that implicated violent video games in the violence of U.S. society.

ISSUE 3

Is Emphasis on Body Image in the Media Harmful to Females Only?

YES: Mary C. Martin and James W. Gentry, from "Stuck in the Model Trap: The Effects of Beautiful Models in Ads on Female Pre-Adolescents and Adolescents," *Journal of Advertising* (Summer 1997)

NO: Michelle Cottle, from "Turning Boys Into Girls," *The Washington Monthly* (May 1998)

ISSUE SUMMARY

YES: Marketing professors Mary C. Martin and James W. Gentry address the literature dealing with advertising images and the formation of body identity for preadolescent and adolescent females. They report a study to explore how social comparison theory influences young women.

NO: *Washington Monthly* editor Michelle Cottle takes the perspective that females are not the only ones influenced by media image. She cites polls and magazine advertising that indicate that males are exposed to images of idealized body type as well, and she argues that these images also have an impact on the male psyche.

There is plenty of evidence to support the idea that young girls are influenced by the body images of models and actresses they see in the media. In her book *The Beauty Myth* (Anchor Books, 1992), Naomi Wolf writes that the typical model or actress is significantly below what the medical establishment considers a "healthy" body weight. The desire to look like a model or actress has contributed to what could be termed an outbreak in eating disorders among females. Wolf warns that 1 out of 10 college women develop an eating disorder while in college, but the desire to be thin often starts as early as age eight for many girls.

Little attention has been given to the self-images of boys, while the unhealthy aspects of eating disorders and idealized body image has been primarily attributed to girls. In the following selections the authors help us to understand this phenomenon on an even broader scale.

Mary C. Martin and James W. Gentry take the position that idealized body image is a female problem, and they attempt to study whether or not social comparison theory (the idea that females compare their own physical attractiveness with models) influences self-esteem. Their studies of fourth- and sixth-graders help to illuminate differential cognitive levels and the way images influence self-perceptions.

Michelle Cottle adds an interesting dimension to the problem of images and idealized body type. She asserts that men's magazines have also taken the approach to making males feel inadequate through images and stories that work against male vanity. The images and stories she describes raise questions about the content of magazines and the way pictures and stories affect us psychologically.

These issues will undoubtedly spark lively discussions about whether or not images and stories actually do shape the way we think about ourselves in relation to idealized images. The psychological effects of media are difficult to assess, even though the presence of images is pervasive, but it is hard to ignore their potential power. The history of media effects research has much to offer in the way we think about the following selections.

Mary C. Martin and James W. Gentry  **YES**

Stuck in the Model Trap

Agrowing concern in our society is the plight of female pre-adolescents and adolescents as they grow up facing many obstacles, including receiving less attention than boys in the classroom, unrealistic expectations of what they can and cannot do, decreasing self-esteem, and being judged by their physical appearance. In particular, girls are generally preoccupied with attempting to become beautiful. As Perry suggests, "Today's specifications call for blonde and thin—no easy task, since most girls get bigger during adolescence. Many become anorexics or bulimics; a few rich ones get liposuction. We make their focus pleasing other people and physical beauty." Further, studies show that self-esteem drops to a much greater extent for female than male pre-adolescents and adolescents, with self-perceptions of physical attractiveness contributing to the drop.

Another growing concern in our society is the role of advertising in contributing to those obstacles. For example, advertising has been accused of unintentionally imposing a "sense of inadequacy" on women's self-concepts. Studies suggest that advertising and the mass media may play a part in creating and reinforcing a preoccupation with physical attractiveness and influence consumer perceptions of what constitutes an acceptable level of physical attractiveness. Further, studies have found that female college students, adolescents, and pre-adolescents compare their physical attractiveness with that of models in ads and that female pre-adolescents and adolescents have desires to be models. An aspiring young model, for example, describes "the model trap":

> Deep down inside, I still want to be a supermodel.... As long as they're there, screaming at me from the television, glaring at me from magazines, I'm stuck in the model trap. Hate them first. Then grow to like them. Love them. Emulate them. Die to be them. All the while praying this cycle will come to an end.

Clearly, such findings raise concern about advertising ethics. Jean Kilbourne, for example, addresses how female bodies are depicted in advertising imagery and the potential effects on women's physical and mental health in her videos *Still Killing Us Softly* and *Slim Hopes*. The use of highly attractive models in ads as an "ethical issue" received little or no attention in published research from 1987 to 1993, but the ethics of that practice have begun to be questioned by consumers and advertisers. For example, a consumer movement against advertising has arisen in the United States. The organization Boycott Anorexic Marketing (BAM) is attempting to get consumers to boycott products sold by companies that use extremely thin models in their ads. Such criticisms of advertising are "much too serious to dismiss cavalierly."

Using social comparison theory as a framework, we propose that female pre-adolescents and adolescents compare their physical attractiveness with that of advertising models. As a result, their self-perceptions and self-esteem may be affected. In response to the criticisms, we conducted a study to assess those unintended consequences of advertising. However, unlike previous empirical studies of those effects, ours incorporated the role of a motive for comparison —self-evaluation, self-improvement, or self-enhancement—which may help to explain the inconsistent findings in the advertising/marketing and psychology literature. Specifically, our premise was that changes in self-perceptions and/or self-esteem may be influenced by the type of motive operating at the time of comparison.

Physical Attractiveness and Self-Esteem in Children and Adolescents

Cultural norms in the United States dictate the importance of being physically attractive, especially of being thin. The emphasis on being physically attractive begins in infancy and continues throughout childhood and adolescence. How physically attractive a child or adolescent perceives him/herself to be heavily influences his/her self-esteem, particularly beginning in fifth grade. However, the effect of self-perceptions of physical attractiveness on self-esteem differs between girls and boys. For example, Harter, in a cross-sectional study of third through eleventh graders, found that self-perceptions of physical attractiveness and levels of global self-esteem appeared to decline systematically over time in girls but not for boys. Other researchers have documented such decreases throughout adolescence for girls. Boys' self-esteem, in contrast, tends to increase from early through late adolescence.

The nature of physical attractiveness differs for male and female children and adolescents as well. Girls tend to view their bodies as "objects," and their physical beauty determines how they and others judge their overall value. Boys tend to view their bodies as "process," and power and function are more important criteria for evaluating their physical self. For example, Lerner, Orlos, and Knapp found that female adolescents' self-concepts derived primarily from body attractiveness whereas male adolescents' self-concepts were related more strongly to perceptions of physical instrumental effectiveness. The difference in body orientation results in girls paying attention to individual body parts and boys having a holistic body perspective. Because the ideal of attractiveness for girls is more culturally salient, girls have a greater likelihood of being negatively affected by the feminine ideal than boys have of being negatively affected by the masculine ideal.

Advertising and Social Comparison

Television commercials and magazine advertisements that contribute to the "body-as-object" focus for female pre-adolescents and adolescents, using difficult-to-attain standards of physical attractiveness to market products, are pervasive. For example, in an analysis of *Seventeen,* a magazine with "the potential to influence a substantial proportion of the adolescent female population," Guillen and Barr found that models' body shapes were less curvaceous than those in magazines for adult women and that the hip/waist ratio decreased from 1970 to 1990, meaning that models' bodies had become thinner over time. In addition, nearly half of the space of the most popular magazines for adolescent girls is devoted to advertisements.

Social comparison theory holds that people have a drive to evaluate their opinions and abilities, which can be satisfied by "social" comparisons with other people. With that theory as a framework, recent studies have found that female college students and female pre-adolescents and adolescents do compare their physical attractiveness with that of models in ads. In turn, those comparisons may result in changes in self-perceptions of physical attractiveness or self-perceptions of body image. Given the importance of self-perceptions of physical attractiveness in influencing female self-esteem, the comparisons may result in changes in self-esteem as well....

Using social comparison theory as a basis, Richins found no support for the hypothesis that exposure to advertising with highly attractive models would temporarily lower female college students' self-perceptions of physical attractiveness. "By late adolescence, however, the sight of extremely attractive models is 'old news' and unlikely to provide new information that might influence self-perception." Martin and Kennedy assessed the effects of highly attractive models in ads on female pre-adolescents and adolescents but found no support for a lowering of self-perceptions. Relying on Festinger's original conception of the theory, those researchers did not account for motive, and appear to have assumed that the motive for comparison was self-evaluation (i.e., girls compare themselves with models in ads to evaluate their own level of physical attractiveness). However, more recent research has shown that social comparisons may occur for other reasons, suggesting that female pre-adolescents and adolescents may compare themselves to models in ads for any one (or a combination) of three motives: self-evaluation, self-improvement, or self-enhancement. For example, Martin and Kennedy found that self-evaluation and self-improvement are common motives when female pre-adolescents and adolescents compare themselves with models in ads. Self-enhancement, in contrast, is not common and does not seem to occur naturally. Similarly, in a series of pretests reported by Martin, self-evaluation and self-improvement were found to be common motives in college students, but self-enhancement was not. Gentry, Martin, and Kennedy, however, found stronger support for self-enhancement in a study using in-depth interviews of first and fifth graders. As girls mature, their motives for comparison apparently vary.

The incorporation of motive may help to clarify the inconsistent findings in the literature. Our subsequent discussion explores possible differential effects of comparisons with advertising models on female pre-adolescents' and adolescents' self-perceptions and self-esteem, depending on whether self-evaluation, self-enhancement, or self-improvement is the primary motive at the time of comparison. We do not examine what motives are occurring naturally, but rather how advertising affects girls when they have a particular motive. Our overriding research question is whether motives make a difference in terms of self-perceptions and self-esteem. Finding differences between motives would clearly encourage consumer educators to stress one motive for social comparison over another. Our hypotheses specify the direction of change for each motive, thus implying response differences between subjects who have a particular comparison motive and subjects in a control group. Finding differences between motives would answer our research question even though differences between a motive group and the control group may not be significant.

Self-Evaluation as a Motive for Comparison

As the motive for comparison, Festinger originally proposed self-evaluation, the judgment of value, worth, or appropriateness of one's abilities, opinions, and personal traits. Information obtained from social comparison is not used for self-evaluation until the age of seven or eight, even though social comparison has been found to occur in children of preschool age. In the context of advertising, given that advertising models represent an ideal image of beauty, we expect comparison to be generally upward. That is, female pre-adolescents and adolescents will generally consider advertising models to be superior in terms of physical attractiveness. Therefore, if self-evaluation is the primary motive at the time of comparison (a girl is attempting to judge the value or worth of her own physical attractiveness or body image against that of advertising models), comparisons are likely to result in lowered self-perceptions and lowered self-esteem....

Method ...

Subjects

Female pre-adolescents and adolescents in grades four (n = 82; mean age = 9.8 years), six (n = 103; mean age = 11.9 years), and eight (n = 83; mean age = 13.8 years) from a public school system in the Midwest participated in the study (total sample size 268). The public school system is in a county where 98% of the population is white and the median family income is $31,144. Although the sample is not representative of all pre-adolescent and adolescent girls in the United States, it does represent a segment of girls most susceptible to problems linked to physical attractiveness such as eating disorders. As an incentive to participate, the subjects took part in a drawing for two prizes of $50 each. In addition, a $500 donation was made to the public school system.

Fourth, sixth, and eighth graders were chosen for the study because research suggests that the period between the fourth and eighth grades is important in girls' development of positive perceptions of the self. It is a period when female bodies are changing drastically and adult definitions of "beauty" are becoming relevant social norms. We suggest that a girl's transition in this time period is more of a discontinuity than a linear transformation because of the conflicting biological and social processes. For example, Martin and Kennedy found, in an experiment with fourth, eighth, and twelfth grade girls, that self-perceptions of physical attractiveness decreased as the subjects got older. Fourth graders' self-perceptions were significantly higher than those of eighth graders, but eighth graders' self-perceptions were not significantly different from those of twelfth graders. Other evidence suggests that self-perceptions of physical attractiveness start to become particularly important during fifth grade. For example, Krantz, Friedberg, and Andrews found a very high correlation between self-perceived attractiveness and self-esteem in fifth graders. . . . The strength of the relationship in fifth graders more than tripled the variance accounted for at the third-grade level.

Classroom teachers administered the questionnaires to the subjects at the schools during an hour of class time. To separate the measurement of covariates from the manipulation, two separate booklets were used. The first booklet contained the covariate measures. After subjects completed that booklet, they handed it in and were given a second booklet with a set of ads and dependent variable measures. The assignment to treatments was randomized by giving each classroom a random assortment of the five types of questionnaires with ads. Teachers administered the questionnaires to minimize any source effects caused by having an unfamiliar authority figure collect the data. To facilitate understanding, the teachers administered the questionnaires orally by reading each question aloud and allowing appropriate time for the subjects to mark their responses.

Advertising Stimuli

Full-color ads were created by cutting and pasting stimuli from magazine ads in *Seventeen, Sassy, Teen,* and *YM.* Those magazines were chosen because they are the top four teen magazines in the United States and because they maintain consistency with respect to type of beauty. The stimuli were cut from original ads in a way that eliminated information about the sources. The ads created were for commonly advertised but fictional brand name adornment products: Satin Colors lipstick, Generation Gap jeans, and Hair in Harmony hair care products. The ads appeared to be professionally prepared, were kept very simple, and were realistic as they included partial- and full-body photos of models extracted from actual hair care, jeans, and lipstick ads.

To ensure that the subjects perceived the models in the ads as highly attractive, means of two items that measured the models' perceived attractiveness were calculated for each of the three ads. On 7-point semantic differential scales, subjects were asked to rate the model in the ad from "very overweight and out of shape, fat" to "very fit and in shape, thin" and "very unattractive, ugly" to "very attractive, beautiful" prior to measurement of the dependent variables. The range of mean responses to those items was 5.1 to 6.4, far above the midpoint value of four. Hence, the subjects perceived the models as highly attractive.

Manipulation of Motives

Motives were manipulated through instructions given prior to exposure to a set of ads, advertising headlines and copy, and a listing exercise. The manipulations were based on the following operational definitions of each motive.

1. Self-evaluation—a girl's explicit comparison of her physical attractiveness with that of models in ads to determine whether she is as pretty as or prettier than the models on specific dimensions such as hair, eyes, and body.
2. Self-improvement—a girl's explicit comparison of her physical attractiveness with that of models in ads to seek ways of improving her own attractiveness on specific dimensions such as hairstyle and makeup.
3. Self-enhancement 1—a girl's explicit comparison of her physical attractiveness with that of models in ads in an attempt to enhance her self-esteem by finding ways in which she is prettier than the model on specific dimensions (inducement of a downward comparison).
4. Self-enhancement 2—a girl's discounting of the beauty of models in ads and, in turn, the avoidance of an explicit comparison of her own physical attractiveness with that of the models in an attempt to protect/ maintain her self-esteem.

Prior to exposure to a set of ads, the subjects were given instructions in which they were shown a drawing of "Amy looking at an advertisement in a magazine" and were told a story about Amy comparing herself with a model in an ad for a particular motive. Then the subjects were asked to look at the ads on the following pages and view the ads as Amy had viewed them.

As consistency in ad design across experimental groups was essential, the headline and copy were the only components manipulated in the four sets of ads designed to induce particular motives. Minor deviations from the ad design were necessary for the control group because their ads did not include a model. The instructions, headlines, and copy were developed from "stories" written by female adolescents in projective tests in previous studies....

The subjects also completed a listing exercise after viewing each ad. They looked at each ad and listed specific ways in which the manipulated motive may have occurred. For example, in the self-improvement condition, subjects were asked to look at the model and "list ideas you get on how to improve your looks." The intent of the study was not to measure naturally occurring motives for social comparison, but rather to investigate how the use of various motives changes cognitive and affective reactions to stimuli showing physically attractive models.

If a subject successfully completed the listing exercises, the manipulation was considered successful. One author analyzed the responses to each listing exercise, coding for the subject's success or failure in completing it. Criteria for a successful response were specific references to aspects of physical attractiveness that were compared in the ad and no indication that another motive was present. For example, for a successful manipulation of self-improvement, one respondent listed the following ideas she got from looking at the model in the ad: "Use the product. Get a perm. Wear lots of make-up and have as pretty of a face as she does."

A response failed if it indicated that no motive or another motive was present. The failed responses were discarded, resulting in seven subjects being dropped (three subjects from the self-evaluation condition, one subject from the self-improvement condition, and three subjects from the self-enhancement 2 condition). For example, one subject in the self-evaluation condition was dropped because, when asked to list "ways in which your hair, face, and body look compared to the model's hair, face, and body," she wrote, "She looks different because I am a different person. I don't really compare to her." One subject in the self-improvement condition was dropped because, when asked to "list the ideas you get from the model on how you could improve the way you look," she wrote, "I could never look like her and will not try. I know that she has to be willing to work to look like she does. I don't worry about the way I look, it's just not at all that important to me." ...

Discussion

In general, our results suggest that motives do play an important role in the study context as we found differential effects for changes in self-perceptions of physical attractiveness, self-perceptions of body image, and self-esteem. Consistent with predictions of social comparison theory, female pre-adolescents' and adolescents' self-perceptions and self-esteem can be detrimentally affected, particularly when self-evaluation occurs: self-perceptions of physical attractiveness were lowered in all subjects.... In sixth graders, self-perceptions of body image were lowered (i.e., body was perceived as larger) in subjects who self-evaluated....

On a positive note, the inclusion of motives shows that detrimental effects do not always occur. That is, positive temporary effects occur when either self-improvement or self-enhancement is the motive for comparison: self-perceptions of physical attractiveness were raised in subjects who self-improved or self-enhanced through downward comparisons.... Self-perceptions and self-esteem were unaffected in most cases in subjects who self-enhanced by discounting the beauty of models.... The only exception occurred when sixth graders' self-perceptions of body image were raised (i.e., body was perceived as skinnier)....

Social comparison theory, as it currently stands, cannot explain all of our results. In particular, how the processes may change over the course of one's lifetime is not articulated theoretically or empirically. A closer examination of the results and some speculation may help to explain the inconsistent and contradictory support for the hypotheses. Though no statistically significant differences were detected, the findings for the fourth graders are interesting and offer some food for thought. Their self-evaluations produced the lowest self-perceptions of physical attractiveness and the highest (i.e., most skinny) self-perceptions of body image in comparison with the other motives. Perhaps in childhood girls (like boys) desire to grow up and "get bigger." Hence, if the fourth graders in our study desired to "get bigger," a skinnier body image would actually represent a "lowering" of self-perceptions. In that case, low self-perceptions of physical attractiveness and skinny self-perceptions of body image after self-evaluation would be consistent, supporting the notion that self-evaluation through comparisons with models in ads has detrimental effects on female pre-adolescents and adolescents.

In comparison with the fourth graders, the sixth graders produced somewhat different results. Sixth graders' self-evaluations produced the lowest self-perceptions of physical attractiveness and the lowest (i.e., the least skinny) self-perceptions of body image in comparison with the other motives. For sixth graders, unlike fourth graders, the direction of changes in self-perceptions of physical attractiveness and body image were consistent. Perhaps a transition occurs between the fourth and sixth grade, from "bigger is better" to "skinnier is better."

In self-esteem, only fourth graders were affected after self-enhancement. Self-esteem was raised in fourth graders who self-enhanced through downward comparisons.... However, self-esteem was lowered in fourth graders who self-enhanced by discounting the beauty of the models.... Martin and Kennedy found that fourth graders aspire to be models more than older adolescents, and perhaps fourth graders are discounting their own future when they discount the beauty of models. Further, fourth graders may be young enough not to realize that not all will grow up to be as beautiful as advertising models. The lack of effects of self-enhancement on sixth and eighth graders' self-esteem may be due to their reluctance to accept that they can look better than advertising models... or that they can discount the beauty of models....

Implications and Directions for Future Research

Our results have implications for advertisers and educators. Educators can use the framework of social comparison theory to instruct children and adolescents about how (i.e., which motives to use) and when (i.e., in what circumstances and with whom) to use others for comparison. With respect to advertising models, children and adolescents may be able to use the processes of self-improvement and self-enhancement to their advantage, as both led to temporary increases in self-perceptions (in comparison with the control group or girls in another manipulated condition). As Martin and Kennedy found, however, self-enhancement is not a naturally occurring motive when female pre-adolescents and adolescents compare themselves with models in ads. Hence, the involvement of educators would be crucial. Not only would emphasis on self-enhancement be advantageous in terms of self-perceptions, but advertisers could benefit as well, as research suggests that making consumers feel physically attractive encourages sales of cosmetic and other adornment products. That possibility is encouraging, but must be viewed with caution until further research has been conducted. Our results suggest that the relationships between motives and self-perceptions and self-esteem are not straightforward and that there are particular times in childhood and adolescence when efforts to instruct young people in how to view ads may be most appropriate. Simply beginning education at a very early age is not the answer. For example, self-enhancement by discounting the beauty of models essentially did not work for fourth graders, as it caused their self-esteem to decrease. Discounting the beauty of models appears to have led fourth graders to discount their own futures in terms of physical attractiveness. In addition, if fourth graders believe "bigger is better," they may not have enough intellectual maturity to realize that "bigger is better" conflicts with the beauty and slenderness of advertising models.

Sixth and eighth graders, in contrast, may be reluctant to accept the notion of discounting models' beauty, hence the lack of effect on their self-esteem. That reluctance might be due partly to their having developed a more sophisticated level of advertising skepticism, as "adolescents have the confidence to rely on their own judgment and the discernment necessary to separate advertising truth from advertising hype." Boush and his coauthors found that self-esteem is related directly to mistrust of advertiser motives and disbelief of advertising claims. Hence, education before sixth grade may be critical to get female pre-adolescents and adolescents to accept the notion of discounting the beauty of advertising models.

The period between the fourth and eighth grades appears to be a critical one on which future research would be beneficial to assess further what role each of the motives has and for what ages. Other issues also warrant attention. For example, in our study, the models in the ads were in their late teens or early adulthood. Future research might address the effects of younger models, as well as more ordinary-looking models, in ads. Another need is to assess whether the type of physical attractiveness is important.... Further, future research should incorporate the role of "esteem relevance" and "perceived control" to determine whether and to what extent those variables account for natural tendencies to have one motive rather than another. In addition, differential levels of esteem relevance and perceived control may lead to different types and levels of responses. For example, cognitive responses (e.g., self-perceptions) may differ from affective responses (e.g., self-esteem) after comparisons with models in ads, which may help to explain the inconsistent results found here and in similar studies.

Finally, some researchers have acknowledged that the minimal effects or lack of effects found in studies assessing temporary changes in self-perceptions or self-esteem may differ from what may be found in the long term. Thornton and Moore concluded that "with long-term comparisons such as this, particularly with the pervasive presence of idealized media images in our culture and the continued, and perhaps increasing, emphasis placed on physical appearance, there exists the potential for bringing about more significant and lasting changes in the self-concept." The motive of self-improvement, however, represents a unique situation in that temporary changes may differ from the long-term changes. When one commonly compares oneself to advertising models for self-improvement, one may eventually realize that the ideal is not as attainable as originally believed. . . .

Given the criticisms of advertising based on its cultural and social consequences, a better understanding of the role of comparison motives and the other issues mentioned here is needed. Such understanding may lead to a unified effort by educators to help prevent detrimental effects on female preadolescents and adolescents. However, a unified effort by educators may not be enough, and a call for legislation to control the use of models in advertising may arise in response to consumer movements such as Boycott Anorexic Marketing (BAM). Advertising researchers must respond with studies to determine more clearly the unintended consequences of advertising.

Turning Boys Into Girls

Ilove *Men's Health* Magazine. There. I'm out of the closet, and I'm not ashamed. Sure, I know what some of you are thinking: What self-respecting '90s woman could embrace a publication that runs such enlightened articles as "Turn Your Good Girl Bad" and "How to Wake Up Next to a One-Night Stand"? Or maybe you'll smile and wink knowingly: What red-blooded hetero chick *wouldn't* love all those glossy photo spreads of buff young beefcake in various states of undress, rippled abs and glutes flexed so tightly you could bounce a check on them? Either way you've got the wrong idea. My affection for *Men's Health* is driven by pure gender politics—by the realization that this magazine, and a handful of others like it, are leveling the playing field in a way that *Ms.* can only dream of. With page after page of bulging biceps and Gillette jaws, robust hairlines and silken skin, *Men's Health* is peddling a standard of male beauty as unforgiving and unrealistic as the female version sold by those dewy-eyed pre-teen waifs draped across the covers of *Glamour* and *Elle*. And with a variety of helpful features on "Foods That Fight Fat," "Banish Your Potbelly," and "Save Your Hair (Before it's Too Late)," *Men's Health* is well on its way to making the male species as insane, insecure, and irrational about physical appearance as any *Cosmo* girl.

Don't you see, ladies? We've been going about this equality business all wrong. Instead of battling to get society fixated on something besides our breast size, we should have been fighting spandex with spandex. Bra burning was a nice gesture, but the greater justice is in convincing our male counterparts that the key to their happiness lies in a pair of made-for-him Super Shaper Briefs with the optional "fly front endowment pad" (as advertised in *Men's Journal*, $29.95 plus shipping and handling). Make the men as neurotic about the circumference of their waists and the whiteness of their smiles as the women, and at least the burden of vanity and self-loathing will be shared by all.

This is precisely what lads' mags like *Men's Health* are accomplishing. The rugged John-Wayne days when men scrubbed their faces with deodorant soap and viewed gray hair and wrinkles as a badge of honor are fading. Last year, international market analyst Euromonitor placed the U.S. men's toiletries market —hair color, skin moisturizer, tooth whiteners, etc.—at $3.5 billion. According to a survey conducted by DYG researchers for *Men's Health* in November 1996, approximately 20 percent of American men get manicures or pedicures, 18 percent use skin treatments such as masks or mud packs, and 10 percent enjoy professional facials. That same month, *Psychology Today* reported that a poll by Roper Starch Worldwide showed that "6 percent of men nationwide actually use such traditionally female products as bronzers and foundation to create the illusion of a youthful appearance."

What men are putting *on* their bodies, however, is nothing compared to what they're doing *to* their bodies: While in the 1980s only an estimated one in 10 plastic surgery patients were men, as of 1996, that ratio had shrunk to one in five. The American Academy of Cosmetic Surgery estimates that nationwide more than 690,000 men had cosmetic procedures performed in '96, the most recent year for which figures are available. And we're not just talking "hair restoration" here, though such procedures do command the lion's share of the male market. We're also seeing an increasing number of men shelling out mucho dinero for face peels, liposuction, collagen injections, eyelid lifts, chin tucks, and, of course, the real man's answer to breast implants: penile enlargements (now available to increase both length and diameter).

Granted, *Men's Health* and its journalistic cousins (*Men's Journal, Details, GQ,* etc.) cannot take all the credit for this breakthrough in gender parity. The fashion and glamour industries have perfected the art of creating consumer "needs," and with the women's market pretty much saturated, men have become the obvious target for the purveyors of everything from lip balm to lycra. Meanwhile, advances in medical science have made cosmetic surgery a quicker, cleaner option for busy executives (just as the tight fiscal leash of managed care is driving more and more doctors toward this cash-based specialty). Don't have several weeks to recover from a full-blown facelift? No problem. For a few hundred bucks you can get a micro-dermabrasion face peel on your lunch hour.

Then there are the underlying social factors. With women growing ever more financially independent, aspiring suitors are discovering that they must bring more to the table than a well-endowed wallet if they expect to win (and keep) the fair maiden. Nor should we overlook the increased market power of the gay population—in general a more image-conscious lot than straight guys. But perhaps most significant is the ongoing, ungraceful descent into middle age by legions of narcissistic baby boomers. Gone are the days when the elder statesmen of this demographic bulge could see themselves in the relatively youthful faces of those insipid yuppies on "Thirtysomething." Increasingly, boomers are finding they have more in common with the *parents* of today's TV, movie, and sports stars. Everywhere they turn some upstart Gen Xer is flaunting his youthful vitality, threatening boomer dominance on both the social and professional fronts. (Don't think even Hollywood didn't shudder when the Oscar for best original screenplay this year went to a couple of guys barely old enough to shave.) With whippersnappers looking to steal everything from their jobs to their women, post-pubescent men have at long last discovered the terror of losing their springtime radiance.

Whatever combo of factors is feeding the frenzy of male vanity, magazines such as *Men's Health* provide the ideal meeting place for men's insecurities and marketers' greed. Like its more established female counterparts, *Men's Health* is an affordable, efficient delivery vehicle for the message that physical imperfection, age, and an underdeveloped fashion sense are potentially crippling disabilities. And as with women's mags, this cycle of insanity is self-perpetuating: The more men obsess about growing old or unattractive, the more marketers will exploit and expand that fear; the more marketers bombard men with messages about the need to be beautiful, the more they will obsess. Younger and younger men will be sucked into the vortex of self-doubt. Since 1990, *Men's Health* has seen its paid circulation rise from 250,000 to more than 1.5 million; the magazine estimates that half of its 5.3 million readers are under age 35 and 46 percent are married. And while most major magazines have suffered sluggish growth or even a decline in circulation in recent years, during the first half of 1997, *Men's Health* saw its paid circulation increase 14 percent over its '96 figures. (Likewise, its smaller, more outdoorsy relative, Wenner Media's *Men's Journal,* enjoyed an even bigger jump of 26.5 percent.) At this rate, one day soon, that farcical TV commercial featuring men hanging out in bars, whining about having inherited their mothers' thighs will be a reality. Now *that's* progress.

Vanity, Thy Name Is Man

Everyone wants to be considered attractive and desirable. And most of us are aware that, no matter how guilty and shallow we feel about it, there are certain broad cultural norms that define attractive. Not surprisingly, both men's and women's magazines have argued that, far from playing on human insecurities, they are merely helping readers be all that they can be—a kind of training camp for the image impaired. In recent years, such publications have embraced the tenets of "evolutionary biology," which argue that, no matter how often we're told that beauty is only skin deep, men and women are hard-wired to prefer the Jack Kennedys and Sharon Stones to the Rodney Dangerfields and Janet Renos. Continuation of the species demands that specimens with shiny coats, bright eyes, even features, and other visible signs of ruddy good health and fertility automatically kick-start our most basic instinct. Of course, the glamour mags' editors have yet to explain why, in evolutionary terms, we would ever desire adult women to stand 5'10" and weigh 100 pounds. Stories abound of women starving themselves to the point that their bodies shut down and they stop menstruating—hardly conducive to reproduction—yet Kate Moss remains the dish du jour and millions of Moss wannabes still struggle to subsist on a diet of Dexatrim and Perrier.

Similarly, despite its title, *Men's Health* is hawking far more than general fitness or a healthful lifestyle. For every half page of advice on how to cut your stress level, there are a dozen pages on how to build your biceps. For every update on the dangers of cholesterol, there are multiple warnings on the horrors of flabby abs. Now, without question, gorging on Cheetos and Budweiser while your rump takes root on the sofa is no way to treat your body if you plan on living past 50. But chugging protein drinks, agonizing over fat grams, and counting the minutes until your next Stairmaster session is equally unbalanced.

The line between taking pride in one's physical appearance and being obsessed by it is a fine one—and one that disappeared for many women long ago.

Now with lads' mags taking men in that direction as well, in many cases it's almost impossible to tell whether you're reading a copy of *Men's Health* or of *Mademoiselle:* "April 8. To commemorate Buddha's birthday, hit a Japanese restaurant. Stick to low-fat selections. Choose foods described as *yakimono*, which means "grilled," advised the monthly "to do list" in the April *Men's Health*. (Why readers should go Japanese in honor of the most famous religious leader in *India's* history remains unclear.) The January/February list was equally thought provoking: "January 28. It's Chinese New Year, so make a resolution to custom-order your next takeout. Ask that they substitute wonton soup broth for oil. Try the soba noodles instead of plain noodles. They're richer in nutrients and contain much less fat." The issue also featured a "Total Body Workout Poster" and one of those handy little "substitution" charts (loathed by women everywhere), showing men how to slash their calorie intake by making a few minor dietary substitutions: mustard for mayo, popcorn for peanuts, seltzer water for soda, pretzels for potato chips....

As in women's magazines, fast results with minimum inconvenience is a central theme. Among *Men's Health's* March highlights were a guide to "Bigger Biceps in 2 Weeks," and "20 Fast Fixes" for a bad diet; April offered "A Better Body in Half the Time," along with a colorful four-page spread on "50 Snacks That Won't Make You Fat." And you can forget carrot sticks—this think-thin eating guide celebrated the wonders of Reduced Fat Cheez-its, Munch 'Ems, Fiddle Faddle, Oreos, Teddy Grahams, Milky Ways, Bugles, Starburst Fruit Twists, and Klondike's Fat Free Big Bear Ice Cream Sandwiches. Better nutrition is not the primary issue. A better butt is. To this end, also found in the pages of *Men's Health* is the occasional, tasteful ad for liposuction—just in case nature doesn't cooperate.

But a blueprint to rock-hard buns is only part of what makes *Men's Health* the preeminent "men's lifestyle" magazine. Nice teeth, nice skin, nice hair, and a red-hot wardrobe are now required to round out the ultimate alpha male package, and *Men's Health* is there to help on all fronts. In recent months it has run articles on how to select, among other items, the perfect necktie and belt, the hippest wallet, the chicest running gear, the best "hair-thickening" shampoo, and the cutest golfing apparel. It has also offered advice on how to retard baldness, how to keep your footwear looking sharp, how to achieve different "looks" with a patterned blazer, even how to keep your lips from chapping at the dentist's office: "[B]efore you start all that 'rinse and spit' business, apply some moisturizer to your face and some lip balm to your lips. Your face and lips won't have that stretched-out dry feeling.... Plus, you'll look positively radiant!"

While a desire to look good for their hygienists may be enough to spur some men to heed the magazine's advice (and keep 'em coming back for more), fear and insecurity about the alternatives are generally more effective motivators. For those who don't get with the *Men's Health* program, there must be the threat of ridicule. By far the least subtle example of this is the free subscriptions for "guys who need our help" periodically announced in the front section of the magazine. April's dubious honoree was actor Christopher Walken:

> Chris, we love the way you've perfected that psycho persona. But now you're taking your role in "Things to Do in Denver When You're Dead" way too seriously with that ghostly pale face, the "where's the funeral?" black clothes, and a haircut that looks like the work of a hasty undertaker.... Dab on a little Murad Murasun Self-Tanner ($21).... For those creases in your face, try Ortho Dermatologicals' Renova, a prescription anti-wrinkle cream that contains tretinoin, a form of vitamin A. Then, find a barber.

Or how about the March "winner," basketball coach Bobby Knight: "Bob, your trademark red sweater is just a billboard for your potbelly. A darker solid color would make you look slimmer. Also, see 'The Tale of Two Bellies' in our February 1998 issue, and try to drop a few pounds. Then the next time you throw a sideline tantrum, at least people won't say, 'look at the crazy *fat* man.' "

Just as intense as the obsession with appearance that men's (and women's) magazines breed are the sexual neuroses they feed. And if one of the ostensible goals of women's mags is to help women drive men wild, what is the obvious corollary objective for men's magazines? To get guys laid—well and often. As if men needed any encouragement to fixate on the subject, *Men's Health* is chock full of helpful "how-tos" such as, "Have Great Sex Every Day Until You Die" and "What I Learned From My Sex Coach," as well as more cursory explorations of why men with larger testicles have more sex ("Why Big Boys Don't Cry"), how to maintain orgasm intensity as you age ("Be one of the geysers"), and how to achieve stronger erections by eating certain foods ("Bean counters make better lovers"). And for those having trouble even getting to the starting line, last month's issue offered readers a chance to "Win free love lessons."

The High Price of Perfection

Having elevated men's physical and sexual insecurities to the level of grand paranoia, lads' mags can then get down to what really matters: moving merchandise. On the cover of *Men's Health* each month, in small type just above the magazine's title, appears the phrase "Tons of useful stuff." Thumbing through an issue or two, however, one quickly realizes that a more accurate description would read: "Tons of expensive stuff." They're all there: Ralph Lauren, Tommy Hilfiger, Paul Mitchell, Calvin Klein, Clinique, Armani, Versace, Burberrys, Nautica, Nike, Omega, Rogaine, The Better Sex Video Series.... The magazine even has those annoying little perfume strips guaranteed to make your nose run and to alienate everyone within a five-mile radius of you.

Masters of psychology, marketers wheel out their sexiest pitches and hottest male models to tempt/intimidate the readership of *Men's Health*. Not since the last casting call for "Baywatch" has a more impressive display of firm, tanned, young flesh appeared in one spot. And just like in women's magazines, the articles themselves are designed to sell stuff. All those helpful tips on choosing blazers, ties, and belts come complete with info on the who, where, and how much. The strategy is brilliant: Make men understand exactly how far short of the ideal they fall, and they too become vulnerable to the lure of high-priced underwear, cologne, running shoes, workout gear, hair dye, hair strengthener, skin softener, body-fat monitors, suits, boots, energy bars, and sex aids. As Mark Jannot, the grooming and health editor for *Men's Journal,* told "Today" show host Matt Lauer in January, "This is a huge, booming market. I mean, the marketers have found a group of people that are ripe for the picking. Men are finally learning that aging is a disease." Considering how effectively *Men's Health* fosters this belief, it's hardly surprising that the magazine has seen its ad pages grow 510 percent since 1991 and has made it onto *Adweek's* 10 Hottest Magazines list three of the last five years.

To make all this "girly" image obsession palatable to their audience, lads' mags employ all their creative energies to transform appearance issues into "a guy thing." *Men's Health* tries to cultivate a joking, macho tone throughout ("Eat Like Brando and Look Like Rambo" or "Is my tallywhacker shrinking?") and tosses in a handful of Y-chromosome teasers such as "How to Stay Out of Jail," "How to Clean Your Whole Apartment in One Hour or Less," and my personal favorite, "Let's Play Squash," an illustrated guide to identifying the bug-splat patterns on your windshield. Instead of a regular advice columnist, which would smack too much of chicks' magazines, *Men's Health* recently introduced "Jimmy the Bartender," a monthly column on "women, sex, and other stuff that screws up men's lives."

It appears that, no matter how much clarifying lotion and hair gel you're trying to sell them, men must never suspect that you think they share women's insecurities. If you want a man to buy wrinkle cream, marketers have learned, you better pitch it as part of a comfortingly macho shaving regimen. Aramis, for example, assures men that its popular Lift Off! Moisture Formula with alpha hydroxy will help cut their shave time by one-third. "The biggest challenge for products started for women is how to transfer them to men," explained George Schaeffer, the president of OPI cosmetics, in the November issue of *Soap-Cosmetics-Chemical Specialties.* Schaeffer's Los Angeles-based company is the maker of Matte Nail Envy, and unobtrusive nail polish that's proved a hit with men. And for the more adventuresome shopper, last year Hard Candy cosmetics introduced a line of men's nail enamel, called Candy Man, that targets guys with such studly colors as Gigolo (metallic black) and Testosterone (gunmetal silver).

On a larger scale, positioning a makeover or trip to the liposuction clinic as a smart career move seems to help men rationalize their image obsession. "Whatever a man's cosmetic shortcoming, it's apt to be a career liability," noted Alan Farnham in a September 1996 issue of *Fortune.* "The business world is prejudiced against the ugly." Or how about *Forbes'* sad attempt to differentiate between male and female vanity in its Dec. 1 piece on cosmetic surgery: "Plastic surgery is more of a cosmetic thing for women. They have a thing about aging. For men it's an investment that pays a pretty good dividend." Whatever you say, guys.

The irony is rich and bittersweet. Gender equity is at last headed our way —not in the form of women being less obsessed with looking like Calvin Klein models, but of men becoming hysterical over the first signs of crows feet. Gradually, guys are no longer pumping up and primping simply to get babes, but because they feel it's something everyone expects them to do. Women, after all, do not spend $400 on Dolce & Gabbana sandals to impress their boyfriends, most of whom don't know Dolce & Gabbana from Beavis & Butthead (yet). They buy them to impress other women—and because that's what society says they should want to do. Most guys haven't yet achieved this level of insanity, but with grown men catcalling the skin tone and wardrobe of other grown men (Christopher Walken, Bobby Knight) for a readership of still more grown men, can the gender's complete surrender to the vanity industry be far behind?

The ad for *Men's Health* web site says it all: "Don't click here unless you want to look a decade younger... lose that beer belly... be a better lover... and more! Men's Health Online: The Internet site For Regular Guys." Of course, between the magazine's covers there's not a "regular guy" to be found, save for the occasional snapshot of one of the publication's writers or editors—usually taken from a respectable distance. The moist young bucks in the Gap jeans ads and the electric-eyed Armani models have exactly as much in common with the average American man as Tyra Banks does with the average American woman. Which would be fine, if everyone seemed to understand this distinction. Until they do, however, I guess my consolation will have to be the image of thousands of once-proud men, having long scorned women's insecurities, lining up for their laser peels and trying to squeeze their middle-aged asses into a snug set of Super Shaper Briefs—with the optional fly front endowment pad, naturally.

POSTSCRIPT

Is Emphasis on Body Image in the Media Harmful to Females Only?

The selections by Martin and Gentry and by Cottle contain negative criticism about advertising, but they also suggest that age affects how susceptible people are to different aspects of advertising images. While one selection focuses on girls at a time in their lives when their bodies are changing, the second selection indicates that adult males, too, can be highly influenced by the images they see and by what seems to be a preoccupation with youth.

These selections also raise questions about the magazine industry and the hypersegmentation by market. If people's tastes and choices of media are being met by a wider variety of specialized publications (or even lifestyle TV channels, such as ESPN or Lifetime), perhaps there is a shift in the idea of a "mass audience." This concept has traditionally meant that the audience was characterized by homogeneity. Perhaps now the audience is less characterized by a sameness, but the content of the media may suggest a "homogenized" ideal for the different groups that make up the audience.

Standards of beauty and success are culturally defined. It is often interesting to pick up magazines or newspapers from other countries or ethnic groups and examine the images in ads to see if specific cultural differences are apparent.

There are many excellent references on the topics raised by this issue. John Tebbel and Mary Ellen Zuckerman have produced a history of magazines entitled *The Magazine in America, 1741-1990* (Oxford University Press, 1991). Books like Naomi Wolf's *The Beauty Myth* (Anchor Books, 1992) and Julia T. Wood's *Gendered Lives: Communication, Gender, and Culture* (Wadsworth, 1994) are particularly insightful regarding the images of women and minorities.

Some videotapes are also available for extended discussion, such as Jeanne Kilbourne's *Still Killing Us Softly* and *Slim Hopes* (Media Education Foundation).

ISSUE 4

Do African American Stereotypes Still Dominate Entertainment Television?

YES: Donald Bogle, from *Primetime Blues: African Americans on Network Television* (Farrar, Straus and Giroux, 2001)

NO: John McWhorter, from "Gimme a Break!" *The New Republic* (March 5, 2001)

ISSUE SUMMARY

YES: Professor and author Donald Bogle offers a comprehensive analysis of African Americans on network series. He traces their role on prime time from the negative stereotypes of the 1950s to the current more subtle stereotypes of the 1990s. Bogle tackles the shows of the 1990s, particularly the popular and controversial *Martin*.

NO: Professor and author John McWhorter counters that stereotypes are diminishing in America. In his review of Bogle's book, McWhorter asserts that Bogle has donned an ideological straitjacket, which blinds him to the strides that African Americans have made in prime time. He concludes that the continued search for stereotypes prevents us from seeing the very real changes that have taken place in the media.

Intense controversy exists about how racial and ethnic groups are portrayed in the media. Many scholars argue that racial representations in popular culture help to mold public opinion and set the agenda for public discourse on race issues in the media and in society as a whole. Do members of an audience identify with the characters portrayed? Do expressions of and images in the media communicate effectively about specific cultures? How much can we learn about other cultures through media portrayals?

Despite such shows as the infamous *Amos 'n' Andy*, portrayals of African Americans were for the most part absent from early television programming. By the 1970s, a number of shows focused on black families, including *Sanford and Son, Good Times*, and *The Jeffersons*. Few shows in the history of television have been as popular as *The Cosby Show*, which debuted in 1984 and attracted white as well as black audiences. These financially successful shows paved the way for programming that highlighted black characters and families. In the 1990s there were many shows that focused on black families or friendship groups. Yet critics noted that the primary audience for these shows was African American viewers, and at the end of the 1990s, the National Association for the Advancement of Colored People (NAACP) challenged the major networks to better integrate the prime-time population.

Both Donald Bogle and John McWhorter discuss the general issues of how minorities are characterized on television. Both are concerned with the issue of equal access, and by implication both are concerned with the issue of the participation of minorities in media industries.

Bogle discusses how decades of television programs, most often sitcoms, have provided a distorted picture of the African American population. His book includes comprehensive analyses of hundreds of shows. In the following selection he examines one of the more popular shows of the 1990s—*Martin*—to demonstrate both the positive and negative aspects of the program. Although he presents the analysis of only one show, he gives a hint of the richness of description to be found in his book. According to Jannette Dates (*TV Quarterly*, Spring 2001) Bogle implies that "television, the medium said by many to show Americans' true values, systematically deterred whites from learning about African American realities and prevented blacks from full participation in the most important means of communication ever invented by mankind" (p. 78).

McWhorter decries the "Can You Find the Stereotype?" game. He accuses Bogle and many others of being blind to the many positive changes in the media environment. Keeping black viewers indignant over their "perceived victimhood" is, he argues, central to the stereotype game. Ultimately, McWhorter, a linguist, argues that it is "just television"—a perspective sure to anger both black and white mass communication scholars.

The issues of race presented in these selections should lead you to think broadly about the roles represented by African Americans within the media, behind the camera, and beyond media. In recent years more writing has begun to emerge that reflects the role of African Americans in the United States and that bespeaks of greater class differentiation and economic interests. An interesting question to ask might be whether or not viewing politically powerful African Americans challenges traditional media roles and representations. For example, have highly visible African American leaders such as Colin Powell challenged media stereotypes? How long might it take to reverse harmful stereotypes that may have been portrayed in media for generations?

Donald Bogle

 **YES**

The 1990s: Free-for-Alls

The restless, politically contentious 1990s closed a century *and* a millennium. The decade was a heady mix of pessimistic low expectations and surprisingly, by decade's end, high hopes for the future. In the early years, as the Bush era came to a close, Americans were faced with a war in the Persian Gulf, unprecedented unemployment statistics, and vast company layoffs as corporations talked of downsizing. The national mood changed, however, once William Jefferson Clinton assumed the presidency with ambitious plans to boost the economy and reform health care. As Clinton appointed more African Americans and women to his cabinet than any American President before him, he looked as if he really might be able to overhaul history and lead (as he would say in his reelection campaign) to a bridge to the next century. The good news was that the economy soared, unemployment was at record lows, and Wall Street profits were at record highs. But along with the boom years came a series of White House scandals that ultimately led to the historic impeachment hearings of William Jefferson Clinton, the President of the United States. Though Clinton remained in office, and high in the opinion polls, the pundits cried that permanent damage had been done to the presidency—and the country.

In the early 1990s, the nation seemed to have mixed feelings about race, racial problems, and racial/cultural identities. Some preferred to believe, as they had in the 1980s, that America had outgrown its racial divisions and conflicts. Affirmative action and quotas, they contended, were unfair and unnecessary. But an entirely different mood arose at colleges and universities, where a traditional Eurocentric view of history and culture was challenged. The rise of multicultural studies marked the new view of the American experience as a mosaic of cultural contributions and insights, its very fabric woven together by the input of Native Americans, Africans, Asians, and Europeans. A new generation of African Americans was more conscious of its cultural roots in this Afrocentric era. Young rap/hip-hop artists celebrated Black life and culture and also examined—with hard-hitting lyrics—long-held American social/political injustices and inequities.

Throughout the era, the nation was stunned by a series of events—many televised—in which race reared its ugly head. Television viewers could daily turn on the tube and witness the Clarence Thomas/Anita Hill hearings, in which

Thomas referred to the Senate investigation of him on charges of sexual harassment as a "high-tech lynching," while Hill emerged as a solitary figure
being judged not by her peers buy by a panel of senators that was all male
and all white. In March 1991, the nightly news shows broadcast a videotape of
four white Los Angeles police officers brutally beating African American mo-
torist Rodney King. Little more than a year later, in April 1992, after those same
police officers were acquitted in a state trial on charges of having used excessive force on King, civil disorders erupted in Los Angeles's African American
community. Fifty-three Americans ended up dead while property damaged to-
taled some $1 billion. Riots also broke out in other parts of the country. At the
end of the 1990s, the nation would learn of a shockingly vicious hate crime
in Texas. A Black man was chained to a pickup truck by three white men who
then dragged him to his death. Mainstream America was forced to acknowledge
that the nation's racial attitudes had not changed as much as many might have
hoped.

In one way or another, all these events would affect television's primetime
African American images.

But in this new decade, television programming was also affected by further changes in the medium itself as the networks continued to see an erosion
of their viewership. By 1990, the number of households wired for cable rose
from 20 percent to 37. In turn, the networks' 67 percent share of American
homes slipped to 57 percent. Viewers in more than half of those cable-wired
households could choose from some fifty channels. The once seemingly undifferentiated TV audience that the three networks had always catered to could
now tune in to cable's Black Entertainment Television or the Food Channel or
the Sci-Fi Channel or the History Channel, all of which successfully tapped the
tastes of specific viewers. Many established cable networks like Lifetime also offered original productions. In the summer of 1998, cable would triumph when
it "captured more TV households than ABC, NBC, CBS and Fox combined *for the
entire month of August.*" By the end of the decade, the future for the networks
looked even bleaker. Of the nation's 100 million households with television,
some 70 million would have cable.

With all the changes in viewer tastes and habits as the twentieth century
drew to a close, network television often appeared frantic in both its search for
and its avoidance of shows centered on African Americans. TV power brokers
like Cosby and Oprah still found the networks receptive to just about anything they wanted to do. A newcomer like Will Smith looked as if he were
his network's darling. For a brief spell, the network Black-cast series was also
fashionable. But as the decade progressed, the three major networks, unable to
come up with hit Black shows, reverted to form and played it safe, airing fewer
and fewer Black-cast series. In their place the new "alternative" networks like
Fox and later UPN and WB became known for taking a chance on weekly Black
material. These networks solidified their power bases by courting the African
American audience, but often with controversial images that might have made
Kingfish and Sapphire [characters from the controversial *Amos 'n' Andy* radio
show that was produced for television starting in 1951] blush....

Martin Mania: The Rise of Martin Lawrence

... Fox hit pay dirt—and heated controversy—with the sitcom *Martin*. The series chronicled the adventures of Insane Martin Payne (Martin Lawrence), the host of a talk show at the Detroit radio station WZUP. Away from work, Martin pursues, beds, and eventually weds the girl of his dreams, Gina (Tisha Campbell), a marketing executive. Also around are Martin's friends Tommy (Thomas Mikal Ford) and Cole (Carl Anthony Payne Jr.) as well as Gina's secretary and close friend, Pam (Tichina Arnold). There were also such characters as Sheneneh Jenkins, Jerome, security guard Otis, and Martin's mother, Mrs. Payne, all of whom were played by Martin Lawrence.

Martin Lawrence was already known for his stand-up comedy. Lawrence had been born Martin Fitzgerald Lawrence (named, so he said, after Martin Luther King Jr. and John Fitzgerald Kennedy) in 1965 in Frankfurt, Germany, where his father, John, was stationed in the air force. By the time Martin was seven, his parents divorced. While his mother, Chlora, took her other children to live in Landover, Maryland, a suburb of Washington, D.C., Martin was left with his father but joined his siblings when he was in the third grade. To keep the family afloat, Chlora Lawrence worked various jobs as a cashier and in department stores.

As a heavy, hyperactive kid nicknamed Chubby, Martin was so disruptive at school that his teachers sometimes permitted him to tell the class jokes if he promised to be quiet afterward. At home, Lawrence watched Jimmie Walker on *Good Times* (maybe that was his biggest mistake), Redd Foxx, and Richard Pryor, all of whom, along with Eddie Murphy, would be influences. "Richard taught me that honest emotions about sex could be really funny on stage," said Lawrence. Slimming down to some ninety pounds at age fifteen, he became a Golden Gloves boxer. Upon graduation from high school in 1984, he performed at local clubs while working as a janitor at a five-and-dime.

The big break came with a 1987 appearance on television's *Star Search*. Not long afterward, he won a supporting role in the syndicated series *What's Happening Now!!* Spike Lee cast him in *Do the Right Thing*. Then came roles in the movies *House Party* and *Boomerang*.

Lawrence continued performing stand-up comedy routines in which he created energetic minidramas, often centered on relationships. He acted all the parts. Discussing a variety of subjects from racism to the use of condoms, he could be both macho and sensitive. When addressing the subject of male sexual boasts, he seemed surprisingly candid. "Brothers, quit braggin' [about your equipment]," he once said. Then he confessed to being minimally endowed. "But I *work* with what I've got," he said. Audiences loved the honesty. "He is *so* large. He's like the first in a new wave of comics behind Robin Harris," said producer Russell Simmons. "He's part of a whole new generation that is a little freer. The energy is different. It's not shock humor. The language is so natural." Still, Lawrence was criticized for his "woman-hating" material. Often Lawrence could revel in graphic discussions about feminine hygiene, odors, and yeast infections.

His stand-up performances reached a wider audience when he became the host of HBO's sexually explicit *Def Comedy Jam*. In many respects, that series served as a launching pad for *Martin*. *Def Comedy Jam's* executive producer, Stan Lathan, called him "a mirror of the current hip-hop generation. The kids are all trying to maintain this macho exterior even though they have a lot of inner sensitivity and insecurities."

Much as Lawrence had done in concerts, his sitcom *Martin* was intended as a new take on contemporary relationships and friendships, done with a hip-hop beat and rhythm. It also set out to comically dramatize the rather traditional sexual/gender attitudes of a young African American male. On its premiere episode, radio host Martin, who specializes in talk about romance and relationships, discussed male sensitivity on the air. When a male listener admits to crying, Martin gets his dander up. What is the world coming to? "You shave your face or your bikini line?" he asks. "Stand up, pull your pants down, man, and look at the front of your drawers. You're missing a flap, girlfriend." Throughout the series, the openly sexist Martin battled his girlfriend Gina for the upper hand. Though she fought him, and though Martin was sometimes made to look foolish, the series glorified rather than challenged his attitudes, not only with Gina but with the world at large.

From the start, the reviewers—to put it mildly—*hated* the series. "Clearly, 'Martin' intends to mine the same misogynistic mucho-macho vein that is a hallmark of 'Def Comedy,'" wrote the *New York Post's* Michele Greppi. "It deserves a deaf ear."

In the *Los Angeles Times*, television critic Howard Rosenberg wrote of the racism of a "world-class crude" episode in which an oversexed Martin struggles to forgo having sex—for two weeks—with his girlfriend, Gina. "Bumping, grinding and pawing, he was all over her in public—his body pumping like a piston, his tongue thrusting lewdly—acting generally like an animal. 'I'm telling you, baby, I gots to have it!'" At one point, as a desperate Martin tries to calm himself down, Gina discovers he is wearing an ice pack on his penis. "That the half hour was endorsed by Fox's standards and practices department for airing at all was bad enough," wrote Rosenberg. "That it was on at 8 p.m.—and thus potentially available to young kids galore—made it an even greater abomination." He added that perhaps "the bottom line here *is* the bottom line, that anything goes on Fox when it comes to making a buck."

Everything about the show seemed caricatured. In the first year, the primary set—Martin's living room—with its bold colors (purples, yellows, greens) looked like something out of a cartoon. The acting too was fast-paced and frenetic, with most cast members playing to the manic rhythm established by Lawrence. There never seemed to be a quiet moment when a character could relax and—heaven forbid—reflect about what he/she was saying. Worse, the scripts presented the characters with too broad a stroke. Martin's friend Cole, with his oversized clothes and his large hats, seemed so dim-witted that one wondered how he survived in the world. Certainly, he didn't look as if he could function in any workplace; one more sign that Black males had nothing to contribute to establishment culture. (Watching actor Payne, viewers must have asked how an actor who was so appealing and refreshing on *The Cosby Show* could have sunk so low. His saving grace was his vulnerability: he almost looked helpless. Somehow he never lost his fundamental charm.) On the other hand, Tommy appeared as if he *might* be on the ball; certainly he wasn't childlike like Cole and certainly he had more common sense than Martin. But no one was sure where Tommy worked. Or if he worked at all. It was as bad as the situation with Kingfish.

Then there was Gina's friend Pam, decked out in her tighter than skintight dresses while the camera gave viewers a lingering, leering look at her. She became the butt of Martin's repeated jokes. The two regularly traded insults. Of course, bickering Black couples were a staple of Black sitcoms; Kingfish and Sapphire; Fred Sanford and Aunt Esther; George Jefferson and Florence. But Sapphire was usually on Kingfish's back because of something stupid he had done. George Jefferson's criticism of Florence—for not being able to cook, for being lazy, or for being late—grew out of his belief that she failed to meet her responsibilities as an employee in his home. In turn, she criticized him for being cheap and pretentious.

But Martin's criticism of Pam were usually tied to her looks. Or her attributes (or lack of) as a woman. He talked about her bad breath, her nappy hair, her figure—and compared her to a horse and a camel. "Why can't I find at least a half decent man?" Pam once asked Gina. "Don't you have any mirrors at home?" said Martin. Pam could match him in the insult department. She made fun of his size and other male inadequacies. For Martin, Gina was always the ideal woman; Pam, the unpleasant leftover, a disgrace to the other sex. Because of the casting, the subtext of the Martin/Pam spats seemed to comment on color. Once again, a lighter African American woman, Gina, played by the lighter actress Tisha Campbell, was the dreamgirl; Pam, played by the browner Tichina Arnold, became a Black woman who cannot meet certain physical standards. As much as Martin yelled and screamed at Pam, he could never directly refer to her color as a sign of her lack of beauty. Never could he call her a *dark* heifer or a *Black* witch. That would have alienated the African American viewer. But for many, color preference was tied in to those battles. In this respect, *Martin* could be pernicious and poisonous.

The characters played by Lawrence himself were the most blatant caricatures. The jivey Jerome, who looked like a reject from *Superfly,* was as sexist as Martin. One afternoon when he eyed Gina walking off with Pam, he felt compelled to *compliment* her by saying, "Girl, you sure is *swollen.*" Unlike Richard Pryor, who could uncover the pathos or pain inside his winos and junkies, Lawrence could never invest a character like Jerome with any insights. At the same time, as his character Mother Emma Payne badgered and blasted Gina (whom she felt was totally inappropriate for her baby Martin), she was one more old-style mammy, a direct descendant of Sapphire's Mama.

Much the same might be said of Sheneneh, one of Lawrence's best-known creations. Living across the hall from Martin, Sheneneh sashayed about wearing opulent extensions in her hair, tight short skirts to emphasize her bulging hips and bodacious backside, tight blouses to showcase her ample breasts. Like Martin's mother, she despised Gina.

Part of the cruel fun was watching Sheneneh dump on Gina and other women. On one episode, the conniving Sheneneh took advantage of Gina and forced her to work in Sheneneh's Sho' Nuf Hair Salon. All sorts of comic horrors transpire here. First Gina was told she must have a professional look. The next thing we know, we see Gina *coiffed* in out-sized curly braids. A customer, Mira, said she needed a pedicure because her corns were fixing to pop. "Why don't you take your shoes off, so we can get started," she was told. "They are off," the woman answered. Sheneneh then used an electric power tool to work on the woman's feet.

Shortly afterward, Mira told Gina, "Look, I got to get my perm. I can't sit here all day. I got *mens* waiting to see me." Gina gave her a perm but without a neutralizer. Mira ended up practically bald, except for patches of hair above her ears and long hair in the back. Sheneneh, however, persuaded Mira that she looked stylish. But Sheneneh let Gina know that Mira "was tore up from the floor up. I damn near threw up."

Throughout, *Martin's* misogyny was apparent (and, sadly, part of the appeal for some misguided males). The series delighted in turning Sheneneh and other women (with the notable exception of Gina and perhaps Pam) into grotesque figures; objects of tawdry jokes and scorn. With her extensions, her eye pops, her competitive attitude toward Gina and other women, Sheneneh was a ribald parody of a pushy, know-it-all, forever attitudinizing, desperately trying-to-be-hip, always-in-your-face young urban Black woman.

Yet *Martin* quickly emerged as a very popular hit. Perhaps young viewers were drawn in by the simple fact that *Martin* was far franker about sex (and the fact that the hero had to have it) than previous Black sitcoms. At times, Martin, like other Black male characters on sitcoms, seemed a tad obsessed with sex. But for viewers, what distinguished Martin was indeed the relationship with Gina. The story line of three of the most popular earlier episodes centered on Martin and Gina as they fought, broke up, and then got back together. Before the final episode, viewers were invited to vote, via a 900 number, on which of the two should apologize. The verdict: Martin should get on his knees. Viewers were always willing to forgive him his trespasses. Hip, loose, free, and very up-front about his desires, he may have struck the young as being an assault (much like Kingfish) on traditional, polite bourgeois society.

Another aspect of his appeal—though his critics would be loath to admit it—was that Martin had a joie de vivre that was infectious; he was something of the indomitable optimist (the opposite of the beleaguered, sometimes cornered Kingfish) with catchphrases that encapsulated his energy and perspective on life. "You go, girl!" "You so crazy!" "Wass Up!" and "Don't go there" caught on and entered the popular lexicon of people who didn't even know of the series.

Martin Lawrence's looks no doubt led viewers not only to feel sorry for him but also to patronize him. Thin and short with large eyes and protruding ears, he was never anyone's idea of a hunk (which, of course, made his slams against Pam seem all the more absurd). All mouth, he was a fiercely unthreatening hero. In this respect, he was obviously similar to Sherman Hemsley's George Jefferson but without the charm or wily intelligence and without the wicked way of turning a line inside out. Martin Lawrence usually bopped and hopped his way through a performance, using his energy rather than any acting talent to create his character. Nonetheless, had the character Martin been tall, muscular, deep-voiced, less hyper, he might have been scary and totally unacceptable. No one would sit by and listen to a buck figure express some of the sexist sentiments of a Martin.

For the same reason, Lawrence no doubt succeeded with his characters Sheneneh, Jerome, and Mama Payne. Despite the fact that they're cruel parodies, they're such outlandish clowns that it's hard not to laugh at them, even though you do so at your own peril. In the minds of viewers, these characters were all the same person: It's Martin—the perpetual runty adolescent—dressed up in the clothes and makeup of Mommy and her friends. You almost feel sorry for this overcaffeinated adolescent's desperate need to get attention—by any means necessary. Yet viewers were always drawn to him. Later in movies like *Life,* Lawrence also extended his talents as an actor.

The demographics indicated that *Martin* was popular with those 18- to 49-year-old viewers that pleased advertisers. To appeal to them even more, the series featured such guest stars as rappers Snoop Doggy Dogg and Biggie Smalls as well as football star Randall Cunningham. But the series also found favor with even younger viewers. *Martin* ranked in the top five among viewers age 12 to 17 and in the top ten with ages 2 to 11. "I'm huge with the under-5 crowd," said star Martin Lawrence. One only wonders about the ideas those poor kids came away with.

As *Martin* continued its run, it was toned down. Later episodes were better, yet more traditional television fare, at times as much influenced by *I Love Lucy* as episodes of *227* and *Amen.* A memorable episode featured Marla Gibbs as an exacting drill sergeant of a housekeeper determined to make Martin and Gina stick to a schedule. The episode played on our knowledge of Gibbs's TV career from the days of *The Jeffersons* to *227.* In some episodes, Judyann Elder and J. A. Preston had funny bits as the parents of Gina. Here the series touched on class friction within the African American community. Some characters on *Martin* almost started to look like actual human beings.

In time, viewers became as familiar with the off-screen Martin Lawrence as with the character he played. The success of the series and the new fame that grew out of it appeared to take a toll on him. He became a favorite of the gossips and the tabloids. In 1993, the press reported that he dumped his manager and co-creator of *Martin,* Topper Carew. The next year, a story broke that Lawrence had failed to perform concert dates in Cleveland, Atlanta, and Buffalo. Lawrence, along with his agent and tour promoter, was sued for fraud and breach of contract for the cancellation of the concerts. Later came news that Lawrence had been arrested after he stood at a busy Los Angeles intersection, screaming and ranting incoherently at passersby. Police discovered that he was carrying a concealed weapon. Another arrest came in August 1996 at California's Burbank airport. There he was charged with carrying a loaded handgun in his luggage. Most damaging to his professional image was a sexual harassment suit filed by his TV co-star Tisha Campbell. Campbell left the show but later returned just before its last episodes were filmed.

By the fifth season, the overall ratings for *Martin* plunged. It ranked number 106 out of approximately 130 shows. Yet Lawrence's Black constituency stuck with the program. It was the third most watched show by African Americans. Still, that couldn't save it. Fox dropped the sit-com in August 1997. Afterward its reruns scored well in syndication.

John McWhorter

 **NO**

Gimme a Break!

I.

Like Donald Bogle, I grew up in Philadelphia watching the increasing presence of black Americans on television. Bogle has some years on me, having been in attendance since the 1960s. My own memories of television begin in the early 1970s, when my mother demanded that I sit by her side to watch the new flood of black shows such as *Good Times, Sanford and Son*, and *The Jeffersons*, as well as mainstream shows attending to race such as *All in the Family* and *Maude*. And, of course, watching the entire run of *Roots* was a required rite of passage, even though it meant staying up past my bedtime for many nights in a row.

A part of this regimen was surely due to black Americans' cultural affection for television. As Bogle notes in his new book, *Primetime Blues: African Americans on Network Television*, a Nielsen survey in 1990 showed that blacks watched an average of seventy hours of television a week, and non-blacks watched an average of forty-seven hours; and it is certainly true that television was a more central ritual in my household than in the homes of my white friends. Yet my mother, a professor of social work, also considered black television a part of my early education in racial consciousness. She regarded the shows as a way to inculcate me with the basics of black history, and with the message that the whole world was not white, and that black America included many people not as fortunate as we were.

As we passed into the 1980s and 1990s, the black presence on television grew so steadily that had I been born later, it would have been impractical to try to find everything that blacks did on the tube. In the 1950s, white racists could be satisfied to find blacks on television only in the very occasional series, a few supporting roles, scattered variety show appearances, and one-shot dramatic productions from which they could easily avert their gaze. Today blacks are so numerous on television in all of its genres, represented in such a wide sociological and psychological range, that the same bigot would feel inundated by the objects of his scorn every time he turned on his set, and incensed at how sympathetically they are portrayed and how intimately they interact with whites.

I have always considered the history of blacks on television to be a clear sign that the color line is ever dissolving in America. But Bogle arrives at the opposite conclusion. His book concedes that progress has been made in a sheerly numerical sense, but it argues that overall the black presence on television has been an endless recycling of a passel of injuriously stereotypical images. It is a "Do the Right Thing" affair, exposing the eternal racism that always lurks behind allegedly positive developments that give the appearance of black progress. But Bogle's pessimistic argument is ultimately owed primarily to the ideological fashions of our moment. It cannot withstand a fair and thorough empirical look at the subject. It is a perfect product of the distortions, some of them benevolently meant, that have dominated the thinking of black intellectuals since the late 1960s.

✐❀✐

But Bogle's early chapters, on the 1950s and 1960s, are masterful, and they put one in mind of his accomplishments in his earlier writings. With *Brown Sugar*, which appeared in 1980, Bogle did the history of black popular entertainment a signature service with a smart survey of black "divas" from Ma Rainey to Donna Summer, bringing to the light of day the work of many figures who had faded from consciousness. His biography of Dorothy Dandridge was published in 1987, and it was a long overdue chronicle of the life and the work of this world-class beauty and gifted actress who was denied the career that she deserved by the naked racism of her era, and died in despair at the age of forty-two.

With the crisp prose and the masterful eye for detail that were evident in those books, Bogle now takes us through black television of the 1940s, 1950s, and 1960s, bringing to light performances barely recorded in accessible sources. Thus we learn that the very first experimental television broadcast by NBC in 1939 was not, say, a half-hour with Jack Benny, but a variety show starring none other than Ethel Waters. Bogle traces Waters's little-known but fascinating television career, which most famously included a stint playing the maid Beulah. *Beulah* was more representative of the black presence on stone-age television than its more frequently discussed contemporary *Amos 'n' Andy*, which even by the early 1950s was a tatty, recidivist affair rooted in an obsolete minstrel humor and thriving more on familiarity than on pertinence.

Beulah is remembered for depicting a black woman who has nothing better to do than center her life around the white family that employs her, other than waiting for her ne'er-do-well boyfriend, Bill, to propose. This was not an exclusively black convention, of course: Shirley Booth's Hazel on *Hazel* and Ann B. Davis's Alice on *The Brady Bunch* occupied similar spaces. What makes *Beulah* so excruciating to watch today is that Beulah is, in addition, none too bright. It is only with the thickest fortification of historical perspective that one can today endure the opening tags, in which Beulah looks us dead in the eye and offers such apercus as the fact that she is "the maid who's always in the kitchen—but never knows what's cookin'...! HYEH HYEH HYEH HYEH...!"...

Bogle is correct in noting that the miraculous Waters managed to draw some kind of character out of the wan scripts. Waters's episodes are the only ones that can be even approximately tolerated today, as she conveys a kind of warmth and sexual affection between her and Bill, and manages to evoke an impression of will and intelligence despite what her lines have her utter. Throughout her life Waters could not help filling empty space with her charisma. Bogle movingly describes an episode of the usually frothy *Person to Person* in 1954, in which Waters diverted the interview into sincere psychological self-revelation. Waters was intense....

II.

The sun began breaking through the clouds in the 1960s, as the civil rights era brought race relations and "the Negro question" to the forefront of American consciousness. Perhaps the most immediately memorable black figure of this era on television is Bill Cosby's erudite Scotty on *I Spy*, portrayed as every bit the equal of his white partner in undercover operations. From the vantage point of our identity politics, however, we instantly note the absence of any racial identity in Scotty, and this is largely true of other blacks in series of this decade, such as Greg Morris on *Mission Impossible*, Lloyd Haines on *Room 222*, and Nichelle Nichols's Uhura on *Star Trek*. For Bogle, as for many analysts, this reflected white America's desire to "tame" the Negro, who was beginning to be seen as a threat.

Certainly this was a part of the story—but it was not until the end of the decade that the salad bowl would triumph over the melting pot as the dominant metaphor for immigration in the minds of most Americans. In an era in which the central objective of civil rights leaders was still integration, many white producers and writers sincerely considered themselves to be doing good by portraying blacks without any particular "cultural" traits. Today, of course, the seams show, and the space to which blacks were assigned on television requires major historical adjustment....

⋅⊙⋅

Drama shows were somewhat more concerned with addressing the tensions that would soon transform the integrationist imperative into a separatist one, though usually more in the name of economic and racial justice than in the name of what we call "diversity." ...

This is all a far cry from Beulah in the Hendersons' kitchen. Still, throughout most of the 1960s there was not a single "black show" proper. This changed in 1968 with *Julia*, starring Diahann Carroll; and the response to this show by black commentators signaled that a new era in black American ideology had arrived. *Julia* portrayed a middle-class widow raising a young son while working as a nurse. With the "assimilated" Carroll's chiseled features and crisp standard English, *Julia* wore the race issue lightly. There was only an occasional episode that depicted Julia encountering and defeating prejudice, which was portrayed as an occasional excrescence rather than the manifestation of a profound moral and social malaise.

Basically, *Julia* was a more sober version of its contemporary *That Girl*. And so black writers, actors, and critics fiercely condemned this little show for neglecting the tragedies of blacks in the inner cities. The Black Power movement was just then forging a new sense of a "black identity" opposed to the mainstream one, which promoted the suffering poor blacks—the blacks most unlike middle-class whites—as the "real" blacks. For this radical (but increasingly pervasive) view, middle-class blacks had some explaining to do. They had deserted their "roots."

The black response to *Julia* was predicated upon this new idea—it is now so deeply ensconced in mainstream black thought that it no longer feels like a "position" at all—that the essence of blackness is suffering. A middle-class nurse living in a nice apartment and interacting easily with whites was obviously "inauthentic." Objections to *Amos 'n' Andy* in the early 1950s were based in part on the fact that even if the show was undeniably amusing, this parody of black reality was one of the only depictions of blacks on television. By the time *Julia* aired, however, black misery and the new "black identity" were not exactly absent from American television. The problem now was not that *Julia* was the only view of blacks on television; the problem was that this side of black life did not deserve to be shown at all.

III.

Fifteen years or so earlier, the critics would have eaten up *Julia* with a spoon. A comparison with *Amos 'n' Andy* is again useful. Bogle presents a list of objections to that show by the NAACP [National Association for the Advancement of Colored People]—and in a full page of complaints, the fact that the show did not address black poverty is not even mentioned. Most black thinkers of the earlier period would have had no more interest in seeing black misfortune dutifully "explored" on television than white viewers had in seeing depictions of Appalachia or the poor rural South; and they would have applauded a portrait of members of their race doing well as a genuine advance from the "mammy" days. And yet the NAACP of the period was certainly interested in the problem of black poverty.

The difference hinged on the contrast between an ideology focused on achievement despite acknowledged obstacles and an ideology predicated upon the treacherous notion that achievement is an extraordinary affair of luck until all the obstacles are removed. This latter view— fatalistic, doctrinaire—instantly casts those people blessed with only ordinary capabilities and not with luck— that is, poor people—as the "real" black people. This ideology remains with us today, pervading the thought of most black American pundits and professors. Bogle is one of their company. In its discussion of *Julia*, his book suddenly begins a disappointing decline into a narrow and numbingly circular litany of complaint. Bogle frames the thirty remaining years of black work on television as an almost unbroken procession of veiled injustice and exploitation.

Bogle at this point falls into the same trap that mars his *Toms, Coons, Mulattoes, Mammies, and Bucks*—or, rather, its revised edition. That book first appeared in 1973, and it was my first primer on blacks in film. It aptly identified five eponymous stereotypes running throughout black roles in American movies, making the useful point that the "blaxploitation" genre, whatever its visceral thrill and the work that it gave black actors, was in essence a recapitulation of the types on view as far back as *The Birth of a Nation*. But in 1989 Bogle updated his book and revealed himself as a man with a hammer to whom everything is a nail. What was a valid and penetrating thesis applied to blacks in film up to the early 1970s came to be reflexively applied to the next fifteen years of American popular culture, with no significant acknowledgment made of the stunning maturation of the black role on the silver screen that occurred during those years.

Is Eddie Murphy an exciting phenomenon, playing lead roles in film after film, and often producing films as well? Not at all, because he is sexually appetitive, and therefore he is merely a recapitulation of the oversexed black "buck" who chases the Camerons' young daughter off a cliff in D.W. Griffith's racist film. Was Lonette McKee's performance in *Sparkle* a signature piece of acting? Not quite, because she is light-skinned, and therefore her sad fate in the plot renders her a "tragic mulatto," despite her character's not being of mixed race. And so on. Richard Pryor, speaking for the ghetto, gets one of Bogle's rare stamps of approval—but with the ominous qualification that he may exemplify a new type aborning, the "Crazy Nigger."

Bogle pigeonholes almost every black contribution to American television from 1970 to 2000 into one of several dogmatic categories. As a result, his inquiry degenerates into a game that one might call "Can You Find the Stereotype?" As the years wear on, the relation of Bogle's analysis to the reality that it is describing grows more and more slender. All large, nurturing black women are "mammies," mere recapitulations of Hattie McDaniel and Beulah. This type includes even Oprah Winfrey, whose inspiring success is thereby rendered suspect. Any feisty black woman who speaks her mind to men is a "Sapphire," the idea being that the Kingfish's shrewish wife on *Amos 'n' Andy* established a "stereotype" about the black female that is now best avoided. And so our pleasure in watching LaWanda Page's immortal Aunt Esther on *Sanford and Son* or Nell Carter's lead character on *Gimme a Break!* must be a guilty one....

In Bogle's doctrinaire framework, it is all but impossible for any black performance to pass as kosher. Instead the analysis of every black character is a "damned if they do, damned if they don't" exercise designed more to feed the flames of indictment of the white man than to illuminate any actual truths. *Benson* was indeed a little dicey in depicting an intelligent, middle-aged black man as a butler in a governor's mansion as late as 1979. Within two years, however, the show's writers had Benson elected state budget director; eventually he became lieutenant governor; and finally he ran against the governor himself.

The series ended with Benson and the governor awaiting the election results to- gether. One would think this series aggressively negated the Beulah stereotype, even at the expense of some plausibility. What counts for Bogle, however, is that the show ends with Benson "by his good white friend's side." Physically, yes—but he was watching the progress of an election in which he had attempted to unseat the man from his livelihood! How would Bogle have contrived his analysis if the series had ended with Benson watching the returns by himself?

It gets worse. If a show addresses racism in history (*Homefront, I'll Fly Away*), then Bogle takes it to mean that racism is safely confined to the past. But then if producers had refrained from depicting slavery and segregation on tele- vision, surely Bogle would have decried this as "whites denying the wrongs of the past." Meanwhile Bogle repeatedly dismisses as "self-congratulatory" shows in which whites denounce racism—though a black character who wears racial indignation on his sleeve merely restores us to the Angry Black Man. In Gary Coleman's savvy comments about racism in *Diff'rent Strokes*, Bogle detects the message that such comments are acceptable "*only* out of the mouths of babes," when in fact black adults had been sounding off about racism for a decade on other shows. This is not serious engagement with a cultural development. It is the promulgation of professional underdog-ism in black America, and as with most such work, it is accomplished only at the expense of empirical seriousness.

IV.

... One of the saddest results of the ideological straitjacket that Bogle imposes upon black television is that it blinds him to some remarkable and histori- cally important performances. In *Gimme a Break!* in the early 1980s, Nell Carter played a live-in housekeeper to a widowed white police officer (Dolph Sweet), and became essentially a surrogate mother to his children. In Bogle's account, "For African American viewers, *Gimme a Break!* was little more than a remake of *Beulah*." But this is only what Bogle and assorted black commentators chose to make of it. The show was quite popular in the black American community, and it owed its popularity not least to the fact that its resemblance to *Beulah* was only superficial.

Beulah was meekly deferent to her employers, but Nell brooked no non- sense from the Chief. Bogle may read this as a revival of "Sapphire" (despite Nell's decidedly unsexual rapport with Sweet), but most of us simply enjoyed seeing a black woman holding her own against a white man. Beulah never knew what was cookin', but Nell ran the house to such an extent that the show barely skipped a beat when Sweet died during the run. Beulah's life outside the house was a cipher, but Nell was depicted as dreaming of a singing career, and Carter could really sing. (I can hear the party-faithful Bogle asking why black people always have to sing and dance; but if Carter hadn't been allowed to use her amazing voice, he would certainly have complained of the suppression of her talent.)

... Few vintage performances are immune from Bogle's straitened stand- point. Sherman Hemsley's loud-mouthed George Jefferson is a retread of the "coon," regardless of the joy that black audiences regularly felt at the sight of

Hemsley's strutting bantam entrance into the lobby of his and Louise's new "dee-luxe apartment in the sky" in the opening credits, which seemed to encapsulate the prospect of advancement without a surrender of pride. Hemsley's cocky yet contoured reading of what could have been a shallow, shrill character was most of what kept this silly show going for eleven seasons. . . .

V.

It is his separatist ideology that ruins Bogle's pleasure. It is also what keeps him from ever addressing the paradoxical nature of his expectations, such as his implication that there should be a moratorium on black participation in certain entertainment clichés long beloved by audiences of any extraction, including black Americans. One comes away from Bogle's book with the impression that he considers black television to have a special therapeutic mission from which the rest of television is exempt. In *Toms, Coons, Mulattoes, Mammies, and Bucks*, he proposed that "black films can liberate audiences from illusions, black and white, and in so freeing can give all of us vision and truth. It is a tremendous responsibility, much greater than that placed on ordinary white moviemakers"; and at the end of *Primetime Blues* he considers television to have "a long way to go in honestly and sensitively recording African American life."

And so Bogle reserves his highest praise for *The Cosby Show*, and for the brooding, quirky, and still-missed 1980s "dramedy" *Frank's Place*, and for the *succes d'estime* drama *I'll Fly Away*, which depicted a black maid working for an integrationist white lawyer in the segregated South of the 1950s. Ever vigilant against the mammy stereotype, and imbued with his evangelical conception of black television, Bogle also appears to have a particular predilection for low-key, dreamy black women, heaping special praise on Louise Beavers of *Beulah*, Gloria Reuben of *ER*, Regina Taylor of *I'll Fly Away*, and Lisa Bonet of *The Cosby Show*.

Working with this, we can construct a future that would presumably meet with Bogle's approval. All black television series would portray financially stable people infused with a combination of intellectual curiosity and good old-fashioned mother wit. All characters would regularly display passionate commitment to uplifting the blacks left behind, while at the same time participating in mainstream society—but with a healthy dose of "authentic" anti-assimilationist resistance as well. All characters would be romantically fulfilled, but within the bounds of carefully considered serial monogamy. Humor would be low-key, avoiding any hint of "raucousness," yet always with one foot in African American folk traditions. Mothers and wives would be portrayed by small, light-skinned women, preferably of dreamy affect, who would never engage their husbands in anything but the most civil conduct. Black characters in mainstream programs would at all times refrain from "nurturing" whites and would display a primary rootedness in black culture, while at the same time refraining from going as far as being perceived as "angry" or as "the Other." In sum: all black shows would essentially be recapitulations of *The Cosby Show*.

I cherished *The Cosby Show* in its early years for gracefully depicting a black family whose lives were not defined by impecuniousness or tragedy: here was where black America was headed, rather than where it had been. Yet the common consensus among black commentators, as Bogle notes, was that the show carried an implication that the black underclass was a marginal issue. Maybe it did. But the real problem was that the show became downright dull. "That's just Ozzie and Harriet," my father groused during its first season. The show's "statement" was eloquent, but after a while it became a weekly sermon, and hard to recognize as entertainment.

Sanford and Son, by contrast, was entertainment. But under Bogle's rule, this show would have had Lamont working his way out of Watts by attending college, while Fred took continuing education classes alongside, all the while giving his white teachers hell as he resisted "assimilation." Instead of giving work to his old chitlin' circuit friend LaWanda Page, and thereby surrendering to the "Sapphire stereotype," Redd Foxx should have let her languish in obscurity while casting a petite, reserved, light-skinned woman—probably given to spells of wide-eyed reverie—as Aunt Esther, with her and Sanford getting along warmly. The show should have been an hour-long drama, so that it might more fully "explore" the "personas" and "issues." In later seasons, Lamont should have entered the corporate world.

But who would have watched this show, or another like it? It is fine for entertainment to be edifying, but it must also be entertaining. Moreover, Bogle's requirements for entertainment would make it even less true to life than he now thinks it is. For there is no room for natural human exuberance in Bogle's ideal. Surely an essential aspect of African American experience—its amazing vitality—would go missing if all black shows were of the gentle and genteel tone of *The Cosby Show, Frank's Place,* and *I'll Fly Away.* Consider Bogle's ideal of "dreamy" women: really, Louise Beavers was never much of an actress; and even Bogle notes Gloria Reuben's "flat voice"; and most viewers considered *A Different World* to have hit its stride only when the similarly flat-voiced Lisa Bonet left the show. I confess that I prefer LaWanda Page to Lisa Bonet any day of the week. And I doubt that I am alone.

This is, after all, commercial television. In the eternal tug-of-war between art and commerce in popular entertainment, commerce has always come out on top, even if art occasionally slips through. More to the point, popular entertainment has always been founded upon character types, from Pierrot and Harlequin to Sapphire and the Kingfish. To assail all such black personages as "stereotypes" is intellectually irresponsible—unless one is prepared to accuse, say, West African villagers of trucking in "stereotypes" in keeping alive the stock characters in their culturally central folk tales. Why is Anansi, the wily spider at the heart of tales passed down the generations in Africa and the Caribbean, any less a stereotype than George Jefferson? This point is all the more significant given that black writers are as complicit as white writers in promulgating these "stereotypes," as Bogle surely agrees.

Bogle is too familiar with popular entertainment and its history not to understand this. But this means that his proposition that black television must shoulder a unique and "tremendous responsibility" cannot be taken seriously, except as another cry of victimhood. That "tremendous responsibility" is just another way to keep black readers eternally indignant at perceived racism in America. Bogle's chronicle of fifty-plus years of black television is more a reflection of the centrality of victimhood to modern black identity than an accurate history of race in this medium and this time. If you put an African American of the 1950s before a television set in 2001, he would surely be stunned and elated by the evidence of progress that would pass before his eyes.

᭜᭜᭜᭜

Bogle is hardly alone in his approach to black television. There now exists a whole literature of books and articles by black writers playing endless rounds of the "Can You Find the Stereotype?" game. This impulse to uncover rot behind all black success runs so deep in so many black writers that many might find it difficult to imagine just what else a survey of black television could be about. Yet there are many, many things that Bogle and the others neglect, because they do not fit the arc of a victimologist's argument.

Thus Bogle zips perfunctorily by the welter of black sitcoms on the new UPN and WB networks. True, the shows put a new low in lowest common denominator, operating at a ding-dong *Laverne & Shirley* level that has been foreign to most white sitcoms since about 1980. And yet these shows are extremely popular with black viewers. The people who recently made a boisterous cartoon such as *The Parkers* the top-rated show among blacks do not share Bogle and his comrades' idea of an evening's entertainment. While Bogle waits for "honesty" and "sensitivity," millions of other African Americans are happily sitting down to *Homeboys in Outer Space, The Wayans Bros., Malcolm & Eddie,* and their ilk.

These sitcoms have been very popular with black audiences, while richer fare, such as the heavily black and highly regarded *Homicide*, has not fared so well; and this is a fact that is worth exploring. Bogle is correct that there has always been a sad dearth of black dramas as opposed to black comedies—but surely this is in part because black audiences have repeatedly been less likely to take them to heart. There are rich issues of culture, class, tradition, and psychology to be mined that could engage even the most essentialist-minded of writers. But Bogle falls short here, preferring to malign the nerdy character of Urkel in *Family Matters* as "deracialized" for not infusing his persona with any identifiable "blackness."

Empirical studies have suggested, contrary to the common wisdom, that blacks are not depicted as criminals on television today out of proportion to their representation in the population. I would have liked to see Bogle ponder this question, charting the evolution of the black criminal on television (in the 1950s, the criminal was usually a working-class white) and possibly refuting the studies in some way. And perhaps because they do not lend themselves to the "Can You Find the Stereotype?" game, Bogle largely neglects black variety shows after Flip Wilson, when these shows, especially in the 1970s, contributed some definitive moments for black viewers. Who could forget little Janet Jackson's imitation of Mae West on *The Jacksons* in the mid-1970s? I also fondly remember Telma Hopkins and Joyce Vincent Wilson's savory skits as working-class Lou-Effie and Maureen on *Tony Orlando and Dawn*.

I do not wish to suggest that there is no basis for an anxiety about stereotypes. I cannot find a positive word to say about Jimmie "J.J." Walker's sad takeover of *Good Times*, even though I was one of the kids in the schoolyards shouting "Dy-no-MITE!!!" And too often black cast members are the ones with the least defined personas, a notable current example being Victoria Dillard's Janelle on *Spin City*, a character whose facelessness after six seasons would be unimaginable in any white character on any program. And yet we are a long, long way from Andy and the Kingfish—a long way even from Scotty.

And why, we must ask in the end, is the issue so urgent at all? To be sure, popular entertainment has an influence upon the formation of identity in America; but the stereotype obsession presumes something more. It presumes that anything short of a "sensitive" and "honest" depiction of black experience constitutes an obstacle to black advancement. This, I think, is a very brittle claim. Granted, it was hardly a picnic when practically the only image of blacks on television was *Amos 'n' Andy*. But given the profoundly richer and more positive situation today, it is difficult to argue that only Bogle's ideal would discourage a black youth from using drugs, or lead a young black woman to work harder in school, or raise the rate of blacks opening small businesses. Quite the contrary. A great many individuals and groups have worked their way up in American history despite the ugly stereotypes in popular entertainment.

In other words, it's just television. Real life happens outside the little box. Yes, there is evidence that television can affect behavior. But if, between 1970 and 2000, blacks had been depicted only "sensitively" and "honestly" on television, their history during the period would certainly have unfolded exactly as it did, with the same ratio of triumphs to setbacks. The assumption that television must carefully reflect reality, and even airbrush reality, but never exaggerate or parody reality—and that it must do so only in the case of blacks—is unwarranted by history or psychology or politics; and it represents a gross misunderstanding of popular entertainment. No form of entertainment has ever achieved such representational justice, and the implication that black Americans are helpless without it renders us passive victims rather than masters of our own fates.

Yet Bogle's book will surely stand as the authoritative source on the subject. It will be endlessly borrowed from university libraries by black undergraduates in classes on "Race and the Media," dutifully writing papers illuminating the "stereotypes" underlying almost anything anyone black has ever done on television. Black thinkers—many of whom, like most busy intellectuals and journalists, do not actually watch much television—will continue to decry "the scarcity of positive portrayals of blacks in the media." And the NAACP will continue to harangue the big networks—which are watched by fewer people each year—as racist for not happening to have included black characters in a particular season's lineup. Never mind that blacks are all over the myriad shows on the dozens of other stations now available on cable, as well as in shows from past seasons on the big networks themselves. (The networks, of course, will eagerly accept their guilt and quickly cast black actors in roles written as race-neutral—with the result that their shows will include various black-white "friendships" devoid of any natural chemistry, as on *The Weber Show,* where the seasoned stage and film actor Wendell Pierce cavorts perfunctorily with white actors looking as if he walked in from some other show, or worse, like a "Negro" token circa 1966. The show's white writers, hip to the "deracialization" gospel, have made certain to include the occasional exchange acknowledging the character's color, which in such a lightweight show only makes the falsity of the whole business stand out even more.)

But, as I say, it's just television. Regardless of the essentialism of thinkers such as Donald Bogle, the African American community is well on its way past its old radical platitudes to a truly integrated—dare I say "deracialized"?—future, which is the only future possible. And for the fortunate people in that future, *Primetime Blues* will serve as a poignant document of a time when black thought in America was unwittingly dominated by an appetite for self-defeat.

POSTSCRIPT

Do African American Stereotypes Still Dominate Entertainment Television?

In this issue, as in a related issue of how the media portrays gender, an important question arises: What are the consequences of long-term exposure to media messages? This question leads naturally to another essential question: What are the unintended consequences of television viewing? Although these selections focus on African Americans, the same concerns apply to other racial and ethnic groups.

Whether race portrayals are changing or not, a number of studies over the years have demonstrated the impact of negative or limited portrayals of blacks and other minorities. Clint C. Wilson and Felix Gutierrez, in *Minorities and the Media: Diversity and the End of Mass Communication* (Sage Publications, 1985), examine portrayals of blacks, Native Americans, Latinos, and Asians. Carolyn Martindale, in *The White Press and Black America* (Greenwood Press, 1986), explores newspaper coverage of race-related news and analyses its deficiencies. Sut Jhally and Justin Lewis write of the impact of *The Cosby Show* on perceptions of African Americans in *Enlightened Racism* (Westview, 1992).

Scholars struggle with how to talk about representation. In Horace Newcomb's *Television: The Critical View*, 6th ed. (Oxford, 2000), Herman Gray has written an important essay about the issue of what he calls representational politics. See also Gray's book *Watching Race: Television and the Struggle for the Sign of Blackness* (University of Minnesota Press, 1997). The two selections represent exactly the problem that scholars have as they try to uncover hidden patterns that undermine equality, acknowledge real strides forward, and demonstrate why certain choices are more positive than others. A number of books over the years have examined the issues of race and representation in media. They include Sasha Torres, ed., *Living Color: Race and Television in the United States* (Duke University Press, 1998) and Janette Dates and William Barlow, eds., *Split Image: African Americans in the Mass Media* (Howard University Press, 1993).

Other attempts to understand race in U.S. society are found in Cornel West's *Keeping Faith: Philosophy and Race in America* (Routledge, 1993) and bell hooks's *Black Looks: Race and Representation* (South End Press, 1992). For a personal look at the lived experience of one author, see *Colored People: A Memoir* by Henry Louis Gates, Jr. (Vintage Books, 1995).

Cultural and Media Studies

Cultural and Media Studies (CMS) is located at the University of Natal–Durban in South Africa. CMS was established to develop strategies of cultural resistance through media and culture after the Soweto uprising of 1976. With the advent of democratic political processes in South Africa, CMS now works in policy research and to develop support for communication projects.

http://www.nu.ac.za/cms/

Freedom Forum

The Freedom Forum is a nonpartisan, international foundation dedicated to free press, free speech, and free spirit for all people. Its mission is to help the public and the news media understand one another better. The newseum area of this site is very intriguing.

http://www.freedomforum.org

Fairness and Accuracy in Reporting

Fairness and Accuracy in Reporting (FAIR) is a national media watch group that offers well-documented criticism of media bias and censorship. FAIR advocates for greater diversity in the press and scrutinizes media practices that marginalize public interest, minority, and dissenting viewpoints.

http://www.fair.org

Television News Archive, Vanderbilt University

Since August 5, 1968, the Television News Archive has systematically recorded, abstracted, and indexed national television newscasts. This database is the guide to the Vanderbilt University collection of network television news programs.

http://tvnews.vanderbilt.edu

Advertising Age

The Web site of *Advertising Age* magazine provides access to articles and features about media advertising, such as history of television advertising.

http://adage.com

PART 2

Media Ethics

*M*edia ethics concerns the delicate balance between society's interests and the interests of individuals, groups, and institutions such as the
press and the government. Questions of ethics are, by definition, issues
of right and wrong. But they are among the most difficult issues we face
because they require decisions of us, even in the face of articulate and
intelligent opposition. What is the appropriate balance between responsibility and liberty? Who should decide where the lines between right
and wrong are to be drawn, and on what values should these decisions
be made? Are all decisions relative to the individual case, or are there
larger, overriding principles to which we should all pledge our allegiance?
Most important, to whom should we entrust the power to make and implement ethical choices? In this section, the reader must grapple with
the questions ethics ask of us and critically examine the purposes and
actions of some of the most fundamental institutions we know.

- Should the Names of Rape Victims Be Reported?

- Should Tobacco Advertising Be Restricted?

- Is Advertising Ethical?

ISSUE 5

Should the Names of Rape Victims Be Reported?

YES: Michael Gartner, from "Naming the Victim," *Columbia Journalism Review* (July/August 1991)

NO: Katha Pollitt, from "Naming and Blaming: Media Goes Wilding in Palm Beach," *The Nation* (June 24, 1991)

ISSUE SUMMARY

YES: President of NBC News Michael Gartner justifies his decision to name the accuser in the William Kennedy Smith rape case, stating that names add credibility to a story. He further argues that a policy of identifying accusers in rape cases will destroy many of society's wrongly held impressions and stereotypes about the crime of rape.

NO: Using examples from the William Kennedy Smith case, journalist and social critic Katha Pollitt identifies six reasons commonly cited by proponents of naming alleged rape victims and argues that not one of them justifies the decision to reveal victims' identities without their consent.

In 1991 a woman stated that she was raped at the Kennedy compound in Palm Beach, Florida, one night during the Easter weekend. After an investigation by the local police, William Kennedy Smith, nephew of Senator Edward M. Kennedy (D-Massachusetts), was charged with the assault. The subsequent trial later that same year resulted in an acquittal for Smith. The case received widespread media coverage, in part because it involved a Kennedy, and in part because the circumstances of the case tapped into the ongoing national debate over so-called acquaintance rape, or date rape. On the night of the incident, Smith and the woman met at an exclusive club, they spent some time drinking and partying, and the woman later drove Smith home and accepted his invitation to take a walk on the beach. According to the woman, the police, and the local prosecutor, what eventually took place that night was rape. Smith, his supporters, and the jury, however, saw it as consensual sex. In addition to raising the question of date rape, the case also provoked controversy because of how various news organizations handled the issue of whether or not to reveal the woman's identity.

Shielding the names and identities of victims of rape has long been a press tradition. But when the William Kennedy Smith story first broke, both the NBC television network and the *New York Times* reported the woman's name; furthermore, the *New York Times* ran a story that gave details on her personal background. These actions sparked controversy among the public and among journalists and media critics.

Who should control the decision to use the names of victims when the media reports rape cases? Should it be only the victims? Considering that the names of other crime victims are generally not withheld, does concealing identities in news coverage of rape perpetuate stereotypes about rape? What rights does the alleged rapist have? What, in short, are the legitimate privacy interests of those involved? How can those interests be balanced with the public interest and the press's responsibility to fully report a story?

These are difficult ethical questions for journalists. In making a decision, how does a journalist balance competing demands, such as the common good versus the rights of an individual, or absolute freedom of the press versus the right to privacy? Does one value predominate over another?

Michael Gartner, president of NBC News, decided to break with journalistic tradition and broadcast the name of the alleged victim of the incident at the Kennedy compound without her consent. In the following memo to his staff dated April 24, 1991, Gartner outlines his reasons for making the controversial decision. Some NBC affiliates complained, and even among his own staff the decision was not unanimously supported, but Gartner maintains that it is usually journalistically responsible to reveal the names of rape victims. Katha Pollitt, in opposition, argues that society's attitudes toward rape justify privacy for rape victims. Naming names is media exploitation, she asserts, and it does not serve a good purpose.

Michael Gartner

 **YES**

Naming the Victim

This past April [1991]—following a woman's allegations that she had been raped by Senator Edward Kennedy's nephew William Kennedy Smith—NBC News broke ranks with a tradition honored by other mainstream news organizations by reporting the name of the alleged victim without her consent. The following day *The New York Times* published the woman's name, asserting that the NBC disclosure had already made her name public knowledge. These decisions set off a great deal of internal discussion at both organizations and in the press at large. In this memo to his staff, Michael Gartner, president of NBC News, justifies his decision.

To the staff:

Why did NBC News name the woman who says she was raped at the Kennedy compound in Florida over the Easter weekend? How was that decision made?

For years, the issue has been debated by journalists and feminists: should the names of rape victims or alleged rape victims be made public? Among journalists, there is no agreement; among feminists, there is no agreement.

At NBC, we debated the journalistic arguments.

Some background: I have been deeply interested in this subject for years, discussing it and debating it. Years ago, I concluded that journalistically it is usually right to name rape victims. Usually, but not always.

Here is my reasoning:

First, we are in the business of disseminating news, not suppressing it. Names and facts are news. They add credibility, they round out the story, they give the viewer or reader information he or she needs to understand issues, to make up his or her own mind about what's going on. So my prejudice is always toward telling the viewer all the germane facts that we know.

Second, producers and editors and news directors should make editorial decisions; editorial decisions should not be made in courtrooms, or legislatures, or briefing rooms—or by persons involved in the news. That is why I oppose military censorship, legislative mandate, and the general belief that we should only print the names of rape victims who volunteer their names. In no other category of news do we give the newsmaker the option of being named. Those are decisions that should be made in newsrooms—one way or another.

Third, by not naming rape victims we are part of a conspiracy of silence, and that silence is bad for viewers and readers. It reinforces the idea that somehow there is something shameful about being raped. Rape is a crime of violence, a horrible crime of violence. Rapists are horrible people; rape victims are not. One role of the press is to inform, and one way of informing is to destroy incorrect impressions and stereotypes.

Fourth, and finally, there is an issue of fairness. I heard no debate in our newsroom and heard of no debate in other newsrooms on whether we should name the suspect, William Smith. He has not been charged with anything. Yet we dragged his name and his reputation into this without thought, without regard to what might happen to him should he not be guilty—indeed, should he not even be charged. Rapists are vile human beings; but a suspect isn't necessarily a rapist. Were we fair? Probably, yes, because he was thrust into the news, rightly or wrongly. But so was Patricia Bowman, and we should treat her the same way journalistically. We are reporters; we don't take sides, we don't pass judgment.

Those are the points made in our internal debates. At NBC News, I first raised the issue when the woman was raped in Central Park. We had one story on Nightly News, and after that I told some colleagues that if that were to become a continuing national story we should debate the question of naming the woman. As it turned out, it did not become a continuing national story, and we did not have the debate at that time.

Two weeks ago, I began debating in my own mind the issue of the Florida case. I joined in the debate with some colleagues from outside NBC News last week. On Monday of this week, I raised the issue with three colleagues within NBC News. We discussed it at some length. Should we do this, and if we did it how should we frame it?

On Tuesday, the discussions continued. They were passionate and spirited, but not mean-spirited. By the end of the day, the debate probably encompassed 30 persons, men and women of all views. There was no unanimity; if a vote had been taken, it probably would have been not to print the name. But I decided, for the reasons listed here, to air the name. The fact that her identity was known to many in her community was another factor—but not a controlling one—in my decision.

There were those—including some involved in the preparation, production and presentation of the piece—who disagreed intellectually. But no one asked to be removed from the story, and everyone did a thorough job. The story was clear and fair and accurate; it was not sensational, and—for those who think it was done for the ratings or the like—it was not hyped or promoted. It was presented as just another very interesting story in a Nightly News broadcast that, that night, was full of especially compelling stories.

At 5:00 P.M., we did send an advisory to affiliates that we were naming the woman, for our Florida affiliates, especially, needed to be told in advance. In the time since, six of our 209 affiliates have complained to us about the decision; at least one, WBZ in Boston, bleeped out the woman's name and covered her picture. Several affiliates said we ran counter to their own policies, but just as we respect their views they respected ours and ran the story. Several other affiliates called to say they agreed with our decision. Most said nothing.

I am particularly proud of the process we went through in reaching our conclusion; in fact, the process was more important than the conclusion. There was vigorous and free debate about an issue of journalism; all sides were discussed. The story was shaped and reshaped as a result of that debate. When we ultimately decided to air the name, everyone involved at least understood the reasons, and everyone then did the usual first-rate work.

Our decision engendered a national debate. Much of the debate has been focused on the wrong issues, but much of it has been focused on the right issue: the crime of rape. The debate itself has raised the awareness of the horribleness of the crime, the innocence of victims, the vileness of rapists. That has been a beneficial side-effect.

Rape is rarely a national story. If another rape becomes a big story, we will have the same debate again. The position at NBC News is this: we will consider the naming of rape victims or alleged rape victims on a case-by-case basis.

NO

Katha Pollitt

Media Goes Wilding in Palm Beach

I drink, I swear, I flirt, I tell dirty jokes. I have also, at various times, watched pornographic videos, had premarital sex, hitchhiked, and sunbathed topless in violation of local ordinances. True, I don't have any speeding tickets, but I don't have a driver's license either. Perhaps I'm subconsciously afraid of my "drives"? There are other things, too, and if I should ever bring rape charges against a rich, famous, powerful politician's relative, *The New York Times* will probably tell you all about them—along with, perhaps, my name. Suitably adorned with anonymous quotes, these revelations will enable you, the public, to form your own opinion: Was I asking for trouble, or did I just make the whole thing up?

In April the media free-for-all surrounding the alleged rape of a Palm Beach woman by William Smith, Senator Ted Kennedy's nephew, took a vicious turn as the *Times*—following NBC, following the *Globe* (supermarket, not Boston, edition), following a British scandal sheet, following *another* British scandal sheet—went public with the woman's name, and a lot more: her traffic violations, her mediocre high school grades, her "little wild streak," her single motherhood, her mother's divorce and upwardly mobile remarriage. Pretty small potatoes, really; she sounds like half my high school classmates. But it did make a picture: bad girl, loose woman, floozy.

Or did it? In a meeting with more than 300 outraged staff members, national editor Soma Golden said that the *Times* could not be held responsible for "every weird mind that reads [the paper]." NBC News chief Michael Gartner was more direct: "Who she is, is material in this.... You try to give viewers as many facts as you can and let them make up their minds." Forget that almost none of these "facts" will be admissible in court, where a jury will nonetheless be expected to render a verdict.

In the ensuing furor, just about every advocate for rape victims has spoken out in favor of preserving the longstanding media custom of anonymity, and in large part the public seems to agree. But the media,[1] acting in its capacity as the guardian of public interest, has decided that naming the victim is an issue up for grabs. And so we are having one of these endless, muddled, two-sides-to-every-question debates that, by ignoring as many facts as possible and by weighing all arguments equally, gives us that warm American feeling that truth must lie somewhere in the middle. Anna Quindlen, meet Alan Dershowitz. Thank you very much, but our time is just about up.

Sometimes, of course, the truth does lie somewhere in the middle. But not this time. There is no good reason to publish the names of rape complainants without their consent, and many compelling reasons not to. The arguments advanced in favor of publicity reveal fundamental misconceptions about both the nature of the media and the nature of rape.

Let's take a look at what proponents of naming are saying.

The media has a duty to report what it knows   Where have you been? The media keeps information secret all the time. Sometimes it does so on the ground of "taste," a waffle-word that means whatever an editorial board wants it to mean. Thus, we hear about (some of) the sexual high jinks of heterosexual celebrities but not about those of socially equivalent closet-dwellers, whose opposite-sex escorts are portrayed, with knowing untruthfulness, as genuine romantic interests. We are spared—or deprived of, depending on your point of view—the gruesome and salacious details of many murders. (Of all the New York dailies, only *Newsday* reported that notorious Wall Street wife-killer Joseph Pikul was wearing women's underwear when arrested. Not fit to print? I was *riveted.*) Sometimes it fudges the truth to protect third parties from embarrassment, which is why the obituaries would have us believe that eminent young bachelors are dying in large numbers only from pneumonia.

And of course sometimes it censors itself in "the national interest." The claim that the media constitutes a fourth estate, a permanent watchdog, if not outright adversary, of the government, has always been a self-serving myth. Watergate occurred almost twenty years ago and has functioned ever since as a kind of sentimental talisman. Like Charles Foster Kane's Rosebud sled. As we saw during the gulf war, the media can live, when it chooses, quite comfortably with government-imposed restrictions. Neither NBC nor *The New York Times,* so quick to supply their audiences with the inside scoop on the Palm Beach woman, felt any such urgency about Operation Desert Storm.

Anonymous charges are contrary to the American way   Anonymous charges are contrary to American *jurisprudence.* The Palm Beach woman has not made an anonymous accusation. Her name is known to the accused and his attorney, and if the case comes to trial, she will have to appear publicly in court, confront the defendant, give testimony and be cross-examined. But the media is not a court, as the many lawyers who have made this argument—most prominently Alan Dershowitz and Isabelle Pinzler of the American Civil Liberties Union's Women's Rights Project—ought to know.

The media itself argues in favor of anonymity when that serves its own purposes. Reporters go to jail rather than reveal their sources, even when secrecy means protecting a dangerous criminal, impeding the process of justice or denying a public figure the ability to confront his or her accusers. People wouldn't talk to reporters, the press claims, if their privacy couldn't be guaranteed—the same greater-social-good argument it finds unpersuasive when made about rape victims and their reluctance to talk, unprotected, to the police. The media's selective interest in concealment, moreover, undermines its vaunted mission on behalf of the public's right to know. Might not the identity of an anonymous informant (one of those "sources close to the White House" or "highly placed observers," for instance) help the public "make up its mind" about the reliability of the statements? I don't want to digress here into the complex issue of protecting sources, but there can be little question that the practice allows powerful people, in and out of government, to manipulate information for their own ends. Interestingly, the *Times* story on the Palm Beach woman concealed (thirteen times!) the names of those spreading malicious gossip about her, despite the *Times*'s own custom of not using anonymous pejoratives. That custom was resuscitated in time for the paper's circumspect profile of William Smith, which did not detail the accusations against him of prior acquaintance rapes that have been published by *The National Enquirer* and the gossip columnist Taki, and which referred only vaguely to "rumors" of "a pattern of aggressiveness toward women in private." (These, the *Times* said, it could not confirm—unlike the accuser's "little wild streak.")

How *did* the *Times* manage to amass such a wealth of dirt about the Palm Beach woman so quickly? It's hard to picture the reporter, distinguished China hand Fox Butterfield, peeking into the window of her house to see what books were on the toddler's shelf. Could some of his information or some of his leads have come, directly or circuitously, from the detectives hired by the Kennedy family to investigate the woman and her friends—detectives who, let's not forget, have been the subject of complaints of witness intimidation? The *Times* denies it, but rumors persist. One could argue that, in this particular case, *how* the *Times* got the story was indeed part of the story—perhaps the most important part.

That anonymity is held to be essential to the public good in a wide variety of cases but is damned as a form of censorship in the Palm Beach case shows that what the media is concerned with is not the free flow of information *or* the public good. What is at stake is the media's status, power and ability to define and control information in accordance with the views of those who run the media.

Consider, for example, the case of men convicted of soliciting prostitutes. Except for the occasional athlete, such men receive virtual anonymity in the press. Remember the flap in 1979 when Manhattan D.A. Robert Morgenthau released a list of recently convicted johns and the *Daily News* and two local radio stations went public with it? Universal outrage! Never mind that solicitation is a crime, that convictions are a matter of public record, that the wives and girlfriends of these men might find knowledge of such arrests extremely useful or that society has a declared interest in deterring prostitution. Alan Dershowitz, who in his syndicated column has defended both the content of the *Times* profile and its use of the woman's name, vigorously supported privacy for johns, and in fact made some of the same arguments that he now dismisses. Reporting, he said, was vindictive, subjected ordinary people to the glaring light of publicity for a peccadillo, could destroy the johns' marriages and reputations, and stigmatized otherwise decent people. Dershowitz did not, however, think privacy for johns meant privacy for prostitutes: They, he argued, have no reputation to lose. Although solicitation is a two-person crime, Dershowitz thinks the participants have unequal rights to privacy. With rape, he treats the rapist and his victim as *equally* placed with regard to privacy, even though rape is a one-person crime.

But here the woman's identity was already widely known   Well, I didn't know it. I did, however, know the name of the Central Park jogger—like virtually every other journalist in the country, the entire readership of *The Amsterdam News* (50,000) and the listening audience of WLIB-radio (45,000). Anna Quindlen, in her courageous column dissenting from the *Times'*s profile naming the Palm Beach woman, speculated that roughly equivalent large numbers of people knew the identity of the jogger as knew that of William Smith's alleged victim before NBC and the *Times* got into the act. Yet the media went to extraordinary lengths to protect the remaining shreds of the jogger's privacy—film clips were blipped, quotes censored.

What separates the jogger from the Palm Beach woman? You don't have to be the Rev. Al Sharpton to suspect that protecting the jogger's identity was more than a chivalrous gesture. Remember that she too was originally blamed for her assault: What was she doing in the park so late? Who did she think she was? It's all feminism's fault for deluding women into thinking that their safety could, or should, be everywhere guaranteed. But partly as a result of the severity of her injuries, the jogger quickly became the epitome of the innocent victim, the symbol, as Joan Didion pointed out in *The New York Review of Books,* for New York City itself (white, prosperous, plucky) endangered by the black underclass. A white Wellesley graduate with a Wall Street job attacked out of nowhere by a band of violent black strangers and, because of her comatose state, unable even to bring a rape complaint—this, to the media, is "real rape." The Palm Beach woman, on the other hand, is of working-class origins, a single mother, a frequenter of bars, who went voluntarily to her alleged attacker's house (as who, in our star-struck society, would not?). The jogger could have been the daughter of the men who kept her name out of the news. But William Smith could have been their son.

Rape is like other crimes and should be treated like other crimes. Isn't that what you feminists are always saying?   As the coverage of the Palm Beach case proves, rape isn't treated like other crimes. There is no other crime in which the character, behavior and past of the complainant are seen as central elements in determining whether a crime has occurred. There are lots of crimes that could not take place without carelessness, naïveté, ignorance or bad judgment on the part of the victims: mail fraud ("Make $100,000 at home in your spare time!"), confidence games and many violent crimes as well. But when my father was burglarized after forgetting to lock the cellar door, the police did not tell him he had been asking for it. And when an elderly lady (to cite Amy Pagnozzi's example in the *New York Post*) is defrauded of her life savings by a con artist, the con artist is just as much a thief as if he'd broken into his victim's safe-deposit box. "The complainant showed incredibly bad judgment, Your Honor," is not a legal defense.

Why is rape different? Because lots of people, too often including the ones in the jury box, think women really do want to be forced into sex, or by acting or dressing or drinking in a certain way, give up the right to say no, or are the sort of people (i.e., not nuns) who gave up the right to say no to one man by saying yes to another, or are by nature scheming, irrational and crazy. They also think men cannot be expected to control themselves, are entitled to take by force what they cannot get by persuasion and are led on by women who, because they are scheming, irrational and crazy, change their minds in mid-sex. My files bulge with stories that show how widespread these beliefs are: The Wisconsin judge who put a child molester on probation because he felt the 3-year-old female victim had acted provocatively; the Florida jury that exonerated a rapist because his victim was wearing disco attire; and so on.

In a bizarre column defending Ted Kennedy's role on the night in question, William Safire took aim at the Palm Beach woman, who was "apparently" not "taught that drinking all night and going to a man's house at 3:30 A.M. places one in what used to be called an occasion of sin." (All her mother's fault, as usual.) The other woman present in the Kennedy mansion that night, a waitress named Michelle Cassone, has made herself a mini-celebrity by telling any reporter who will pay for her time that she too believes that women who drink and date, including herself, are "fair game."

By shifting the debate to the question of merely naming victims, the media pre-empts a discussion of the way it reports all crimes with a real or imaginary sexual component. But as the *Times* profile shows, naming cannot be divorced from blaming. When the victim is young and attractive (and in the tabloids *all* female victims are attractive), the sexual element in the crime is always made its central feature—even when, as in the case of Marla Hanson, the model who was slashed by hired thugs and whose character was savaged in *New York,* there is no sexual element. I mean no belittlement of rape to suggest it was one of the lesser outrages visited on the Central Park jogger. She was also beaten so furiously she lost 80 percent of her blood and suffered permanent physical, neurological and cognitive damage. Yet, paradoxically, it was the rape that seized the imagination of the media, and that became the focus of the crime both for her defenders and for those who defended her attackers.

Naming rape victims will remove the stigma against rape Of all the arguments in favor of naming victims, this is the silliest, and the most insincere. Sure, NBC's Michael Gartner told *Newsweek,* the consequences will be "extraordinarily difficult for this generation, but it may perhaps help their daughters and granddaughters." How selfish of women to balk at offering themselves on the altar of little girls yet unborn! If Gartner wishes to make a better world for my descendants, he is amply well placed to get cracking. He could demand non-sensationalized reporting of sex crimes; he could hire more female reporters and producers; he could use NBC News to dispel false notions about rape—for example, the idea that "who the woman is, is material." Throughout the country there are dozens of speakouts against rape at which victims publicly tell of their experiences. Every year there are Take Back the Night marches in Manhattan. Where are the cameras and the reporters on these occasions? Adding

misery to hundreds of thousands of women a year and—as just about every expert in the field believes—dramatically lowering the already abysmal incidence
of rape reporting (one in ten) will not help my granddaughter; it will only make
it more likely that her grandmother, her mother and she herself will be raped
by men who have not been brought to justice.

This argument is, furthermore, based on a questionable assumption. Why
would society blame rape victims less if it knew who they were? Perhaps its
censure would simply be amplified. Instead of thinking, If ordinary, decent,
conventional women get raped in large numbers it *can't* be their fault, people
might well think, Goodness, there are a lot more women asking for it than we
thought. After the invasion of Kuwait, in which scores of women were raped by
Iraqi soldiers, there was no dispensation from the traditional harsh treatment
of rape victims, some of whom, pregnant and in disgrace, had attempted sui-
cide, gone into hiding or fled the country. One woman told *USA Today* that she
wished she were dead. America is not Kuwait, but here, too, many believe that
a woman can't be raped against her will and that damaged goods are damaged
goods. (Curious how publicity is supposed to lessen the stigma against rape
victims but only adds to the suffering of johns.)

One also has to wonder about the urgency with which Gartner and the
other male proponents of the anti-stigma theory, with no history of public
concern for women, declare themselves the best judge of women's interests and
advocate a policy that they themselves will never have to bear the consequences
of. Gartner cited, as did many others, the *Des Moines Register* profile of a named
rape victim but neglected to mention that the victim, Nancy Ziegenmeyer, vol-
unteered the use of her name, seven months after reporting the crime—in other
words, after she had had a chance to come to terms with her experience and
to inform her family and friends in a way she found suitable. (Ziegenmeyer, by
the way, opposes involuntary naming.) Why is it that, where women are concerned, the difference between choice and coercion eludes so many? Rapists,
too, persuade themselves that they know what women really want and need.

**William Smith's name has been dragged through the mud. Why should his
accuser be protected?**   Actually, William Smith has been portrayed rather favorably in the media. No anonymous pejoratives for him: He is "one of the
least spoiled and least arrogant of the young Kennedys" (*Time*); an "unlikely villain" (*Newsweek*); "a man of gentleness and humor," "the un-Kennedy," "a good
listener" (*The New York Times*); from a "wounded," "tragic" family (*passim*).
Certainly he has been subjected to a great deal of unpleasant media attention,
and even if he is eventually found innocent, some people will always suspect
that he is guilty. But no one forced the media to sensationalize the story; that
was a conscious editorial decision, not an act of God. Instead of heaping slurs
on the Palm Beach woman in order to even things up, the media should be
asking itself why it did not adopt a more circumspect attitude toward the case
from the outset.

The tit-for-tat view of rape reporting appeals to many people because of
its apparent impartiality. Feminists of the pure equal-treatment school like it
because it looks gender neutral (as if rape were a gender-neutral crime). And

nonfeminist men like it because, while looking gender neutral, it would, in practice, advantage men. "Should the press be in the business of protecting certain groups but not others—," wrote *Washington Post* columnist Richard Cohen, "alleged victims (females), but not the accused (males)? My answer is no." Cohen, like Michael Gartner, presents himself as having women's best interests at heart: "If rape's indelible stigma is ever to fade, the press has to stop being complicitous in perpetuating the sexist aura that surrounds it." Thus, by some mysterious alchemy, the media, which is perhaps the single biggest promoter of the sexist aura surrounding crimes of violence against women, can redeem itself by jettisoning the only policy it has that eases, rather than augments, the victim's anguish.

Behind the tit-for-tat argument lies a particular vision of rape in which the odds are even that the alleged victim is really the victimizer—a seductress, blackmailer, hysteric, who is bringing a false charge. That was the early word on the Palm Beach woman, and it's hard not to conclude that publicizing her identity was punitive: She's caused all this trouble, is visiting yet more "tragedy" on America's royal family, and had better be telling the truth. In fact, the appeal of naming the victim seems to rest not in the hope that it "may perhaps" someday make rape reporting less painful but in the certainty that right now it makes such reporting *more* painful, thereby inhibiting false accusations. Although studies have repeatedly shown that fabricated rape charges are extremely rare, recent years have seen a number of cases: Tawana Brawley, for example, and Cathleen Crowell Webb, who recanted her testimony after finding Jesus and then hugged her newly freed, no-longer-alleged-assailant on the *Donahue* show. A year ago a Nebraska woman who admitted filing a false charge was ordered by a judge to purchase newspaper ads and radio spots apologizing to the man she had accused. (She was also sentenced to six months in jail.) It is not unknown for other criminal charges to be fabricated, but has anyone ever been forced into a public apology in those cases? The tenor of the equal-publicity argument is captured perfectly by the (female) letter writer to *Time* who suggested that newspapers publish both names and both photos too. Why not bring back trial by ordeal and make the two of them grasp bars of red-hot iron?

⚜

Fundamentally, the arguments about naming rape victims center around two contested areas: acquaintance rape and privacy. While the women's movement has had some success in expanding the definition of rape to include sexual violation by persons known to the victim—as I write, *The New York Times* is running an excellent series on such rape, containing interviews with women named or anonymous by their choice (atonement?)—there is also a lot of backlash.

The all-male editorial board of the *New York Post*, which rather ostentatiously refused to print the Palm Beach woman's name, has actually proposed a change in the law to distinguish between "real rape" (what the jogger suffered) and acquaintance rape, confusedly described as a "sexual encounter, forced or not," that "has been preceded by a series of consensual activities." *Forced or not?*

At the other end of the literary social scale, there's Camille (No Means Yes) Paglia, academia's answer to Phyllis Schlafly, repackaging hoary myths about rape as a bold dissent from feminist orthodoxy and "political correctness." Indeed, an attack on the concept of acquaintance rape figures prominently in the many diatribes against current intellectual trends on campus. It's as though the notion of consensual sex were some incomprehensible French literary theory that threatened the very foundations of Western Civ. And, come to think of it, maybe it does.

Finally, there is the issue of privacy. Supporters of naming like to say that anonymity implies that rape is something to be ashamed of. But must this be its meaning? It says a great deal about the impoverishment of privacy as a value in our time that many intelligent people can find no justification for it but shame, guilt, cowardice and prudishness. As the tabloidization of the media proceeds apace, as the boundaries between the public and the personal waver and fade away, good citizenship has come to require of more and more people that they put themselves forward, regardless of the cost, as exhibit A in a national civics lesson. In this sense, rape victims are in the same position as homosexuals threatened with "outing" for the good of other gays, or witnesses forced to give painful and embarrassing testimony in televised courtrooms so that the couch potatoes at home can appreciate the beauty of the legal process.

But there are lots of reasons a rape victim might not want her name in the paper that have nothing to do with shame. She might not want her mother to know, or her children, or her children's evil little classmates, or obscene phone callers, or other rapists. Every person reading this article probably has his or her secrets, things that aren't necessarily shameful (or things that are) but are liable to misconstructions, false sympathy and stupid questions from the tactless and ignorant. Things that are just plain nobody's business unless you want them to be.

Instead of denying privacy to rape victims, we should take a good hard look at our national passion for thrusting unwanted publicity on people who are not accused of wrong-doing but find themselves willy-nilly in the news. ("How did it *feel* to watch your child being torn to pieces by wild animals?" "It felt terrible, Maury, terrible.") I've argued here that society's attitudes toward rape justify privacy for rape complainants, and that indeed those attitudes lurk behind the arguments for publicity. But something else lurks there as well: a desensitization to the lurid and prurient way in which the media exploits the sufferings of any ordinary person touched by a noteworthy crime or tragedy. Most of the people who have spoken out against anonymity are journalists, celebrity lawyers, media executives and politicos—people who put themselves forward in the press and on television as a matter of course and who are used to taking their knocks as the price of national attention. It must be hard for such people to sympathize with someone who doesn't want to play the media game —especially if it's in a "good cause."

I'm not at all sure there is a good cause here. Titillation, not education, seems the likely reason for the glare on the Palm Beach case. But even if I'm unduly cynical and the media sincerely wishes to conduct a teach-in on rape, the interests of the public can be served without humiliating the complainant.

Doctors educate one another with case histories in which patients are identified only by initials and in which other nonrelevant identifying details are changed. Lawyers file cases on behalf of Jane Doe and John Roe and expect the Supreme Court to "make up its mind" nonetheless.

If the media wants to educate the public about rape, it can do so without names. What the coverage of the Palm Beach case shows is that it needs to educate itself first.

Note

1. I use "media" in the singular (rather than the strictly grammatical plural) because I am talking about the communications industry as a social institution that, while hardly monolithic (as the debate over naming shows), transcends the different means—"media" plural—by which the news is conveyed.

POSTSCRIPT

Should the Names of Rape Victims Be Reported?

During the extensive televised coverage of the William Kennedy Smith trial, a dot was used to cover the woman's face. After the trial's conclusion, the woman herself went public and gave a handful of print and broadcast interviews.

With regard to rape and other sex crimes, the media must answer questions beyond whether or not to name the victims. Do common news practices, for example, yield biases that perpetuate myths and injustice? Helen Benedict, in *Virgin or Vamp: How the Press Covers Sex Crimes* (Oxford University Press, 1992), harshly critiques the manner in which newspapers have handled sex crimes.

Ethical guidelines require journalists to make specific choices as they balance freedom and responsibility in their day-to-day reporting. In making decisions, journalists are most often guided by the practices of the profession, their education, their on-the-job socialization, and the written codes of the organizations for which they work. Debates such as the one presented here are inevitable when traditional practices come under scrutiny.

The history of journalism has borne witness to many styles of approaching a story. In his book *Goodbye Gutenberg: The Newspaper Revolution of the 1980s* (Oxford University Press, 1980), Anthony Smith says, "Investigation has become the most highly praised and highly prized form of journalism, taking the place of opinion leadership, the historic purpose of the press." He suggests that the investigative reporter typically finds him- or herself in the position of both judge and jury—the authority to whom the public turns to get the whole story.

Ethical issues are not easily resolved: We should always struggle to discuss them, think about them, and let them guide our consciences. Only when we cease thinking about them is it too late to do anything about them.

There are many books on different styles of journalism, and the biographies of such people as Horace Greeley, William Randolph Hearst, Joseph Pulitzer, and even Rupert Murdoch show how each individual shaped a special time in journalism history. Other sources that describe journalistic themes and public reaction include Ben H. Bagdikian's *The Information Machines: Their Impact on Men and the Media* (Harper & Row, 1971); the Roper Organization's *Trends in Public Attitudes Toward Television and Other Media, 1969-1974* (Television Information Office, 1975); and John P. Robinson's *Daily News Habits of the American Public*, ANPA New Research Center Study No. 15 (September 22, 1978). Also, among the periodicals that cover journalistic styles and practices are *Columbia Journalism Review, Editor and Publisher,* and *American Society of Newspaper Editors (ASNE) Newsletter.*

Further readings on ethics and the media include Everette Dennis, Donald Gillmore, and Theodore Glasser, eds., *Media Freedom and Accountability* (Greenwood Press, 1989) and Bruce Swain, *Reporters' Ethics* (Iowa State University Press, 1978), which examine a number of issues that reporters must face. More recent books include *Ethical Issues in Journalism and the Media* edited by Andres Beasly and Ruth Chadwick (Routledge, Chapman & Hall, 1992) and *Good News: Social Ethics and the Press* by Clifford G. Christians, John P. Ferre, and Mark Fackler (Oxford University Press, 1993).

ISSUE 6

Should Tobacco Advertising Be Restricted?

YES: Joseph R. DiFranza et al., from "RJR Nabisco's Cartoon Camel Promotes Camel Cigarettes to Children," *Journal of the American Medical Association* (December 11, 1991)

NO: George J. Annas, from "Cowboys, Camels, and the First Amendment—The FDA's Restrictions on Tobacco Advertising," *The New England Journal of Medicine* (December 5, 1996)

ISSUE SUMMARY

YES: Doctor Joseph R. DiFranza and his colleagues report a national study that examines the possibility of children being tempted to smoke because of the tobacco industry's use of images that appeal to and are remembered by children. Because of the profound health risks, DiFranza et al. call for restrictions on tobacco ads.

NO: Attorney George J. Annas agrees that the tobacco industry has marketed products to children, but he maintains that efforts to restrict advertising are inappropriate, perhaps even illegal. He argues that some of the restrictions that have been placed on tobacco advertisements violate the First Amendment.

The marketing of tobacco products has been controversial for some time, but discussions have become more heated in recent years as the extent of the tobacco industry's knowledge of nicotine as an addictive drug and the long-term effects of smoking on a person's health has come into question. Court cases and public scrutiny of the tobacco industry have led to legal sanctions and restrictions on the marketing of tobacco products, most specifically with regard to tobacco ads that appeal to children. Although tobacco industry officials state that they do not try to induce children to smoke, evidence indicates that advertising strategies do, indeed, target a potential audience of young people. Research shows that most long-term smokers begin smoking at the age of 12 or 13 and become hooked for life.

In the following selections, Joseph R. DiFranza and his colleagues raise ethical concerns about the effects of the tobacco industry's using appeals that may tempt children to start smoking, and they explain how advertising effectively reaches consumers. Arguing from a legal position, George J. Annas examines the Federal Drug Administration's current efforts to restrict advertising, particularly to the youth market. Citing several precedents regarding the restriction of advertising, he draws the conclusion that current governmental efforts to curb ads will remain ineffective and may violate the advertisers' First Amendment right to free speech.

This issue brings up several topics for discussion. One important question is whether or not children should be protected from activities and behaviors that may have long-term negative effects. Also, should advertisers exercise standards regarding the products they promote? Should the tobacco industry divulge all of their research regarding the hazards of smoking? Do ethical standards change when appeals are made to children as potential consumers?

Annas raises another important ethical dimension: How far can the First Amendment be used in defending free speech? Since the Bill of Rights was written—over 200 years ago—the type of "speech" that Americans engage in has changed dramatically. Does the right of free speech extend to advertising?

Advertising has traditionally been classified as "commercial" speech, which gives greater license to its use. Should commercial speech also be subject to a more stringent interpretation when the rights of children are involved? If so, should other products be given special consideration? At what point does censorship enter into the picture? Also, if tobacco advertising can be restricted, what about advertising for other potentially harmful products?

Issues involving tobacco advertising are timely and important. Many states have enacted laws to encourage counteradvertising to promote the health benefits of not smoking. The figures of Joe Camel and the Marlboro Man have been banned from all advertising. A range of data suggests that antismoking campaigns have different levels of effects. In many ways, antismoking campaigns use many of the same tools and techniques to get the public's attention as do the advertisers of tobacco products. What can be learned from these campaigns about strategies for instituting long-term behavior change?

Joseph R. DiFranza et al.

RJR Nabisco's Cartoon Camel Promotes Camel Cigarettes to Children

With the number of US smokers declining by about 1 million each year, the tobacco industry's viability is critically dependent on its ability to recruit replacement smokers. Since children and teenagers constitute 90% of all new smokers, their importance to the industry is obvious. Many experts are convinced that the industry is actively promoting nicotine addiction among youth.

Spokespersons for the tobacco industry assert that they do not advertise to people under 21 years of age, the sole purpose of their advertising being to promote brand switching and brand loyalty among adult smokers. However, industry advertising expenditures cannot be economically justified on this basis alone. This study was therefore undertaken to determine the relative impact of tobacco advertising on children and adults.

There is abundant evidence that tobacco advertising influences children's images of smoking. In Britain, the proportion of children who gave "looks tough" as a reason for smoking declined after tough images were banned from cigarette advertisements. Children as young as the age of 6 years can reliably recall tobacco advertisements and match personality sketches with the brands using that imagery. In fact, cigarette advertising establishes such imagery among children who are cognitively too immature to understand the purpose of advertising. Subsequently, children who are most attuned to cigarette advertising have the most positive attitudes toward smoking, whether or not they already smoke. Children who are more aware of, or who approve of, cigarette advertisements are more likely to smoke, and those who do smoke buy the most heavily advertised brands.

Historically, one brand that children have not bought is Camel. In seven surveys, involving 3400 smokers in the seventh through 12th grades, conducted between 1976 and 1988 in Georgia, Louisiana, and Minnesota, Camel was given as the preferred brand by less than 0.5%. In 1986, Camels were most popular with smokers over the age of 65 years, of whom 4.4% chose Camels, and least popular among those 17 to 24 years of age, of whom only 2.7% preferred Camels.

From Joseph R. DiFranza, John W. Richards, Jr., Paul M. Paulman, Nancy Wolf-Gillespie, Christopher Fletcher, Robert D. Jaffe, and David Murray, "RJR Nabisco's Cartoon Camel Promotes Camel Cigarettes to Children," *Journal of the American Medical Association*, vol. 266, no. 22 (December 11, 1991), pp. 3149–3152. Copyright © 1991 by The American Medical Association. Reprinted by permission. References omitted.

In 1988, RJR Nabisco launched the "smooth character" advertising campaign, featuring Old Joe, a cartoon camel modeled after James Bond and Don Johnson of "Miami Vice." Many industry analysts believe that the goal of this campaign is to reposition Camel to compete with Philip Morris' Marlboro brand for the illegal children's market segment. To determine the relative impact of Camel's Old Joe cartoon advertising on children and adults, we used four standard marketing measures.

1. Recognition. We compared the proportions of teenagers and adults aged 21 years and over who recognize Camel's Old Joe cartoon character.
2. Recall. We compared the ability of teenagers and adults to recall from a masked Old Joe advertisement the type of product being advertised and the brand name.
3. Appeal. We compared how interesting and appealing a series of Old Joe cartoon character advertisements were to teenagers and adults.
4. Brand preference. We compared brand preferences of teenaged smokers prior to the Old Joe cartoon character campaign with those 3 years into the campaign to determine if the campaign had been more effective with children or with adults, and to determine if Camel had been repositioned as a children's brand.

Methods

Subjects

Since adolescent brand preferences may vary from one geographic location to another, we selected children from Georgia, Massachusetts, Nebraska, New Mexico, and Washington, representing five regions. One school in each state was selected based on its administration's willingness to participate. Schools with a smoking prevention program focused on tobacco advertising were excluded.

A target of 60 students in each grade, 9 through 12, from each school was set. In large schools, classes were selected to obtain a sample representative of all levels of academic ability. Students were told that the study concerned advertising and were invited to participate anonymously.

Since adult brand preferences are available from national surveys, adult subjects were recruited only at the Massachusetts site. All drivers, regardless of age, who were renewing their licenses at the Registry of Motor Vehicles on the days of the study during the 1990–1991 school year were asked to participate. Since licenses must be renewed in person, this is a heterogeneous population.

Materials

Seven Camel Old Joe cartoon character advertisements were obtained from popular magazines during the 3 years prior to the study. One ad was masked to hide all clues (except Old Joe) as to the product and brand being advertised.

The survey instrument collected demographic information and information on past and present use of tobacco, including brand preference. Children were considered to be smokers if they had smoked one or more cigarettes during the previous week. Previously validated questions were used to determine children's intentions regarding smoking in the next month and year and their attitudes toward the advertised social benefits of smoking.

Subjects rated the ads as "cool or stupid" and "interesting or boring." Subjects were asked if they thought Old Joe was "cool" and if they would like to be friends with him. Each positive response to these four questions was scored as a one, a negative response as a zero. The "appeal score" was the arithmetic sum of the responses to these four questions, with the lowest possible score per respondent being a zero and the highest a four.

Procedure

Subjects were first shown the masked ad and asked if they had seen the Old Joe character before. They were then asked to identify the product being advertised and the brand name of the product. Subjects who could not answer these questions were required to respond "Don't know" so they would not be able to write in the correct answer when the unmasked advertisements were shown. The subjects were then shown, one at a time, the six unmasked advertisements and asked to rate how the advertisements and the Old Joe cartoon character appealed to them. Subjects then completed the remainder of the survey instrument.

Adolescent brand preference data from this study were compared with the data obtained by seven surveys completed prior to the kickoff of Camel's Old Joe cartoon character campaign early in 1988.

Tests of significance were made using the Two-tailed Student's t Test for continuous data and the x^2 and Fisher's Exact Test for discrete data. A P value of less than .05 was used to define statistical significance.

The study was conducted during the 1990–1991 school year.

Results

A total of 1060 students and 491 subjects from the Registry of Motor Vehicles were asked to participate. Usable surveys were obtained from 1055 students (99%) and 415 license renewal applicants (84.5%). Seventy drivers were under 21 years of age, leaving 345 adults aged 21 years or older. Students ranged in age from 12 to 19 years (mean, 15.99 years) and adults from 21 to 87 years (mean, 40.47 years). Females represented 51.0% of the students and 54.8% of the adults.

Children were much more likely than adults to recognize Camel's Old Joe cartoon character (97.7% vs 72.2%). It is not plausible that the children were simply saying they had seen Old Joe when they had not, since they also demonstrated a greater familiarity with the advertisement on the two objective measures.

When shown the masked advertisement, the children were much more successful than the adults in identifying the product being advertised (97.5% vs 67.0%) and the Camel brand name (93.6% vs 57.7%). Even when the analysis was limited to those subjects who were familiar with the Old Joe cartoon character, children were still more likely than adults to remember the product (98.6% vs 89.6%) and the Camel brand name (95.0% vs 79.1%). This confirms that Old Joe cartoon advertisements are more effective at communicating product and brand name information to children than to adults.

Because Massachusetts adults may not be representative of adults in the other four states where children were surveyed, the above analyses were repeated comparing only Massachusetts children and adults. In all cases the differences between adults and children were significant and of even greater magnitude, excluding the possibility that the above findings were due to a lighter level of advertising exposure in the Massachusetts area.

On all four measures, the children found the Camel cartoon advertisements more appealing than did the adults. Children were more likely to think the advertisements looked "cool" (58.0% vs 39.9%) or "interesting" (73.6% vs 55.1%). More of the children thought Old Joe was "cool" (43.0% vs 25.7%) and wanted to be friends with him (35.0% vs 14.4%).

The brand preference data revealed a dramatic reversal in the market segment pattern that existed prior to Camel's Old Joe cartoon character campaign. Camel was given as the preferred brand by 32.8% of children up to the age of 18 years who smoked, 23.1% of Massachusetts adult smokers aged 19 and 20 years, and 8.7% of those 21 years of age and over. The figures for the Massachusetts adults were significantly higher than the national market share for Camel, 4.4%, suggesting that Massachusetts adults may be more familiar with the Old Joe Camel campaign than adults in general. Camel cigarettes are now most popular with children and progressively less popular with older smokers.

About equal proportions of adults (28.2%) and children (29.0%) reported some current cigarette use, making it unlikely that this factor influenced any of the above findings. Although there were some statistically significant differences in the responses of children from different regions, these were not the focus of this study.

When compared with nonsmokers, children who were currently smoking gave higher approval ratings to the advertisements. Approving attitudes toward cigarette advertisements seem to precede actual smoking. Among the nonsmoking children, those who either were ambivalent about their future smoking intentions or expressed a definite intention to smoke were more approving of the advertisements than those children who intended not to smoke.

Children were more likely to smoke if they believed that smoking is pleasurable and that it makes a person more popular, all common themes in cigarette advertising. Among nonsmoking children, those who believed that smoking would make them more attractive were eight times more likely to express an intention to smoke in the next year.

Comment

Our data demonstrate that in just 3 years Camel's Old Joe cartoon character had an astounding influence on children's smoking behavior. The proportion of smokers under 18 years of age who choose Camels has risen from 0.5% to

32.8%. Given that children under 18 years account for 3.3% of all cigarette sales, and given a national market share of 4.4% for Camel, we compute that Camel's adult market share is actually 3.4%. Given a current average price of 153.3 cents per pack, the illegal sale of Camel cigarettes to children under 18 years of age is estimated to have risen from $6 million per year prior to the cartoon advertisements to $476 million per year now, accounting for one quarter of all Camel sales.

From both a legal and moral perspective, it is important to determine if the tobacco industry is actively promoting nicotine addiction among youngsters. However, from a public health perspective it is irrelevant whether the effects of tobacco advertising on children are intentional. If tobacco advertising is a proximate cause of disease, it must be addressed accordingly. In the following discussion we will examine the evidence produced by this study, the marketing practices of the tobacco industry as a whole as revealed in industry documents, and the marketing practices used by RJR Nabisco, in particular, to promote Camel cigarettes. The quotations cited below are from tobacco industry personnel and from documents obtained during litigation over Canada's ban of tobacco advertising.

Our data show that children are much more familiar with Camel's Old Joe cartoon character than are adults. This may be because children have more exposure to these advertisements, or because the advertisements are inherently more appealing to youngsters. The tobacco industry has long followed a policy of preferentially placing selected advertisements where children are most likely to see them. For example, print advertisements are placed in magazines "specifically designed to reach young people." Paid cigarette brand promotions appear in dozens of teen movies. Camels are featured in the Walt Disney movies *Who Framed Roger Rabbit?* and *Honey I Shrunk the Kids.*

The industry targets poster advertisements for "key youth locations/ meeting places in the proximity of theaters, records [sic] stores, video arcades, etc." It is common to see Old Joe poster advertisements in malls, an obvious gathering spot for young teens. Billboards, T-shirts, baseball caps, posters, candy cigarettes, and the sponsorship of televised sporting events and entertainment events such as the Camel "Mud and Monster" series are all used to promote Camels. All are effective marketing techniques for reaching children.

The fact that children are much more attracted to the themes used in the Old Joe cartoon character advertisements may also explain why they are more familiar with them. The themes used in tobacco advertising that is targeted at children are the result of extensive research on children conducted by the tobacco industry to "learn everything there was to learn about how smoking begins." Their research identifies the major psychological vulnerabilities of children, which can then be exploited by advertising to foster and maintain nicotine addiction.

The marketing plan for "Export A" cigarettes describes their "psychological benefits"; "Export smokers will be perceived as ... characterized by their self-confidence, strength of character and individuality which makes them popular and admired by their peers."

Consider a child's vulnerability to peer pressure. According to one industry study, "The goading and taunting that exists at the age of 11 or 12 to get nonsmokers to start smoking is virtually gone from the peer group circles by 16 or 17." If peer influence is virtually gone by the age of 16 years, who is the intended target group for RJR-MacDonald's Tempo brand, described as individuals who are "[e]xtremely influenced by their peer group"? (RJR-MacDonald is a wholly owned subsidiary of RJR Nabisco.) The recommended strategy for promoting this brand is the "[m]ajor usage of imagery which portrays the positive social appeal of peer group acceptance." In one Camel advertisement, a cowboy (a Marlboro smoker?) is being denied admission to a party because "only smooth characters [ie, Camel smokers] need apply". It appears that Camel advertisements are also targeted at individuals who are influenced by their peer group.

Children use tobacco, quite simply, because they believe the benefits outweigh the risks. To the insecure child, the benefits are the "psychological benefits" promised in tobacco advertisements: confidence, an improved image, and popularity. Children who believe that smoking will make them more popular or more attractive are up to 4.7 times more likely to smoke.

Previous research makes it clear that children derive some of their positive images of smoking from advertising. Children who are aware of tobacco advertising, and those who approve of it, are also more likely to be smokers. Children's favorable attitudes toward smoking and advertising precede actual tobacco use and correlate with the child's intention to smoke, suggesting that the images children derive from advertising encourage them to smoke. Our data confirm these earlier findings. Among nonsmoking children, those who were more approving of the Old Joe advertisements were more likely either to be ambivalent about their smoking intentions or to express a definite intention to smoke. Nonsmoking children who believed that smoking would make them more popular were eight times more likely to express an intention to smoke in the future.

Since a child's intention to smoke is considered to be a good predictor of future smoking behavior, it seems reasonable to conclude that a belief in the psychological benefits of smoking, derived from advertising, precedes, and contributes to, the adoption of smoking.

There are other lines of evidence indicating that tobacco advertising increases the number of children who use tobacco. In countries where advertising has been totally banned or severely restricted, the percentage of young people who smoke has decreased more rapidly than in countries where tobacco promotion has been less restricted. After a 24-year decline in smokeless tobacco sales, an aggressive youth-oriented marketing campaign has been followed by what has been termed "an epidemic" of smokeless tobacco use among children, with the *average* age for new users being 10 years.

Many of the tobacco industry documents cited above provide abundant evidence that one purpose of tobacco advertising is to addict children to tobacco. In the words of one advertising consultant, "Where I worked we were trying very hard to influence kids who were 14 to start to smoke." Two marketing strategy documents for Export A also reveal that it is the youngest children they are after. "Whose behavior are we trying to affect?: new users." The goal is "[o]ptimizing product and user imagery of Export 'A' against young starter smokers." The average age for starter smokers is 13 years.

The industry also researches the best ways of keeping children from quitting once they are "hooked on smoking." The purpose of one tobacco industry study was to assess the feasibility of marketing low-tar brands to teens as an alternative to quitting. The study found that for boys, "[t]he single most commonly voiced reason for quitting among those who had done so . . . was sports." The tobacco industry's sponsorship of sporting events, such as the Camel Supercross motorcycle race, should be seen in relation to its need to discourage teenage boys from quitting. Similarly, its emphasis on slimness serves as a constant reinforcement of teenage girls' fears of gaining weight as a result of quitting.

Our study provides further evidence that tobacco advertising promotes and maintains nicotine addiction among children and adolescents. A total ban of tobacco advertising and promotions, as part of an effort to protect children from the dangers of tobacco, can be based on sound scientific reasoning.

NO

George J. Annas

Cowboys, Camels, and the First Amendment

T he Marlboro Man and Joe Camel have become public health enemies number one and two, and removing their familiar faces from the gaze of young people has become a goal of President Bill Clinton and his health care officials.[1] The strategy of limiting the exposure of children to tobacco advertisements is based on the fact that almost all regular smokers begin smoking in their teens. This approach is politically possible because most Americans believe that tobacco companies should be prohibited from targeting children in their advertising.

Shortly before the 1996 Democratic National Convention, the President announced that he had approved regulations drafted by the Food and Drug Administration (FDA) to restrict the advertising of tobacco products to children. At the convention, Vice-President Al Gore told the delegates, "Until I draw my last breath, I will pour my heart and soul into the cause of protecting our children from the dangers of smoking."[2] In a press conference at the White House immediately following the announcement, Health and Human Services Secretary Donna Shalala said, "This is the most important public health initiative in a generation. It ranks with everything from polio to penicillin. I mean, this is huge in terms of its impact."[3]

No one doubts that a substantial reduction in the number of teenage smokers would mean a substantial reduction in the number of adult smokers when these teenagers grow up, and this reduction would have a major effect on health and longevity. Since almost 50 million Americans smoke, the result of reducing the number of young smokers substantially would indeed be "huge in terms of its impact." The real question is not whether the goal is appropriate but whether the means proposed to reach it are likely to be effective. In this regard, the FDA regulations may be unsuccessful for either of two related reasons: the implementation of the regulations may not reduce the number of teenagers who start smoking, or some of the regulations may be found to violate the First Amendment.

From George J. Annas, "Cowboys, Camels, and the First Amendment—The FDA's Restrictions on Tobacco Advertising," *The New England Journal of Medicine,* vol. 335, no. 23 (December 5, 1996), pp. 1779–1783. Copyright © 1996 by The Massachusetts Medical Society. Reprinted by permission.

The Regulations

The FDA's new regulations are designed to reduce the demand for tobacco products among teenagers, which is consistent with the goal of the Healthy People 2000 program to reduce by half (to 15 percent) the proportion of children who use tobacco products.[1,4] The FDA has somewhat modified the time line: the goal of its regulations is to cut underage smoking by half in seven years. Although the FDA has never before asserted jurisdiction over cigarettes or smokeless tobacco, the agency bases its claim to jurisdiction over these two types of products on its authority to regulate medical devices, defining cigarettes as a "drug-delivery device." Of course, this means that the FDA also defines nicotine as a drug. The regulations apply to sellers, distributors, and manufacturers of tobacco products. Sellers may not sell cigarettes or smokeless tobacco to anyone under the age of 18 years and must verify the age of purchasers under 26 by checking a form of identification bearing a photograph, in a "direct, face-to-face exchange." Exceptions are sales through mail orders and vending machines located in facilities that persons under the age of 18 years are not permitted to enter at any time. The distribution of free samples is also outlawed, as is the sale of cigarettes in packs of fewer than 20 (so-called kiddie packs). All cigarettes and smokeless tobacco products must bear the following statement: "Nicotine delivery devices for persons 18 or older."[1]

The most controversial portions of the regulations deal with advertising. One section outlaws all outdoor advertising within 1000 feet of public playgrounds and elementary and secondary schools. Advertising is restricted to "black text on a white background."[1] This restriction applies to all billboards but not to "adult publications." Such publications are defined by the regulations as "any newspaper, magazine, periodical or other publication... whose readers younger than 18 years of age constitute 15 percent or less of the total readership as measured by competent and reliable survey evidence; and that is read by fewer than 2 million persons younger than 18 years of age."[1] Tobacco manufacturers and distributors are prohibited from marketing any item (other than cigarettes or smokeless tobacco) that bears a brand name used for cigarettes or smokeless tobacco and are prohibited from offering any gift to a person purchasing cigarettes or smokeless tobacco products.[1] Finally, "no manufacturer, distributor, or retailer may sponsor or cause to be sponsored any athletic, musical, artistic, or other social or cultural event, or any entry or team in any event, [under] the brand name [of a tobacco product] (alone or in conjunction with any other words)."[1] Such events, may, however, be sponsored under the name of the corporation that manufactures the tobacco product, provided that the corporate name existed before 1995 and does not include a brand name.

The Legal Challenge

Tobacco companies have already filed suit to enjoin enforcement of the regulations. According to FDA Commissioner David Kessler, the FDA decided to assert its jurisdiction over cigarettes when the scientific community determined that the nicotine in tobacco products is addictive, and when the FDA concluded that the tobacco companies were probably manipulating the levels of nicotine to maintain their market of addicted users.[5] Under the legislation that gives the FDA its authority, a drug is any product "intended to affect the structure or any function of the body." The FDA contends that cigarettes and smokeless tobacco can be properly viewed as devices for delivering the drug nicotine, because they meet all three independent criteria for determining whether a product is a drug-delivery device: "a reasonable manufacturer would foresee that the product will be used for pharmacologic purposes [or] that consumers actually use it for such purposes [or] the manufacturer experts or designs the product to be used in such a manner."[5]

The primary argument of the tobacco companies is that Congress has consistently refused to give the FDA jurisdiction over tobacco products, and until now, the FDA itself has consistently said that it has no jurisdiction over such products. Moreover, the companies assert that if the FDA had jurisdiction over cigarettes as a drug or drug-delivery device, the FDA would have to ban them as not being "safe," which Congress has repeatedly refused to do or permit.

The second argument used by the tobacco companies, which is the focus of this article, is that the regulations violate the First Amendment of the U.S. Constitution by restricting the right to free speech in advertising. Congress could vote to give the FDA authority over tobacco but could not, of course, change the First Amendment.

The First Amendment and Advertising

The basic test used to determine whether the government can ban advertising is set out in the Supreme Court's 1980 opinion in *Central Hudson Gas & Electric Corporation v. Public Service Commission of New York.*[6] This case involved a regulation that prohibited electric utilities from advertising to promote the use of electricity. The court adopted a four-part test to determine whether this regulation was constitutional: (1) to be protected by the First Amendment, the advertising must concern a lawful activity and not be misleading, (2) for the ban to be valid, the state's interest in banning the advertising must be "substantial," (3) the ban must "directly advance" the state's interest, and (4) it must be no more extensive than necessary to further the state's interest.[6] In *Central Hudson,* the Supreme Court concluded that although the state had a substantial interest in energy conservation that was advanced by the ban on advertising, the ban nonetheless failed the fourth part of the test. The ban failed that part because it was overly broad, prohibiting the promotion of potentially energy-saving electric services, and there was no proof that a more limited restriction of advertising could not have achieved the same goal. The court suggested, as an example, that a narrower regulation could have required "that the advertisements include information about the relative efficiency and expense of the offered services."

In 1986, in *Posadas de Puerto Rico Associates* v. *Tourism Company of Puerto Rico,* the Supreme Court upheld a ban on advertisements for casino gambling in Puerto Rico.[7] The court held that this ban met the four parts of the test in

Central Hudson. Adding that the government could ban advertising for any activity that it could outlaw, the court said it would be "a strange constitutional doctrine which would concede to the legislature the authority to totally ban a product or activity, but deny to the legislature the authority to forbid the stimulation of demand for the product or activity through advertising."[7] The court gave a number of other examples of "vice" products or activities, including cigarettes, alcohol beverages, and prostitution, which struck many in the public health community as warranting restricted advertising. Of course, fashions change, and many states now promote and advertise gambling, in the form of lotteries and casinos, as good for the financial health of the government. Nonetheless, in the wake of the May 1996 decision in *44 Liquormart* v. *Rhode Island*,[8] the most recent and comprehensive case involving free speech in advertising, it is unlikely that *Posadas* will continue to be invoked. Moreover, the four-part test in *Central Hudson* will be more strictly applied in the future.

The *44 Liquormart* Case

In *44 Liquormart v. Rhode Island,* a liquor retailer challenged the Rhode Island laws that banned all advertisements of retail liquor prices, except at the place of sale, and prohibited the media from publishing any such advertisements, even in other states. 44 Liquormart had published an advertisement identifying various brands of liquor that included the word "wow" in large letters next to pictures of vodka and rum bottles. An enforcement action against the company resulted in a $400 fine. After paying the fine, 44 Liquormart appealed, seeking a declaratory judgment that the two statutes and the implementing regulations promulgated under them violated the First Amendment.

The U.S. District Court declared the ban on price advertising unconstitutional because it did not "directly advance" the state's interest in reducing alcohol consumption and was "more extensive than necessary to serve that interest."[9] The Court of Appeals reversed the decision, finding "inherent merit" in the state's argument that competitive price advertising would lower prices and that lower prices would induce more sales.[10] In reviewing these decisions, the Supreme Court unanimously found that the state laws violated the First Amendment, but no rationale for this opinion gained more than four votes. Justice John Paul Stevens (who wrote the principal opinion) began his discussion by quoting from an earlier case involving advertisements of prices for prescription drugs:

> Advertising, however tasteless and excessive it sometimes may seem, is nonetheless dissemination of information as to who is producing and selling what product, for what reason, and at what price. So long as we preserve a predominantly free enterprise economy, the allocation of our resources in large measure will be made through numerous private economic decisions. It is a matter of public interest that those decisions, in the aggregate, be intelligent and well informed. To this end, the free flow of commercial information is indispensable.[8]

Justice Stevens went on to note that "complete speech bans, unlike content-neutral restrictions on the time, place, or manner of expression... are particularly dangerous because they all but foreclose alternative means of disseminating certain information."[8] Bans unrelated to consumer protection, Stevens noted further, should be treated with special skepticism when they "seek to keep people in the dark for what the government perceives to be their own good." Stevens moved on to apply *Central Hudson's* four-point test. He concluded that "there is no question that Rhode Island's price advertising ban constitutes a blanket prohibition against truthful, nonmisleading speech about a lawful product." Stevens also agreed that the state has a substantial interest in "promoting temperance."

But can the state meet part three of the test, by showing that the ban is effective in advancing this interest? Four justices defined the third part of the test as requiring the state to "bear the burden of showing not merely that its regulation will advance its interest but also that it will do so 'to a material degree.' "[8] This requirement is necessary because of the "drastic nature" of the state's ban: "the wholesale suppression of truthful, nonmisleading information." Justice Stevens concluded that Rhode Island did not meet this requirement and could not do so without "any findings of fact" or other evidence. The common-sense notion that prohibitions against price advertising will lead to higher prices and thus lower consumption (an assumption made in *Central Hudson*) was found insufficient to support a finding that the restriction of advertising would "significantly reduce market-wide consumption."[8] "Speculation or conjecture" does not suffice.[9]

As for the fourth part of the test, Justice Stevens concluded that the ban also failed because Rhode Island did not show that alternative forms of regulation that do not limit speech, such as limiting per capita purchases or using educational campaigns that address the problem of excessive drinking, could not be equally or more effective in reducing consumption. All nine members of the Supreme Court agreed with this conclusion. Finally, Justice Stevens (again on behalf of four justices) argued that in *Posadas* the court had wrongly concluded that since the state could ban a product or activity, it could ban advertising about it. He argued that the First Amendment was much stronger than that decision implied, noting "We think it quite clear that banning speech may sometimes prove far more intrusive than banning conduct," and thus it is not true that "the power to prohibit an activity is necessarily 'greater' than the power to suppress speech about it.... The text of the First Amendment makes clear that the Constitution presumes that attempts to regulate speech are more dangerous than attempts to regulate conduct."[8] Stevens also rejected the idea that "vice" activities have less protection from the First Amendment than other commercial activities, noting that the distinction would be "difficult, if not impossible, to define."

Free Speech and the FDA Regulations

Selling cigarettes and smokeless tobacco to persons under the age of 18 is illegal is all states, so advertising to this age group is not protected by the First Amendment. Nor does outlawing vending machines that children have access to pose a problem with respect to the First Amendment. Because the FDA regulations are intended to apply only to children and do not foreclose alternative sources of information, it is impossible to predict with certainty how the Supreme Court will respond to a First Amendment challenge (assuming the court finds that the FDA has authority in this area). Nonetheless, the areas of primary concern can be identified.

Bans will be subject to a higher standard of review than restrictions. Forms of advertising that are banned include the distribution of products (other than cigarettes and smokeless tobacco) with the tobacco brand name or insignia on them, the placement of billboards within 1000 feet of playgrounds and elementary and secondary schools, and the use of brand names for sporting and cultural events. If the court adopts the strict version of the third part of the test in *Central Hudson*, the FDA will have to present evidence that these bans will reduce underage smoking to a material degree. Moreover, to meet the fourth part of the test, which the court unanimously found was not met in *44 Liquormart*, the FDA must also show that no other, less restrictive method, such as antismoking advertising or better enforcement of existing laws, would work as well. This will be difficult, especially since the FDA commissioner has already said he believes that antismoking advertising is effective in helping young people understand the risks of smoking and that, after the publication of its rules, the agency plans "to notify the major cigarette and smokeless-tobacco companies that it will begin discussing a requirement that they fund an education program in the mass media."[5] The court could decide that a nonspeech ban should have been tried first.

Restrictions on advertising may be easier to uphold, but even they are not obviously permissible. The tobacco companies spend $6 billion a year in advertising and promotion, about $700 million of which is spent on magazine advertisements.[11] The core antiadvertising regulation requires that advertisements on all billboards and in publications that do not qualify as adult publications be limited to black text on a white background.[1] This is a restriction (not a ban) and does not prohibit the inclusion of factual information (such as the price of liquor, which was at issue in *44 Liquormart*). The rationale for these rules is that images in bright colors, of which Joe Camel is the primary example, entice children to start smoking or continue to smoke. Since no objective information is being banned or restricted, the court may find that such a restriction need meet only a common-sense test.[12] If, however, the court takes a more sophisticated view of advertising—which is largely focused on image rather than text—it may well hold that the same rules apply and that therefore the burden of proof is on the FDA to demonstrate that such a restriction would reduce underage smoking to a material degree. No study has yet been able to show evidence of this effect. Consistent with the view that "pop art" should be protected at least as much as text is the view that advertising images are forms designed to elicit certain responses and as such are entitled to at least as much protection from the First Amendment as objective information.

Drastic restrictions on advertising may also be ineffective or even counterproductive. In Britain, for example, where both Joe Camel and the Marlboro

Man are outlawed and tobacco advertisers are prohibited from using anything that suggests health, fresh air, or beauty, creative advertisers have found other ways to promote tobacco products. Advertisements for Silk Cut cigarettes feature various images of silk being cut (e.g., scissors dancing a cancan in purple silk skirts and a rhinoceroses whose horn pierces a purple silk cap), and Marlboro advertisements portray bleak and forbidding western U.S. landscapes with the words, "Welcome to Marlboro Country." It has been suggested that by using such surreal images, tobacco advertisers may be appealing to fantasies of death and sexual violence that have a powerful (if unconscious) appeal to consumers.[13] Such imagery may actually have greater appeal for teenagers than Joe Camel. U.S. advertising agencies have already experimented with black-and-white, text-only advertisements. One agency proposed that the required phrase, "a nicotine-delivery device," can be used in conjunction with the phrase ".cyber cigarettes" on one line, under the phrase (in larger type) "pleasure.com" and a sideways smiling face, formed by a colon, a hyphen, and a closed parenthesis[:-)], to suggest that nicotine is a pleasure of the cyberspace age.[14]

The FDA knows it has a First Amendment problem here. In its comments accompanying the regulations, the agency argues that it is not required to "conclusively prove by rigorous empirical studies that advertising causes initial consumption of cigarettes and smokeless tobacco."[1] In fact, the FDA says it is impossible to prove this. Instead, the agency argues it need only demonstrate that there is "more than adequate evidence" that "tobacco advertising has an effect on young people's tobacco use behavior if it affects initiation, maintenance, or attempts at quitting."[1] The FDA's position follows from the conclusion of the Institute of Medicine:

> Portraying a deadly addiction as a healthful and sensual experience tugs against the nation's efforts to promote a tobacco-free norm and to discourage tobacco use by children and youths. This warrants legislation restricting the features of advertising and promotion that make tobacco use attractive to youths. The question is not, "Are advertising and promotion the causes of youth initiation?" but rather, "Does the preponderance of evidence suggest that features of advertising and promotion tend to encourage youths to smoke?" The answer is yes and this is a sufficient basis for action, even in the absence of a precise and definitive causal chain.[11]

The Surgeon General has reached a similar conclusion:

> Cigarette advertising uses images rather than information to portray the attractiveness and function of smoking. Human models and cartoon characters in cigarette advertising convey independence, healthfulness, adventure-seeking, and youthful activities—themes correlated with psychosocial factors that appeal to young people.[15]

The Supreme Court may make an exception for tobacco advertisements because of the clear health hazards and the use of restrictions instead of bans, but the extent of the restrictions will have to be justified. In this regard, the 15 percent young-readership rule for publications is difficult to justify as either not arbitrary or not more restrictive than necessary. The FDA admits, for example, that its rule would require the following magazines to use black-and-white, text-only advertisements: *Sports Illustrated* (18 percent of its readers are under the age of 18), *Car and Driver* (18 percent), *Motor Trend* (22 percent), *Road and Track* (21 percent), *Rolling Stone* (18 percent), *Vogue* (18 percent), *Mademoiselle* (20 percent), and *Glamour* (17 percent).[1] The FDA seems particularly offended by "a cardboard Joe Camel pop-out" holding concert tickets in the center of *Rolling Stone.*[5] (Some Americans might wish to censor the photograph of a naked Brooke Shields on the cover of the October 1996 issue as well, although that image is clearly protected by the First Amendment.) A 25 percent rule, for example, would exempt all these magazines.

The FDA justifies the 15 percent rule by arguing that young people between the ages of 5 and 17 years constitute approximately 15 percent of the U.S. population and that "if the percentage of young readers of a publication is greater than the percentage of young people in the general population, the publication can be viewed as having particular appeal to young readers."[1] A similar argument can, of course, be made with regard to sporting and cultural events— some of which may have very few young people in attendance.[15] On the other hand, the billboard restrictions seem to have a more solid justification.

Tobacco companies profit handsomely by selling products that cause serious health problems and contribute to the deaths of millions of Americans. There is also little doubt that nicotine is physically addictive and that it is in the interest of tobacco companies to get children addicted early, since very few people take up smoking after the age of 18 years. The FDA admits, however, that it cannot prove that cigarette advertising causes children to begin to smoke, and the agency has not tried alternative measures, such as strictly enforcing current laws that prohibit sales to minors and engaging in a broad-based educational campaign against smoking, to reduce the number of children who smoke. Until the FDA either proves that cigarette advertising causes children to start smoking or uses methods of discouraging smoking that stay clear of the First Amendment, bans and restrictions on advertising will raise enough problems with the First Amendment to ensure that they will be tied up in court for years. This does not mean, however, that no immediate legal actions can be taken against tobacco companies. In a future article, I will discuss current trends in litigation against these companies and assess the likely impact of antismoking lawsuits on the tobacco companies.

References

1. Food and Drug Administration, Department of Health and Human Services. Regulations restricting the sale and distribution of cigarettes and smokeless tobacco to protect children and adolescents. Fed Regist 1996;61 (168):44, 396-618.
2. Gore speech: "America is strong. Bill Clinton's leadership paying off." New York Times, August 29, 1996: B12.
3. Press Briefing by Secretary of HHS Donna Shalala, FDA Commissioner David Kessler, and Assistant Secretary Phil Lee. White House, Office of Press Secretary, August 23, 1996.
4. Trends in smoking initiation among adolescents and young adults—United States, 1980–1989. MMWR Morb Mortal Wkly Rep 1995;44:521–5.

5. Kessler DA, Witt AM, Barnett PS, et al. The Food and Drug Administration's regulation of tobacco products. N Engl J Med 1996; 335:988–94.
6. Central Hudson Gas & Electric Corp. v. Public Service Commission of New York, 447 U.S. 557 (1980).
7. Posadas du Puerto Rico Associates v. Tourism Company of Puerto Rico, 478 U.S. 328 (1986).
8. 44 Liquormart, Inc. v. Rhode Island, 116 S. Ct. 1495 (1996).
9. 44 Liquor Mart, Inc. v. Racine, 829 F. Supp. 543 (R.I. 1993).
10. 44 Liquor Mart, Inc. v. Rhode Island, 39 F. 3d 5 (1st Cir. 1994).
11. Committee on Preventing Nicotine Addiction in Children and Youths. Institute of Medicine. Growing up tobacco free: preventing nicotine addiction in children and youths. Washington, D.C.: National Academy Press, 1994:131.
12. Glantz L. Regulating tobacco advertising: the FDA regulations and the First Amendment. Am J Public Health (in press).
13. Parker-Pope T. Tough tobacco-ad rules light creative fires. Wall Street Journal. October 9, 1996:B1.
14. Brownlee L. How agency teams might cope with U.S. ad restraints. Wall Street Journal. October 9, 1996:B1.
15. Department of Health and Human Services. Preventing tobacco use among young people: a report of the Surgeon General. Washington, D.C.: Government Printing Office, 1994:195.

POSTSCRIPT

Should Tobacco Advertising Be Restricted?

There are several resources available with which to further examine this issue. The government report on the Hearing Before the Committee on Labor and Human Resources of the United States Senate, 101st Congress, Second Session, on the Tobacco Product Education and Health Protection Act of 1990 (Senate Hearing 101-707, available in most government repository libraries on microfiche) is one of the first fully documented sources on the tobacco industry's disclosure of addictive agents in cigarettes.

Simon Chapman has written a book on the techniques and marketing tools used for cigarette advertising entitled *Great Expectorations: Advertising and the Tobacco Industry* (Comedia Publishing Group, 1986). Bruce Maxwell and Michael Jacobson have examined appeals to certain target audiences in their book *Marketing Disease to Hispanics: The Selling of Alcohol, Tobacco, and Junk Foods* (Center for Science in the Public Interest, 1989).

There are a number of good, general references on advertising, including Roland Marchand's *Advertising the American Dream* (University of California Press, 1985) and Robert Goldman's *Reading Ads Socially* (Routledge, 1992).

Among books that are critical of the advertising industry in general, a recent text lends itself to the discussion of the potential for the regulation of the advertising industry: Matthew P. McAllister's *The Commercialization of American Culture: New Advertising, Control and Democracy* (Sage Publications, 1995).

ISSUE 7

Is Advertising Ethical?

YES: John E. Calfee, from "How Advertising Informs to Our Benefit," *Consumers' Research* (April 1998)

NO: Russ Baker, from "The Squeeze," *Columbia Journalism Review* (September/October 1997)

ISSUE SUMMARY

YES: John E. Calfee, a former U.S. Trade Commission economist, takes the position that advertising is very useful to people and that the information that advertising imparts helps consumers make better decisions. He maintains that the benefits of advertising far outweigh the negative criticisms.

NO: Author Russ Baker focuses on the way in which advertisers seek to control magazine content and, thus, go beyond persuasion and information into the realm of influencing the content of other media.

Professor Dallas Smythe first described commercial media as a system for delivering audiences to advertisers. This perception of the viewing public as a "market" for products as well as an audience for advertising—a main source of media revenue—reflects the economic orientation of the current media system in America. The unplanned side effects of advertising, however, concern many critics. For example, socialization into consumption, consumerism, materialism, and high expectations are one set of concerns. Many of these questions have often been asked: Is advertising deceptive? Does it create or perpetuate stereotypes? Does it create conformity? Does it create insecurity in order to sell goods? Does it cause people to buy things that they do not really need?

John E. Calfee addresses some of these questions in the following selection, but he focuses on how the information in ads benefits consumers. He takes the position that advertising is in the public interest and that even controversies about ads may be beneficial because they can result in competitive pricing for consumers. Citing some specific cases, he states that individuals can learn about important issues (such as health) through ads. He even considers what he calls "less bad" ads, which give consumers important negative information that can be useful to their well-being.

In the second selection, Russ Baker provides many different examples to show that the advertising industry has become too large and too powerful. He maintains that by giving corporations too much say in magazine and newspaper copy, advertisers may ultimately distort free press and free inquiry. When publishers bow to corporate control over material that is not advertising, they may lose focus and become mere extensions of advertisers.

These two selections raise concerns about the ethical nature of ads. Calfee focuses only on the good that advertising does, while Baker addresses the ethical nature of the control that corporations and advertising have in influencing media content. Both authors examine important concepts of fairness, honesty, and integrity in the world of advertising.

John E. Calfee

 **YES**

How Advertising Informs to Our Benefit

A great truth about advertising is that it is a tool for communicating information and shaping markets. It is one of the forces that compel sellers to cater to
the desires of consumers. Almost everyone knows this because consumers use
advertising every day, and they miss advertising when they cannot get it. This
fact does not keep politicians and opinion leaders from routinely dismissing
the value of advertising. But the truth is that people find advertising very useful
indeed.

Of course, advertising primarily seeks to persuade and everyone knows
this, too. The typical ad tries to induce a consumer to do one particular thing
—usually, buy a product—instead of a thousand other things. There is nothing
obscure about this purpose or what it means for buyers. Decades of data and
centuries of intuition reveal that all consumers everywhere are deeply suspicious of what advertisers say and why they say it. This skepticism is in fact
the driving force that makes advertising so effective. The persuasive purpose of
advertising and the skepticism with which it is met are two sides of a single process. Persuasion and skepticism work in tandem so advertising can do its job in
competitive markets. Hence, ads represent the seller's self interest, consumers
know this, and sellers know that consumers know it.

By understanding this process more fully, we can sort out much of the
popular confusion surrounding advertising and how it benefits consumers.

How useful is advertising? Just how useful is the connection between advertising and information? At first blush, the process sounds rather limited. Volvo
ads tell consumers that Volvos have side-impact air bags, people learn a little
about the importance of air bags, and Volvo sells a few more cars. This seems
to help hardly anyone except Volvo and its customers.

But advertising does much more. It routinely provides immense amounts
of information that benefits primarily parties other than the advertiser. This
may sound odd, but it is a logical result of market forces and the nature of
information itself.

The ability to use information to sell products is an incentive to create
new information through research. Whether the topic is nutrition, safety, or
more mundane matters like how to measure amplifier power, the necessity of

From John E. Calfee, "How Advertising Informs to Our Benefit," *Consumers' Research* (April 1998).

achieving credibility with consumers and critics requires much of this research to be placed in the public domain, and that it rest upon some academic credentials. That kind of research typically produces results that apply to more than just the brands sold by the firm sponsoring the research. The lack of property rights to such "pure" information ensures that this extra information is available at no charge. Both consumers and competitors may borrow the new information for their own purposes.

Advertising also elicits additional information from other sources. Claims that are striking, original, forceful or even merely obnoxious will generate news stories about the claims, the controversies they cause, the reactions of competitors (A price war? A splurge of comparison ads?), the reactions of consumers and the remarks of governments and independent authorities.

Probably the most concrete, pervasive, and persistent example of competitive advertising that works for the public good is price advertising. Its effect is invariably to heighten competition and reduce prices, even the prices of firms that assiduously avoid mentioning prices in their own advertising.

There is another area where the public benefits of advertising are less obvious but equally important. The unremitting nature of consumer interest in health, and the eagerness of sellers to cater to consumer desires, guarantee that advertising related to health will provide a storehouse of telling observations on the ways in which the benefits of advertising extend beyond the interests of advertisers to include the interests of the public at large.

A cascade of information   Here is probably the best documented example of why advertising is necessary for consumer welfare. In the 1970s, public health experts described compelling evidence that people who eat more fiber are less likely to get cancer, especially cancer of the colon, which happens to be the second leading cause of deaths from cancer in the United States. By 1979, the U.S. Surgeon General was recommending that people eat more fiber in order to prevent cancer.

Consumers appeared to take little notice of these recommendations, however. The National Cancer Institute decided that more action was needed. NCI's cancer prevention division undertook to communicate the new information about fiber and cancer to the general public. Their goal was to change consumer diets and reduce the risk of cancer, but they had little hope of success given the tiny advertising budgets of federal agencies like NCI.

Their prospects unexpectedly brightened in 1984. NCI received a call from the Kellogg Corporation, whose All-Bran cereal held a commanding market share of the high-fiber segment. Kellogg proposed to use All-Bran advertising as a vehicle for NCI's public service messages. NCI thought that was an excellent idea. Soon, an agreement was reached in which NCI would review Kellogg's ads and labels for accuracy and value before Kellogg began running their fiber-cancer ads.

The new Kellogg All-Bran campaign opened in October 1984. A typical ad began with the headline, "At last some news about cancer you can live with." The ad continued: "The National Cancer Institute believes a high fiber, low fat diet may reduce your risk of some kinds of cancer. The National Cancer

Institute reports some very good health news. There is growing evidence that may link a high fiber, low fat diet to lower incidence of some kinds of cancer. That's why one of their strongest recommendations is to eat high-fiber foods. If you compare, you'll find Kellogg's All-Bran has nine grams of fiber per serving. No other cereal has more. So start your day with a bowl of Kellogg's All-Bran or mix it with your regular cereal."

The campaign quickly achieved two things. One was to create a regulatory crisis between two agencies. The Food and Drug Administration thought that if a food was advertised as a way to prevent cancer, it was being marketed as a drug. Then the FDA's regulations for drug labeling would kick in. The food would be reclassified as a drug and would be removed from the market until the seller either stopped making the health claims or put the product through the clinical testing necessary to obtain formal approval as a drug.

But food advertising is regulated by the Federal Trade Commission, not the FDA. The FTC thought Kellogg's ads were non-deceptive and were therefore perfectly legal. In fact, it thought the ads should be encouraged. The Director of the FTC's Bureau of Consumer Protection declared that "the [Kellogg] ad has presented important public health recommendations in an accurate, useful, and substantiated way. It informs the members of the public that there is a body of data suggesting certain relationships between cancer and diet that they may find important." The FTC won this political battle, and the ads continued.

The second instant effect of the All-Bran campaign was to unleash a flood of health claims. Vegetable oil manufacturers advertised that cholesterol was associated with coronary heart disease, and that vegetable oil does not contain cholesterol. Margarine ads did the same, and added that vitamin A is essential for good vision. Ads for calcium products (such as certain antacids) provided vivid demonstrations of the effects of osteoporosis (which weakens bones in old age), and recounted the advice of experts to increase dietary calcium as a way to prevent osteoporosis. Kellogg's competitors joined in citing the National Cancer Institute dietary recommendations.

Nor did things stop there. In the face of consumer demand for better and fuller information, health claims quickly evolved from a blunt tool to a surprisingly refined mechanism. Cereals were advertised as high in fiber and low in sugar or fat or sodium. Ads for an upscale brand of bread noted: "Well, most high-fiber bran cereals may be high in fiber, but often only one kind: insoluble. It's this kind of fiber that helps promote regularity. But there's also a kind of fiber known as soluble, which most high-fiber bran cereals have in very small amounts, if at all. Yet diets high in this kind of fiber may actually lower your serum cholesterol, a risk factor for some heart diseases." Cereal boxes became convenient sources for a summary of what made for a good diet.

Increased independent information   The ads also brought powerful secondary effects. These may have been even more useful than the information that actually appeared in the ads themselves.

One effect was an increase in media coverage of diet and health. *Consumer Reports*, a venerable and hugely influential magazine that carries no advertising, revamped its reports on cereals to emphasize fiber and other ingredients (rather than testing the foods to see how well they did at providing a complete diet for laboratory rats). The health-claims phenomenon generated its own press coverage, with articles like "What Has All-Bran Wrought?" and "The Fiber Furor." These stories recounted the ads and scientific information that prompted the ads; and articles on food and health proliferated. Anyone who lived through these years in the United States can probably remember the unending media attention to health claims and to diet and health generally.

Much of the information on diet and health was new. This was no coincidence. Firms were sponsoring research on their products in the hope of finding results that could provide a basis for persuasive advertising claims. Oat bran manufacturers, for example, funded research on the impact of soluble fiber on blood cholesterol. When the results came out "wrong," as they did in a 1990 study published with great fanfare in *The New England Journal of Medicine*, the headline in *Advertising Age* was "Oat Bran Popularity Hitting the Skids," and it did indeed tumble. The manufacturers kept at the research, however, and eventually the best research supported the efficacy of oat bran in reducing cholesterol (even to the satisfaction of the FDA). Thus did pure advertising claims spill over to benefit the information environment at large.

The shift to higher fiber cereals encompassed brands that had never undertaken the effort necessary to construct believable ads about fiber and disease. Two consumer researchers at the FDA reviewed these data and concluded they were "consistent with the successful educational impact of the Kellogg diet and health campaign: consumers seemed to be making an apparently thoughtful discrimination between high- and low-fiber cereals," and that the increased market shares for high-fiber non-advertised products represented "the clearest evidence of a successful consumer education campaign."

Perhaps most dramatic were the changes in consumer awareness of diet and health. An FTC analysis of government surveys showed that when consumers were asked about how they could prevent cancer through their diet, the percentage who mentioned fiber increased from 4% before the 1979 Surgeon General's report to 8.5% in 1984 (after the report but before the All-Bran campaign) to 32% in 1986 after a year and a half or so of health claims (the figure in 1988 was 28%). By far the greatest increases in awareness were among women (who do most of the grocery shopping) and the less educated: up from 0% for women without a high school education in 1984 to 31% for the same group in 1986. For women with incomes of less than $15,000, the increase was from 6% to 28%.

The health-claims advertising phenomenon achieved what years of effort by government agencies had failed to achieve. With its mastery of the art of brevity, its ability to command attention, and its use of television, brand advertising touched precisely the people the public health community was most desperate to reach. The health claims expanded consumer information along a broad front. The benefits clearly extended far beyond the interests of the relatively few manufacturers who made vigorous use of health claims in advertising.

A pervasive phenomenon   Health claims for foods are only one example, however, of a pervasive phenomenon—the use of advertising to provide essential health information with benefits extending beyond the interests of the advertisers themselves.

Advertising for soap and detergents, for example, once improved private hygiene and therefore, public health (hygiene being one of the under-appreciated triumphs in twentieth century public health). Toothpaste advertising helped to do the same for teeth. When mass advertising for toothpaste and tooth powder began early in this century, tooth brushing was rare. It was common by the 1930s, after which toothpaste sales leveled off even though the advertising, of course, continued. When fluoride toothpastes became available, advertising generated interest in better teeth and professional dental care. Later, a "plaque reduction war" (which first involved mouthwashes, and later toothpastes) brought a new awareness of gum disease and how to prevent it. The financial gains to the toothpaste industry were surely dwarfed by the benefits to consumers in the form of fewer cavities and fewer lost teeth.

Health claims induced changes in foods, in non-foods such as toothpaste, in publications ranging from university health letters to mainstream newspapers and magazines, and of course, consumer knowledge of diet and health.

These rippling effects from health claims in ads demonstrated the most basic propositions in the economics of information. Useful information initially failed to reach people who needed it because information producers could not charge a price to cover the costs of creating and disseminating pure information. And this problem was alleviated by advertising, sometimes in a most vivid manner.

Other examples of spillover benefits from advertising are far more common than most people realize. Even the much-maligned promotion of expensive new drugs can bring profound health benefits to patients and families, far exceeding what is actually charged for the products themselves.

The market processes that produce these benefits bear all the classic features of competitive advertising. We are not analyzing public service announcements here, but old-fashioned profit-seeking brand advertising. Sellers focused on the information that favored their own products. They advertised it in ways that provided a close link with their own brand. It was a purely competitive enterprise, and the benefits to consumers arose from the imperatives of the competitive process.

One might see all this as simply an extended example of the economics of information and greed. And indeed it is, if by greed one means the effort to earn a profit by providing what people are willing to pay for, even if what they want most is information rather than a tangible product. The point is that there is overwhelming evidence that unregulated economic forces dictate that much useful information will be provided by brand advertising, and *only* by brand advertising.

Of course, there is much more to the story. There is the question of how competition does the good I have described without doing even more harm elsewhere. After all, firms want to tell people only what is good about their brands, and people often want to know what is wrong with the brands. It turns out that competition takes care of this problem, too.

Advertising and context   It is often said that most advertising does not contain very much information. In a way, this is true. Research on the contents of advertising typically finds just a few pieces of concrete information per ad. That's an average, of course. Some ads obviously contain a great deal of information. Still, a lot of ads are mainly images and pleasant talk, with little in the way of what most people would consider hard information. On the whole, information in advertising comes in tiny bits and pieces.

Cost is only one reason. To be sure, cramming more information into ads is expensive. But more to the point is the fact that advertising plays off the information available from outside sources. Hardly anything about advertising is more important than the interplay between what the ad contains and what surrounds it. Sometimes this interplay is a burden for the advertiser because it is beyond his control. But the interchange between advertising and environment is also an invaluable tool for sellers. Ads that work in collaboration with outside information can communicate far more than they ever could on their own.

The upshot is advertising's astonishing ability to communicate a great deal of information in a few words. Economy and vividness of expression almost always rely upon what is in the information environment. The famously concise "Think Small" and "Lemon" ads for the VW "Beetle" in the 1960s and 1970s were highly effective with buyers concerned about fuel economy, repair costs, and extravagant styling in American cars. This was a case where the less said, the better. The ads were more powerful when consumers were free to bring their own ideas about the issues to bear.

The same process is repeated over again for all sorts of products. Ads for computer modems once explained what they could be used for. Now a simple reference to the Internet is sufficient to conjure an elaborate mix of equipment and applications. These matters are better left vague so each potential customer can bring to the ad his own idea of what the Internet is really for.

Leaning on information from other sources is also a way to enhance credibility, without which advertising must fail. Much of the most important information in advertising—think of cholesterol and heart disease, antilock brakes and automobile safety—acquires its force from highly credible sources *other* than the advertiser. To build up this kind of credibility through material actually contained in ads would be cumbersome and inefficient. Far more effective, and far more economical, is the technique of making challenges, raising questions and otherwise making it perfectly clear to the audience that the seller invites comparisons and welcomes the tough questions. Hence the classic slogan, "If you can find a better whisky, buy it."

Finally, there is the most important point of all. Informational sparseness facilitates competition. It is easier to challenge a competitor through pungent slogans—"Where's the beef?", "Where's the big saving?"—than through a step-by-step recapitulation of what has gone on before. The bits-and-pieces approach makes for quick, unerring attacks and equally quick responses, all under the watchful eye of the consumer over whom the battle is being fought. This is an ideal recipe for competition.

It also brings the competitive market's fabled self-correcting forces into play. Sellers are less likely to stretch the truth, whether it involves prices or subtleties about safety and performance, when they know they may arouse a merciless response from injured competitors. That is one reason the FTC once worked to get comparative ads on television, and has sought for decades to dismantle government or voluntary bans on comparative ads.

'Less-bad' advertising   There is a troubling possibility, however. Is it not possible that in their selective and carefully calculated use of outside information, advertisers have the power to focus consumer attention exclusively on the positive, i.e., on what is good about the brand or even the entire product class? Won't automobile ads talk up style, comfort, and extra safety, while food ads do taste and convenience, cigarette ads do flavor and lifestyle, and airlines do comfort and frequency of departure, all the while leaving consumers to search through other sources to find all the things that are wrong with products?

In fact, this is not at all what happens. Here is why: Everything for sale has something wrong with it, if only the fact that you have to pay for it. Some products, of course, are notable for their faults. The most obvious examples involve tobacco and health, but there are also food and heart disease, drugs and side effects, vacations and bad weather, automobiles and accidents, airlines and delay, among others.

Products and their problems bring into play one of the most important ways in which the competitive market induces sellers to serve the interests of buyers. No matter what the product, there are usually a few brands that are "less bad" than the others. The natural impulse is to advertise that advantage —"less cholesterol," "less fat," "less dangerous," and so on. Such provocative claims tend to have an immediate impact. The targets often retaliate; maybe their brands are less bad in a different respect (less salt?). The ensuing struggle brings better information, more informed choices, and improved products.

Perhaps the most riveting episode of "less-bad" advertising ever seen occurred, amazingly enough, in the industry that most people assume is the master of avoiding saying anything bad about its product.

Less-bad cigarette ads   Cigarette advertising was once very different from what it is today. Cigarettes first became popular around the time of World War I, and they came to dominate the tobacco market in the 1920s. Steady and often dramatic sales increases continued into the 1950s, always with vigorous support from advertising. Tobacco advertising was duly celebrated as an outstanding example of the power and creativity of advertising. Yet amazingly, much of the advertising focused on what was wrong with smoking, rather than what people liked about smoking.

The very first ad for the very first mass-marketed American cigarette brand (Camel, the same brand recently under attack for its use of a cartoon character) said, "Camel Cigarettes will not sting the tongue and will not parch the throat." When Old Gold broke into the market in the mid-1920s, it did so with an ad campaign about coughs and throats and harsh cigarette smoke. It settled on the slogan, "Not a cough in a carload."

Competitors responded in kind. Soon, advertising left no doubt about what was wrong with smoking. Lucky Strike ads said, "No Throat Irritation—No Cough... we... removed... harmful corrosive acids," and later on, "Do you inhale? What's there to be afraid of?... famous purifying process removes certain impurities." Camel's famous tag line, "more doctors smoke Camels than any other brand," carried a punch precisely because many authorities thought smoking was unhealthy (cigarettes were called "coffin nails" back then), and smokers were eager for reassurance in the form of smoking by doctors themselves. This particular ad, which was based on surveys of physicians, ran in one form or another from 1933 to 1955. It achieved prominence partly because physicians practically never endorsed non-therapeutic products.

Things really got interesting in the early 1950s, when the first persuasive medical reports on smoking and lung cancer reached the public. These reports created a phenomenal stir among smokers and the public generally. People who do not understand how advertising works would probably assume that cigarette manufacturers used advertising to divert attention away from the cancer reports. In fact, they did the opposite.

Small brands could not resist the temptation to use advertising to scare smokers into switching brands. They inaugurated several spectacular years of "fear advertising" that sought to gain competitive advantage by exploiting smokers' new fear of cancer. Lorillard, the beleaguered seller of Old Gold, introduced Kent, a new filter brand supported by ad claims like these: "Sensitive smokers get real health protection with new Kent," "Do you love a good smoke but not what the smoke does to you?" and "Takes out more nicotine and tars than any other leading cigarette—*the difference in protection is priceless*," illustrated by television ads showing the black tar trapped by Kent's filters.

Other manufacturers came out with their own filter brands, and raised the stakes with claims like, "Nose, throat, and accessory organs not adversely affected by smoking Chesterfields. First such report ever published about any cigarette," "Takes the fear out of smoking," and "Stop worrying... Philip Morris and only Philip Morris is entirely free of irritation used [sic] in all other leading cigarettes."

These ads threatened to demolish the industry. Cigarette sales plummeted by 3% in 1953 and a remarkable 6% in 1954. Never again, not even in the face of the most impassioned anti-smoking publicity by the Surgeon General or the FDA, would cigarette consumption decline as rapidly as it did during these years of entirely market-driven anti-smoking ad claims by the cigarette industry itself.

Thus advertising traveled full circle. Devised to bolster brands, it denigrated the product so much that overall market demand actually declined. Everyone understood what was happening, but the fear ads continued because they helped the brands that used them. The new filter brands (all from smaller manufacturers) gained a foothold even as their ads amplified the medical reports on the dangers of smoking. It was only after the FTC stopped the fear ads in 1955 (on the grounds that the implied health claims had no proof) that sales resumed their customary annual increases.

Fear advertising has never quite left the tobacco market despite the regulatory straight jacket that governs cigarette advertising. In 1957, when leading cancer experts advised smokers to ingest less tar, the industry responded by cutting tar and citing tar content figures compiled by independent sources. A stunning "tar derby" reduced the tar and nicotine content of cigarettes by 40% in four years, a far more rapid decline than would be achieved by years of government urging in later decades. This episode, too, was halted by the FTC. In February 1960 the FTC engineered a "voluntary" ban on tar and nicotine claims.

Further episodes continue to this day. In 1993, for example, Liggett planned an advertising campaign to emphasize that its Chesterfield brand did not use the stems and less desirable parts of the tobacco plant. This continuing saga, extending through eight decades, is perhaps the best documented case of how "less-bad" advertising completely offsets any desires by sellers to accentuate the positive while ignoring the negative. *Consumer Reports* magazine's 1955 assessment of the new fear of smoking still rings true:

> " . . . companies themselves are largely to blame. Long before the current medical attacks, the companies were building up suspicion in the consumer by the discredited 'health claims' in their ads. . . . Such medicine-show claims may have given the smoker temporary confidence in one brand, but they also implied that cigarettes in general were distasteful, probably harmful, and certainly a 'problem.' When the scientists came along with their charges against cigarettes, the smoker was ready to accept them."

And that is how information works in competitive advertising.

Less-bad can be found wherever competitive advertising is allowed. I already described the health-claims-for-foods saga, which featured fat and cholesterol and the dangers of cancer and heart disease. Price advertising is another example. Prices are the most stubbornly negative product feature of all, because they represent the simple fact that the buyer must give up something else. There is no riper target for comparative advertising. When sellers advertise lower prices, competitors reduce their prices and advertise that, and soon a price war is in the works. This process so strongly favors consumers over the industry that one of the first things competitors do when they form a trade group is to propose an agreement to restrict or ban price advertising (if not ban all advertising). When that fails, they try to get advertising regulators to stop price ads, an attempt that unfortunately often succeeds.

Someone is always trying to scare customers into switching brands out of fear of the product itself. The usual effect is to impress upon consumers what they do not like about the product. In 1991, when Americans were worried about insurance companies going broke, a few insurance firms advertised that they were more solvent than their competitors. In May 1997, United Airlines began a new ad campaign that started out by reminding fliers of all the inconveniences that seem to crop up during air travel.

Health information is a fixture in "less-bad" advertising. Ads for sleeping aids sometimes focus on the issue of whether they are habit-forming. In March 1996, a medical journal reported that the pain reliever acetaminophen, the active ingredient in Tylenol, can cause liver damage in heavy drinkers. This fact immediately became the focus of ads for Advil, a competing product. A public debate ensued, conducted through advertising, talk shows, news reports and pronouncements from medical authorities. The result: consumers learned a lot more than they had known before about the fact that all drugs have side effects. The press noted that this dispute may have helped consumers, but it hurt the pain reliever industry. Similar examples abound.

We have, then, a general rule: sellers will use comparative advertising when permitted to do so, even if it means spreading bad information about a product instead of favorable information. The mechanism usually takes the form of less-bad claims. One can hardly imagine a strategy more likely to give consumers the upper hand in the give and take of the marketplace. Less-bad claims are a primary means by which advertising serves markets and consumers rather than sellers. They completely refute the naive idea that competitive advertising will emphasize only the sellers' virtues while obscuring their problems.

Russ Baker

 **NO**

The Squeeze

> In an effort to avoid potential conflicts, it is required that Chrysler Corporation be alerted in advance of any and all editorial content that encompasses sexual, political, social issues or any editorial that might be construed as provocative or offensive. Each and every issue that carries Chrysler advertising requires a written summary outlining major theme/articles appearing in upcoming issues. These summaries are to be forwarded to PentaCom prior to closing in order to give Chrysler ample time to review and reschedule if desired.... As acknowledgment of this letter we ask that you or a representative from the publication sign below and return to us no later than February 15.
>
> — from a letter sent by Chrysler's ad agency, PentaCom, a division
> of BBDO North America, to at least fifty magazines

Is there any doubt that advertisers mumble and sometimes roar about reporting that can hurt them? That the auto giants don't like pieces that, say, point to auto safety problems? Or that Big Tobacco hates to see its glamorous, cheerful ads juxtaposed with articles mentioning their best customers' grim way of death? When advertisers disapprove of an editorial climate, they can—and sometimes do—take a hike.

But for Chrysler to push beyond its parochial economic interests—by demanding summaries of upcoming articles while implicitly asking editors to think twice about running "sexual, political, social issues"—crosses a sharply defined line. "This is new," says Milton Glaser, the *New York* magazine co-founder and celebrated designer. "It will have a devastating effect on the idea of a free press and of free inquiry."

Glaser is among those in the press who are vocally urging editors and publishers to resist. "If Chrysler achieves this," he says, "there is no reason to hope that other advertisers won't ask for the same privilege. You will have thirty or forty advertisers checking through the pages. They will send notes to publishers. I don't see how any good citizen doesn't rise to this occasion and say this development is un-American and a threat to freedom."

Hyperbole? Maybe not. Just about any editor will tell you: the ad/edit chemistry is changing for the worse. Corporations and their ad agencies have clearly turned up the heat on editors and publishers, and some magazines are

From Russ Baker, "The Squeeze," *Columbia Journalism Review* (September/October 1997). Copyright © 1997 by Russ Baker. Reprinted by permission of *Columbia Journalism Review*.

capitulating, unwilling to risk even a single ad. This makes it tougher for those who do fight to maintain the ad-edit wall and put the interests of their readers first. Consider:

- A major advertiser recently approached all three newsweeklies—*Time, Newsweek,* and *U.S. News*—and told them it would be closely monitoring editorial content. So says a high newsweekly executive who was given the warning (but who would not name the advertiser). For the next quarter, the advertiser warned the magazines' publishing sides it would keep track of how the company's industry was portrayed in news columns. At the end of that period, the advertiser would select one—and only one—of the magazines and award all of its newsweekly advertising to it.

- An auto manufacturer—not Chrysler—decided recently to play art director at a major glossy, and the magazine played along. After the magazine scheduled a photo spread that would feature more bare skin than usual, it engaged in a back-and-forth negotiation with that advertiser over exactly how much skin would be shown. CJR's source says the feature had nothing to do with the advertiser's product.

- Kimberly-Clark makes Huggies diapers and advertises them in a number of magazines, including *Child, American Baby, Parenting, Parents, Baby Talk,* and *Sesame Street Parents.* Kimberly-Clark demands—in writing in its ad insertion orders—that these ads be placed only "adjacent to black and white happy baby editorial," which would definitely not include stories about, say Sudden Infant Death Syndrome or Down's syndrome. "Sometimes we have to create editorial that is satisfactory to them," a top editor says. That, of course, means something else is likely lost, and the mix of the magazine is altered.

- Former Cosmo Girl Helen Gurley Brown disclosed to *Newsday* that a Detroit auto company representative (the paper didn't say which company) asked for—and received—an advance copy of the table of contents for her bon voyage issue, then threatened to pull a whole series of ads unless the representative was permitted to see an article titled "How to Be Very Good in Bed." Result? "A senior editor and the client's ad agency pulled a few things from the piece," a dispirited Brown recalled, "but enough was left" to salvage the article.

Cosmo is hardly the only magazine that has bowed to the new winds. Kurt Andersen, the former *New York* magazine editor—whose 1996 firing by parent company, K-III was widely perceived to be a result of stories that angered associates of K-III's founder, Henry R. Kravis—nonetheless says that he always kept advertisers' sensibilities in mind when editing the magazine. "Because I worked closely and happily with the publisher at *New York*, I was aware who the big advertisers were," he says. "My antennae were turned on, and I read copy thinking, 'Is this going to cause Calvin Klein or Bergdorf big problems?' "

National Review put a reverse spin on the early-warning-for-advertisers discussion recently, as *The Washington Post* revealed, when its advertising director sent an advance copy of a piece about utilities deregulation to an energy supplier mentioned in the story, as a way of luring it into buying space.

And Chrysler is hardly the only company that is aggressive about its editorial environment. Manufacturers of packaged goods, from toothpaste to toilet paper, aggressively declare their love for plain-vanilla. Colgate-Palmolive, for example, won't allow ads in a "media context" containing "offensive" sexual content or material it deems "antisocial or in bad taste"—which it leaves undefined in its policy statement sent to magazines. In the statement, the company says that it "charges its advertising agencies and their media buying services with the responsibility of pre-screening any questionable media content or context."

Procter & Gamble, the second-largest advertising spender last year ($1.5 billion), has a reputation as being very touchy. Two publishing executives told Gloria Steinem, for her book *Moving Beyond Words*, that the company doesn't want its ads near anything about "gun control, abortion, the occult, cults, or the disparagement of religion." Even nonsensational and sober pieces dealing with sex and drugs are no-go.

Kmart and Revlon are among those that editors list as the most demanding. "IBM is a stickler—they don't like any kind of controversial articles," says Robyn Mathews, formerly of *Entertainment Weekly* and now *Time*'s chief of makeup. She negotiates with advertisers about placement, making sure that their products are not put near material that is directly critical. AT&T, Mathews says, is another company that prefers a soft climate. She says she often has to tell advertisers, "We're a *news* magazine. I try to get them to be realistic."

Still, the auto companies apparently lead the pack in complaining about content. And the automakers are so powerful—the Big Three pumped $3.6 billion into U.S. advertising last year—that most major magazines have sales offices in Detroit.

After *The New Yorker*, in its issue of June 12, 1995, ran a Talk of the Town piece that quoted some violent, misogynist rap and rock lyrics—along with illustrative four-letter words—opposite a Mercury ad, Ford Motor Company withdrew from the magazine, reportedly for six months. The author, Ken Auletta, learned about it only this year. "I actually admire *The New Yorker* for not telling me about it," he says. Yet afterwards, according to *The Wall Street Journal*, the magazine quietly adopted a system of warning about fifty companies on a "sensitive advertiser list" whenever potentially offensive articles are scheduled.

It is the Chrysler case, though, that has made the drums beat, partly because of Chrysler's heft and partly because the revelation about the automaker's practice came neatly packaged with a crystalline example of just what that practice can do to a magazine.

In the advertising jungle Chrysler is an 800-pound gorilla—the nation's fourth-largest advertiser and fifth-largest magazine advertiser (it spent some $270 million at more than 100 magazines last year, behind General Motors, Philip Morris, Procter & Gamble, and Ford). Where it leads, other advertisers may be tempted to follow.

The automaker's letter was mailed to magazines in January 1996, but did not come to light until G. Bruce Knecht of *The Wall Street Journal* unearthed it this April in the aftermath of an incident at *Esquire*. The *Journal* reported that *Esquire* had planned a sixteen-page layout for a 20,000-word fiction piece by accomplished author David Leavitt. Already in page proofs and scheduled for the April '97 issue, it was to be one of the longest short stories *Esquire* had ever run, and it had a gay theme and some raw language. But publisher Valerie Salembier, the *Journal* reported, met with then editor-in-chief Edward Kosner and other editors and voiced her concerns: she would have to notify Chrysler about the story, and she expected that when she did so Chrysler would pull its ads. The automaker had bought four pages, the *Journal* noted—just enough to enable the troubled magazine to show its first year-to-year ad-page improvement since the previous September.

◆

Kosner then killed the piece, maintaining he had editorial reasons for doing so. Will Blythe, the magazine's literary editor, promptly quit. "I simply can't stomach the David Leavitt story being pulled," he said in his letter of resignation. "That act signals a terrible narrowing of the field available to strong, adventuresome, risk-taking work, fiction and nonfiction alike. I know that editorial and advertising staffs have battled—sometimes affably, other times savagely—for years to define and protect their respective turfs. But events of the last few weeks signal that the balance is out of whack now—that, in effect, we're taking marching orders (albeit, indirectly) from advertisers."

The Chrysler letter's public exposure is a rough reminder that sometimes the biggest problems are the most clichéd: as financial concerns become increasingly paramount it gets harder to assert editorial independence.

After the article about *Esquire* in the *Journal*, the American Society of Magazine Editors—the top cops of magazine standards, with 867 members from 370 magazines—issued a statement expressing "deep concern" over the trend to give "advertisers advance notice about upcoming stories." Some advertisers, ASME said, "may mistake an early warning as an open invitation to pressure the publisher to alter, or even kill, the article in question. We believe publishers should—and will—refuse to bow to such pressure. Furthermore, we believe editors should—and will—follow ASME's explicit principle of editorial independence, which at its core states: 'The chief editor of any magazine must have final authority over the editorial content, words, and pictures that appear in the publication.' "

On July 24, after meeting with the ASME board, the marketing committee of the Magazine Publishers of America—which has 200 member companies that print more than 800 magazines—gathered to discuss this issue, and agreed to work against prior review of story lists or summaries by advertisers. "The magazine industry is united in this," says ASME's president, Frank Lalli, managing editor of *Money*. "There is no debate within the industry."

How many magazines will reject Chrysler's new road map? Unclear. Lalli says he has not found any publisher or editor who signed and returned the Chrysler letter as demanded. "I've talked to a lot of publishers," he says, "and I don't know of any who will bow to it. The great weight of opinion among publishers and editors is that this is a road we can't go down."

Yet Mike Aberlich, Chrysler's manager of consumer media relations, claims that "Every single one has been signed." Aberlich says that in some cases, individual magazines agreed; in others a parent company signed for all its publications.

CJR did turn up several magazines, mostly in jam-packed demographic niches, whose executives concede they have no problem with the Chrysler letter. One is *Maxim*, a new book aimed at the young-men-with-bucks market put out by the British-based Dennis Publishing. "We're going to play ball," says *Maxim*'s sales manager, Jamie Hooper. The startup, which launched earlier this year, signed and returned the Chrysler letter. "We're complying. We definitely have to."

At *P.O.V.*, a two-and-a-half-year-old magazine backed largely by Freedom Communications, Inc. (owners of *The Orange County Register*) and aimed at a similar audience, publisher Drew Massey says he remembers a Chrysler letter, can't remember signing it, but would have no problem providing advance notice. "We do provide PentaCom with a courtesy call, but we absolutely never change an article." Chrysler, alerted to *P.O.V.*'s August "Vice" issue, decided to stay in. Massey argues that the real issue is not about edgy magazines like *P.O.V.*, but about larger and tamer magazines that feel constrained by advertisers from being adventurous.

Hachette Filipacchi, French-owned publisher of twenty-nine U.S. titles, from *Elle* to *George*, offered Chrysler's plan for a safe editorial environment partial support. Says John Fennell, chief operating officer: "We did respond to the letter, saying we were aware of their concern about controversial material and that we would continue—as we have in the past—to monitor it very closely and to make sure that their advertising did not appear near controversial things. However, we refused to turn over or show or discuss the editorial direction of articles with them."

⋆◈⋆

It has long been a widely accepted practice in the magazine industry to provide "heads-up"—warnings to advertisers about copy that might embarrass them—say, to the friendly skies folks about a scheduled article on an Everglades plane crash, or to Johnnie Walker about a feature on the death of a hard-drinking rock star. In some instances, advertisers are simply moved as far as possible from the potentially disconcerting material. In others, they are offered a chance to opt out of the issue altogether, ideally to be rescheduled for a later edition.

In the 1980s, Japanese car makers got bent out of shape about news articles they saw as Japan-bashing, says *Business Week*'s editor-in-chief, Stephen B. Shepard, a past ASME president. Anything about closed markets or the trade imbalance might be seen as requiring a polite switch to the next issue.

Chrysler, some magazine people argue, is simply formalizing this long-standing advertiser policy of getting magazine executives to consider their special sensitivities while assembling each issue. But Chrysler's letter clearly went beyond that. PentaCom's president and c.e.o., David Martin, was surprisingly blunt when he explained to *The Wall Street Journal* the automaker's rationale: "Our whole contention is that when you are looking at a product that costs $22,000, you want the product to be surrounded by positive things. There's nothing positive about an article about child pornography."

Chrysler spokesman Aberlich insists the brouhaha is no big deal: "Of the thousands of magazine ads we've placed in a year, we've moved an ad out of one issue into the next issue about ten times a year. We haven't stopped dealing with any magazine." He compares placing an ad to buying a house: "You decide the neighborhood you want to be in." That interesting metaphor, owning valuable real estate, leads to other metaphors—advertisers as editorial NIMBYs (Not In My Back Yard) trying to keep out anybody or anything they don't want around.

As for the current contretemps, Aberlich says it's nothing new, that Chrysler has been requesting advance notice since 1993. "We sent an initial letter to magazines asking them to notify us of upcoming controversial stuff —graphic sex, graphic violence, glorification of drug use." But what about the updated and especially chilling language in the 1996 letter, the one asking to look over editors' shoulders at future articles, particularly *political, social* material and *editorial that might be construed as provocative*? Aberlich declines to discuss it, bristling, "We didn't give you that letter."

⋯⊙⋯

How did we get to the point where a sophisticated advertiser dared send such a letter? In these corporate-friendly times, the sweep and powers of advertisers are frenetically expanded everywhere. Formerly pure public television and public radio now run almost-ads. Schools bombard children with cereal commercials in return for the monitors on which the ads appear. Parks blossom with yogurt- and sneaker-sponsored events.

Meanwhile, a growing number of publications compete for ad dollars—not just against each other but against the rest of the media, including news media. Those ads are bought by ever-larger companies and placed by a shrinking number of merger-minded ad agencies.

Are magazines in a position where they cannot afford to alienate any advertiser? No, as a group, magazines have done very well lately, thank you. With only minor dips, ad pages and total advertising dollars have grown impressively for a number of years. General-interest magazines sold $5.3 billion worth of advertising in 1987. By 1996 that figure had more than doubled, to $11.2 billion.

Prosperity can enhance independence. The magazines least susceptible to advertiser pressures are often the most ad-laden books. Under its new editor-in-chief, David Granger, the anemic *Esquire* seems to be getting a lift, but *GQ* had supplanted it in circulation and in the serious-article business, earning many National Magazine Awards. This is in part because it first used advertiser-safe service pieces and celebrity profiles to build ad pages, then had more space to experiment and take risks.

Catherine Viscardi Johnston, senior vice president for group sales and marketing at *GQ*'s parent company, the financially flush Condé Nast, says that in her career as a publisher she rarely was asked to reschedule an ad—perhaps once a year. Meddling has not been a problem, she says: "Never was a page lost, or an account lost. Never, never did an advertiser try to have a story changed or eliminated."

At the other extreme, *Maxim*, which signed the Chrysler letter, does face grueling ad-buck competition. The number of new magazine startups in 1997 may well exceed 1,000, says Samir Husni, the University of Mississippi journalism professor who tracks launches. And *Maxim*'s demographic—21- to 24-year-old males—is jam-packed with titles.

This is not to say that prosperity and virtue go hand in hand. Witness Condé Nast's ad-fat *Architectural Digest*, where editor-in-chief Paige Rense freely admits that only advertisers are mentioned in picture captions. The range of standards among magazines is wide.

And that range can be confusing. "Some advertisers don't understand on a fundamental level the difference between magazines that have a serious set of rules and codes and serious ambitions, and those that don't," says Kurt Andersen. "The same guy at Chrysler is buying ads in *YM* and *The New Yorker*."

If it is up to editors to draw the line, they will have to buck the industry's impulse to draw them even deeper into their magazines' business issues. Hachette Filipacchi's U.S. president and c.e.o., David Pecker, is one who would lower the traditional ad-edit wall. "I actually know editors who met with advertisers and lived to tell about it," he said in a recent speech. Some editors at Hachette—and other news organizations—share in increased profits at their magazines. Thus, to offend an advertiser, it might be argued, would be like volunteering for a pay cut. So be it; intrepid editors must be prepared to take that.

Ironically, in fretting over public sensibilities, advertisers may not be catering to their consumers at all. In a recent study of public opinion regarding television—which is even more dogged by content controversies than magazines—87 percent of respondents said it is appropriate for network programs to deal with sensitive issues and social problems. (The poll was done for ABC, NBC, and CBS by the Roper Starch Worldwide market research firm.) Asked who should "have the most to say about what people see and hear on television," 82 percent replied that it ought to be "individual viewers themselves, by deciding what they will and will not watch." Almost no one—just 9 percent—thought advertisers should be able to shape content by granting or withholding sponsorship. Even PentaCom admitted to the *Journal* that its own focus groups show that Chrysler owners are not bothered by Chrysler ads near controversial articles.

So what's eating these folks? Partially, it may be a cultural phenomenon. Ever since magazines began to attract mass audiences and subsidize subscription rates with advertising, many magazines have chased readers—just as networks chase viewers now—with ever more salacious fare. But corporate executives have often remained among the most conservative of Americans. Nowhere is this truer than in heartland locations like Chrysler's Detroit or Procter & Gamble's Cincinnati.

Ad executives say one factor in the mix is sponsors' fear of activist groups, which campaign against graphic or gay or other kinds of editorial material perceived as "anti-family." Boycotts like the current Southern Baptist campaign against Disney for "anti-family values" may be on the rise, precisely because advertisers do take them seriously. This, despite a lack of evidence that such boycotts do much damage. "Boycotts have no discernible impact on sales. Usually, the public's awareness is so quickly dissipated that it has no impact at all," says Elliot Mincberg, vice-president and general counsel of People For the American Way, a liberal organization that tracks the impact of pressure groups. Why, then, would advertisers bother setting guidelines that satisfy these groups at all? "They're trying to minimize their risk to *zero*," says an incredulous Will Blythe, *Esquire*'s former literary editor.

Yet not every advertiser pines for the bland old days. The hotter the product, it seems, the cooler the heads. The "vice" peddlers (booze & cigarettes), along with some apparel and consumer electronics products, actually like being surrounded by edgy editorial copy—unless their own product is zapped. Party *on*!

Even Chrysler's sensitivities appear to be selective. *Maxim*'s premier issue featured six women chatting provocatively about their sex lives, plus several photos of women in scanty come-hither attire, but Chrysler had no grievances.

⋅⟨⟩⋅

The real danger here is not censorship by advertisers. It is self-censorship by editors. On one level, self-censorship results in omissions, small and large, that delight big advertisers.

Cigarettes are a clear and familiar example. The tobacco companies' hefty advertising in many a magazine seems in inverse proportion to the publication's willingness to criticize it. Over at the American Cancer Society, media director Susan Islam says that women's magazines tend to cover some concerns adequately, but not lung cancer: "Many more women die of lung cancer, yet there have hardly been any articles on it."

To her credit, *Glamour*'s editor-in-chief, Ruth Whitney, is one who has run tobacco stories. She says that her magazine, which carries a lot of tobacco advertising, publishes the results of every major smoking study. But Whitney concedes they are mostly short pieces. "Part of the problem with cigarettes was—we did do features, but there's nobody in this country who doesn't know cigarettes kill." Still, everybody also knows that getting slimmer requires exercise and eating right, which has not prevented women's magazines from running that story in endless permutations. Tobacco is in the news, and magazines have the unique job of deepening and humanizing such stories.

Specific editorial omissions are easier to measure than how a magazine's world view is altered when advertisers' preferences and sensitivities seep into the editing. When editors act like publishers, and vice versa, the reader is out the door.

Can ASME, appreciated among editors for its intentions, fire up the troops? The organization has been effective on another front—against abuses of special advertising sections, when advertisements try to adapt the look and feel of editorial matter. ASME has distributed a set of guidelines about just what constitutes such abuse.

To enforce those guidelines, ASME executive director Marlene Kahan says the organization sends a couple of letters each month to violators. "Most magazines say they will comply," she reports. "If anybody is really egregiously violating the guidelines on a consistent basis, we'd probably sit down and have a meeting with them." ASME can ban a magazine from participating in the National Magazine Awards, but Kahan says the organization has not yet had to do that. In addition, ASME occasionally asks the organization that officially counts magazine ad pages, the Publishers Information Bureau, not to count advertising sections that break the rules as ad pages—a tactic that ASME president Lalli says tends to get publishers' attention.

Not everyone in the industry thinks ASME throws much of a shadow. "ASME can't bite the hand that feeds them," says John Masterton of *Media Industry Newsletter*, which covers the magazine business. During Robert Sam Anson's brief tenure as editor of *Los Angeles* magazine, the business side committed to a fifteen-page supplement, to be written by the editorial side and called "The Mercedes Golf Special." Mercedes didn't promise to take any ads, but it was hoped that the carmaker would think kindly of the magazine for future issues. The section would appear as editorial, listed as such in the table of contents. Anson warned the business side that, in his opinion, the section would contravene ASME guidelines, since it was in effect an ad masquerading as edit. A senior executive told him not to worry—that at the most they'd get a "slap on the wrist." The section did not run in the end, Anson says, because of "deadline production problems."

◦◉◦

The Chrysler model, however—with its demand for early warnings, and its insistence on playing editor—is tougher for ASME to police. Special advertising sections are visible. Killed or altered articles are not. And unless it surfaces, as in the *Esquire* case, self-censorhip is invisible.

One well-known editor, who asks not to be identified, thinks the problem will eventually go away. "It's a self-regulating thing," he says. "At some point, the negative publicity to the advertisers will cause them to back off."

Of course, there is nothing particularly automatic about that. It takes an outspoken journalistic community to generate heat. And such attention could backfire. The *Journal*'s Knecht told the audience of public radio's *On the Media* that his reporting might actually have aggravated the problem: "One of the negative effects is that more advertisers who weren't aware of this system have gone to their advertising agencies and said, 'Hey, why not me too! This sounds like a pretty good deal!'"

Except, of course, that it really isn't. In the long run everybody involved is diminished when editors feel advertisers' breath on their necks. Hovering there, advertisers help create content that eventually bores the customers they seek. Then the editors of those magazines tend to join the ranks of the unemployed. That's just one of the many reasons that editors simply cannot bend to the new pressure. They have to draw the line—subtly or overtly, quietly or loudly, in meetings and in private, and in their own minds.

POSTSCRIPT

Is Advertising Ethical?

Since a number of media technologies have become vehicles for advertising (such as the Internet and even broadcast/cable infomercials), questions about the ethics of advertising have taken yet another turn. In some ways, the current presence of advertising raises questions that are very basic to the phenomenon of advertising. Do the ads we see register on our conscious or subconscious minds? Do ads really make us buy things or think of things in a certain way? Do we perceptually "screen" unwanted information?

In recent years some of the basic questions about ads have shifted because our "use patterns" of media have changed. Today a prime-time network television program has more ad time than ever before. Remote controls allow viewers to "zap" through commercials on tape or change channels when commercials appear. Ads in the form of company logos are displayed on clothing and other personal items, which have, in turn, emphasized brand affiliation and status.

Since the development of the advertising industry, the question of advertising ethics has periodically resurfaced. *The Journal of Advertising Ethics* is a good source to begin investigating what leaders in the industry themselves say about ethical practices, but articles are often tied to specific products or issues. There have been some defenses of the ad industry, such as Yale Brozen's *Advertising and Society* (New York University Press, 1974) and Theodore Levitt's article "The Morality(?) of Advertising," *Harvard Business Review* (July/August 1970).

Stuart Ewen and Elizabeth Ewen's *Channels of Desire: Mass Images and the Shaping of American Consciousness* (McGraw-Hill, 1982) offers the idea that advertising in Western society has had a major influence on public consciousness. Stuart Ewen's more recent book *PR! A Social History of Spin* (Basic Books, 1996) also investigates the origin, effect, and impact of the public relations industry in America.

On the Internet ...

Center for Media and Public Affairs

The site for the Center for Media and Public Affairs (CMPA) offers information about ongoing debates concerning media fairness and impact, with particular attention to political campaigns and political journalism.

http://www.cmpa.com

Poynter Online: Research Center

The Poynter Institute for Media Studies provides extensive links to information and resources on all aspects of media, including political journalism. This is a good general resource with an extensive list of references.

http://www.poynter.org/research/index.htm

Pew Research Center for People and the Press

The purpose of the Pew Research Center for People and the Press Web site is to serve as a forum for ideas on the media and public policy through public opinion research. This site serves as an important information resource for political leaders, journalists, scholars, and public interest organizations.

http://people-press.org

Society of Professional Journalists

The Web site for *The Electronic Journalist*, the online service for the Society of Professional Journalists (SPJ), will lead you to a number of articles on media ethics, accuracy, media leaders, and other topics.

http://www.spj.org

NewsLink

The *American Journalism Review*'s NewsLink Web site provides links to newspapers around the country. You may access regional and national coverage, as well as smaller publications in specific regions. Links to organizations that are concerned with the ethics and quality of media coverage may be found on this site, as well.

http://www.ajr.org

NewspaperLinks

The Newspaper Association of America's NewspaperLinks Web site provides a state-by-state search for newspaper links. International newspaper links as well as college newspaper links can also be found on this site.

http://newspaperlinks.com/home.cfm

PART 3

Media and Politics

*T*he presence of media has changed the relationship between government, politics, and the press. Media have changed democratic practices such as campaigns, voting, and debating. How can we evaluate the performance of the press in these all-important events? What are the principles and practices of campaigns and of the operation of the press? What part do media play in the creation of negativity concerning politics? Are media biased?

- Do the Mass Media Undermine Openness and Accountability in Democracy?

- Is Negative Campaigning Bad for the American Political Process?

- Do the Media Have a Liberal Bias?

ISSUE 8

Do the Mass Media Undermine Openness and Accountability in Democracy?

YES: J. M. Balkin, from "How Mass Media Simulate Political Transparency," *Cultural Values* (1999)

NO: Roger Cotterrell, from "Transparency, Mass Media, Ideology, and Community," *Cultural Values* (1999)

ISSUE SUMMARY

YES: Yale Law School professor J. M. Balkin argues that without media, openness and accountability are impossible in contemporary democracies. However, he also states that television tends to convert political coverage into entertainment. Current focus on the "horse race" aspects of campaigns and personal scandal is detrimental to media's central mission of communicating information, holding officials accountable, and uncovering secrets.

NO: University of London legal theory professor Roger Cotterrell suggests that Balkin's argument implicitly assumes that there is a political reality or "truth," which he argues is illusory. He contends that transparency in media coverage should emphasize breach of trust as the justification for publicizing personal conduct and treat scandal as the public revelation of these breaches of trust.

The issues addressed in these selections are broad. What is the appropriate role of the press in politics? As the founding fathers of America provided in the Bill of Rights, one of the inalienable rights of the citizenry should be the freedom of the press. They intended for the media to have their voice protected by the government so that the public can have access to crucial information pertaining to society.

In reality these freedoms impose a lot of pressure on the media. How deeply do we trust the press to be the watchdog of the government? What is the proper balance between freedom and obligations? If the press polices the government, then who or what polices the press, particularly when the press is part of big business?

What criteria should we use to judge the practices of the media? What should be the standards of media accountability? Denis McQuail, in *Mass Communication Theory*, 3rd ed. (Sage Publications, 1994), offers four central values: freedom, order, diversity, and information quality. Media freedom implies lack of constraint and is usually measured in terms of the degree of control over news content by government or by corporate owners. Editorial freedom from the outside is easier to measure than is the control exerted by managers or editors and in the professional socialization process. Central to freedom are issues of editorial freedom, internal (journalistic) press freedom, and creative freedom. The value of order has sometimes been called the correlational function of media: providing channels for communication by many groups through bringing the country together in times of crisis, and by supporting social and civic order, while also paying attention to the needs and concerns of minorities. Diversity presumes that the more different channels of communication there are, the better. That the information provided should be of high quality seems self-evident and important to creating a society of informed individuals ready to participate in democratic decision making. Central tenets of journalism designed to produce high-quality information are fairness and accuracy, impartiality, and comprehensive and relevant information.

Perhaps there is no more important function of the press than in its contribution to the political process. J. M. Balkin holds the media to very high standards and concludes that they fail to meet these standards. Openness and democratic accountability are political goals that can only be accomplished in today's complex world with mass media coverage. Politicians can undermine this transparency through rhetorical and media manipulation. One way that media cooperates in this charade, maintains Balkin, is by converting political coverage into forms of entertainment for mass consumption. When "entertaining" stories crowd out substantive public issues, both political life and public discourse suffer. Balkin demonstrates the many ways in which media, wittingly and unwittingly, participate in this process.

Roger Cotterrell takes direct aim at the fundamental assertion that media should somehow "transparently" give access to the unvarnished truth of political reality. Instead, he argues, we must see the community nature of the interaction between press and politics, wherein each is required to account for its actions, understandings, and commitments. Such an approach, concludes Cotterrell, legitimizes the coverage of personal conduct or scandal as necessary public revelation of breaches of trust.

J. M. Balkin

 **YES**

How Mass Media Simulate Political Transparency

Introduction

This essay concerns the mass media's contributions to the political values of openness and democratic accountability that go by the name of 'transparency'. In fact, the metaphor of transparency encompasses three separate political virtues, which often work together but are analytically distinct. The first kind of transparency is informational transparency: knowledge about government actors and decisions and access to government information. Informational transparency can be furthered by requiring public statements of the reasons for government action, or requiring disclosure of information the government has collected. A second type of transparency is participatory transparency: the ability to participate in political decisions either through fair representation or direct participation. A third kind of transparency is accountability transparency: the ability to hold government officials accountable—either to the legal system or to public opinion—when they violate the law or when they act in ways that adversely affect people's interests.[1]

In theory, at least, mass media can make the political system more 'transparent' in all three respects: mass media can help people understand the operations of government, participate in political decisions, and hold government officials accountable. In practice, however, its effects are often quite different. In the age of mass media, democratic governments and politicians may find it useful to simulate the political virtues of transparency through rhetorical and media manipulation. This simulated transparency does not serve the underlying political values that motivate the metaphor of transparency. Instead, it is a transparency that obscures and obfuscates, that frustrates accountability and hides important information in a mass of manufactured political realities. It is a form of transparency that is not transparent at all.

Today political transparency is virtually impossible without some form of mass media coverage. However, mass media can frustrate the values of political transparency even while appearing to serve those values. When politicians and political operatives attempt to simulate transparency and appropriate the

From J. M. Balkin, "How Mass Media Simulate Political Transparency," *Cultural Values*, vol. 3, no. 4 (1999). Copyright © 1999 by *Cultural Values*. Reprinted by permission of Taylor & Francis Ltd.

rhetoric of openness and accountability, the mass media does not always counteract the simulation. Indeed, it may actually tend to proliferate it.

People often oppose transparency to secrecy. However, governments and politicians can manipulate the presentation and revelation of information to achieve the same basic goals as a policy of secrecy and obfuscation. There are two basic strategies: divert audience attention, and supplement politics with new realities that crowd out and eventually displace other political realties and political issues. In this way political transparency can be defeated by what appear to be its own mechanisms: proliferating information, holding political officials accountable, and uncovering things that are secret.[2]

Strategies of Simulation

The very metaphor of transparency suggests a medium through which we view things. We want the medium to be transparent to vision so that we can accurately view what is on the other side.[3]

This metaphor assumes:

1. That the medium is conceptually separate from the object on the other side; and
2. That the process of seeing through the medium does not substantially alter the nature of the object viewed.

Both of these assumptions turn out to be false when the medium is television and the object to be viewed is governance. The medium is not conceptually distinct from the operations of governance because governance occurs through using the medium. Moreover, seeing things through the medium of television substantially alters the object being viewed. Indeed, television creates its own political reality: a televised politics and a public sphere of discourse organised around media coverage of politics. This sphere of discourse is self-reflexive and self-reproducing—television coverage of politics is part of politics, and hence media discourse about politics continually supplements and alters the politics that it purports to portray.

How do mass media simulate and subvert political transparency? The basic idea is simple. Sometimes the most effective strategy for hiding something may be to leave it out in the open, and merely alter the context in which people view it. Instead of hiding facts, one should instead seek to change background realities. Large law firms in the United States have long understood this point. When faced with requests for discovery in civil cases, they understand that simply stonewalling to avoid the disclosure of sensitive information is not always the most effective strategy. Instead they can adopt a dual strategy of aggressive overcompliance coupled with strategic manoeuvre. They flood the other side with so much information and so many documents—most of them extraneous —that the other side lacks the time or ability to find the relevant information. At the same time, the law firm can raise continual technical objections to the progress of discovery, without ever ultimately withholding anything.[4]

These tactics are most useful against a weaker, smaller opponent with less information processing and filtering resources. They are designed to demoralise the other side, raise the costs of litigation, and divert time and energy from the most important substantive questions in the lawsuit. In this way one can use the discovery process—which is, after all, designed to achieve a certain kind of informational transparency—to undermine the values of transparency. One can use the form of transparency to achieve substantial obscurity.

This example demonstrates the two basic strategies for simulating transparency: diversion of attention and supplementation of reality. The goal is to consume the opponent's time and attention. Equally important, one tries to shift the ground of battle to issues of information management and technical questions of procedure. In short, one creates a new practical legal reality for the opponent. This new reality competes with and displaces the substantive issues that originally motivated the lawsuit. In other words, the skilfully played discovery battle creates new objects of contention: it produces ever new things to be concerned about, to become angry about, and to fight about.

In the public arena, simulation of transparency also uses diversion and supplementation. But although the public is trying to obtain information, it is not in the same position as a litigant. Politicians and the mass media do not necessarily regard the public as an adversary. Rather politicians seek to shape and benefit from public opinion, and mass media seek to entertain the public and maintain public attention and influence. Nevertheless, in achieving these ends politicians and the media, both collectively and agonistically, divert audience attention and supplement politics with new political realities.

The Special Role of Television

One can well understand why politicians would want to divert attention from information that is detrimental to their interests. But why would the mass media have an interest in simulating transparency? Indeed, the media's interests are quite different than those of politicians. Nevertheless, the media's collective efforts also subvert the political values of transparency, even—and perhaps especially—when media and politicians view each other as adversaries.

Many different kinds of mass media can simulate transparency. But the dominant medium of political communication in our age—and hence the dominant medium of political transparency—is television. To understand how television simulates transparency, we must understand how television shapes what we see through it. When we use television to understand politics, we see things in the way that television allows them to be seen. At the same time, television creates new forms of political reality that exist because they are seen on television.

Television tends to emphasise entertainment value. It subjects culture to a Darwinian process: The less entertaining is weeded out, the more entertaining survives to be broadcast. Hence coverage of public events, politics, and even law must eventually conform to the requirements of 'good television', that is, the kind of television that grabs and keeps viewers' attention by absorbing and entertaining them (Balkin, 1998).[5]

Television encourages coverage that focuses on the personal celebrity of participants and on the sporting elements of political conflict (Fallows, 1996; Postman, 1985). Over time, television coverage of politics tends to focus less on substantive policy issues than on the techniques of securing political advantage and political viability (Fallows, 1996; Bennett, 1996). The question of 'who's winning' and how are they achieving this victory tends to dominate television coverage. In one sense stories about backstage political manoeuvring and spin control offer a kind of transparency, because they purport to give viewers an 'inside' account of the strategic considerations of politicians and public officials. But in another sense they divert attention from substantive policy debates. Given the limited time available for broadcast and the limited attention of audiences, 'inside' stories about strategy and jockeying for political advantage tend to crowd out stories about substantive policy questions.

Moreover, because politicians understand how important mass media have become to retaining power and influencing citizens, television helps create a new reality populated by spin doctors, pollsters, pundits and media consultants. Thus eventually political life begins to conform more closely to the image of politics that television portrays it to be. Television portrays a world of image manipulation and spin control largely devoid of substantive debate or reasoned analysis. Because television is so central to successful mass politics, it eventually helps produce the very elements that it portrays. We might call this a self-fulfilling representation.

Television coverage of law has analogous effects. Television converts law into a form of entertainment suitable for consumption by lay audiences (Postman, 1985). Television has created a world of law-related shows and legal commentators whose basic goal is to describe law in ways that are comprehensible to television audiences and that can hold their attention. This means, among other things, that law must become entertaining (Balkin, 1992). Certain features of law—the thrust and parry of contention in lawsuits and criminal trials—seem tailor made for television coverage. But the image of law that television portrays reshapes the adversary system in television's image. Law-as-entertainment seems to bring the legal system closer to the public, but it actually substitutes a transformed product—televised law. Public imagination about law used to be nourished by television dramas and made-for-TV movies; now it is increasingly shaped by television coverage of legal events themselves which are served up as popular entertainment and displayed through the lens of television commentary (Balkin, 1992).[6]

In a very short time the Internet has become an important medium of political communication that rivals television. The Internet is not yet televisual; it employs mostly text and still pictures. Even so, the Internet has shaped and enhanced the effects of television in three ways. First, the Internet has helped to shorten the news cycle of reporting, in part because stories can be constantly updated on the Internet with relative ease. A shorter news cycle tends to promote more continuous television coverage of news events, especially on cable networks. Second, because the Internet makes mass distribution of information relatively inexpensive, it helps proliferate new kinds of information from new sources—including gossip and second-hand reports—that television can pick up and disseminate, assuming that the information passes muster under existing standards of television journalism. Third, for similar reasons, the Internet makes possible new journalistic sources that compete with television coverage, and new journalistic practices that may occasionally affect the form and content of television coverage and the standards of television journalists. Hence, the Internet can help exacerbate television's tendency to emphasise celebrity, inside strategy and gossip, and television's conversion of law and politics into forms of entertainment, even though the Internet is not yet a fully televisual medium.

Media Events

Media events are familiar methods of manipulating political transparency. Politicians stage events specifically designed to be covered by the mass media. Media events show politicians engaged in the business of governing or carefully deliberating over public policy issues. Another class of media event shows the politician with his or her family, participating in casual activities, or in a seemingly unguarded and intimate moment.[7]

Media events that involve displays of governance are designed to look governmental, and media events involving displays of personal affect are designed to look spontaneous. American politics has employed media events for many years. The Reagan Administration developed them to a high art form.[8] Almost all public presidential appearances now consist in some form of media event, merging the act of governance with media display. The Clinton Administration has used media events to great advantage: As President [Bill] Clinton lost the ability to push large scale reforms through a recalcitrant Congress, he increasingly took to governing through small scale initiatives like encouraging the adoption of school uniforms. These initiatives were announced and touted in a series of media events designed to make his presidency appear active, robust, and engaged with popular sentiments and concerns.[9]

Media events perform a *jujitsu* move on the political values of transparency. The goal of political transparency is to help people watch over the operations of government and the behaviour of government officials. The point of the media event is to encourage watching. The media event is a form of political exhibitionism that simulates effective governance and personal candour.

By demanding our attention, and the attention of the news media, media events appear to offer us substantive information although what they actually offer is largely political image and showmanship. Moreover, by commanding media attention, media events trade on a fundamental difficulty facing all forms of political transparency. This is the problem of audience scarcity.

Most individuals have only limited time and attention to devote to public issues. Political values of transparency do not demand that citizens spend all of their time on public subjects. Rather, they make information available to individuals so that they can use it if they so choose. But when there is too much information, filtering necessarily occurs. This filtering occurs both in terms of what media decide to cover and what individuals decide to watch. Media companies must pick and choose among hundreds of possible subjects to discuss.

Individuals must choose among thousands of hours of potential coverage of public events.

The need for filtering enhances the power of media events. By flooding the media with ready made press releases and staged pageants that function as 'good television', politicians provide media with easily edited programming that can be strung together in televised sequences. Providing media with 'good television' allows politicians to capture more and more of the media's coverage. This diverts media attention from information that might actually be more useful to the political goals of participation, information, and accountability.

Moreover, media events do not simply add new information to the mix; they also drive out other forms of coverage through a sort of Gresham's law of mass media. The media event is deliberately designed to be a watchable, ready-made form of political entertainment, one that can be easily chopped up and edited for news broadcasts. It is relatively cheap to cover, and easy to broadcast. News organisations quickly learn that it takes less effort to accept what is given them by politicians than to develop entertaining news programming on their own.[10]

For these reasons media events can affect the behaviour of news organisations that are fully aware of their simulated character. Well-planned media events can displace other forms of reporting that take greater time and effort to produce. By thrusting entertainment in our face, politicians effectively keep us from watching other things. And because politicians, and especially presidents, increasingly govern through media events, news organisations feel an obligation to cover them. Media events, in short, both divert political attention and supplement political reality.

The Public and the Private

Many people have noted and decried the mass media's increasing intrusion into the private lives of public figures. Although coverage of entertainers' and sports figures' private lives has been common for many years, the phenomenon has clearly invaded political life as well. The Clinton scandals have made possible discussion of private sexual conduct in the mainstream press that would have been unthinkable only a few years before.[11]

Media coverage of the private lives of public figures is actually a form of informational transparency, although not necessarily one that serves democratic values. Increasingly the mass media have endeavoured to make the private lives of public figures transparent to the ordinary viewer. For many people this evolution of journalistic standards is a travesty, because it diverts attention from 'public' issues. But as noted before, increasing intrusion into private lives does not merely divert attention—it also helps create and supplement public discourse; it fosters new political realities that cannot easily be avoided.... Repeated focus on the 'private' eventually alters the boundaries between public and private; it changes the nature of what is appropriately withheld from public scrutiny. Revelations of the previously 'private' also alter the meaning of 'public discourse' or 'public issues'. The very pervasiveness and availability of information (or rumours) about the private lives of public officials reinforces the idea that such private behaviour is not wholly private—that it raises public issues about which the public should be concerned. . . .

Many journalists defend their evolving practices using language that sounds very much like a defence of political transparency: The public, they argue, has a right to know. Moreover, although some revelations may ultimately prove immaterial to political issues, journalists should place all potentially relevant information before the public and let the public choose whether it is relevant to democratic decision making.[12] This rhetoric has three effects.

First, it equates public knowledge about (for example) the President's sexual habits with public knowledge about the details of foreign or domestic policy, and with information that government collects on private citizens through surveillance.

Second, by making these new forms of knowledge part of democratic decision-making, journalists change the contours of public discourse and the definition of a 'public issue'. Journalists do not simply respect the existing boundaries of the public and the private but actively reshape them. Merely by talking about sexual scandal and encouraging others to do so, journalists make these topics part of public discourse and public comment.

Third, by adding formerly excised information about sexual conduct to public discourse, journalists inevitably create competition for public attention between stories about politicians' private lives and stories about other aspects of public concern, for example, the details of public policy debates. In this competition, stories about sexual and personal matters are likely to grab a greater share of attention. By adding sexual scandal to the mix of competing stories, journalists change the odds that other forms of information will survive the inevitable filtering that occurs when information is too plentiful. It is somewhat like introducing a particularly virulent weed into a flower garden: one should not be surprised if the weed monopolises increasing amounts of space while less hardy plants are choked off.

This effect occurs even if the public does not think that 'private' or sexual matters are appropriate to judging the performance of public officials. For what draws audience attention is not what the public regards as relevant to public policy but what it regards as entertaining. For example, polls have repeatedly suggested that most Americans do not think President Clinton's alleged peccadillos undermine their confidence in his performance as president, although they have undermined their respect for him.[13] Nevertheless, the details of the Lewinsky scandal formed continuous fodder for talk shows, and for months consumed a considerable portion of nightly news broadcasts. Reports about scandal grab attention even if the scandal itself is considered irrelevant to public policy by the very public that watches the reports. As a result, the purported expansion of information in the name of 'the public's right to know' is effectively a contraction of public discourse, because audience time is limited. Through a Darwinian mechanism, information about sexual scandal proliferates and drives out information that constitutes or could potentially constitute other elements of public discourse.

The very question of what is appropriately a 'public issue' or an 'appropriate' story to broadcast is not based on a fixed set of standards. Rather, it is the product of the joint activities of all who call themselves journalists, and depends on their existing professional standards and their expectations about likely public reaction to their reports. Because each journalist has the potential ability to alter the mix of stories competing in the public sphere, journalists as a whole face a collective action problem in maintaining the boundaries of what is public and what is private. If one journalist changes the contours of the public through a series of revelations, other journalists may feel compelled to follow along. Journalists may feel duty bound to report whatever is in fact in the public sphere of discussion. Once one journalist has broken a story, it has been inserted into the public arena, thus lessening the sense of responsibility felt by other journalists.[14] Moreover, once a story has been inserted into public discussion, the incentives of media actors follow a familiar logic: Because journalists believe that certain kinds of stories are more likely to gain valuable and limited audience attention than others, they must respond when other journalists produce stories likely to garner the lion's share of attention because of their salacious or dramatic elements. The result is a self-amplifying focus or a 'feeding frenzy' around certain topics (Sabato, 1991).

It is important to recognise that this effect can occur even though all journalists do not share the same standards of what is newsworthy. It can occur even though mainstream or high prestige journalists usually demand more corroboration or more reliable sources than other journalists before they will publish a story. For example, journalists in traditional metropolitan dailies take great pains to distinguish their standards and practices from those of Matt Drudge's Drudge Report. Drudge's Internet-based column regularly acts as a foil to the journalistic standards of the mainstream media. However, once a journalist like Drudge publishes a story, this sends a few journalists scurrying to confirm it. If they cannot confirm it according to their higher standards, the story does not spread to more mainstream outlets. However, once there is confirming evidence —as judged by the standards of a given group of professional journalists—there is pressure on those journalists to repeat the substance of the story. Eventually this creates a sort of cascade effect. This cascade occurs even if there are different groups of journalists with different standards of verification. And once a story breaks through a certain level of 'mainstream' journalistic judgement, it is very difficult to stop the story.[15]

Fourth, by arguing that the public has a right to know about 'private' issues, journalists can present themselves as more devoted to transparency than journalists of the past. While journalists previously would have killed stories about private sexual behaviour, contemporary journalists can claim that they are offering a freer, more open form of public debate in which they no longer play the role of paternalistic gatekeepers. Some journalists can even convince themselves that they are empowering the public through these revelations. But instead of empowering their audiences or increasing information, journalists may in fact simply be altering the mix of stories presented to the public; the practical effect may be a contraction of the scope of public discourse.

However, we should not lay blame for these changes entirely at the feet of journalists and media executives. In fact, politicians themselves have contributed to the gradual change in the contours of public discussion. Politicians, like other public figures, have discovered over time that in a world shaped by television, it is increasingly important to communicate not only information but also ethos. Public figures hope to persuade and possibly manipulate their audiences by presenting themselves as likeable or down-to-earth characters that a television audience can relate to. Using television to humanise public figures is related to the rise of media events as a form of governance.

By displaying their personalities for consumption by television audiences, public figures simulate yet another form of transparency—the transparency of ethos. The television audience gains access to what the public figure is 'really' like 'up close and personal'. Celebrities and public figures who appear regularly on television try to garner high popularity ratings by appearing close to their viewers. In this respect television differs somewhat from motion pictures; movie actors may deliberately attempt to establish aloofness or distance from their fans. Fans of television actors, on the other hand, often think themselves closer to the actors as people.

Politicians have learned that the appearance of intimacy or the production of an attractive ethos on television is very helpful to political success. As a result, many public figures have attempted to project as far as possible a personable, warm, or approachable image appropriate for television. Public figures who appear distant, cold, or uncaring on television generally succeed in spite of their appearance.

In order to simulate a transparency of ethos, politicians and public figures have been collapsing the distance between the public figure and his or her private persona for some time. They have attempted to connect with viewers and voters by emphasising their emotional availability, friendliness, and closeness to voters in ways dictated by the medium of television. Successful politicians have always run on character issues and emphasised their own good character. But television culture gradually changes the sort of character the successful politician must portray. To succeed as a television personality, politicians have tended to emphasise elements of their persona that might otherwise be thought 'private'; they have shown more and more of their (seemingly) 'private' sides to the public. They show themselves to be 'family people'. They engage in confessional displays, revealing private features of their past, their family's past, or their family's current difficulties. They provide seemingly unguarded moments of revelation and deep connection to the voters. They emote on cue in public. To a large extent this presentation of the private side of a politician's life is a fabrication—it is the work of publicity agents and campaign staffs. Nevertheless, politicians persist in it because it works well in terms of the dominant medium of political communication—television.

But this simulated transparency comes at a cost. Simulating a transparent ethos for television necessarily reconfigures the boundaries between publicity and privacy. The more politicians attempt to use television as a means of establishing closeness to their constituents, the more they erase the boundaries between the public official and what they promote as his or her private persona. The exhibition of a private persona for public consumption invites the public to expect that elements of the private appropriately merge with a politician's public persona and hence are appropriate subjects of public discussion. Politicians have manipulated television imagery for so long that they have helped to create the very erasure of public and private persona that now haunts them.[16] They have been willing accomplices in the creation of a new political culture that sees private aspects of a person's life as politically relevant, that collapses older boundaries between public and private. The [recent] wave of media propagated scandals in the United States is the price we are currently paying for the construction of a simulated transparency between governments and the governed.[17]

Conclusion

To some extent the phenomena I have described in this essay are simply the by-products and imperfections of a normally functioning democratic system. Taken to an extreme, however, they can prove troublesome. My sense is that the Clinton/Lewinsky scandal[, for example]—which produced the first presidential impeachment in over a century—is a pathological tendency rather than an instance of democratic politics as usual. There may be little that can be done at this point to remedy the damage this particular scandal . . . created. But we can well ask what we should do for the future.

The most direct approach, in the form of censorship or regulations on political speech, is surely unconstitutional, and is destined in any case to fail. Instead of attempting to block these tendencies, one must rather supplement them with healthier ones. The public must demand a more diverse coverage and news organisations must provide it. But the problem lies not so much in failure of will as in the structure of news creation and dissemination. In the same way that stock markets have rules to prevent avalanches of panic selling, news organisations should consider creating structural methods of diversifying their coverage even in times of intense political and cultural scandal. These structural provisions cannot be the product of government fiat but rather must come from within media organisations themselves. In the United States, at any rate, government's role must be limited to supplementing existing broadcasting with more balanced fare.

One might object that news organisations cover media events, politicians and scandals in the way that they do because they are behaving rationally given the incentives to increase or maintain audience share. That may be true, but one can also say that sellers in a market panic are also behaving rationally given what other people are doing. Rational behaviour occurs against a background of incentives produced by structures. Our goal should be to understand how existing structures operate and to change them for the better.

Notes

1. This accountability can be direct accountability (for example, the ability to sue), indirect accountability (holding officials accountability to one's agents or elected representatives) or accountability to some other body that acts in the public interest, like a court of law.

2. Jean Baudrillard (1994) is famous for his emphasis on the emergence of 'simulacra' —signs which constitute their own reality. He describes a historical progression in which images first depict reality, then distort it, then hide the fact that the reality they depict is missing, and finally produce their own 'hyperreality'. In this progression, 'simulations' begin as false representations of reality; they end as the basic building blocks of a hyperreality. My concern in this essay is somewhat different from Baudrillard's and I do not adopt his language of 'simulations' versus 'simulacra'. I am particularly interested in the ways that mass media can divert audience attention and supplement political reality. The example of law firm discovery practices offered in the next section of text suggests that diversion of attention and supplementation of reality are old stratagems that can arise without mass media. Indeed, these techniques are ancient military stratagems described in Sun Tzu's famous treatise *The Art of War* (1991). For this reason, I would not describe diversion and supplementation as creating a new hyperreality. Nevertheless, I do agree with Baudrillard (and with McLuhan, for that matter) that the rise of mass media (and particularly televisual mass media) has important effects on our sense of what is important in life as well as what is real.

3. In the case of transparency of participation or accountability, we want to make the medium 'transparent' to political will so that what is on the other side of the medium will respond efficaciously to assertions of political will.

4. See Hare (1994, p. 47), noting attempts to subvert meaningful discovery by responding to specific inquiries with volumes of documents, undifferentiated as to subject matter.; Dombroff (1984; 1988 Supp., p. 35); T. N. Tanke Corp. v. Marine Midland Mortgage Corp., 136 F. R. D. 449, 456 (W. D. N. C. 1991) (ordering documents to be produced in a manner clearly indicating which documents respond directly to plaintiff's request); Holben v. Coopervision, Inc., 120 F. R. D. 32 (E. D. Pa. 1988) (finding response to interrogatories seeking information concerning test results was improper where defendant unloaded information in bulk).

5. This is not a claim of technological determinism. What we call the medium of television involves not only electronic systems of delivery but social relations: the economics and culture of television production. The definition of 'good television' has changed over the years, and continues to evolve. Nevertheless, it has tended to evolve in the way I have described.

6. Broadcast of legislative and court proceedings offer yet another example of how transparency can be simulated. C-SPAN and C-SPAN2 cover only hearings and debates; they do not show the actual places where most public policy decisions are made. Moreover, there are strict limits on where the cameras can be aimed, so that the audience does not know whether a Senator or congressman is speaking to a full audience or an empty house, or whether the person sitting five feet away from the speaker is listening attentively, is sleeping through the eloquent appeal or has collapsed in a drunken stupor. On C-Span's coverage and camera restrictions, see Sharkey (1996); Grimes (1995); Anon. (1995).

7. Members of the candidates' family can serve as props in these pageants. A well-known example is the news coverage of President Clinton dancing with his wife Hillary in a seemingly unguarded moment during a vacation in the Virgin Islands. The photographs seemed to reveal a moment of unrehearsed marital harmony in the midst of the President's troubles in the Paula Jones lawsuit and the Monica Lewinsky investigation, but some have speculated that the private moment was planned for public consumption (Smith 1988). See also Harris (1998), speculating on the status of the Clinton marriage after the President and First Lady are seen dancing closely at a state dinner for Vaclav Havel.

8. See Hertsgaard (1988, pp. 6, 52–53, 341), describing the Reagan Administration's institutionalisation of the practice of presenting the media with pre-packaged news stories.

9. Note that media events are normally staged by people at the top of the political hierarchy rather than by subordinates whose decisions may actually have more direct effects on individuals. One does not expect motor vehicle department workers, welfare caseworkers, probation officers, or other members of the bureaucracy to engage in media events on a regular basis.

10. See Fallows (1996, pp. 146-7), arguing that journalists tend to rely on accessible, familiar sources of information; Behr and Iyengar (1993, pp. 222-6), describing how politicians set agendas for journalists.

11. See. e.g., Baker (1998) ('pornographic reporting'); Goodman (1998) (describing coverage of the Lewinsky scandal as 'unusually salacious.'); Gumbel (1998) (American political commentators and comedians have made sexually explicit references that would have been unthinkable prior to the scandal); Gurdon (1998) (documenting media's practice, as a result of the Lewinsky coverage, of attaching warnings to their broadcasts to alert viewers unaccustomed to torrents of sexually explicit reporting).

12. See, e.g. Overholser (1998); Newport (1998) (Lewinsky scandal has resulted in press practice of releasing unfettered information to the public).

13. See, e.g., Burke (1998) (citing a *New York Times*/CBS poll documenting that the public's view of the President's moral character has sunk to its lowest level, but that most Americans still believe Clinton to be a vigorous leader); Anon. (1998) (citing a CBS survey recording Clinton's approval rating at 67%, despite the fact that most Americans claimed to respect the President less as a person). Indeed, the release of the videotape of President Clinton's grand jury testimony on September 21, 1998 actually resulted in a temporary increase in his overall approval ratings (Connelly 1998; Baer 1998; Lawrence 1998).

14. See Williams (1998) (crediting the Drudge report with producing an unedited flood of Lewinsky scandal coverage); Noah (1998) (arguing that the Drudge Report, by 'scooping' the mainstream media, escalated the intensity and explicitness of the Lewinsky coverage).

15. Thus, the question is not whether journalists will publish unconfirmed stories about private sexual behaviour because someone else who lacks their investigatory standards publishes these stories. The question is whether journalists will publish 'private' information, which is believed to be true by their existing journalistic conventions of investigation after someone else has published it. Once that happens, there are very strong pressures to disseminate it.

16. This applies, with some modifications, to the British Royal Family and its current problems. Beginning in the 1950's Queen Elizabeth II attempted to use television as a device to modernise the monarchy by portraying the British royal family as a model family that Britons could relate to. The result of this campaign over the years was to make the British monarchy more human, and thus more 'transparent' to the public. However, the campaign had an unintended side effect—it turned the royal family into television characters and television celebrities. Princess Diana was the most obvious example of this tendency. The problem with making British Royalty into television celebrities was that it also increased the public's and the media's sense of entitlement to know about the details of their private lives. Formerly the British Royals were wrapped around a veil of secrecy that supported the public's image of them as role models and icons of respectability. But under the glare of publicity, they were revealed to be just as dysfunctional—if not more so—than the average British family. Their image and the British public's confidence in them have suffered as a result. See, e.g., Anon. (1997) (describing coverage of the death of Princess Diana in context of the historical evolution of the cult of celebrity surrounding the British royal family); Judd (1994) (noting that after many years of pretending to be the ideal family, the British royal family

has been revealed to be dysfunctional); Zweininiger-Bargielowska (1993) (comparing the lurid press coverage of today with high hopes held for the British Royal family in the 1950s); Hoggart (1987) (describing how media coverage has revealed unpleasant facts about the royal family).

17. Bill Clinton, for example, won two presidential elections by consistently making voters feel that he personally cared about them. Indeed, one of the clichés most often used to describe President Clinton's personal style is his famous remark delivered in the 1992 campaign that 'I feel your pain'. Clinton has proven himself a master at pushing himself—his emotions, his desires, his empathy, his appetites, even his moments of personal pain—at the American public. Clinton is the master emotional exhibitionist, which is why he is also one of the most effective politicians of his time. Nevertheless, he who lives by ethos shall die by ethos. It is no accident that accusations of bad character have continuously swirled around President Clinton. His political style—which is also his personal style—actively invites discussion of his character because so much of his appeal comes from his personality and his apparent emotional closeness to the voting public.

References

Anon. 1998: Dow Rises on Poll Support for Clinton, *Financial Times* (London), September 15, p. 52.

Anon. 1997: The Modernizer. *New Statesman*, September 5, p. 5.

Anon. 1995: Better TV on Capitol Hill. *Boston Herald*, January 4, p. 22.

Baer, Susan 1998: New Attack Launched on Starr. *Baltimore Sun*, September 23, p. 1A.

Baker, Russell 1998: The Great Media Meltdown. *New York Times*, September 19, p. A15.

Balkin, J.M. 1998: *Cultural Software: A Theory of Ideology*. New Haven, CT: Yale University Press.

Balkin, J.M. 1992: What is a Postmodern Constitutionalism? *Michigan L. Rev.* 92: 1966.

Baudrillard, Jean 1994: *Simulacra and Simulation*. Sheila Faria Glaser, trans. Ann Arbor, MI: University of Michigan Press.

Behr, Roy and Iyengar, Shanto 1993: The Media: American Politics in the Television Age. New York: Macmillan.

Bennett, W. Lance 1996: News: *The Politics of Illusion*. New York: Longman.

Biddle, Frederick 1995: Is ABC's Image Going-up in Smoke? *Boston Globe*, August 23, p. 56.

Burke, Richard L. 1998: The Testing of a President. *New York Times*, September 16, p. A24.

Connelly, Marjorie 1998: The Testing of a President. *New York Times*, September 23, p. A24.

Dombroff, Mark A. 1984 & 1988 Supp.: *Dombroff on Unfair Tactics* §1.19.

Fallows, James 1996: *Breaking the News*. New York: Pantheon Books.

Gitlin, Josh 1998: Press Report Coverage on Scandal is Hardly Honor-Roll Caliber. *Los Angeles Times*, October 22, p. A5.

Goodman, Ellen 1998: At Last, A Sex Scandal Without a Gender Gap. *Boston Globe*, September 20, p. F7.

Grimes, Charlotte 1995: In Congress, Viewers Get Big Picture. *Washington Post*, March 30, p. 5B.

Gumbel, Andrew 1998: Clinton Crisis. *Independent* (London), September 15, p. 4.

Gurdon, Hugo 1998: TV Viewers Warned in Advance. Daily Telegraph (London), September 14, p. 2.

Hare, Francis H. et. al., 1994: *Full Disclosure: Combating Stonewalling and Other Discovery Abuses*. Washington, D.C.: Alta Press.

Harris, John 1998: A Definite Focus on Public Policy. *Washington Post*, September 18, p. A20.

Hertsgaard, Mark 1988: *On Bended Knee*. New York: Farrar, Strauss, Giroux.

Hoggart, Simon 1987: The Big Bang: The Press and the British Royal Family. *New Republic*, November 23.

Holben v. Coopervision, Inc., 120 F.R.D. 32 (E.D. Pa. 1988).

Judd, Denis 1994: Royally Screwed. *New Statesman and Society*, October 23, p. 16.

Kurtz, Howard 1998: Report Faults Lewinsky Coverage. *Washington Post*, October 21, p. D1.

Kurtz, Howard 1996: Ted Koppel: Firmly Anchored. *Washington Post*, May 28, p. B1.

Lawrence, J.M. 1998: Political Experts: Dirt Likely to Reflect Badly on Congress. *Boston Herald*, October 3.

Newport, Frank 1998: A Matter of Trust. *American Journalism Review*, July, p. 30.

Noah, Timothy 1998: The Media's Struggle Against Sex Addiction. *New Republic*, February 23, p. 15.

Overholser, Geneva 1998: Pushing the Limits. *Washington Post*, October 10, p. 23A.

Postman, Neil 1985: *Amusing Ourselves to Death*. New York: Penguin Books.

Quindlen, Anna 1994: Talking About the Media Circus. *New York Times*, June 26, at p. A28.

Sabato, Larry J. 1991: *Feeding Frenzy: How Attack Journalism has Transformed American Politics*. New York: Macmillan.

Sharkey, Joe 1996: Full Senate Session on Cable. *New York Times*, January 1, p. B1.

Smith, Liz 1998: Those Hillary Pix. *Newsday*, January 16, p. A15.

Snoddy, Raymond 1998: Making the Media Squirm. *The Times* (London), August 21, features section.

Sun Tzu 1991: *The Art of War*. Thomas Cleary, trans. New York and London: Shambala.

T.N. Tanke Corp. v. Marine Midland Mortgage Corp., 136 F.R.D. 449 (W.D.N.C. 1991).

Williams, Margot 1998: For the Unsatiated, Sites for Clinton-Lewinsky News. *Washington Post*, August 17, p. F23.

Zweininiger-Bargielowska, Ina 1993: Royal Rations. *History Today*, December, p. 13.

Roger Cotterrell

 **NO**

Transparency, Mass Media, Ideology, and Community

In his paper... Jack Balkin (1999) examines how 'mass media *simulate* political transparency' (my emphasis). Use of the word 'simulate' here is, I want to argue, both revealing and problematic. To simulate something is to offer not the real thing, whatever that might be, but something that mimics the real. It is to hold up an illusion. What is simulated by the media, according to Balkin, is 'transparency', and transparency is the availability of information on matters of public concern, the ability of citizens to participate in political decisions, and the accountability of government to public opinion or legal processes. But he claims that what we sometimes mistake as transparency in political processes or public events is actually something wholly different. It is an *absence* of relevant knowledge of political and public affairs, of participation and accountability; an absence *disguised* by an overload of information on politically irrelevant or unenlightening matters. In particular, mass media produce and use information to *divert attention* from important matters, to change or confuse the meanings of events, to turn public concerns into matters of entertainment. Far from focusing on matters of public interest in a way that respects that public interest, they increasingly blur the public-private line. They intrude into the private lives of public figures, pleading the public's 'right to know'. The result is 'a simulated transparency between governments and the governed'.

I

Much of what Balkin writes about the nature and importance of media practices in shaping perceptions of politics and influencing the character of political debate is insightful and important. But I think that the idea of simulated transparency is ultimately unhelpful. It suggests that we can recognise what a real, non-simulated transparency would be. More specifically it suggests that we know what true or substantive political issues are as opposed to 'manufactured political realities' (his term). Because simulated transparency 'obscures and obfuscates', there must be, Balkin implies, a real politics, if we could find

From Roger Cotterrell, "Transparency, Mass Media, Ideology, and Community," *Cultural Values*, vol. 3, no. 4 (1999). Copyright © 1999 by *Cultural Values*. Reprinted by permission of Taylor & Francis Ltd.

it, that would not be obscured or obfuscated. This seems to me to be highly problematic.

Balkin's initial clarification of the concept of transparency is useful and careful. He makes clear that transparency is not just a matter of the availability of knowledge, but also of various kinds of participation and accountability. It could be all or some of these, depending on circumstances. But after this clarification at the beginning of his paper little more is said about the kind of knowledge that contributes to transparency (though much is said about types of information which he sees as not contributing to it), or what kinds of participation and accountability contribute to transparency. The assumption seems to be that the criteria of publicly valuable knowledge, participation and accountability in this context can be assumed. Secondly, although participation and accountability are important aspects of transparency in Balkin's conception, it is significant that as his paper progresses most attention is given to the information-knowledge aspect of transparency. The focus is very much on the way that media agendas and practices shape the kinds of information presented and the ways in which this presentation occurs.

The effect of this approach is frequently to imply that transparency requires certain kinds of knowledge or information that could, as he puts it, '... bring us closer to understanding the workings of government' (p. 404), and that what these kinds of information are is not in issue. In any case the media do not supply them. The kinds of media information received by the public often amount to 'obfuscation' and 'obscurity'. They 'divert' attention and 'supplement' politics. Media practices may involve 'manipulating' transparency and 'driving out' information. It is not clear what exactly is being obscured, supplemented, manipulated, obscured or driven out. But 'political image and showmanship' tend to take the place of 'substantive information'. The culture of scandal not only 'disguises political life' but 'fosters it, multiplies it, mutates it, supplements and eventually substitutes for it'.

I think that there is something reminiscent here of an old distinction between true and false consciousness which bedevilled theories of ideology, and which in other writings Balkin has been anxious to avoid (see especially, Balkin 1998, pp. 116–8, 122, 126). In his paper on transparency he does not refer to ideology at all. But he refers, throughout, to processes that somehow cloud, transform or supplement the real with the simulated and manufactured (so creating new realities). In Marxist-oriented literature on ideology the production and maintenance of false consciousness was usually seen as obscuring 'true' consciousness. For Balkin it seems that there is a true or real politics (or at least a shared ideal of such a politics) which gets distorted, obscured and ultimately abolished by the false political messages of the media and its 'manufactured political realities'. His focus on the mass media, as a major instrument of this, even recalls to some extent (especially when he refers to governance through media) Louis Althusser's once celebrated thesis about 'state apparatuses' that sustain ideology (Althusser, 1984). The comparison can be taken far enough to suggest that Balkin, like Althusser before him, is fundamentally concerned with apparatuses (such as mass media) that help to represent to individuals an imaginary relationship to their (political) conditions of existence, and so contribute towards defining their social identity in certain respects.[1]

The concept of ideology is useful in making sense of the mechanisms or practices Balkin describes (Cotterrell, 1995, chap. 12). But to write, as he does, about mechanisms of diversion, distortion, substitution and simulation in media practice suggests we know or agree about what 'real' transparency would be, what attention 'really' should be fixed on, or what an 'undistorted' politics might be and how it could be recognised. In other words, it suggests that we have some idea of what a true (or at least truer) representation of politics might require and how the media falsify this truth. But theorists of ideology never showed how true consciousness, undistorted by false consciousness, was to be identified.[2] Similarly, it is not possible to say what 'real' as opposed to 'simulated' political transparency is. For example, Balkin suggests that the 'Clinton/ Lewinsky scandal' is '... a pathological tendency rather than an instance of democratic politics as usual' (p. 407), but he admits that this is only his *sense* of the matter. How is pathology to be identified? Thus, we need conceptions that do not set up impossible (even if implicit) confrontations between true and false politics, or real and simulated transparency. The complex processes of knowledge transmission need to be understood non-judgementally. Then it may become possible to treat transparency not as an ideal betrayed by reality, but as a process operating differently in different contexts.

There may be some warrant for saying that the cause of Balkin's conceptual difficulties in his paper on simulated transparency arises from his having side-stepped the true-false dichotomy without confronting it. In other writings he has made much use of the concept of ideology, treating it as an inevitable medium in which individuals understand and evaluate the world around them and their identity within it (Balkin, 1991, pp. 1151–3; and generally, Balkin, 1998). He firmly denies that ideology is *necessarily* false consciousness, because ideologies are sometimes liberating, progressive or empowering (see, e.g., 1991, p. 1138; 1998, pp. 126, 272, 273); in any event we cannot avoid ideological thought (1998, p. 128). The implication, therefore, is that ideology is not false, distorting or obscuring when ideological systems of thought bring us closer to some real understanding or progress or the means of reaching it. In other circumstances it can be. So the real-false opposition lurks behind the analysis.[3] In my view, however, we should adopt a view of ideology that discards this problematic opposition.

II

How can this be done? In the context of the mass media's production of news or information, ideological communication might be thought of as the conveying of an impression or message that what we watch, hear, read or understand is complete, a *totality of understanding* in relation to the matter concerned, the 'whole picture' or 'whole story'. The opposite of ideological communication in this context is the conveying of an impression or message that there is always more to be said or known, the story is incomplete, there is always another viewpoint, the facts are inevitably not fully in, final judgement cannot be made (even though provisional judgements must be), what is available is not 'the truth' but plausible accounts, and information and interpretations presently available are fated for revision and possible contradiction. Seen in this way the true-false opposition disappears from the concept of ideology. Ideological accounts are partial rather than false. Their ideological character lies precisely in their denial of their partiality. They mislead by proclaiming, as true and complete, information or ideas that are not necessarily false, but necessarily partial and incomplete. They appear to present the truth of the matter when they offer a selection of facts and a range of opinion. What is misleading or distorting in ideology, therefore, is the illusion created that all knowledge on a particular matter is available and being presented; that there is nothing more of fundamental significance to know.[4]

It is easy to see why mass media tend to produce accounts that are ideological in this sense. The illusion of completeness is much valued. People seek shortcuts towards apparently complete (that is, adequate for practical purposes) knowledge. The 'one-stop' information source that summarises many others is a feature of a contemporary world with too much information to digest. It is useful to the extent that the user can assume that nothing of importance is lost by not referring to the sources summarised. Matters of selection and interpretation of knowledge must be ignored to make this assumption. The selling of knowledge, as news or other information, is most effectively done the more that knowledge can be assimilated to a commodity. And this depends on specific items of knowledge being seen as reliable, objective and complete; packaged commodities. The mass marketing of knowledge-as-commodity occurs most obviously in the mass media. Hence journalistic practice downplays interpretation or asserts the complete separability for practical purposes of fact and opinion. It emphasises 'the truth about', 'the whole story', 'objectivity' and 'the facts' because these labels identify a commodity that can be conveniently packaged, such as news stories in a newspaper or a television bulletin.

Thoughtful readers of a particular newspaper may be aware that the stories printed in it have a particular 'slant' because the paper has its known political line. In that sense it might well be said that something more (or less) than objective fact is being presented. But readers who share the newspaper's ideological viewpoints are unlikely to be troubled by such observations. They may be entirely content to know that the paper they read conforms to the ideological outlook they share (which for them is usually mere common sense). In the light of this knowledge they can judge its presentation of news as objective, factual and reliable. This is because it shares their certainties; it assumes as truth what they know to be truth; it will not challenge what they know cannot seriously be challenged, or declare untrue what they know to be true. It will present the commodity of fact as they understand that commodity, and will do so in accepted, familiar, ultimately unthreatening ways.

Sociological literature analyses the production processes by which news is 'manufactured' as an eternal recurrence (Rock, 1973). Created in a never-ending process, it must (from the producer's point of view) be marketed as scarce and, wherever possible, 'exclusive'. But news and media information in general is a rapidly wasting commodity—today's news sheet becomes tomorrow's rubbish wrapper. The dissipation of the value of news as a commodity, almost as soon as it is sold or distributed, carries advantages in itself. It avoids, at least for many purposes, the difficult legal problems associated with the protection of knowledge as a kind of property. In other settings where knowledge is considered for certain purposes as a commodity (for example, expert, technical or scientific knowledge or other intellectual products of creativity) the issue of how this commodity can be protected legally is addressed by means of intellectual property law.

It is tempting, if misleading, to think of transparency as a condition in which it becomes possible to see undistorted (or a less distorted) reality. This idea seems implicit in Balkin's essay. But, if this conception of transparency is discarded along with the idea of true (or truer) consciousness, which it implies, a different and more politically useful conception is available. Transparency can then be seen as a process which presupposes that (i) there is always more to know on any matter, (ii) there is always another side to every story and (iii) one account never cancels out a different one but merely supplements it, even through contradiction. Transparency as a process involves not just availability of information but active participation in acquiring, distributing and creating knowledge. It also involves responsibility for providing personal accounts. In other words, it involves 'accountability'; the willingness and responsibility to try to give a meaningful and accurate account of oneself, or of circumstances in which one is involved, or of which one is aware; and, beyond that, a responsibility to try honestly to define the relation of one's account to the variety of other accounts given in connection with the relevant matter. Thus, what is involved is not real as opposed to simulated transparency but a process founded on a conception of knowledge opposite to that of knowledge-as-commodity; a conception that sees knowledge as always incomplete, always to be questioned, broadened and extended, enriched and refined, supplemented and controverted. Because the process of transparency treats knowledge in this way, it requires for its fulfilment moral obligations of accountability in the sense referred to above.

So it is possible to identify tensions between transparency and media interests without necessarily making any claims or implications as to what 'real' transparency in any given situation might be. The key is in the tension between, on the one hand, an idea of knowledge-as-commodity, which is likely to be particularly congenial to media interests, and, on the other, an idea of a transparency process that denies any finished or objective character of knowledge and emphasises uncertainty, questioning and the challenging of accounts against other accounts as central to this process.

III

In this paper, Balkin describes the way mass media tend to turn serious political matters into entertainment (and see, Balkin, 1998, pp. 80–1). Clearly this points to very important matters. But I think that the term 'entertainment' is no less problematic here than the term 'simulate'. Its meaning is too imprecise to allow analysis of the variety of ways in which media attempt to commodify political or other kinds of information or communication. Entertainment suggests that people enjoy, or find diverting, attractive, interesting, captivating or unmissable, for any of a variety of reasons, what is presented to them. But it is possible to separate the different kinds of value that they might find in what is presented by mass media. One kind might be called 'gossip value'. For example, it is entertaining to learn information about people we know personally, things happening in our locality, or people with whom we have some connection through environmental proximity or personal experience. Beyond this it is of interest to know facts about familiar institutions, or to have questions raised about them. The value of the information comes from its relating to aspects of an environment of some kind of which we are part or to which we have traditional links—for example, living in the same neighbourhood, city or county, or sharing common roots, language, experience or background.

Another quite different kind of value which communicated ideas or information may have is utility value. The knowledge is instrumentally useful. On television, gardening, cookery, do-it-yourself or keep fit programmes seek to convey instrumentally useful information as entertainment. A third kind of communication may have value because it arouses empathy, evokes human interest or stirs the emotions. News reports about starving people in another country may hardly be thought of as entertainment but may be gripping and powerful because they engage emotions of sympathy and compassion. Similarly, the (real or fictional) stories or personalities of people on the television screen may engage feelings or make us think through our own response to other people's dilemmas. At least momentarily, we have an affective link with them, and are part of an affective community of concern or empathy. We might even feel we have come to know these people in some sense. Finally, communications may have propagandist or reassurance value, because they assert ultimate values or beliefs that we share. They confirm or reinforce what we believe in or claim to believe in. At a much deeper level (as perhaps in the best drama or literature) what is communicated may demand a clarification, refinement or questioning of familiar beliefs and values, making us explore anew their integrity or coherence.

In thinking of the ways in which mass media transform politics into entertainment it is important to distinguish these different kinds of values that may attach to what is relayed by the media. Balkin notes the way that media presentation of political life has altered distinctions between the public and the private so that politicians' private lives are the subject of media scrutiny. He sees this as media trivialisation of serious political issues in pursuit of entertainment value, broadly interpreted. But a different way to view the matter is as knowledge that relates to different kinds of relations of community, rather than knowledge that relates either to public or private life.

This is an important change of focus because it tends to break down the public-private distinction that Balkin uses as his point of reference, even while he recognises its contingent and constructed nature. The four kinds of values of communicated ideas or information, referred to above, relate to different types of social relations: respectively, first, relations of chance proximity, common environment or shared tradition; secondly, instrumental relations of common or convergent purposes; thirdly, affective or emotionally-based relations; and, fourthly, relations based on shared beliefs or ultimate values. These imply different kinds of relationship of community (Cotterrell, 1997) and that individuals may have interests in what is communicated that vary with these different kinds of relationships to which knowledge or information may relate.

The public-private dichotomy tends to postulate a single kind of politically-relevant relationship in which individuals find themselves: the relationship of individual and state. The private sphere, seen in these terms, is that of individuals and their personal ties to family, work and free associations; the public sphere is that of the state and government. But it is not necessary to refer to media coverage of the Clinton-Lewinsky affair to note that this distinction is highly unstable. In Britain, debate and discussion around aspects of the private life of Diana, Princess of Wales, increasingly appeared as holding keys to public issues about the monarchy as an institution. Again, the 'outing' of gay politicians and other public figures is sometimes defended (by those who do the 'outing') on the grounds that to hide or disguise one's private persona in creating a public one in this context is a betrayal of identity and of solidarity. Lines between public and personal life can become unclear insofar as people's identity and responsibilities are seen in terms of different kinds of group memberships they hold, or different kinds of social relationships in which they are seen to be implicated. Thus, Diana's life became an object of general interest particularly in the context of affective relations in which she was involved. In part this interest arises because the monarchy's modern tie to the people in Britain has been engineered sporadically in terms of the idea of a first family of the nation, to which subjects have been encouraged to feel affectually tied.[5]

If the identity of individuals is, as Balkin has claimed elsewhere (1998, p. 18; 1995, p. 1228), assigned to them by 'culture', this idea can be refined by saying that their identity conferred on them by others is formed by the relations of community in which they are involved. If we recognise instrumental, affective, belief-based, and local or traditional, types of relations of community we can similarly recognise that what is germane to an individual's identity in this sense varies with the kinds of relationships involved. And, again, the kind of knowledge of individuals and their actions that is relevant in assessing these relationships depends on the nature of the relationships. If the tie of monarchy to subjects is supposed to be, or has been shaped to be, in some measure an affective one, then matters germane to the affective or emotional aspects of life are relevant knowledge in understanding and negotiating that relationship.

The point can be generalised across all the different types of relations of community. Relevant knowledge depends on the nature of the relations of community in which people are involved. It does not depend on the drawing of a sharp line between the public and the private. Thus, where ties are essentially merely instrumental (for example, a purely business relationship) the knowledge that is relevant in managing those ties, evaluating them or understanding them is properly restricted to knowledge of capacities relevant to projects undertaken (for example, relating to skills and motivation). Where relations are affective, knowledge of personal and emotional intimacies may be relevant. Where relations are founded on an assumption of shared beliefs or ultimate values a knowledge of the individual's ultimate values and belief commitments is relevant. For example, if the judges of a supreme court have as part of their perceived or proclaimed role the protection of the assumed common values of the nation, it is highly relevant to citizens to have knowledge of the personal beliefs and ultimate values of these judges in so far as these may colour their decisions. Again, where relationships of community are merely those of shared environment or common locality, the knowledge the neighbours need to have of each other may be merely that which bears on 'neighbour reliability'; essentially knowledge of a limited range of negative features of individuals that could make them a threat to their neighbours (for example, a history of personal violence, or of paedophile tendencies).

Looking at matters in this way suggests that it is not particularly easy to define what kinds of knowledge are properly conveyed in the 'public interest'. Especially so, when it is recognised that actual social relations (for example between those who govern and those governed) may involve complex interactions of the four ideal types of relations of community discussed above. The public 'right to know' depends on how the public is defined, and in relation to what matters. And that definition in turn depends on the relations to what matters. And that definition in turn depends on the relations of community involved. We might say that there is no right to know that does not relate to a specific community setting. The public right to know depends on the nature of the social relationships to which knowledge relates.

If we return to the mass media, it is clear that the work of journalists is concerned with all of the four ideal types of relations of community I have tried to distinguish. It concerns them insofar as they are thought to relate to the lives and experience of readers or viewers. What limit is there on the amount of knowledge that can legitimately be asked for? How far does transparency go? If I know a person X, I am likely to be interested in information about X. There is a potentially unlimited interest in 'gossip knowledge'. What is the limit properly to be put to that interest? The answer is surely that I have no right to knowledge about X unless I am actually or potentially affected in a relatively direct way by X's actions, in relations of community that X and I are held to share.

An understanding of transparency seems, then, to require acceptance of several premises. First, transparency is a process, not a kind of knowledge or understanding, and still less a matter of 'the truth' about some matter or other. Secondly, the transparency process is potentially unending because there are always new accounts or revelations that can be sought, another side of the story to tell. Thirdly, the kind of knowledge that it is proper to seek depends not on the maintenance or negotiation of a public-private divide but on the complex interplay of relations of community that link the objects of media curiosity with those who watch or read about these objects. These relations of community are abstract and extremely varied (including, for example, links with people I do not know in another part of the world insofar as their experiences engage my feelings or values, or the links of shared local environment or common or convergent purposes). Fourthly, the appropriate limits of knowledge to be sought of acts or persons are determined ultimately by whether those acts or persons significantly affect the viewer or reader, within the context of the relations of community that link the object of knowledge with the recipient of knowledge.

IV

There is a calculatedly portentous moment towards the end of the 1981 Hollywood movie *Absence of Malice*—a film that presents a nice moral tale of journalistic ethics and unjustified media intrusion into private lives. The moment occurs when the chastened journalist (Sally Field) has to tell in print the deeply embarrassing story of her own malpractice. Questioned about her account of events by a fellow journalist deputed to write up the painful news story, she is asked finally about her testimony, 'That's true, isn't it?' and replies 'No, but it's accurate'. The script line marks her belated recognition of the difference between transparency and the commodification of knowledge. The package of recorded facts and observations, accurately recorded from their sources, tells a plausible story. But it is not to be mistaken for 'the truth', the whole story (if that were possible), with all its innumerable justifications, explanations and excuses. An account has merely been added to the record.

In law, also, witnesses promise to tell the whole truth and nothing but the truth, but they merely give their own accounts. The accusatorial system recognises in its practices the impossibility of truth, but affirms the importance of transparency as a process. Because of the limited time available in the courtroom the process is brought to an end with arbitrary finality when an understanding 'beyond reasonable doubt' or merely 'on the balance of probabilities' has been achieved.

The commodification of knowledge in the media tends to obscure the nature of transparency as a process. So does the human desire for certainty, in legal processes as elsewhere,[6] as well as the unavoidable necessity of relying on imperfect knowledge in the practical affairs of everyday life, as though the knowledge were complete. The most important certainty in social relations may, however, be that which comes from being in a secure relationship of *trust*. Each of the types of community I referred to earlier can be thought of as relations in which people trust others in bonds of mutuality: the trust, for example, between traders who have made a deal, between politicians and those who elect them, between friends or neighbours.

When Balkin points justifiably to the prominence of scandal as the subject matter of mass media reporting he treats the emphasis on scandal as somehow pathological. Indeed, he sees it as a ' . . . cultural virus that spreads like an epidemic through the public sphere' (p. 404). But again, the matter might be read differently. A scandal can be defined as a betrayal of expectations based on normal conditions of mutual interpersonal trust in social relations of community. Politicians often seek to bolster their popular support by presenting themselves, or allowing themselves to be portrayed, as the personal friend of each and every citizen, as the folksy representative of local concerns, as the protector of shared values and beliefs or in some other way that builds bonds of community with citizens beyond those of pure instrumentality. In other words, they are tempted to offer more than just the promise of governing efficiently

—of instrumental success. They offer themselves to the electors not merely in a relationship of instrumental community, but also, for example, of affective community or community of belief. Thus they expose themselves to the risk of being judged in terms of those relationships. Scandal is best defined as the perceived betrayal of the trust that underpins one or more of these relationships of community. Political scandal is a perceived betrayal of such relationships as they are held to exist between rulers and ruled.

In this sense, scandal is the most normal thing imaginable in politics. Far from being 'a pathological tendency', it is the stuff of everyday political life and is likely to remain so. The reason is clear. All social life, it has been suggested here, is lived in relations of community of various kinds. If this is so, it is, regrettably, one of the most obvious features of those relations that the conditions of trust on which they depend are endlessly betrayed. What is remarkable, and perhaps ultimately a cause for optimism about the human condition, is the way in which, despite all betrayals, relations of community keep getting repaired or renewed in new forms.

Notes

1. Althusser 1984, pp. 17, 36; Balkin 1995, pp. 1225, 1230; Balkin 1991, pp. 1151–3; Balkin 1998, pp. 18, 79–80, 270–1. Like Althusser, Balkin (1998, pp. 1, 173) stresses the importance of studying 'distinct and analyzable mechanisms' of ideology.

2. In his own writings of ideology, Balkin seeks to avoid this problem by treating 'truth' as a transcendent ideal; that is, a value presupposed in discourse even though the content of the value remains inevitably and permanently indeterminate (see Balkin 1998, chap. 7). But the question of how the ideal can be operationalised in order to distinguish 'empowering' from 'distorting' knowledge (Balkin 1998, p. 126) seems to remain.

3. Thus, in a particularly revealing comment, Balkin (1987, p. 426n) has claimed that every ideology 'involves a partially true as well as a partially false vision of the world'. More recently (1991, p. 1138n) he has declared that his conception of ideology is closer to that of the anthropologist Clifford Geertz than to 'the more traditional Marxist conception' and he cites Geertz' essay 'Ideology as a Cultural System' in support. But this does not really help to avoid the true-false dichotomy. In that essay Geertz (1973) declares: 'It is ... not truth that varies with social, psychological, and cultural contexts but the symbols we construct in our unequally effective attempts to grasp it' (p. 212). Thus an idea of ultimate truth confronting ideology's more or less imperfect understandings remains firmly in the picture. In his newest discussion of ideology, Balkin (1998, chap. 7) asserts the necessity of a transcendent ideal of truth against which ideological thought or debate can be compared. He sees inquiries into false consciousness as problematic but not because of difficulties of the true-false dichotomy as such. Rather, he sees the problems as lying in the incoherence or unhelpfulness of the idea of the objective interests of social classes as the particular measure by which to assess the falsity of individuals' thought or belief (1998, pp. 116–8). He maintains the true-false dichotomy, stating that via the mechanisms of ideology 'truth and falsity, deception and empowerment enter through the same door' (1998, p. 19; and 1995, p. 1232).

4. For an elaboration of this conception of ideology see Cotterrell 1995, chap. 1.

5. See Nairn 1994; and on the modern beginnings of this, Bagehot 1963, pp. 85–6.

6. A classic source is Frank 1963.

References

Althusser, L. 1984: Ideology and Ideological State Apparatuses (Notes Towards an Investigation). In Althusser, *Essays on Ideology.* London: Verso, pp. 1–60.

Bagehot, Walter 1963. *The English Constitution* [orig. 1867]. London: Collins.

Balkin, Jack M. 1987: Taking Ideology Seriously: Ronald Dworkin and the CLS Critique. *University of Missouri-Kansas City Law Review,* 55, pp. 392–433.

Balkin, Jack M. 1991: Ideology as Constraint. *Stanford Law Review,* 43, pp. 1133–69.

Balkin, Jack M. 1995: Ideology as Cultural Software. *Cardozo Law Review,* 16, pp. 1221–33.

Balkin, Jack M. 1998: *Cultural Software: A Theory of Ideology.* New Haven: Yale University Press.

Balkin, Jack M. 1999: How Mass Media Simulate Political Transparency. *Cultural Values,* vol. 3: 4.

Cotterrell, Richard 1995: *Law's Community: Legal Theory in Sociological Perspective.* Oxford: Clarendon Press.

Cotterrell, Richard 1997: A Legal Concept of Community. *Canadian Journal of Law and Society,* 12, pp. 75–91.

Frank, Johann 1963: *Law and the Modern Mind* [1930]. Garden City, NJ: Anchor.

Geertz, Clifford 1973: *The Interpretation of Cultures: Selected Essays.* New York: Basic Books.

Nairn, Tom 1994: *The Enchanted Glass: Britain and Its Monarchy,* rev. edn. London: Vintage.

Rock, Paul 1973: News as Eternal Recurrence. In S. Cohen and J. Young (eds.), *The Manufacture of News: Social Problems, Deviance and the Mass Media.* London: Constable, pp. 73–80.

POSTSCRIPT

Do the Mass Media Undermine Openness and Accountability in Democracy?

Although the focus of these selections is on the asserted obligation of the press to promote transparent communication of the political process, and the failure of the press to do so due to its focus on entertaining stories rather than substantive ones, the issues of press performance are much larger. The public image of the press may have improved in recent years, but journalists are still not well respected by the American public. Despite an avowed adherence to the tenets of the First Amendment, few members of the public take it as seriously as do mass communication students and practioners. For example, when freedom of access and a citizen's privacy clash, many come down on the side of the citizen. So while much of the public would agree with sentiments like "the press should be free" and "the press should uncover abuses of power," that allegiance becomes uncomfortable when members of the public see individuals, even politicians, "attacked" by the press. The broadcast news industry legitimately points to the ratings of news programs to support their news decisions —decisions that critics argue focus more on the entertainment value of news than on the important issues of our time.

Thomas Patterson charges that press behavior has weakened our political process. In "Bad News, Period," *PS: Political Science and Politics* (March 1996), he discusses the emergence of "attack journalism" and its impact on both politicians and the general public. He reveals the myth behind claims of a liberal bias in the media and offers instead the evidence of a media that is simply negative. James Fallows, in *Breaking the News: How the Media Undermine American Democracy* (Pantheon Books, 1996), argues that the media's self-aggrandizement gets in the way of solving American's real problems. In *The News About News: American Journalism in Peril* (Knopf, 2002), *Washington Post* editors Leonard Downie and Robert G. Kaiser share their dismay about changing standards of journalism, particularly those changes wrought by commercial interests. In a report of a committee of concerned journalists charged with engaging journalists and the public in a careful examination of what journalism is supposed to be, Bill Kovach and Tom Rosenstiel, in *The Elements of Journalism: What Newspeople Should Know and the Public Should Expect* (Crown, 2001), outlines nine principles, with freedom as the core value of responsible journalism.

ISSUE 9

Is Negative Campaigning Bad for the American Political Process?

YES: Larry J. Sabato, Mark Stencel, and S. Robert Lichter, from *Peepshow: Media and Politics in an Age of Scandal* (Rowman & Littlefield, 2000)

NO: William G. Mayer, from "In Defense of Negative Campaigning," *Political Science Quarterly* (Fall 1996)

ISSUE SUMMARY

YES: Larry J. Sabato, professor of government, Mark Stencel, politics editor for Washingtonpost.com, and S. Robert Lichter, president of the Center for Media and Public Affairs, assert that the line dividing public life and private life is more blurred than ever. The authors state that this is creating an age of scandal. They conclude that this focus on politics-by-scandal results in disaffected voters, discouraged political candidates, and news devoid of analysis of policy issues and substantive debate.

NO: William G. Mayer, assistant professor of political science, defends negative campaigning as a necessity in political decision making. He argues that society must provide the public with the substantive information needed to make informed decisions at the polls and insists that this must occur during political campaigns. Therefore negative campaigns are needed so that citizens can make intelligent choices concerning their leaders.

Probably nothing has so transformed the American political process as the emergence of television as a force in elections. Today many more people see candidates on television than hear them in person. Candidates appear on a variety of media formats—television and radio talk shows, late-night entertainment programs, morning news and information programs, online, and even MTV. Never before have candidates used the power of media to such a comprehensive extent to reach potential voters.

But clearly the public is fed up with political campaigns. Voter apathy is high, as is public disgust with candidates and with politics itself. Viable candidates choose not to run rather than to subject themselves and their families to the scrutiny of the press. Many point the finger of blame at a relentless negativism governing the coverage and the conduct of political campaigns that favor a horse-race mentality, leap at opportunities to "go negative," and gleefully break stories of private failures.

Larry J. Sabato, Mark Stencel, and S. Robert Lichter indict campaigning, indeed much of American politics, in their volume *Peepshow: Media and Politics in an Age of Scandal,* from which the following selection has been taken. Marvin Kalb, executive director of the Shorenstein Center on the Press, bills this volume as a serious study of how scandal coverage has corrupted political coverage and ultimately criticizes journalists, candidates, and voters for degrading politics. Sabato et al. argue that the voracious appetites for scandal exhibited by all three of these groups contribute to the success of attack journalism. Furthermore, by focusing so much attention on the lives of public servants, the press squanders what little chance it has to engage the electorate. This leads to a greater chance that citizens will elect people who should not be in public office.

What should be the rules for politicians and journalists in an era of media preoccupation with private lives and political scandal? Despite the incivility of present campaigns, do we want to return to an era in which private lives were never considered appropriate for public discussion? Does it matter if candidates have experimented with drugs, joined subversive organizations as college students, evaded war service, or had affairs? What changes would make political campaigns and their coverage more substantive?

Sabato et al. and William G. Mayer call for a definition of negativity. To Sabato et al., negative campaigns have harmful effects on the political process. Mayer counters that negative campaigning is beneficial to the public and allows people to distinguish between the candidates. Each author reviles misleading campaign rhetoric and calls for careful policing of false assertions. Sabato et al. and Mayer see a need for media to be more careful in the information they provide, but Mayer challenges the common perception that negativity is bad. Rather than a bland campaign where each candidate speaks in favor of broad generalities, let records and behaviors be revealed and debated, he says. The character issue is real, and there must be a way for people to judge the character of those they elect. Otherwise, the information needed to discriminate among candidates will never emerge. And, the political process will be further diminished.

Larry J. Sabato, Mark Stencel,
and S. Robert Lichter

 **YES**

Peepshow: Media and Politics
in an Age of Scandal

The Scene of the Crime

The line political reporters draw between private and public life is perhaps more blurry than ever before. With increasing regularity, that blurry line is the smudged chalk outline of an ambitious politician.

For both politicians and journalists, deciding when private matters are the public's business is almost always challenging. Competition from new and alternative news sources makes those decisions even more complicated. Mainstream news outlets—newspapers, magazines, broadcast and cable television— no longer serve as almost exclusive gatekeepers of information about those who hold or seek elected office. At the same time, evolving public standards and increasing competitive pressures for a shrinking news audience are changing the ways editors and producers determine when and how to delve into the private lives of political figures. These forces make some editorial decisions seem almost arbitrary....

The press attention focused on the thirteen-month investigation and impeachment of President Clinton has put the press on trial for both its excesses and its oversights. To some, the coverage of President Clinton's sexual relationship with a former low-level White House functionary was an alarming invasion of privacy, a political smear. To others, it was a criminal matter that prompted a long-overdue examination of a pattern of reckless behavior that endangered the moral and ethical standing of the presidency. At the state and local level, candidates now regularly answer probing media questions about adultery, substance abuse and other private behavior—queries that even presidential candidates once weren't expected to answer. Nonetheless, many stories about politicians' private lives still never make it into print or on the air, even after news about those with similar pasts and public responsibilities is reported.

Just what are the rules for politicians and journalists in the aftermath of Washington's biggest sex scandal? When are a public official's or candidate's private affairs fair game and when are they out of bounds? The public, the press and those they cover are divided....

From Larry J. Sabato, Mark Stencel, and S. Robert Lichter, *Peepshow: Media and Politics in an Age of Scandal* (Rowman & Littlefield Publishers, 2000). Copyright © 2000 by Rowman & Littlefield Publishers, Inc. Reprinted by permission. Notes omitted.

[A] Pew Center's poll... suggests that a candidate's personal life is not a major campaign issue for most Americans, even in presidential politics. In a September 1999 survey, strong majorities thought the press should almost always report stories about a presidential candidate's spousal abuse (71 percent), income tax evasion (65 percent), exaggerated military record (61 percent) and exaggerated academic record (61 percent). But there was significantly less interest in reports about a candidate's ongoing affairs (43 percent), sexuality (38 percent), past drinking (36 percent) or cocaine use (35 percent). Less than a quarter of those surveyed (23 percent) said the press should almost always report on a past affair or marijuana use. Less than a third said the press should routinely delve into other personal issues—psychiatric treatment, antidepressant use, even abortions.

Editorial judgment is not always, if ever, a perfect reflection of public opinion. News organizations have a journalistic obligation to try to inform all readers and viewers, even the sizable minority to whom a candidate's or elected official's personal morality is a decisive voting issue. In the Pew Center poll, for example, a significantly higher percentage of Republicans than Democrats said the press should cover many of the personal issues mentioned above, with the division as high as 27 percent on stories about ongoing affairs.

Scandal coverage also can have positive effects on the political process. Intense scrutiny by the press and political opponents can drive away scalawags, increase public accountability and foster realistic attitudes about the human fallibility of elected leaders. But the costs of today's politics-by-scandal outweigh any remedial effects. While public trust in politicians is near all-time lows, confidence in the media is no higher, and participants on both sides say the emphasis on scandal is reducing voter turnout, distracting from important policy debates and discouraging the best politicians and best journalists....

Precedent

The press is on trial with readers and viewers. The charge: Unnecessary violation of the privacy of politicians and their families. Mainstream American political journalism offers an indicting array of examples in recent years, including coverage of extramarital affairs, office romances, divorces, drug use, drinking, sexuality, illegitimate children and plain, unsubstantiated rumor. Individual cases can be made to justify almost any news story that fell into these categories. Collectively, however, the predominance of such so-called character questions is eroding the credibility of political journalists and turning American democracy into a sort of peepshow or soap opera. Public opinion surveys suggest that journalists have stepped over the line most—but not all—Americans would set for legitimate editorial inquiry. Whether reporters, editors and producers are in fact guilty of violating the standards of their own profession depends on whether there really are any standards in an age of multimedia competition among information sources....

The Verdict

Colin L. Powell was preparing to step before more than three dozen television cameras and deliver the news that had already seeped out: The popular retired Army general and first black chairman of the Joint Chiefs of Staff would sit out the 1996 campaign for the White House. Polls showed that Powell was the only Republican likely to best incumbent Democrat Bill Clinton on Election Day a year hence. But as NBC anchorman Tom Brokaw broke into the day's programming to present Powell's news conference, he said one reason for the general's decision was well known. "It is widely believed that his wife, Alma, had a major role in this decision," Brokaw said. "She has a long history of depression, and that no doubt would get a very vigorous examination by not only the general's political opponents but also by reporters."

In fact, the press had already explored the issue of Alma Powell's depression. Dick Polman and Steve Goldstein of the *Philadelphia Inquirer* first reported that she used medication to treat depression. The news was mentioned briefly in a long, front-page story about Powell's possible candidacy more than two weeks earlier. "A close family friend said the Powells consider her condition a minor situation but understand it has to be considered in a family decision of this magnitude," the *Inquirer* reported. *Newsweek* magazine confirmed the report a week later, giving Alma Powell's depression and "worries about the family's privacy" slightly more play than the *Inquirer* in a long article about Powell's campaign contemplation and a sidebar about his wife's role.

At Powell's news conference, however—after Brokaw had already cut away to analyze the ongoing event—the general contradicted the anchorman's introduction. Alma's depression was not a major factor in his decision to sit out the race, he said in answer to a reporter's question, "and we found no offense in what was written about it."

> My wife has depression. She's had it for many, many years, and we have told many, many people about it. It is not a family secret. It is very easily controlled with proper medication, just as my blood pressure is sometimes under control with proper medication.
>
> And you obviously don't want your whole family life out in the press, but when the story broke we confirmed it immediately, and I hope that people who read that story who think they might be suffering from depression make a beeline to the doctor, because it is something that can be dealt with very easily.

Increasing media scrutiny no doubt takes its toll on public figures and their families. The promise of higher pay in the private sector (without prying personal examinations by the press) is appealing. At the same time, the fear that intrusive reporters are driving "good people" out of politics is perhaps overstated, as it was in Colin Powell's case. Media scrutiny can also be a deterrent to scoundrels who might seek political office. In some ways, the consequences of intensive press focus on the private lives of politicians are as great on the press itself as they are on those in politics, at least as measured by public confidence in the credibility of reporters and reporters' confidence in themselves. But the focus of public debate about the issue of political privacy is almost always on the quality candidates who are driven from the process, and the mediocre political figures who are left behind.

Political commentary bemoaning significant numbers of congressional retirements in the 1990s contributed to the sense that the best political leaders are abandoning public service. In the three election cycles that ran from 1991 to 1996, twenty-nine members of the Senate retired, including a record thirteen members in 1996. That was more than the total number of Senate retirements in the previous six cycles. In the same three election cycles, 162 members of the House voluntarily relinquished their seats at the end of their terms. That included a record sixty-five House retirements in 1992, when a check-kiting scandal involving the House of Representatives bank endangered many incumbents' chances for reelection.

The situation was very different in 1998. Even in the midst of the Monica Lewinsky investigation and embarrassing revelations about the personal lives of several prominent Republican congressmen, just four senators and twenty-three members of the House gave up their seats. Both 1998 figures were well below the average number of congressional retirements since 1950. The dropoff in congressional departures suggests that the high number of retirements earlier in the 1990s might have had less to do with the burdens of service than with the political shifts that gave Republicans control of both chambers of Congress for the first time since 1955.

Congressional retirements have indeed depleted the ranks of House and Senate moderates, making the legislative branch a less civil and more partisan place to work. That increasing partisanship also makes Congress a firetrap for political scandal and intrigue. The way the media frames political debate contributes, too, particularly in pyrotechnic talk television and radio formats that give prominence to those who most disagree on an issue. The redistricting process after the 1990 census was another factor. The creation of many minority districts meant that those running for other seats were campaigning in far less ideologically diverse areas. The isolation of certain voting blocs after 1990, particularly of ethnic voters, meant many candidates did not need to appeal to a broad range of voters to win their races.

Some fret that this political climate is only favorable to partisan, blow-dried, sound-biting politicians. But any long-term observer or member of Congress will tell you that the body's current membership is, in general, far better informed, better educated, and in many ways better at communicating than in the past. The vast majority are bright and able, and achieve a fair amount, whether or not one agrees with the object of the members' efforts. This is one subject on which serious reporters, academics, and politicians are agreed. Fifty years ago, many good people served in Congress who could not be elected in the television age. Being good on TV, however, does not mean being a bad public servant. To the contrary, it means one has the communication skills to build support for a public agenda. This can be critical in a country with a growing population that cares much less about politics than in the past.

People who lament the passing of the so-called golden age of public service either have poor memories or weren't alive at all. If law enforcement had been as tough and as thorough in investigating public officials fifty years ago as it is today, and if Congress itself had policed its members then to the extent that it does now, it would have been a good year when a dozen members were not indicted. The degree of corruption in politics is no higher now than in decades past. Reforms passed after Watergate, especially financial disclosure requirements, ensure that the degree of corruption may in fact be far less than it once was. The sins of the past are simply forgotten, because reporters frequently failed to report them and law enforcement failed to pursue them.

The same is true in presidential politics, despite an even more intense media spotlight on nearly every corner of a White House candidate's life. While Bill Clinton may be deficient in his personal morality, he is also one of the smartest and most knowledgeable individuals ever to sit in the Oval Office. And despite the scrutiny that will inevitably follow Clinton's tumultuous two terms, the initial crop of major party contenders who set out to run for the White House in 1999 included a two-term incumbent vice president, a former vice president, a former senator, two former Cabinet secretaries, a current governor, a House committee chairman, three current senators and two former White House advisers.

The field of prospective presidents in 2000 offers more experience and more diversity of views and is arguably a better crop of candidates than in 1960, when the field included three future presidents, one of whom was an incumbent vice president, and one future vice president—all of whom served in the Senate. Further, the presidential debates of the 1960 campaign did not include any discussion of the New Frontier, the Great Society, or the dramatic gestures of international peace and détente on which the three future presidents running that year would base their legacies. Nostalgia should not blind our assessment of past political campaigns, heroes and villains.

All of this is not to minimize the impact of attack journalism on the electoral process. While ambition has provided a healthy antidote to the poison pens of some reporters, the "politics of personal destruction" inevitably takes its toll. A democracy is based on electing human representatives with human failings. But some qualified candidates will remain on the sidelines rather than submit themselves and their families to a grueling personal examination by the press and their opponents. Even candidates standing on top of the polls have stood aside.

Moreover, the level of scrutiny once applied only to candidates for the highest offices is being applied farther down the ballot. In Georgia, for example, Lieutenant Governor Pierre Howard dropped out of the 1998 Democratic gubernatorial contest, relinquishing his front-runner status fifteen months before the election because of the impact on his family. Howard's announcement came two months after the leading Republican in the race, Mike Bowers, confessed to a long-standing extramarital affair that cost him critical support among his party's conservative wing. At the August 1997 news conference announcing his decision, Howard denied he was bowing out of the race to prevent any Bowers-like revelation about himself. "There is nothing in my background that worried me and caused me to want to get out of the race," Howard told suspicious reporters. Almost two weeks later, Jim Wooten, editor of the *Atlanta Journal*'s editorial page, wrote that suspicions lingered nonetheless.

People looking for some dark reason that he withdrew are likely to find it to be nothing more than he stated: His family was not into it. Neither was he.

Since Howard's abrupt announcement, the state has been abuzz with speculation. The most plausible explanation, after 10 days of conversation with people in politics—an industry that rivals journalism in its inability to keep a secret—is that there are no secrets to keep.

And that is the level of scrutiny applied to a *former* gubernatorial candidate.

The public and the press are deeply divided on the importance and the impact of this kind of reporting. A 1998–1999 survey conducted by the Pew Research Center for the People and the Press for the Committee for Concerned Journalists clearly showed this divide.... About half of those in the news survey—49 percent of national media and 56 percent of local outlets—said news organizations' coverage of the personal and ethical aspects of public figures is intended to drive controversy. In contrast, almost three-quarters of the public —72 percent—said news organizations are more interested in the controversy than in reporting the news on such stories. The division is more dramatic when asked about journalists' roles as public watchdogs. Almost 90 percent in the media said criticism by news organizations keeps political leaders from "doing things that should not be done." Only a small majority of the public, 55 percent, agrees—down from 67 percent in a 1985 poll. At the same time, a growing number said press criticism was keeping political leaders "from doing their jobs"—39 percent in the 1998–1999 survey, up from 17 percent in the 1985 poll.

Many journalists contend that their readers and viewers are hypocritical on these questions. They point to increased circulation and TV ratings of scandal news to make their case. After all, almost 50 million Americans tuned in to see Barbara Walters's exclusive March 1999 television interview with Monica Lewinsky on ABC's *20/20*, despite numerous polls in the preceding months suggesting the public had had its fill of news about the former White House aide. While there may be a certain amount of truth to this argument, it misses one key point: Increases in readership and television viewing measured against usual audience size are relatively small shifts, since the overall growth in circulation and network TV audiences stagnated long ago. In other words, the increased audience for scandal coverage is by and large an increase among the relatively small subset of the population who are already news consumers, not the growing number of news "disconnecteds" who have already turned off or tuned out.

"Gotcha" journalism is not the driving force behind these diminishing news audiences. But news coverage driven by values contrary to the public's only contributes to the public's sense that the media does not share their interests. Journalists themselves are beginning to recognize this as a problem. In the aforementioned Pew poll, more than half of news professionals surveyed —57 percent nationally and 51 percent locally—agreed that "journalists have become out-of-touch with their audiences."

Personal scrutiny also ensures that journalists are quite literally "out of touch" with some of the figures they cover. One immediate consequence of political journalists' increased focus on the private lives of politicians is decreased access. In 1998, Idaho representative Helen Chenoweth challenged a news story

in the *Spokane Spokesman-Review*, which reported that she had lied in denying an affair with a married business partner. (She was asked about it directly
by a reporter during an interview in a previous campaign.) Later, when the
Spokesman-Review sought to interview Chenoweth for other news stories and
profiles, she said she was too busy. "I know my staff was just looking out for
my best interests as far as my time," she said, dismissing a reporter's questions
about her interview policy after a candidate debate late in the campaign.

The losers in Chenoweth's feud with the *Spokesman-Review* were not the
publication's reporters but the representative's constituents who read the newspaper and depend on it to relay their questions and her answers. However, there
was no public outcry about Chenoweth's refusal to answer the newspaper's
questions. In fact, she was reelected to a third term with 55 percent of the
vote. The *Spokesman-Review* was right to report the discrepancies between its
reporter's notes and Chenoweth's claim that she had never lied about her relationship. Nonetheless, the public will not side with reporters who they think
are only interested in asking questions that they have no interest in seeing
answered. This puts reporters and editors in an impossible bind.

The mission of the popular press is not to be popular. And in blaming
the press for the sins about which it reports, the public—and even some critics—may be shooting the messenger. But ignoring public attitudes about press
behavior could have grave consequences for the media as well as the political process. In combination with court rulings and high jury awards against
reporters and declining public support for First Amendment press rights, diminished public confidence in the media poses more than a business threat
to journalism's future. It is a potential threat to the very idea of an unrestricted press that was key to the nation's founding, its survival, and its future.
Meanwhile, readers and viewers may increasingly turn to alternative sources
of information . . . for pseudonews that does not stand up to traditional journalistic standards of balance and accuracy. Reporters, editors and producers
cannot be stubborn or cavalier about public attitudes. Ignoring these threats
is as self-destructive as the reckless personal behavior of politicians that today's
journalists so meticulously document.

So far, the threats to journalism's future and the tabloidization of political coverage are not causing news organizations to hemorrhage talent. As with
elected office itself, ambition almost guarantees that there will be hungry, talented young reporters interested in covering politics and government. These
high-profile beats are still prime assignments in most newsrooms. More generally, journalism still provides opportunities to watch history being made and
to get to know those who make it.

Nonetheless, some prominent national journalists have left their daily
beats to try to reform their profession and the process of political discourse.
Some have become nonprofit crusaders for better media. For example, former *Washington Post* political reporter Paul Taylor joined former CBS News
anchorman Walter Cronkite before the 1996 presidential race to mount their
own campaign to convince the major television networks to give free airtime
to candidates. Tom Rosenstiel, a former reporter for the *Los Angeles Times* and
Newsweek, now serves as director of the Project for Excellence in Journalism and

vice chairman of the Committee of Concerned Journalists, where he has led efforts to raise standards and organize support for sensible journalistic reforms.

Some news organizations have embraced a new kind of social responsibility journalism, championed by the Pew Center for Civic Journalism, a nonprofit initiative financed by the Pew Charitable Trusts. No longer willing merely to report the news, some journalists see it as their duty to improve American society. This kind of reporting—which often uses extensive polling, focus groups, voter interviews and public forums to define an editorial agenda—represents a well-intentioned desire by journalists to reconnect with their audience. However, it is also a manifestation of the same editorial idealism that has led to the press emphasis on "character questions." Ultimately, journalism that does not reflect its audience's interests will lose that audience. But it is risky to assume that journalists will be any more successful at representing their readers and viewers when reporting on issues of public concern than they have been when reporting on the private lives of elected officials. These well-meaning journalistic experiments, with their potential to reengage the public, deserve careful attention and close scrutiny.

At the same time, the interactive nature of Internet journalism is pushing some for-profit online news operations in the same direction as the new civic journalists. These online editorial experiments, involving such unconventional media forces as America Online (AOL) and Yahoo!, also have potential to change the direction of mainstream reporting—and are attracting innovative and reform-minded talent from the ranks of traditional journalism. Former ABC News political reporter and Pentagon spokeswoman Kathleen deLaski went to America Online in 1996 to try to develop a new kind of political communication. The idea of covering politics in the interactive medium that AOL offered was enticing "because I thought political journalism could be better when the consumer is choosing what he/she wants to learn," deLaski said. At the same time, the former broadcast reporter said working online was a welcome alternative to the direction of political news on television:

> I went to AOL because I felt I was not serving the viewing audience well when I was on the campaign trail as a TV reporter. I would pick the five sentences of description each day and two sound bites that I could cram into my one-minute and thirty-second spot for ABC News to sum up the candidate's day. The stories often began, "Dogged by the polls. . . ." If you watched one of my stories, you had no idea what the candidate stood for. You learned how his day went versus the other guy's day.

Editorial experimentation in the nonprofit and corporate worlds offers evidence that some thoughtful journalists recognize the problems in their profession and are devoting their careers to addressing them. News organizations must be careful not to drive journalism's "best and brightest" reformers from their ranks.

One unanticipated consequence of media overcoverage of politicians' personal lives is a desensitizing effect among readers and viewers. Eventually, the public will tune out coverage of stories about which it has little interest, no matter how big the headlines or how prominent the TV news reports, as public reaction to the Monica Lewinsky scandal demonstrated. Even private behavior of legitimate public concern can fade into a mix of sensational news, like the blur of celebrity headlines on the cover of a supermarket tabloid. Revelations that once doomed candidacies and careers (such as Republican Nelson Rockefeller's divorce or Democrat Gary Hart's liaisons) are shrugged off later, as was the case with Republican Bob Dole's affair before his first divorce and President Clinton's Oval Office escapades. To some, this effect shows growing maturity on the part of voters and the press. But it also suggests a dangerous opportunity for politicians to exploit the public's scandal fatigue and convince voters to overlook failings that should raise legitimate questions about their fitness to serve.

The public itself has little time or interest in modern politics. By focusing so much attention on the personal lives of public servants, the press squanders what little chance it has to engage the electorate, to remind voters about the connections between public policy and their own personal lives. Voters are willing to devote only so much time to the study of politics. If coverage of personal politics dominates the news, then the public learns less about the matters that ought to be foremost in their minds when they vote. The less informed voters are when they walk into their polling places, the greater the chance that they will elect people who should not be in public office. The election of a real political cad or scoundrel would be the most tragic and ironic consequence of a media process that is intended to protect the public from just such a decision. . . .

The media elite often seems removed from the average news consumer who buys a daily newspaper or a weekly newsmagazine and watches the occasional news show. But those elites are far more closely tied to average citizens than they themselves believe or would want to admit. In the end, the news establishment depends on casual news readers and viewers to support their empires, many of which are already on shaky financial ground. That being true, news executives must be responsive to reasonable and thoughtful public opinion whenever it is manifested. (Many outside the news business are surprised to discover just how few letters or calls it can take to change a newspaper's policy about this or a TV station's approach to that.)

The obverse relationship deserves emphasis. Citizens have the responsibility to shake off the tendency to be mere spectators and passive news receptacles. In a democracy, whether we like it or not, whether it is the ideal or not, citizens themselves must set the rules and, even more critically, enforce those rules with their eyes, their ears, and their pocketbooks.

Public standards and news standards do not always correspond, and public opinion should not substitute for news judgment. But public accountability can be a force that helps guide editorial decision-makers through their most difficult questions about what is news and what is not.

NO

William G. Mayer

In Defense of Negative Campaigning

When televised presidential debates were first held in 1960, many commentators deplored them for their shallow, insubstantial nature. But when scholars write about those debates today, they almost invariably comment about how much better the Kennedy–Nixon encounters seem than any of the more recent presidential debates. Students to whom I have shown excerpts from these debates usually have the same reaction. Compared to the Great Confrontations of [today], the 1960 debates seem more civil, more intelligent, more substantive. Especially noticeable is what is missing from the 1960 debates: the nastiness, the evasions, the meaningless memorized one-liners designed only to be featured on the postdebate newscasts, the boos and applause from the studio audience.

Nostalgia is not in general a helpful tool in policy analysis. Claims about how wonderful things were back in some past golden age usually do severe violence to the facts of history. But it is difficult to avoid the conclusion that American election campaigns have become significantly worse over the last three decades.... [T]here has been a burst of activity—including study commissions, academic research, grassroots organizing, and legislative proposals, as well as the usual quota of lamentation and hand-wringing—all with the intention of figuring out why things have gotten so bad and what we can do to make them better.

This nascent reform movement has a number of specific targets and criticisms, but one of the most widely mentioned is negative campaigning. Whenever commentators compile a catalogue of the most heinous sins in current American politics, negative campaigning and attack advertising usually wind up near the top of the list. As a 1990 *New York Times* article noted, "Ever since the Willie Horton commercial that skewered Michael S. Dukakis's presidential campaign, politicians have been competing to express their outrage over the notion that negative campaigning and superficial news coverage have mired American politics in a swamp of trivia." ...

From William G. Mayer, "In Defense of Negative Campaigning," *Political Science Quarterly*, vol. 111, no. 3 (Fall 1996). Copyright © 1996 by The Academy of Political Science. Reprinted by permission of *Political Science Quarterly*. Notes omitted.

Many elected officials share the sense of outrage. As former Senator Howard Baker declared in 1985:

> There is one singular new development in American politics that violates fair play, and that is negative advertising, the paid commercial, usually on TV or radio, that is a smear attack on a decent person. Not only is the negative ad the sleaziest new element in politics, it may also be the most dangerous. The first victim is the person under attack. But the greater victim is the integrity and credibility of the political system itself.

To many observers, the problem is sufficiently serious to require laws and regulations that would discourage or penalize negative campaigning.... One frequently made proposal... would require any candidate who uses radio or television commercials to attack another candidate to deliver the attack in person. Another suggestion is to allow television and radio stations to charge higher rates for negative commercials than for positive ones. Some critics have even argued that the United States should follow the example of Venezuela and bar candidates entirely from referring to their opponents by name or by picture in their ads.

Whether any of these proposals stands a reasonable chance of being enacted is unclear.... The more likely result, at least in the short run, is a concerted effort on the part of civics groups, journalists, and commentators to create a climate of opinion that would discourage or penalize negative campaigning and that would try to convince voters that the very act of negative campaigning casts the candidate who engages in it in a highly unfavorable light....

There is little doubt that contemporary American election campaigns do fall short of the standards commended in our civics books. But in the laudable desire to improve our campaigns, surprisingly little attention has been paid to the easy, almost reflexive assumption that negative campaigning is bad campaigning: negative speeches and advertising are always morally wrong and damaging to our political system. In part, perhaps, the problem is one of semantics. Negative campaigning certainly sounds bad: it's so, well, you know, negative. But if we move beyond the label, what really is so bad about negative campaigning?

The purpose of this article, as its title indicates, is to challenge the accepted wisdom about negative campaigning. Negative campaigning, in my view, is a necessary and legitimate part of any election; and our politics—and the growing movement to reform our election campaigns—will be a good deal better off when we finally start to acknowledge it.

The Value of Negative Campaigning

What exactly is negative campaigning? Most people who use the term seem to have in mind a definition such as the following: Negative campaigning is campaigning that attacks or is critical of an opposing candidate. Where positive campaigning dwells on the candidate's own strengths and merits, and talks about the beneficial policies he would adopt if elected, negative campaigning focuses on the weaknesses and faults of the opposition: the mistakes they have made, the flaws in their character or performance, the bad policies they would pursue. And the more one focuses on the reality and consequences of such practices, the more clear I think it becomes that negative campaigning is not the plain and unmitigated evil that it is frequently portrayed to be. To the contrary, negative campaigning provides voters with a lot of valuable information that they definitely need to have when deciding how to cast their ballots.

To begin with, any serious, substantive discussion of what a candidate intends to do after the election can only be conducted by talking about the flaws and shortcomings of current policies. If a candidate is arguing for a major change in government policy, his first responsibility is to show that current policies are in some way deficient. If the economy is already growing rapidly with low rates of inflation, if the "environmental crisis" has been greatly exaggerated, if present policies have largely eliminated the possibility that nuclear arms will actually be used, then everything the candidates are proposing in these areas is useless, even dangerous. The need for such proposals becomes clear only when a candidate puts them in the context of present problems— only, that is to say, when a candidate "goes negative." ...

But the information and analysis embodied in negative campaigning are also valuable on their own terms, for they tell us something extremely relevant about the choices we are about to make. We need to find out about the candidates' strengths, it is true, but we also need to learn about their weaknesses: the abilities and virtues they don't have; the mistakes they have made; the problems they haven't dealt with; the issues they would prefer not to talk about; the bad or unrealistic policies they have proposed. If one candidate performed poorly in his last major public office, if another has no clear or viable plan for dealing with the economy, if a third is dishonest, the voters really do need to be informed about such matters. I need hardly add that no candidate is likely to provide a full and frank discussion of his own shortcomings. Such issues will only get a proper hearing if an opponent is allowed to talk about them by engaging in negative campaigning.

Finally, negative campaigning is valuable if for no other reason than its capacity to keep the candidates a bit more honest than they would be otherwise. One doesn't have to have a lot of respect for the truth and intelligence of current campaign practices in order to conclude that things would be a lot worse without negative campaigning. If candidates always knew that their opponents would never say anything critical about them, campaigns would quickly turn into a procession of lies, exaggerations, and unrealistic promises. Candidates could misstate their previous records, present glowing accounts of their abilities, make promises they knew they couldn't keep—all with the smug assurance that no one would challenge their assertions. Every campaign speech could begin with the words, "I think I can say without fear of contradiction...."

The Need for Clarity

In presenting earlier versions of this article, I have frequently encountered [this] surprising reaction: that I have actually overstated and mischaracterized the opposition to negative campaigning. As one panel discussant put it,

"Nobody criticizes *all* negative campaigning. When people criticize negative campaigning, they're not worried about attacks that are true and deal with significant issues. What they're upset about is that so much of this attack advertising is misleading or nasty or about made-up issues that have no real relevance to governing. *That's* what the furor's all about."

To this argument, I would make two responses. First, I would urge anyone who thinks I am overstating the case to read through a substantial part of the writing that has built up recently around the question of negative campaigning. What you will find is that the vast majority of this work ... does, indeed, indict all campaign activities that are aimed at criticizing one's opponents, regardless of the particular issues they deal with, without even investigating whether the attacks are true or not. Very occasionally, one will come across an author who notes, usually in passing, that perhaps not all negative campaigning is bad, that some of it may even serve a useful purpose. But only a very small percentage of the writing on negative campaigning includes this qualification; most writing on the topic criticizes *all* negative campaigning, without any attempt to draw distinctions about its truth, relevance, or civility. . . .

If the problem really is with campaign ads that are misleading or irrelevant or nasty, why not just say so? Why not abandon the attack on negative campaigning and go after misleading campaigning or trivial campaigning instead? . . . As many studies of the policy development process have emphasized, the way a problem is defined has a major effect on the kinds of "solutions" that will be proposed to cope with it.

This has clearly been true of the current effort to improve the conduct of American election campaigns. By defining the problem as one of negative campaigning, critics have naturally been led to look for solutions that would make it more difficult for candidates to criticize their opponents. What all of these proposals have in common, not surprisingly, is that they are targeted at negative campaigning as a generic, undifferentiated category. They would apply, in other words, to all advertising that criticizes one's opponents; they do not even attempt to distinguish between truthful and misleading attacks, or between trivial and relevant issues. And thus, to the extent they are successful, they will not only eliminate scurrilous and unfair attacks, but also those that are true, relevant, responsible, and serious.

There is, in short, a need for much greater care and clarity in thinking and writing about negative campaigning.

The Character Issue

Given the likely consequences of an attempt to limit or discourage critical comments of any kind, many commentators might want to modify their definition of negative campaigning. Perhaps what they really mean is something more like this: "Critical comments about your opponents' policy proposals are acceptable. But critical comments about your opponents' character, ability, or personal behavior are wrong. That's what negative campaigning is."

This argument, of course, is simply one variant of another common theme in the recent public debate about election campaigns. Whenever a candidate's personal character or behavior are questioned by his opponents or by the media, a number of voices will be heard insisting that such matters have no legitimate place in our elections and that campaigns should stick "strictly to the issues." But this argument, too, is fundamentally mistaken. Its basic flaw is the failure to appreciate the fact that candidates for public office are not computer programs with lengthy sets of preestablished policy subroutines, but flesh-and-blood human beings.

Campaign promises are at best only a rough guide to the actual decisions that a public official will make when in office.... Whatever the cause, it is striking how many of the most important policy initiatives of the last thirty years were never discussed in the previous campaign, or were taken by presidents who had promised or implied that they would do otherwise. The issue positions assumed during a campaign, in other words, are short-lived and changeable; a better guide to what a candidate will do is often provided by his personality and character.

Once a public official does reach a decision, there is surely no guarantee that it will automatically be promulgated and executed with the full force of law.... They must... be good managers and political strategists, meet frequently with other elected officials, lead public opinion, persuade the recalcitrant, and attract and retain talented staff. And all of these are matters of ability, temperament, and character.

For both of those reasons, candidate character and behavior are entirely relevant issues, more important than many policy questions. Indeed, if you examine the records of the last few presidents, what strikes you is how their most serious failings—at least in the minds of the voters—were not brought on by their policy views, but by their character flaws: Nixon's dishonesty and vindictiveness, Carter's inability to work with other elected officials, Reagan's management style, Bush's general disinterest in domestic policy. Small wonder, then, that public opinion polls continually show that voters are highly concerned about the personal qualities of the people on the ballot.

After acknowledging this, however, the issues become somewhat murkier. Character matters, but what particular character traits would recommend or disqualify a candidate? Does sexual promiscuity make for a bad president? Does avoiding the draft? Many of the most important character traits, moreover, are remarkably difficult to assess. We not know something about how to determine if a candidate is promiscuous, but how do we "prove" that he is vindictive or paranoid or unintelligent? If a candidate loses his temper at a campaign stop, is this an isolated incident or a sign of a deep-seated mean streak? When a candidate cheats on his wife, is this a regrettable but common human failing, or a symptom of a larger personality disorder?

There are no simple answers to such questions; but particularly in elections for executive offices such as president, governor, or mayor, where character flaws can have such important repercussions, I think we are well advised to cast the net widely....

Furthermore, when difficult and border-line cases do arise as to whether a particular behavior or character trait is relevant to a candidate's performance in office, the bias should clearly be in favor of reporting and discussing the issue. If many voters believe that such matters are irrelevant, then presumably they can be trusted to ignore the issue when deciding how to cast their own ballots. But the final say should rest with the electorate, not with the reporters, political consultants, or fair campaign practice committees who might wish to screen such matters from public attention.

And if issues of character and behavior should be discussed, then they should be examined in both their positive and negative aspects. If candidates are free to portray themselves as leaders or deep thinkers or good managers or highly moral, then their opponents should be free to contest these claims. If Joseph Biden wanted to project an image as a passionate orator, fine. But the campaign manager for one of his leading opponents should then have been allowed to point out that some of Biden's passion and rhetoric were borrowed.

The Role of the Media

Another possible line of reply to the argument presented here is that I have left one important element out of the equation: the news media. If the purpose of negative campaigning is to expose the candidates' weaknesses and shortcomings, and to prevent lies and misrepresentations, then perhaps we can rely on television, newspapers, and magazines to help perform these functions. . . .

But when it comes to the need for negative campaigning, the news media cannot substitute for the candidates. Yes, the media will often be negative— but about the wrong things and in the wrong ways. Two major characteristics of the American news media, amply verified in a long list of studies, make them ill suited to perform the functions that have traditionally been served by negative campaigning. In the first place, the media have a long-standing aversion to issues of any kind—positive or negative—or to detailed discussions of the candidates' previous performance and governing abilities. As one recent analysis of the media performance literature has noted:

> Countless studies of campaign journalism (both print and broadcast) have shown that the news invariably focuses on the campaign as a contest or race. News reports on the candidates' standing in public opinion polls, their advertising strategies, the size of the crowds at their appearances, their fundraising efforts, and their electoral prospects far surpass coverage detailing their issue positions, ideology, prior experience, or decision-making style.

This same sort of disproportion can be found in negative articles about the campaign. If a candidate makes a major gaffe, if his poll ratings are slipping, if there is in-fighting among his advisers—all these will be reported promptly and in exhaustive detail. But do not expect such detailed examination of the shortcomings in a candidate's economic policies, his environmental record, or his plans for dealing with the Middle East. The media's past record suggests that they are unlikely to provide it. Studies of campaign advertising, by contrast, usually conclude that political commercials have far more substantive content than is generally appreciated. Moreover, according to a recent study by Darrell West, negative spots usually have more specific and issue-based appeals than positive commercials.

A second obstacle to the media's attempt to "police" an election campaign are the norms of objectivity and nonpartisanship that govern most major American news outlets. What exactly objectivity means, and whether the media always live up to that standard, are complex and difficult questions, but ones that need not concern us here.... [T]he media are generally averse to saying anything explicit about the issues that could be construed as judgmental, interpretive, or subjective. As Michael Robinson and Margaret Sheehan found in their study of news coverage during the 1980 election:

> As reluctant as the press is about saying anything explicit concerning the leadership qualities of the candidates, the press is markedly more reluctant to assess or evaluate issues.... [We found] an almost total refusal by [CBS and UPI] to go beyond straightforward description of the candidate's policy positions. During the last ten weeks of Campaign '80, CBS failed to draw a single clear inference or conclusion about a single issue position of a single candidate—UPI as well.

How do the media cover issues, then? The answer is that they report on what the candidates themselves are saying.... As a result, the only kinds of policing of the issues that the media will undertake on their own initiative are questions that can clearly and unambiguously be labeled as matters of fact. If a candidate makes a blatant factual error—by misquoting a report, or claiming that nuclear missiles can be called back after they are launched, or adding items to his resume that never actually occurred—the media will sometimes call him on it.... Even the recent profusion of ad watches, which represents a more self-consciously aggressive attempt to scrutinize the candidates, generally adheres to these same guidelines.

In most campaigns, however, the most significant issue controversies are not matters of fact, but questions that require a substantial amount of judgment and interpretation. Would George McGovern's proposed defense cuts have left America unprotected? Was Jimmy Carter avoiding the issues in 1976? Was Ronald Reagan a warmonger?... Did George Bush have any vision for America's future?... On these and similar controversies, the media's record is that they will publicize these issues only if a candidate's opponents have talked about them first....

But even if the news media were to adopt a new set of norms and were willing to police our election campaigns, it is doubtful that we would want to put this burden primarily on their shoulders. The right of any individual or group to criticize, to object, to dissent is one of the signal achievements of American democracy, enshrined in the First Amendment. To say that we should restrict or penalize negative campaigning is to say, in effect, that candidates should now largely abdicate that right and rest content with whatever the media decide to broadcast or publish. If candidates did agree to abide by such strictures, they would thus be renouncing many of the most important duties we have traditionally expected from our best leaders and political heroes: such tasks as articulating grievances; speaking on behalf of the ignored and the forgotten; taking an unappreciated problem, bringing it to public attention, and thereby compelling the system to take action.

On a more general level, it has become increasingly clear over the last thirty years to both liberals and conservatives that some of the most difficult challenges facing American democracy in the twenty-first century concern the enormous power vested in the mass media, an entity that is self-selected, demographically and ideologically unrepresentative, increasingly monopolistic, almost entirely unregulated, and not directly accountable to the voters. There are no easy solutions for this complicated set of issues; but the very fact that these questions are so difficult strongly commends the wisdom of one general maxim: we ought to be extremely leery about any proposal that wants to increase the power of the media by asking them to take on one more function that has traditionally been performed by the candidates or the political parties. If candidates abuse their power of negative campaigning, the voters retain the ultimate power of punishing them at the polls. But what real alternative do the voters have if our election campaigns are improperly policed by CBS News or *The New York Times?*

What Restrictions on Negative Campaigning Would Mean for American Politics

Of the proposals ... for reducing or restricting negative campaigning, it is unclear how many would actually accomplish their intended goal....

But let us suppose, for a moment, that one or another of these proposals would be effective: it would significantly reduce the volume of negative campaigning and make it considerably more difficult for a candidate to attack or criticize his opponent. What impact would this have on the character of American politics?

The most obvious consequence, of course, is that it would deprive the electorate of a lot of valuable information, and thereby make it that much more difficult for the voters to make intelligent choices about the people they elect to public office. Like our political system generally, our electoral system is based on the belief that good decisions are more likely to result from a full, thorough, and unrestricted discussion of the issues. As the Supreme Court stated in one of the most important free speech cases of the twentieth century, there is

> a profound national commitment to the principle that debate on public issues should be uninhibited, robust, and wide-open, and *that it may well include vehement, caustic, and sometimes unpleasantly sharp attacks on government and public officials.*

Deprived of the important information conveyed in negative campaigning, the voters would be in the position of a blackjack player who must decide how to play his hand without getting to look at his hole card. He may, of course, stumble into the right decision, but the odds are surely better if he knows all the cards he has been dealt.

But beyond this general enfeebling of democracy, any limitation on negative campaigning is likely to have important systemic consequences for our politics. In congressional elections, restrictions on negative campaigning would almost certainly work to the advantage of incumbents, making them even more entrenched and difficult to unseat. . . .

In the end, a challenger in a congressional election stands almost no chance of winning unless he "goes negative": unless, in other words, he can succeed in raising doubts about the incumbent's character, voting record, and attention to the district. . . .

Any move to limit negative campaigning, in short, would just add one more weapon to the already formidable arsenal with which incumbents manage to entrench themselves in office. . . .

And the more negative campaigning is discouraged or penalized, the more likely it becomes that all voters will ever learn about how the challenger performed in his previous position is the candidate's own highly colored version of that record. Thus, in a close election . . . where the campaign could make a difference in the final outcome, limits on negative campaigning would be distinctly to the advantage of the challenger.

It is no accident that when various commentators recommended a moratorium on negative campaigning during the last few weeks of the 1992 presidential race, Bill Clinton readily agreed to the idea and George Bush tried to resist it. Both major-party campaigns understood quite well that Bush's only chance for victory lay in a negative campaign against Clinton. To be sure, there is something a little sad about an incumbent president whose best argument as to why he should be reelected is to say, in effect, "Sure, I may not have been a very good president—but my opponent would be even worse." But the fact that this argument is sad does not mean that it may not be in some cases entirely valid.

The Search for Better Campaigns

To defend negative campaigning, of course, is not to deny that positive campaigning is also important. What our politics really needs is a mixture of the two. A candidate who is challenging an incumbent should be required to show the weaknesses and shortcomings of his opponent, and then to indicate how and why he would do better. An incumbent should defend his own record, and then (since that record is unlikely to be entirely without blemish) should be able to point out the ways in which the challenger would be deficient. The point is that both are valid ways of appealing to and informing the electorate— just as economic affairs and foreign policy are both relevant issues.

The effort to stamp out negative campaigning thus deals a double blow to any attempt to improve the quality of future American election campaigns. It seeks to deny the voters important information that is relevant to their decisions; but it also helps divert attention from the many serious problems that genuinely afflict our campaigns. Most of the practices that are condemned on the grounds of negative campaigning are actually objectionable for very different reasons. Sending a forged letter about one's opponent, as the Nixon people did in 1972, is wrong, not because it is negative campaigning, but because it's a lie. Demanding that your opponent take a drug test isn't objectionable because it's negative, but because the issue it raises is trivial. Calling your opponent "unChristian" is wrong because it is a misuse of religion. Accusing a congressional incumbent of taking too many junkets would be wrong if it takes such incidents out of context. (It may also be a real indication that the incumbent is neglecting his duties and abusing the perquisites of office.)

There is a simple test that can be applied to all of these issues. If you think that a particular campaign practice is wrong because it is an instance of negative campaigning, then it follows that the same behavior would be acceptable just as long as it was done in a positive manner. So, if negative campaigning is the real villain in all of these cases, sending a forged letter that attacks an opponent is wrong, but forging a letter that says positive things about one's own candidate is acceptable. Or: it's wrong to criticize your opponent for failing to take a drug test, but it's okay if you yourself take a drug test and then trumpet the results as proof of your spectacular fitness for office. It's wrong to call your opponent "unChristian," but acceptable to call yourself "the Christian candidate in this election."

Rather than trying to limit or discourage negative campaigning as a generic category, we ought to recognize that some negative campaigning is good and some negative campaigning is bad—and then think more carefully about the kinds of moral criteria that really should make a difference. . . . Probably the most significant problem with campaign advertising, positive and negative, is that so much of it is misleading, taking votes and actions out of context, or implying connections between events that may be completely unrelated. Many ads also deal with matters of highly questionable relevance that tell us little or nothing about either candidates' ideology or fitness for office. It also seems clear that many voters are troubled by the incivility of many negative ads, the tone of which is frequently harsh and mean-spirited. All of these are real and serious problems, eminently worthy of our best efforts to rectify them. But we will make little progress in this direction by a war against negative campaigning.

POSTSCRIPT

Is Negative Campaigning Bad for the American Political Process?

A 1996 Freedom Forum poll found that three-quarters of American voters believe that the press has a negative impact on U.S. presidential campaigns, detracts from a discussion of the issues, gives undue advantage to front-running candidates, is often confusing and unclear, and even discourages good people from running for president. Despite the criticism, these same voters rely heavily on journalists to provide the information needed to make informed voter decisions. They turn to journalists for information about the candidates, particularly their issue positions, and for information about how election outcomes will affect voters.

The implications of these arguments for judgments about negativity in political campaigns are important. It seems clear that people are unhappy with current political coverage. People want more information, and they want it tailored to their questions and their needs. Political Internet sites are perhaps one answer. They are proliferating; yet, even these suffer from the familiar problem of too much trivia and too little debate. It remains to be seen whether or not the advent of new technology will be able to fulfill its promise of creating a more positive dialogue between candidate and voter.

Lest a reader begin to feel too self-righteous about these issues, let us remember the complicity of the viewing public. Candidate debates attract small numbers of viewers; political scandal sells. Just as in television entertainment, what the public gets is influenced by what the public selects from the available options. Certainly with the advent of cable niche programming, the public can select much more informative and less scandal-oriented programming than ever before. Thus, the critique that implicates the press and the politician also implicates the viewer.

A number of books try to analyze the consequences of negativity. One book that has specifically tackled the history and problem of campaign advertising is *Going Negative: How Attack Ads Shrink and Polarize the Electorate,* by Stephen Ansolabehere and Shano Iyengar (Free Press, 1997). Examining the consequences for the voter are Joseph Capella and Kathleen Hall Jamieson in *Spiral of Cynicism* (Oxford University Press, 1997). See also, Justin Lewis, "Reproducing Political Hegemony in the U.S.," *Critical Studies in Mass Communication* (vol. 16, no. 3, 1999) and Victor Kamber, "Poison Politics," *California Journal* (vol. 28, no. 11, 1997). For a journalistic take on the issue, see Mike McCurry, "Getting Past the Spin," *The Washington Monthly* (July/August 1999).

ISSUE 10

Do the Media Have a Liberal Bias?

YES: Bernard Goldberg, from *Bias: A CBS Insider Exposes How the Media Distort the News* (Regnery Publishing, 2002)

NO: James Wolcott, from "Fox Populi?" *Vanity Fair* (August 2001)

ISSUE SUMMARY

YES: Journalist Bernard Goldberg looks at the common phrase, "the media elite have a liberal bias," and gives examples of the way coverage becomes slanted, depending upon the reporter's or anchor's perception of the subject's political stance.

NO: Journalist James Wolcott examines the impact of Fox television network's conservative approach, as evidenced by the news programs that feature right-wing pundits and pro-Republican views. He contends that Fox's news and public affairs coverage attained the highest ratings when appealing to the "angry white male."

Two important concepts are covered in the following selections; one takes on the traditional complaint that people in the media—the newsmakers and the on-air personalities—have a liberal bias, which presents the public with a critical view of the government and policies. The other concept is more fundamental; it asks whether or not a diversity of viewpoints is really available in the media so that the consumer can be informed appropriately and make up his or her mind depending upon the messages conveyed.

Years of media analysis and theory underscore these issues and include such topics as "agenda setting," "status conferral features," "media functions," and "uses and gratifications." Research in any of these areas will shed greater light on the complexity of media content and audience interpretation of messages.

These selections by Goldberg and Wolcott also present a more "popular" approach to media commentary. Each is written from a distinctly personal viewpoint, which demonstrates that the "sender" of any message (in this case the author) can easily insert his or her own beliefs into a persuasive message. When viewed in this way, the question of whether or not the media can possibly present "neutral" messages takes on greater meaning. But while Goldberg and Wolcott both present their messages in print, the topic they are covering is broadcasting—which is subject to an even broader range of filters, gatekeepers, and audiences.

Goldberg writes from the perspective of a one-time CBS insider who criticized the media (and in particular, Dan Rather at CBS) for what he says are clearly liberal interpretations of information. He cites many examples, and seems to assume that his readers will agree with his interpretations. In doing so, he makes value judgments about issues that perhaps reveal a bias of his own.

Wolcott shows that at least now, since the introduction of Fox News, more "conservative" viewpoints are aired to appeal to a different audience from that of the more mainstream networks' newscasts. However, he talks of a range of diversity on the Fox network, and in doing so, creates a position that the media has a diversity of viewpoints available to viewers. He too, may be considered polemical in his critique.

One of the most important questions to consider as you read the following selections is whether or not any possible bias indicates a transmission of viewpoints or values. If the media lead us to think a certain way, then this may be an important issue to consider. If the media serve as one method among many for the socialization of the individual, then perhaps the topic is less important. Often the importance—and the bias—are in the eye of the beholder. By thinking and talking about this issue and news, you may find yourself having to take a position on the topic. Once you think you understand this concept, why not apply it to other forms of media, like music, film, or television?

Bernard Goldberg

 **YES**

The News Mafia

I can't say the precise moment it hit me, but I do know that it was on a Sunday night while I was watching the HBO series *The Sopranos*. That's when I started noticing that the wise guys in the mob and the news guys at the networks had the same kind of people skills.

Maybe Tony had somebody killed. Or maybe just roughed up. Or it might have been only words, something he said to his psychiatrist. I'm not sure. But the more I watched the more I saw how striking the similarities are between the Mafia and the media.

And, let the record show, I mean no disrespect to the Mafia.

In between hijacking trucks and throwing people off bridges, the wise guys are always going on about honor and loyalty and family, the holy trinity as far as guys with names like Tony Soprano and Paulie Walnuts are concerned. These are people who are exquisitely and monumentally delusional, of course. But it's this fundamental belief—that despite the bad PR, deep down where it really counts, they are just a bunch of honorable men who care about the important things in life and only hurt people who hurt them—that allows the wise guys to crush anyone who gets in their way.

It's the same with the News Mafia....

Trust me. I'm speaking from up-close-and-personal firsthand experience, from twenty-eight years on the inside as a news correspondent with one of the three big families, CBS News....

<<<>>>

February 13, 1996, was the day I committed my unpardonable sin and began to die....

I said out loud what millions of TV news viewers all over America know and have been complaining about for years: that too often, Dan [Rather] and Peter [Jennings] and Tom [Brokow] and a lot of their foot soldiers don't deliver the news straight, that they have a liberal bias, and that no matter how often the network stars deny it, it is true....

Actually I didn't *say* the networks were biased—I *wrote* it in one of the most important and widely read newspapers in the entire country, the *Wall*

From Bernard Goldberg, *Bias: A CBS Insider Exposes How the Media Distort the News* (Regnery Publishing, 2002). Copyright © 2002 by Medium Cool, Inc. Reprinted by permission of Regnery Publishing, Inc., Washington, D.C.

Street Journal, whose editorial page liberals love to hate. In an op-ed piece, I wrote, "There are lots of reasons fewer people are watching network news, and one of them, I'm more convinced than ever, is that our viewers simply don't trust us. And for good reason.

"The old argument that the networks and other 'media elites' have a liberal bias is so blatantly true that it's hardly worth discussing anymore. No, we don't sit around in dark corners and plan strategies on how we're going to slant the news. We don't have to. It comes naturally to most reporters."

As my old buddy Wayne, who's never set foot in a newsroom in his life, put it, "What's the big deal; *everybody* knows that's true." Maybe, Wayne, but there's a big difference between when Rush Limbaugh or Bill Buckley says it and when a CBS News correspondent says it.

This was coming from the inside, from one of Rather's guys. Limbaugh could rave on about the liberal media all he wanted and the media elites would brush him off like a flake of dandruff on a blue suit. If William F. Buckley had written, word for word, what I had written, Dan Rather would have yawned and jumped in his limousine and headed for lunch at The Four Seasons.

Limbaugh and Buckley and all those other "right-wingers"—everybody to the right of Lenin is a "right-winger," as far as the media elites are concerned—were all a bunch of Republican partisans.

But I wasn't. I was a newsman. One of *their* newsmen! I had done a thousand stories for Walter Cronkite and Dan Rather on the *CBS Evening News* and later as the senior correspondent on *48 Hours*, the prime-time show Rather fronted. They don't let you stick around for more than two decades if you've got a political ax to grind. No, I was what The Dan and his nominal bosses in the front office call all of their reporters and producers: objective ... fair ... balanced.

I'll bet anything those are the exact words CBS News would have used to defend me if I had reported a story for the *Evening News* that came down hard on big business or the military or even the church. CBS News would have said, *Bernie has a well-deserved reputation for being objective, fair, and balanced, and we stand by Bernie and our story.*

But this piece I had written for the *Wall Street Journal* wasn't about business or the military or the church or any other safe target. Writing about the evils of business or the military or the church is like taking a walk in the park. I had just taken a stroll through a field of land mines. Taking on the pope is one thing. Taking on the media elites is quite another. And taking them on from the inside—violating their sacred code of *omerta*—is a sin.

A mortal sin.

It's funny how some of the biggest, most dramatic changes in our lives happen almost by accident. If we hadn't gone to that particular drugstore to buy toothpaste and tissues on that particular day, we might not have met an old friend whom we hadn't seen in years, who invited us to a party where we met somebody's accountant, who walked us over to this schoolteacher whom we fell in love with and married. Go to a different drugstore and wind up with a different life.

Which brings us to Hurricane Andrew, the costliest natural disaster in the entire history of the United States, which just happened to blow through my house and thousands of others in South Florida in 1992. This brought me into contact for the very first time with a good ol' boy named Jerry Kelley, a chain-smoking, fifty-something building contractor who grew up in Enterprise, Alabama, and who makes Gomer Pyle sound like Laurence Olivier.

Without Hurricane Andrew there would have been no Jerry Kelley. And without Jerry Kelley there would have been no *Wall Street Journal* op-ed piece that changed my life forever.

Jerry Kelley saved my family and me. He repaired the damage the hurricane had done to our house. He was always there when we needed him. And we became friends, a kind of odd couple. We talked often, mostly about politics and current events, which he loved.

And on February 8, 1996, Jerry Kelley called me at home, wondering whether I had caught the *CBS Evening News* that night.

"Did you see that 'Reality Check' story on Dan Rather tonight?" he wanted to know, sounding even more like a cracker than he usually did, if that was possible. Jerry wasn't an angry kind of guy, but he was pretty hot that night. I told him I missed the Dan Rather newscast and asked what the problem was.

"The problem," he said, "is that you got too many snippy wise guys doin' the news, that's what the problem is." We went around like this for a while, and he told me to get a tape of the news and watch it. Then "you tell me if there's a problem."

Fair enough. The next day I went into the CBS News bureau in Miami to watch a videotape of the story that had Jerry so worked up.

The reporter was Eric Engberg, a Washington correspondent whose "Reality Check" was about presidential candidate Steve Forbes and his flat tax, which was the centerpiece of the Forbes campaign.

Not exactly a sexy subject. So what's the big deal, I wondered. But as I watched the videotape, it became obvious that this was a hatchet job, an editorial masquerading as real news, a cheap shot designed to make fun of Forbes—a rich conservative white guy, the safest of all media targets—and ridicule his tax plan.

Still, blasting the flat tax wasn't in the same league as taking shots at people who are against affirmative action or abortion, two of the more popular targets of the liberal media elites. How worked up was I supposed to get... *over the flat tax?*

But the more I watched the more I saw that this story wasn't simply about a presidential candidate and a tax plan. It was about something much bigger, something too much of big-time TV journalism had become: a showcase for smart-ass reporters with attitudes, reporters who don't even pretend to hide their disdain for certain people and certain ideas that they and their sophisticated friends don't particularly like.

Rather introduced Engberg's piece with the standard stuff about how it would "look beyond the promises to the substance" of the Forbes flat tax.

Television news anchors enjoy using words like "substance," mostly because a half-hour newscast (about twenty-one minutes after commercials) has so little of it.

Engberg's voice covered pictures of Steve Forbes on the campaign trail. "Steve Forbes pitches his flat-tax scheme as an economic elixir, good for everything that ails us."

Scheme? Elixir? What the hell kind of language is that, I wondered? These were words that conjured up images of con artists, like Doctor Feelgood selling worthless junk out of the back of his wagon.

But that was just a little tease to get us into the tent. Then Engberg interviewed three different tax experts. Every single one of them opposed the flat tax. Every single one! Where was the fairness and balance Rather was always preaching about? Wasn't there any expert—*even one*—in the entire United States who thought the flat tax *might* work?

Of course there was. There were Milton Friedman and Merton Miller, both of the University of Chicago and both Nobel Prize winners in economics. There was James Buchanan of George Mason University, another Nobel laureate. There were also Harvey Rosen of Princeton, William Poole of Brown, and Robert Barro of Harvard. All of them were on the record as supporting the flat tax to one degree or another.

Engberg could have found a bunch of economists to support the flat tax, *if he had wanted to.* But putting on a supporter of the flat tax would have defeated the whole purpose of the piece; which was to have a few laughs at Steve Forbes's expense.

There is absolutely no way—not one chance in a million—that Engberg or Rather would have aired a flat-tax story with that same contemptuous tone if Teddy Kennedy or Hillary Clinton had come up with the idea.

But even if you opposed the flat tax, even if you thought it was a bad idea that helped only the wealthiest Americans—fat cats like Steve Forbes himself—what about simple journalistic fairness? What about presenting two sides? Isn't that what Rather was always saying CBS News was about: objectivity, fairness, balance?

And then Engberg crossed that fuzzy little line that's supposed to separate news from entertainment. He decided it was time to amuse his audience. And who could blame him? The flat tax didn't have much pizzazz by showbiz standards. The audience might lose interest and, God forbid, change the channel. In the United States of Entertainment there is no greater sin than to bore the audience. A TV reporter could get it wrong from time to time. He could be snippy and snooty. But he could not be boring.

Which is why Eric Engberg decided to play David Letterman and do a takeoff of his Top Ten list.

"Forbes's Number One Wackiest Flat-Tax Promise," Engberg told the audience, is the candidate's belief that it would give parents "more time to spend with their children and each other."

Wacky? This was a perfectly acceptable word in the United States of Entertainment to describe, say, a Three Stooges movie. Or *Hamlet*, starring Jerry Lewis. Or *My Fair Lady*, with Chris Rock playing Professor Higgins.

But "wacky" seemed an odd word to describe a serious idea to overhaul America's ten-trillion-page tax code that enables lobbyists to donate tons of money to politicians who then use this same Byzantine tax code to hand out goodies to the very same special interests that just gave them all that money. If anything is "wacky," it's the *current* tax system, not an honest attempt to replace it with something new.

Besides, what Forbes meant is that since many Americans—not just the wealthy—would pay less tax under his plan, they might not have to work as many hours and might actually have more time to spend at home with their families. Maybe it's true and maybe it isn't, but is "wacky" the fairest and most objective way to describe it?

Can you imagine, in your wildest dreams, a network news reporter calling Hillary Clinton's health care plan "wacky"? Can you imagine Dan Rather or any other major American news anchorman allowing it?

And finally, the coup de grâce, the knife to Steve Forbes's throat as Engberg went on camera to end his story. The "on camera," as we call it in the TV news business, is when the reporter gets to look the viewer in the eye and deliver a sermonette. This is when the reporter, if he hasn't been slanting the news up to this point, will often give you a little editorial just to make sure you know how you're supposed to think about the subject at hand. Eric Engberg ended his little vaudeville act thus: "The fact remains: The flat tax is a giant, untested theory. One economist suggested, before we put it in, we should test it out someplace—like Albania." Engberg flashed his signature smirk and signed off—"Eric Engberg, CBS News, Washington."

There is junk science, junk food, and junk bonds. This was junk journalism.

I don't believe for a second that Eric Engberg woke up that morning and said, "I think I'll go on the air tonight and make fun of Steve Forbes." The problem is that so many TV journalists simply don't know what to think about certain issues until the *New York Times* and the *Washington Post* tell them what to think. Those big, important newspapers set the agenda that network news people follow. In this case the message from Olympus was clear: We don't like the flat tax. So neither did Eric Engberg, and neither did anyone at CBS News who put his story on the air. It's as simple as that.

That the flat tax was a conservative idea only made the job of bashing it more fun. Yes, it's true that a number of conservative politicians came out against it. Lamar Alexander, for one, called it "a truly nutty idea." But Alexander, and some others who came out against Forbes's version of the flat tax—like Pat Buchanan, who said it was a plan that favored "the boys down at the yacht basin"—just happened to be running for president against Steve Forbes. That raises a few legitimate questions about their motives.

Make no mistake: the flat tax *is* fundamentally conservative. In *Newsweek*, George Will wrote, "In the 1990s conservatism had two genuinely radical proposals for domestic reform, proposals that would have fundamentally altered the political culture. Term limits for members of Congress would have ended careerism, today's strongest motive for entering, and for particular behavior in, politics. A flat tax would have taken the tax code out of play as an instrument for dispensing political favors, and would have put out of business a parasite class of tax lawyers and lobbyists in Washington."

By and large, the angst over the flat tax came from the Left. Which makes perfect sense. Liberals have an uneasy feeling about tax cuts in general and are downright hostile to the kinds of cuts that benefit the wealthy in particular, even if they also help a lot of other Americans. They may argue against the flat tax on economic grounds, which is fair enough since there are legitimate questions and concerns about a flat-tax rate. But much of the opposition from the Left had little to do with economics. It was visceral, from the same dark region that produces envy and the seemingly unquenchable liberal need to wage class warfare.

Paul Begala, the political strategist who worked on both the 1992 and 1996 Clinton-Gore campaigns, charmingly explained the Left's philosophy on people with money when, according to Bob Woodward's *The Agenda*, he told Treasury Secretary Robert Rubin, "F**k them [the rich]."

Karl Marx couldn't have said it better.

So the Left routinely uses words like "scheme" instead of the more neutral "plan" to describe tax cuts that favor "the wrong people." Sometimes they put the word "risky" before "scheme" to make it sound really scary. Al Gore did precisely that, about a hundred times a day, when he was running for president against George W. Bush. I understand why Al Gore and other liberals call something they don't like a "scheme." Politicians and partisans are allowed to do that. But should supposedly objective people like news reporters, people like Eric Engberg, use that kind of loaded language? Should a journalistic enterprise like CBS News—which claims to stand for fairness and objectivity—allow words like "scheme" and "wacky" in what is supposed to be a straight news story about a legitimate candidate running for president of the United States?

Engberg's piece—its strident, mocking tone, its lack of objectivity, its purposeful omission of anyone who supported the flat tax—was like a TV campaign commercial paid for by *Opponents of the Steve Forbes Flat Tax*.

From top to bottom the Engberg piece was breathtaking in its lack of fairness. So how could CBS put it on the air? Well, news fans, here's one of those dirty little secrets journalists are never supposed to reveal to the regular folks out there in the audience: a reporter can find an expert to say anything the reporter wants—*anything!* Just keep calling until one of the experts says what you need him to say and tell him you'll be right down with your camera crew to interview him. If you find an expert who says, "You know, I think that flat tax just might work and here's why . . ." you thank him, hang up, and find another expert. It's how journalists sneak their own personal views into stories in the guise of objective news reporting. Because the reporter can always say, "Hey, I didn't say the flat tax stinks—the guy from that Washington think tank did!"

It happens all the time.

I don't know Steve Forbes. I've never met him. I don't even buy his magazine. *And I had never voted for a Republican candidate for president in my entire life!* But he was a serious, intelligent man seeking the most important job in our country; and what CBS News had just done to him was shameful and not worthy of an important network news organization.

So I called Jeff Fager, who had just taken over as executive producer of the *CBS Evening News*. I had known Jeff for more than ten years. I asked him how in the world he could have put that story on the air. Fager didn't remember any details of the Engberg report. That's how *un*controversial it was to him.

I told Fager I had been complaining privately about bias at CBS News for years, that I always kept it in-house, but this time was different. This time, I told him, I was going to write about it, and then maybe he and the other people who decide what gets on the air would listen.

Jeff Fager is an interesting guy. Funny. Smart. Easygoing. But in some way he's *too* cool. Nothing fazes him. Jeff is the kind of guy who never suffers a crisis of confidence, not on the outside where you could tell, anyway. From what I could tell by working with him over the years, Jeff is someone who is more in touch with his "inner self" than all those self-esteem gurus who show up on PBS during a pledge drive *put together*. Which is probably why he wasn't upset with the Engberg hatchet job. So I sat down and started writing the op-ed piece.

The way I saw it, I wasn't taking on Engberg or Rather or CBS News for airing one snooty story about some politicians tax plan. For me, this was about a nagging problem that none of the big shots would take seriously. It was about the liberal biases that overwhelm straight news reporting.

NO

James Wolcott

Fox Populi?

What ever happened to the Angry White Male? Where did all that apoplexy go? In the early 90s, an irate mob of palefaces seemed to materialize out of the crackling static of talk radio, their fists and faces clenched, intent on righting the crooked path America had taken. This posse was riled. Jutting their jaws like Charlton Heston accepting an ovation from gun nuts, taking their marching orders from Rush Limbaugh, its members were fed up with the entire menu of liberal intrusion: high taxes, gay rights, feminist scolding, yuppie snobbery, multiculturalism, affirmative action, political correctness, sexual-harassment suits, speed limits, seat-belt laws, immigrants flooding the borders and stealing jobs nobody else wanted, restrictions on assault weapons, and the incense aroma of Oprah. They felt like a persecuted minority themselves as the complexion of America began to shade from white to beige. The Angry White Male insurgence crested with the Republican sweep of the Congress in 1994, when voters seemed to rise up like a militant sack of marshmallows—the pudgy-wudgy Newt Gingrich their rebel leader—and mutinied against a political system that had too long discounted their complaints and stigmatized them as the poster boys of patriarchy.

How swiftly this macho uprising went poof. Like Bigfoot, the Angry White Male showed himself only to retreat into the berry bushes, replaced on the political stage by the Soccer Mom. The most popular and plausible explanation for this rapid fade is that the public turned against A.W.M.'s after Republican freshmen on the Hill overplayed their hand with the government shutdown of 1995, as a foolhardy Gingrich was rope-a-doped by the wily Bill Clinton. What appeared at the time to be a temporary defeat dissolved into a complete rout. Not only did Gingrich's switchblade gang of budget cutters and regulations slashers lose the "big mo" (momentum) until they were left with no mo' mo, their followers also seemed to take a powder. As John DiIulio, President [George W.] Bush's current adviser on faith-based initiatives, said later in a panel discussion, "Despite this earthquake election, within two years this supposedly new, cohesive, powerful block of angry white male voters had disappeared. They were gone."

No, not gone. The A.W.M.'s had only beaten a strategic retreat to bandage their egos and regroup. In October of 1996, a month before Bill Clinton beat Bob Dole in the presidential election, Rupert Murdoch launched Fox News Channel, a 24-hour news service that would provide a punchy alternative to the liberal mush of mainstream media. Named as Fox News czar was Roger Ailes, a former Republican strategist who produced Rush Limbaugh's TV show and prides himself on being a man of robust appetites and convictions in a world of salad-eating, do-goody conformists. He told *Newsweek* [in 2001], "The media elite think they're smarter than the rest of those stupid bastards, and they'll tell you what to think. To a working-class guy, that's bulls—t." (Rush Limbaugh is what Roger Ailes would be if he had Limbaugh's golden pipes and a richer vocabulary.) Despite his track record, Ailes assured doubters and cynics that Fox News Channel wouldn't function as a conservative propaganda spout. He told a reporter from E! Online News that Fox News would be a fat-free, no-frills operation. "We're going to provide straight, factual information," he said, "with less 'spin' and less 'face time' for anchors." Its motto—"We Report. You Decide" —proclaimed that Fox would be the Joe Friday of news coverage, just the facts, ma'am. perhaps Ailes found himself snowballed by the realities of broadcasting, or perhaps he was casting a reverse spell, for Fox News Channel couldn't bear less resemblance to his original outline. Some of its star anchors could give Sufi dancers spinning tips, and if they grabbed any more "face time," they would have to be fed intravenously on the set. Fox News Channel has become a vanity showcase catering to the Angry White Male in his autumn plumage.

⋅⟨⊙⟩⋅

Since its inception, Fox News has been a solid winner on cable, its ratings gains boosted in part by the hapless competition, which opened up a passing lane. Like the Baltimore Orioles, CNN is in an awkward rebuilding phase, patching its age-cracks with a youth injection of somewhat untried talent. For unfathomable reasons, MSNBC pads its prime-time weekday schedule with clip-job filler such as *Headliners & Legends*, which is introduced by Matt Lauer as if he rued the day he didn't read the fine print in his contract, and has allowed its entire weekend lineup to molder with recycled junkeroo. This is not to deny or play down Fox News's brash accomplishments as it [recently prepared] to celebrate its fifth birthday. In an otherwise lackluster period for Murdoch's News Corp., the channel has profitably thrived. "The home of brash talker Bill O'Reilly stayed in the black a second quarter in a row and saw its ratings soar by 120%," the New York *Daily News* reported. . . . Ailes's outfit works fast, hits hard, stamps its stories with its own identity, and exudes button-popping confidence, an esprit de corps CNN is groping to regain.

Individually, however, this confidence has inflated into camera-hog hubris. Before long, Fox News may have to add more headroom in the studio to accommodate hosts such as O'Reilly, Neil Cavuto, Brit Hume, Sean Hannity, and Tony Snow, who editorialize as if dictating a stern memo to God. (They have more opinions than thoughts, and more thoughts than ideas.) Years of being massaged with the perks and sweets lavished on a well-known talking head—cocktail parties, rising lecture fees, proximity to power brokers, beckoning glances on the shuttle—have rounded off their anger into a sleek contempt for those who don't share their views, a complacent sneer. Just as Rush Limbaugh has turned into the country-club Republican he routinely scorns (listen to his celebrity-golf-tournament stories), the anchors at Fox news are elitists who act as if they're fighting for you, the average bozo. Like Gingrich, they're corporate apologists posing as populists—inside-the-Beltway outsiders. How apt that after Gingrich stepped down as Speaker of the House he was hired by Fox as an on-air political consultant. The first network with an agenda, Fox News Channel is the continuation of the Gingrich Revolution by other means.

> Folks in Tonopah, Ariz., and other hamlets from Bangor, Maine, to Gold Beach, Ore., don't expect very much from the federal government—only that it be respectful of their beliefs.
>
> — Bill O'Reilly, in his syndicated column (*New York Post*, April 29, 2001).

Then again, these folks could get a mite upset if a flood or tornado tore into their hamlet and federal assistance were slow to arrive while they were snoring on cots in the high-school gym. They might flip their John Deere caps or pop their hair curlers if their Social Security checks or tax refunds failed to make it to the mailbox, or their Medicare benefits stopped, or lax oversight led to brown drinking water and salmonella du jour. As Republicans discovered when they were smacked sideways by the outcry over the government shutdown, folks also expect Washington museums and national parks to be open when they visit—that's part of their beliefs, too. However, the marching-band refrain of Fox News is that the majority of Americans want less government, less regulation, and a stringier safety net.

Beating the bass drum is its biggest star, Bill O'Reilly, host of *The O'Reilly Factor* and the channel's craggiest rock formation of Rugged Individualism. A former TV newsman at CBS and ABC, O'Reilly first came to prominent notice on the syndicated tabloid show *Inside Edition*. A tall, imposing man who uses his size and gruff, mercurial manner to destabilize the normally dead air of the studio (imagine Tom Synder with a broader sense of mission, Synder being content to complain about freeway traffic and slow elevators), O'Reilly is willing to scrap with anyone, which often makes for good TV. In the middle of a question or response, his eyes sometimes flip an existential switch that says, "Ah, what's the point? This is all a farce anyway," and his voice tails off into annoyed futility. His unpredictability extends to his political opinions—but only so far. Although not a doctrinaire Republican like Snow, Hume, Fred Barnes, and Hannity, a barbershop quartet of Bushspeak, O'Reilly proclaims through his every word and defiant cock of the head that he made it where he is today without any handouts from those bleeding hearts in Washington, and if he succeeded without any coddling, so can you. Stand up, be a man! You too, lady! Following the Rush Limbaugh personality-cult playbook, O'Reilly has capitalized on his Fox News success by repackaging his on-air sound bites—he begins each show with a "Talking Points" memo—into No. 1 bestsellerdom with his straight-shooting, back-patting manifesto, *The O'Reilly Factor*.

O'Reilly's posturing as a working-class hero has been derided as pure salami. His background, as Michael Kinsley pointed out in *Slate*, is middle-class.

He grew up in Levittown, New York, and his father's salary as an accountant, $35,000 a year in the 60s, would translate as a six-figure salary today. Kinsley took his funniest swipes at O'Reilly's account of being a graduate student at Harvard's Kennedy School of Government, where he felt like a pair of brown shoes in a sea of tasseled loafers. "The notion that the Kennedy School of Government, populated by swells out of P.G. Wodehouse, reached out to O'Reilly, a poor orphan out of Dickens," beggars credulity, Kinsley wrote. He accused O'Reilly of reverse snobbery, quoting as evidence a passage in a *Newsweek* profile (the same article where Ailes positioned himself as a John Lennon defender of the working class) in which O'Reilly spurned Starbucks for a Long Island coffee shop, "where cops and firemen hang out." You know, real guys like him, not those latte punks. (O'Reilly invited Kinsley on his show to rebut the *Slate* editor's contentions, subjecting him to a rough cross-examination and hoping to reduce him to coffee grounds.)

Like O'Reilly, Neil Cavuto, the host of Fox's afternoon business-news hour and of his own weekend show, *Cavuto on Business*, also buttonholes the camera like a regular guy who's had it up to here with these fancy-cuff-link types who think they can tell us how to run our lives. His "Common Sense" commentaries, like O'Reilly's "Talking Points" memos to the viewer, are sprinkled with barstool icebreakers such as "Hey, maybe it's just me, but..." and "I don't care how the heck I sound saying this, but I gotta tell ya..." But, unlike O'Reilly, Cavuto doesn't use his soapbox simply to pipe up for the little guy; he uses it also to stick up for America's most mistreated and unloved minority, the oppressed rich. Irked over the trimming and second-guessing of President Bush's tax cut, Cavuto squawked that those in the higher brackets were being penalized by these moves. "Why? Because they're rich, that's why, and because they can take it, that's why. And because no one will defend them, that's really why. I mean, when is the last time you saw a lobbying group for rich folks, or the last time you heard anyone say anything good about rich people? Think hard, I dare ya, it ain't gonna happen." Cavuto's weeping-violin cantata for downtrodden billionaires whose wealth can't buy them love or influence was almost touching in its pathos and lack of contact with planet Earth. Had he occupied a tree stump in Sherwood Forest, Cavuto would no doubt have preached, "Take from the rich, give to the poor—that's all anybody in the woods is talkin' about. And you won't hear it from this humble hut dweller that Robin Hood doesn't cut a dashing figure in his feathered cap. But let's get real—do you have any idea on the upkeep of a castle these days? Believe me, all that armor and all those 12-course banquets don't come cheap. To me, Prince John is the real victim here. And if that upsets some of you 'merry men,' too bad—because when I see a worthy nobleman getting robbed, I, for one, don't feel very merry."

Bossy as he can be, Bill O'Reilly will at least lean back now and then and let a guest finish an occasional sentence. Cavuto has an itchier trigger finger. He's a chronic, smart-aleck interrupter, breaking his guests' answers into bits of peanut brittle and always trying to top them with quippy comebacks. He interrupts everyone, but sets up his fragmentation campaign with liberals less besotted with yacht owners than he. Former secretary of labor Robert Reich, vainly trying to have a grown-up conversation about Bush's tax proposals, was peppered with darts from Cavuto that were capped with the parting question "Admit it, you hate rich people, don't you?" "Oh, Neil," Reich sighed. In fairness, Cavuto can be amiable as well, parrying viewer E-mails about his wardrobe choices and how large his head is with self-deprecating humor. When his pet causes are involved, however, he reverts to Mr. Prosecutor.

Fox News might argue that it is within its hosts' prerogative to belt out their opinions through their interviews, commentaries, and responses to viewer feedback. At least their political bias is honestly out in the open and not masked by subtle eyebrow semaphores—Peter Jennings's virtuoso specialty. Personal advocacy is one thing, corporate advocacy another, and when the topic bar in a discussion of Bush's proposals urges, "Cut 'Em Already!" (as it did when Cavuto interviewed Senator Charles Grassley), such propagandizing gives lie to the boast "Fair and Balanced." To Fox News fans, its conservative slant is vital and necessary to offset the liberal bias saturating the news media, but, spank my brain as I may, I can't recall a moment on CNN when Judy Woodruff buttered up a liberal Democrat as the words "Soak the Rich!" were bannered across the screen, or PBS's Jim Lehrer waved a six-shooter and demanded that the Fed lower interest rates (a thumping refrain from both O'Reilly and Cavuto). Whatever the political leanings of their on-air talent, traditional news outlets still believe in the formal appearance of objectivity, in letting the audience draw its own conclusions after hearing both boring sides, which is why their broadcasts look so namby-pamby pitted against the partisan thrust and pugilistics of Fox News, whose slogan ought to be "We Exhort. You Comply."

❧

Today the Angry White Male may be more cranky than angry, but he's still male, which leads one to speculate about the existence of a special chromosome for pompous conviction, an undiscovered blowhard gene. Notably, the only anchor in the prime-time Fox News team who does not begin or end the broadcast with an editorial sermonette is its only woman, Paula Zahn, the host of *The Edge*. Perhaps Zahn's reluctance to hotdog the issue of the day is a personal reticence, or reflects her network broadcast experience on CBS, where she was backup anchor to Dan Rather on the evening news and co-host of *CBS This Morning*, not the sort of jobs conducive to Mau-Mauing. Whatever the reason, Zahn is the Fox host who listens most, interrupts least, and doesn't ask questions as if she already knew the answers, then flash disapproval when the answer isn't to her liking. She's Fox's golden fig leaf—her show is the sole hour in the prime-time lineup that doesn't play like a dramatic reading of that morning's Republican National Committee memo. (In between her show and O'Reilly's comes *Hannity & Colmes*, dominated by Republican parrot Sean Hannity.) While no one would wish Zahn to turn pundit, her political self-effacement reinforces the impression that on Fox News brainwashing the audience—er, influencing public opinion—is serious man's work, rhetorical heavy lifting.

If one program could serve as proxy for all others, it would be *Special Report* with Brit Hume, a nightly hour-long political-news show that is hosted in Hume's absence by Tony Snow, who looks like Hume's younger, more outgoing brother. Whoever is sitting in the host's chair, it is a program that bleeds Republican blue. A former White House correspondent for ABC News, Hume was an occasional contributor to *The American Spectator*, outlet for the infamous "Arkansas Project," and a longtime critic of liberal bias in the news. Snow, who also writes a syndicated column, served in George Bush Sr.'s administration in a number of capacities, including Deputy Assistant to the President for Media Affairs; he also did his bit in the politics of personal destruction by playing matchmaker, introducing Linda Tripp, an acquaintance from his Bush days, to literary agent Lucianne Goldberg. Two of the regulars among the "Fox all-stars" who jaw at the sum-up of each show are *McLaughlin Group* alumni and co-hosts of Fox News's *The Beltway Boys*, Fred Barnes and Mort Kondracke. Barnes is also the executive editor of *The Weekly Standard*, a perishingly thin opinion journal whose frequent ads on Hume's program tout its inside status with the Bush administration. (Like Fox News, *The Weekly Standard* is owned by Rupert Murdoch.) Other rotating pundits include Bill Sammon, a correspondent for *The Washington Times* and author of that impartial, poetic study *At Any Cost: How Al Gore Tried to Steal the Election*, and Jeff Birnbaum of *Fortune* magazine, who's gravitating so far to the right he'll soon be sitting on Fred Barnes's lap.

One of the absurdities of Hume's *Special Report* is that it is so claustrophobically right-wing that anyone who appears on the panel contracts a slow-moving case of Stockholm syndrome. For diversity of opinion and complexion, the all-stars call upon the presence of Juan Williams, host of daily call-in show *Talk of the Nation* on National Public Radio [NPR]. To Yosemite Sam conservatives, always hopping mad about something, the soothing voices of NPR—where the women sound like they're making a clay pot on the turntable and the men sound as if they want to help—are the pigeon coos of modestly upscale liberalism, progressivism as a tone poem. When the camera is on Williams, however, he starts to wobble, unsure of himself, trapped in enemy territory and grappling with a shallow identity crisis—wait, I'm an NPR guy . . . drilling in Alaska, that's gotta be bad for the caribou or whatever's up there . . . but, hey, these conservatives make a lotta sense . . . I can't see me driving a solar car anytime soon . . . I wish the other guys would quit glaring at me—before choking at the plate and coughing up conventional twaddle such as (actual quote): "You know what? If Americans driving around in their S.U.V.'s with their bumper stickers that say SAVE THE EARTH say . . . , 'Wait a minute, I can't get gasoline,' or 'Gasoline prices are going up—I'm goin' with Dick Cheney.'" (Dick Cheney, he's our man, if he can't find oil, no one can.) If this indoctrination through osmosis persists, Williams is going to walk into the Washington studio one day as a black man and walk out a disgruntled honky—then he'll really blend. Another familiar is Mara Liasson, White House correspondent for NPR and likewise an amenable moderate, though more willing to contest Fred Barnes's smug, supremely self-deluded complacencies. Only in the Mir-space-station confinement of the Fox

News studio could mild, occasional demurrers such as Kondracke, Williams, and Liasson be considered foils. (The dour Hume sometimes scowls as if even this lukewarm moderation is more than he can stomach.)

⋘❂⋙

Not every show on Fox News hews or skews to a party line. *Bulls & Bears*, a stock-market roundup hosted by Brenda Buttner, has a lively serve-and-volley that makes *Wall $treet Week with Louis Rukeyser* seem like sands trickling through the hourglass. (Fox News has fortified its business coverage with a new show hosted by Terry Keenan, a recent defector from CNN, and a tie-in program with *Forbes* magazine.) *Fox News Watch*, a media-analysis roundtable moderated by Eric Burns, is sharper and more creatively angled than CNN's *Reliable Sources*, one of Fox's beat cops being Jeff Cohen of Fairness and Accuracy in Reporting (FAIR), who's farther to the left than any other talking head on cable. Cohen's presence is a credit to Fox News, even if he is outnumbered by one-note johnnies Cal Thomas and Jim Pinkerton, syndicated columnists who appear to keep their brains in a jar between broadcasts. Fox's morning show, *Fox & Friends*, which has been eating into Don Imus's simulcast on MSNBC, has a jumpy rhythm and silly irreverence, ducking the sob stories and fawning celebrity interviews that constipate most network morning shows. John Gibson, a high-profile import from MSNBC, is too freewheeling and contrary a host to pin down politically (he's more of a Groucho Marxist: "Whatever it is, I'm against it"), and the daytime anchors have that special spray-on shine that you could find on any anchorperson.

At the knuckled core, however, Fox News Channel is an ideological animal, which gives it a more aggressive pounce than its competitors have and a more coherent identity. Unlike CNN, it doesn't have to look in the mirror and re-arrange its features to figure out what it is and wants to be. Fox News only looks in the mirror to adjust its samurai stare in its role as right-wing enforcer. It isn't the conservatism of Fox News Channel that chafes, it's how narrow, philistine, and unself-reflective that conservatism is. It represents the complete reversal of a conservation once devoted to tradition, civic ideals, stewardship of natural resources, personal tolerance, and cultural aspiration—the quest for enduring, sustaining roots reflected in G. K. Chesterton, Russell Kirk, and, once upon a time, William F. Buckley Jr.'s *National Review*—to a power politics intent on giving corporate interests complete reign, even if it means despoiling the environment, militarizing space, and cramming the entire lardass country into one giant S.U.V. As a viewer watches Fox News Channel regularly, the other dominoes of the game plan click into place: an end to legal abortion, the privatization of Social Security, a never questioning support of Israeli might, a salivating worship of weaponry (a *Forbes on Fox* guest jovially raved about a new assault rifle, "It's gonna bring all the fun back in killing people"), crediting the economic success of the Clinton presidency to anyone but Bill Clinton, and glorifying Ronald Reagan as the quintessence of American majesty—our

Great White Father rosily enshrined in permanent sunset. Say this for Hume, O'Reilly, and company, they don't pretend to be "compassionate conservatives." Their populism may be fraudulent, but their objectives and determination are, to lift a phrase from Saul Bellow, baked in their faces. At Fox News Channel, it takes a bully to run a bully pulpit.

POSTSCRIPT

Do the Media Have a Liberal Bias?

Media bias may seem to be a fairly simple, and perhaps not very powerful, topic but it shows how complex the relationship among senders and receivers of messages may be. The real issue has to do with whether the media tell us what to think or what to think about.

There is no doubt that the audiences for news are changing. People may be getting more information from the Internet or other sources—but here the possibility of bias may become even more important. As newsmakers understand how audiences use news, we might well expect to see different values and approaches designed to reach different audiences. How do media transmit values from one generation to another? Why do we seek out opinions that often confirm what we already believe? Changes in human behavior are often so subtle that we take them for granted. But when we do this, we undermine how important the media are in helping us understand our relationships to our environment and to our social groups.

An important step in considering this issue is to try to understand the nature of news. As Goldberg and Wolcott have shown, messages in media have multiple purposes. As news and other media content become more available, we need to consider the possible bias of any message and ask several questions: Where does the message come from? Where did the information originate? What types of supporting evidence separate opinion from fact?

We also need to be aware of different styles of news over the years. In the 1970s "ambush journalism" was popular—journalists often appeared to be stalking subjects, and much criticism was given to the "hard news" approach. Presently, the issue tends to be more about the journalist's personality and role as a gatekeeper of information. In this case, any personal interests or biases of the journalist become very important.

In recent years, a few books that are primarily memoirs of journalists have taken strong views on the role of the journalist and the way the field of journalism has grown over the years. Among some of the interesting sources in this area are Tom Wicker's *On the Record* (Bedford/St. Martin's, 2002) and Ted Koppel's *Off Camera* (Alfred A. Knopf, 2000), which are particularly good sources for a discussion of the topic of bias. Bill O'Reilly's recent book, *The No-Spin Zone* (Broadway Books, 2001), became a *New York Times* best-seller.

For other books that suggest changes in journalistic style and political differences in the United States, you may want to consult Nina J. Easton's *Gang of Five* (Simon & Schuster, 2000), about media use in the post-Reagan conservative era, or Lisa McGirr's *Suburban Warriors* (Princeton University Press, 2002), about the U.S. political shift toward conservatism.

On the Internet . . .

American Civil Liberties Union

This official site of the American Civil Liberties Union (ACLU) provides a general introduction of issues involving individual rights.

http://aclu.org

The Federal Communications Commission

This official site of the Federal Communications Commission (FCC) provides comprehensive information about U.S. federal media rules and guidelines.

http://www.fcc.gov

Student Press Law Center

The Student Press Law Center (SPLC) Web site provides the full text of *SPLC Report* magazine, news and information on laws and rulings that affect the student press, an online legal clinic, and the fill-in-the-blanks form for public records requests for each state.

http://www.splc.org

The National Freedom of Information Coalition

The National Freedom of Information Coalition is a coalition of various state First Amendment and open government organizations. This Web site provides information on the NFOIC as well as news articles pertaining to freedom of information.

http://www.nfoic.org

PART 4

Regulation

*F*or the media, the First Amendment entails both rights and responsibilities. How to ensure that these responsibilities will be met is the subject
of much of communications law and legislative action. What are the
valid limits of the rights of free speech and the press? How should society
respond when First Amendment rights are in conflict with other individual rights? What changes will new technology force upon our operation
of these rights? The issues in this section deal with who should be responsible for media content and with the rights of groups who find that
content inappropriate.

- Should Internet Access Be Regulated?

- Do Ratings Work?

- Have the Direction and Power of the FCC Changed?

ISSUE 11

Should Internet Access Be Regulated?

YES: Michael A. Banks, from "Filtering the Net in Libraries: The Case (Mostly) in Favor," *Computers in Libraries* (March 1998)

NO: American Civil Liberties Union, from "Censorship in a Box: Why Blocking Software Is Wrong for Public Libraries," in David Sobel, ed., *Filters and Freedom: Free Speech Perspectives on Internet Content Controls* (Electronic Privacy Information Center, 1999)

ISSUE SUMMARY

YES: Author Michael A. Banks explains that as more people turn to libraries for Internet access, libraries and communities have been forced to come to grips with the conflict between freedom of speech and objectional material on the World Wide Web and in Usenet newsgroups. He adds that software filters are tools that help librarians keep inappropriate materials out of the library.

NO: The American Civil Liberties Union (ACLU) concludes that mandatory blocking software in libraries is both inappropriate and unconstitutional. Blocking censors valuable speech and gives librarians, educators, and parents a false sense of security when providing minors with Internet access, argues the ACLU.

$\mathbf{T}$his is an issue that becomes more complex the more one thinks about it. Should public libraries make adult pornography sites available to minor children? Obviously no would be most people's first response. Should software that blocks or filters objectionable material on the Internet be installed in public libraries? Obviously yes would again be the first response. So, is it okay to limit the sites available within a library for adults and children? Or, should only children be limited? Should children only be allowed access to terminals in the children's section? If so, then shouldn't children also be denied access to the many books in the library that cover the same topics?

Beyond these thorny philosophical questions of what constitutes censorship and what constitutes protection lurk some surprisingly practical issues. If software that filters out "unacceptable" sites is adopted, then who controls what children or adults can download from the "information superhighway"? Who determines what children should and should not access and what is offensive? In short, who writes the filtering programs, and what is eliminated? This is a case in which an easy solution—filtering software—has long-term consequences for repressing freedom of speech and access to information.

Teens present a particularly difficult age group when considering this issue. They are interested in many of the sites that would be blocked by filtering software, and most would agree that teens need to know information about sexual issues that would certainly be blocked by most existing filters.

Libraries face engrossing issues. Long the champion of freedom of speech, they have generally fought attempts to ban books. Although the Internet presents similar issues, libraries can lose big with their constituents by their actions. And the political climate that produced the Communications Decency Act, which made transmission of indecent material over the Internet a criminal act, has spawned many suits against libraries for decisions made in the online arena. Some have installed filtering software and have faced suits by the American Civil Liberties Union (ACLU). Others have kept access open and faced community outrage. Although the Communications Decency Act was declared unconstitutional by the Supreme Court, libraries do not know what liabilities they may face from patrons offended by what they see others access in public areas. In one case, a university library posted a notice that it could not control or censor what individual university students viewed but that those students should be aware that if other nearby library patrons found the material offensive, the viewer could be liable for charges of sexual harassment.

The case of libraries facing online access issues is only one specific example in the larger debate on the issues that we face as technology becomes more accessible in public institutions. In the following selection, Michael A. Banks argues for filtering the Internet; not everything there is appropriate for everybody. Some discrimination is called for, he asserts, and filtering software is the least intrusive manner of accomplishing that goal. The ACLU argues against filters as a voluntary alternative to government regulation of Internet content. Filters are now viewed as architectural changes that may facilitate the suppression of speech far more effectively than congressional lawmaking ever could.

Michael A. Banks  **YES**

Filtering the Net in Libraries

The year is 1967. A patron finds a book in your library containing detailed instructions for making dynamite, and uses that information to build a bomb that he uses to destroy a neighbor's house. Now, you are being sued—and you may be charged with complicity in a crime.

Or, it's 1972, and last month you refused to allow a young patron to withdraw books from the "adult" section of your library. Despite the long-standing rule that anyone under 12 is restricted to the juvenile and reference sections, a lawsuit is brought, naming you, library staff, and trustees as defendants.

Absurd? Unthinkable? Indeed, yes—in those times. But such scenarios are possible now, with one major difference. Rather than allowing access to the "wrong" sort of books, or denying access to certain books, today's focus is on whether to allow Internet access. As more and more people turn to local libraries for Internet access, the possibility of such conflicts becomes more probable. This situation has forced more than a few libraries to pass judgment on what Internet content is appropriate for adults and children to see. The task is simple in theory, but complex in practice. Exactly what should you permit, and what should you block? And why?

At the same time, some communities and/or individuals are demanding that libraries abstain from such judgment. For example, late in December 1997 a community group in Virginia filed suit against the public library system in Louden County in order to block an Internet usage policy. Among other things, the police specified that library computers used for Internet access be equipped with filtering software, to protect children from pornography and other objectionable material on the Web and in Usenet newsgroups. The lawsuit claims that the use of such software is a violation of free speech rights since material that adults may want to access is also blocked.

In short, even though you are not expected to have on hand every magazine and every book in the world, you are expected by many to provide access to the full Internet. Since, as the Virginia case proves, there are no hard and fast definitions of what constitutes community standards, the judgment calls are difficult, to say the least. Then there are the widely varying expectations of patrons as to their rights in using library equipment—often quite independent of any perceived community standards. All of this leaves some librarians trying to

From Michael A. Banks, "Filtering the Net in Libraries: The Case (Mostly) in Favor," *Computers in Libraries*, vol. 18, no. 3 (March 1998). Copyright © 1998 by Information Today, Inc. Reprinted by permission of Information Today, Inc., 143 Old Marlton Pike, Medford, NJ 08055.

answer the question: Do you prefer to be liable for "infringing" on freedom of speech, or do you prefer to be liable for the effects of exposure to objectionable text and images?

To Block, or Not to Block

The decision to apply blocks is an unfortunate situation, indeed, but one that many libraries will have to face over the next few years. With fewer than 40 percent of American households on the Internet, more and more people are turning to libraries for Internet access. Even patrons who have Internet access at home also use library computers to get online, a matter of convenience during library visits. This means that, sooner or later, someone is going to have a problem with what they or others can or cannot access on the Internet. So, what do you do? Allow everyone access to everything, or try to control what is available?

On the whole, I feel that it is simpler to opt for blocking or filtering Internet access. That way, you don't risk offending employees and patrons who don't want to see objectionable material. This is to say, the "liability" is less than if you permit wide-open Internet access because once that genie is out of the bottle, there is no turning back. If there are objections to blocking in your community, they can be sorted out and problems rectified (not the case if you don't block and minors are accessing Internet pornography through your system). The only questions that remain are what you filter out, and how.

No Newsgroups Is Good Newsgroups?

For those concerned about Internet security, I advise blocking all Usenet newsgroup access. Usenet newsgroups, in existence since 1979, are one of the oldest components of the Internet. Today, this venerable element is fast becoming all but useless. Why? Because nearly all of the 20,000-plus newsgroups are clogged and choked with "spam," mass advertising of useless moneymaking schemes, con games, and porno sites. In some newsgroups, it is impossible to sort out the worthwhile postings from the spam, thanks to the perpetrators' attempts to disguise the true nature of their postings. Also, many postings are literal traps and ambushes. As I'll show you below, the simple act of opening a newsgroup posting can cause your browser to be taken over completely. Certain Web pages can do the same thing but, fortunately, there are ways to defend against this happening—but only if you use Netscape.

This is why you might be wise to block all Usenet newsgroup access. Simply not installing the newsgroup reader element of your Web browser will do the trick. Or, you can rely on filtering software that blocks objectionable newsgroups. Remember, though, that almost any newsgroup can contain objectionable material—or the ambushes to which I referred above.

What About Filters?

I see filters as part of a complete Internet security program. There are a dozen or more good Web/newsgroup filters available, each as good as the next in certain respects. There's not enough room to cover all of them here, but I will provide an overview of a few of the better products. Before I do that, though, let's take a quick look at what filtering programs do.

Acting as a Web browser "supervisor," a filtering program prevents access to sites considered inappropriate for the person using the browser. The decision as to what is inappropriate is usually based on listings compiled by the software manufacturer or by one of the Internet rating services. (Some companies also accept recommendations from users for sites to be blocked or unblocked.) Most programs block "adult" or sexual material, as well as sites with racist or bigotry-oriented themes. Sites promoting drug abuse are also blocked, along with adult online chat rooms. Various criteria are used to select sites to block, including the use of keywords, selective filtering of domains, and manual selection.

Unfortunately, filtering programs can be quite literal. At least one will not let you access a site or page carrying the surname or title "Sexton," because the word "sex" is contained in that name. However, if the software allows you to unblock sites manually, this problem can be overcome easily enough. With that in mind, you will want to ask yourself these questions when selecting a filtering program:

- Is the program updatable? Most filtering programs provide online updates of blocked site lists, sometimes by subscription. Relying on such updates is a good idea, as thousands of new potentially objectionable sites come online each month. The publishers that provide updates can catch almost all of these, and they do all the work for you.
- Can I unblock selected sites? Sometimes a filtering program mistakenly blocks a site that is not offensive. When this is the case, you should be able to unblock that site.
- Can I block selected sites? Despite all their efforts, the companies that publish blocking software cannot catch every objectionable site. Thus, you will want to be able to add sites to the blocked list.

In addition to altering lists of blocked sites, you may want to be able to alter the criteria that a filtering program uses to block sites on its own. This allows you to make up your own rules as to what is blocked, and why. The more versatility in this area, the better.

The following programs are among the better ones available. Since most blocking programs feature explanations of their blocking criteria at their Web sites, and some provide lists of blocked sites, I urge you to visit the Web site for each.

Cyber Patrol: Cyber Patrol is among the more successful Web filtering programs. It is used by America Online, AT&T WorldNet, Bell Atlantic, British Telecom, and CompuServe, among other online services and Internet service providers (ISPs), and it is bundled with some PCs. You can set up Cyber Patrol to control access to the Internet and newsgroups based on a variety of criteria. Or, you can grant access only to Cyber Patrol's list of approved sites (some 40,000) and block the rest of the Web. A particularly interesting feature of the program is an option that blocks users from typing in or viewing objectionable words or phrases, based in part on a default list of profanity. A special subscription service provides online updates to Cyper Patrol's blocked site lists. For more information, and to download a free trial version, visit http://www.cyberpatrol.com.

CYBERsitter: CYBERsitter is an interesting filtering/blocking program that runs in the background at all times and claims to be virtually impossible to detect or defeat. It works on several fronts. By default, it not only blocks access to adult-oriented Web sites, but also to newsgroups and images. In addition, Web pages and newsgroup posting are filtered to remove offensive language. Blocking and filtering are based on lists provided with the program, but you can add your own words to the lists. When filtering, CYBERsitter examines words and phrases in context, in order to eliminate some of the ambiguity of blocking. For more information about CYBERsitter, or to download a free trial version of the program, visit http://www.solidoak.com.

NetNanny: NetNanny is designed to manage Internet and computer access. You can use it to monitor, screen, or block access to anything that is on or running into, out of, or through a computer, online or off. The outgoing block can be useful in preventing users from using search engines to find and link to objectionable sites.

The program comes with a list of blocked Internet sites and other parameters that it uses to block still more sites. The list and parameters can be updated at no charge at the NetNanny Web site, and you can add your own screening specifications. NetNanny is available for Windows or DOS. See http://www.netnanny.com for more information.

Net Shepherd: Net Shepherd is an Internet content rating service that filters the results of Alta Vista searches. Its PICS-compliant ratings database can be used with Microsoft Internet Explorer or Net Shepherd's own daxHOUND program, a content filtering tool. For additional information on Net Shepherd, visit http://www.netshepherd.com. Information about daxHOUND (and a download) can be found at http://www.netshepherd.com/products/daxHOUND2.0/daxhound.htm.

SurfWatch: SurfWatch is a filter that screens for unwanted material on the Internet. As with other filter and blocking programs, SurfWatch can be used with almost any Web browser. Various levels of access control are available, and the program cannot be easily disarmed by deleting it or by other means. SurfWatch screens Web sites, newsgroups, ftp and gopher sites, and Web chat rooms. Blocking is based on a list of sites generated by in-house research and customer reports. Online updates are available via subscription.

SurfWatch alone doesn't permit you to modify the list of sites, nor does it attempt to block sites that are violent in nature or include material that is hateful or otherwise potentially inappropriate. A free add-on called SurfWatch Manager lets you edit the list of blocked sites. Full information on SurfWatch, along with its list of blocked sites, is available at http://www.surfwatch.com.

X-STOP: The appropriately named X-STOP is a program designed for use by libraries and other institutions and businesses that provide Internet access. It selectively blocks and filters sites based on a variety of criteria. The program allows you to alter the criteria it uses for filtering. It also monitors outgoing words in order to prevent users from looking up objectionable sites with search engines. For more information, see http://www.xstop.com.

Ambushed by Java and JavaScript Risks

Even if you use a filtering program with your computer systems, you can still run into security problems, thanks to Java and JavaScript. You are probably aware of the many security risks associated with Java, a programming language that is used to transmit small computer programs, called "applets" to Internet users' computers, where they are free to run and do things like collect data from hard drives. Filtering programs cannot detect everything a Java program will do, so it is possible to transmit objectionable content with a Java applet. Thus, it is usually a good idea to disable Java on your browsers. It is true that Java-related risks are fewer since so many "loopholes" involving Java have been exposed. But you never know what someone is cooking up. Besides, the Java-less Web surfer usually misses nothing more than animations that slow down browsing anyway.

JavaScript can pose a slightly greater risk, for two reasons. First, there have been no warnings about problems created by JavaScript. Indeed, I expect this to be the first you've heard of such problems. JavaScript can be used to direct your browser to any page on the Web, alter its configuration, and pull other nasty tricks. This being the case, it is best to disable JavaScript when visiting Web sites unfamiliar to you, and when reading newsgroup messages, in which JavaScript can be used to take over browsers.

Second, the JavaScript language is far easier to use, and thus accessible to more people, than Java. This means that the risk of exposure to malevolent JavaScript code is greater. What can JavaScript do to your system? For openers, JavaScript can be used to take control of a browser from a Web page or a Usenet newsgroup posting in two different ways. With a simple line of code, someone can set up a page so that, should your mouse cursor pass over a link or an image (loaded or not), your browser will be forced to "go to" (load) a specified page on the Web. This happens without clicking on anything.

A more insidious JavaScript trick can take over your browser and re-open it without menus or controls, on top of all other applications. Here again, the perpetrator of this trick can put anything he or she wants to appear in your browser window. This not only forces you to look at the perpetrator's message or images, but also disrupts your browsing session. And it can get worse. I have seen this set up so that you are forced to see the same page—or a series of pages —over and over again. Even if you exit the browser, it will reopen and display whatever the perpetrator wants it to display. This has been used extensively by pornography site purveyors to force Web surfers to their sites and to keep them there. Worse, the code required to do the things just described can be hidden, so that you cannot see it even if you view a Web page's source.

The only defense against this is to disable JavaScript. This is easily done with Netscape. Unfortunately, you cannot disable JavaScript if you are using Microsoft Internet Explorer 4. Mircosoft does not "support" JavaScript, and so does not allow you to turn it off.

Summing up My Position

The arguments against restricting Internet access are many, and at times they sound shrill. However, the fact remains that not everything on the Internet is appropriate for everybody, just as not every book or magazine published is appropriate for everybody. This being the case, some discrimination is called for in choosing what a public institution makes available from the Internet. For example, even though libraries make many magazines available, they do not subscribe to *Hustler* because that would be an inappropriate addition to their collections. In this same vein, just because libraries provide access to the Internet, they do not need to provide access to the entire Internet.

I believe that much of the problem here stems from the differences between not subscribing to *Hustler* and not receiving Internet content that is pornographic, racist, or otherwise objectionable. In the former instance, you need do nothing to avoid a subscription; in the latter, action is necessary to keep pornographic content out of the library. The need to take action in order to avoid questionable Internet material unfortunately confuses some people into mistaking positive proaction for repressing action. No one demands that libraries subscribe to *Hustler,* and so I feel that no one should demand that libraries grant full and unrestricted access to the Internet to everyone.

Obviously, posted rules are not enough to limit access to pornography or other objectionable Internet content. Even those who do not want to access such content may have it forced on them. All this being the case, it behooves libraries to provide practical limits to Internet access. At present, filtering and/or blocking Internet content is the only means of even partially controlling access to offensive or objectionable material. Even though filtering sometimes results in legitimate sites being blocked—a problem that can be rectified manually—it is a practical action.

Those who might object on the basis of some specious "freedom of speech" issue should consider the Internet as an analog to real-world books and magazines. In this light, it is easy to see the absurdity of uncontrolled Internet access for children and other patrons. If the sort of content access that some advocate for the Internet were to be applied to conventional library content, *Hustler* magazine, neo-Nazi books and pamphlets, and worse objectionable material would have to be placed in juvenile and children's as well as general library collections. This is what uncontrolled access to the Internet in a public venue can be.

American Civil Liberties Union  **NO**

Censorship in a Box

Introduction

In libraries and schools across the nation, the Internet is rapidly becoming an essential tool for learning and communication. According to the American Library Association, of the nearly 9,000 public libraries in America, 60.4 percent offer Internet access to the public, up from 27.8 percent in 1996. And a recent survey of 1,400 teachers revealed that almost half use the Internet as a teaching tool. But today, unfettered access to the Internet is being threatened by the proliferation of blocking software in libraries.

America's libraries have always been a great equalizer, providing books and other information resources to help people of all ages and backgrounds live, learn, work and govern in a democratic society. Today more than ever, our nation's libraries are vibrant multi-cultural institutions that connect people in the smallest and most remote communities with global information resources.

In 1995, the National Telecommunications and Information Administration of the U.S. Department of Commerce concluded that "public libraries can play a vital role in assuring that advanced information services are universally available to all segments of the American population on an equitable basis. Just as libraries traditionally make available the marvels and imagination of the human mind to all, libraries of the future are planning to allow everyone to participate in the electronic renaissance."

Today, the dream of universal access will remain only a dream if politicians force libraries and other institutions to use blocking software whenever patrons access the Internet. Blocking software prevents users from accessing a wide range of valuable information, including such topics as art, literature, women's health, politics, religion and free speech. Without free and unfettered access to the Internet, this exciting new medium could become, for many Americans, little more than a souped-up, G-rated television network.

This special report by the American Civil Liberties Union [ACLU] provides an in depth look at why mandatory blocking software is both inappropriate and unconstitutional in libraries. We do not offer an opinion about any particular blocking product, but we will demonstrate how all blocking software censors valuable speech and gives libraries, educators and parents a false sense of security when providing minors with Internet access.

Like any technology, blocking software can be used for constructive or destructive purposes. In the hands of parents and others who voluntarily use it, it is a tool that can be somewhat useful in blocking access to some inappropriate material online. But in the hands of government, blocking software is nothing more than censorship in a box.

The ACLU believes that government has a necessary role to play in promoting universal Internet access. But that role should focus on expanding, not restricting, access to online speech.

Reno v. ACLU: A Momentous Decision

Our vision of an uncensored Internet was clearly shared by the U.S. Supreme Court when it struck down the 1996 Communications Decency Act (CDA), a federal law that outlawed "indecent" communications online.

Ruling unanimously in *Reno v. ACLU,* the Court declared the Internet to be a free speech zone, deserving of at least as much First Amendment protection as that afforded to books, newspapers and magazines. The government, the Court said, can no more restrict a person's access to words or images on the Internet than it could be allowed to snatch a book out of a reader's hands in the library, or cover over a statue of a nude in a museum.

The nine Justices were clearly persuaded by the unique nature of the medium itself, citing with approval the lower federal court's conclusion that the Internet is "the most participatory form of mass speech yet developed," entitled to "the highest protection from governmental intrusion." The Internet, the Court concluded, is like "a vast library including millions of readily available and indexed publications," the content of which "is as diverse as human thought."

Blocking Software: For Parents, Not the Government

In striking down the CDA on constitutional grounds, the Supreme Court emphasized that if a statute burdens adult speech—as any censorship law must—it "is unacceptable if less restrictive alternatives were available."

Commenting on the availability of user-based blocking software as a possible alternative, the Court concluded that the use of such software was appropriate for *parents.* Blocking software, the Court wrote, is a "reasonably effective method by which parents can prevent their children from accessing material which the *parents* believe is inappropriate." [Emphasis in the original]

The rest of the Court's decision firmly holds that government censorship of the Internet violates the First Amendment, and that holding applies to government use of blocking software just as it applied when the Court struck down the CDA's criminal ban.

In the months since that ruling, the blocking software market has experienced explosive growth, as parents exercise their prerogative to guide their children's Internet experience. According to analysts at International Data Corporation, a technology consulting firm, software makers sold an estimated $14 million in blocking software last year, and over the next three years, sales of blocking products are expected to grow to more than $75 million.

An increasing number of city and country library boards have recently forced libraries to install blocking programs, over the objections of the American Library Association and library patrons, and the use of blocking software in libraries is fast becoming the biggest free speech controversy since the legal challenge to the CDA.

How Does Blocking Software Work?

The best known Internet platform is the World Wide Web, which allows users to search for and retrieve information stored in remote computers. The Web currently contains over 100 million documents, with thousands added each day. Because of the ease with which material can be added and manipulated, the content on existing Web sites is constantly changing. Links from one computer to another and from one document to another across the Internet are what unify the Web into a single body of knowledge, and what makes the Web unique.

To gain access to the information available on the Web, a person uses a Web "browser"—software such as Netscape Navigator or Microsoft's Internet Explorer—to display, print and download documents. Each document on the Web has an address that allows users to find and retrieve it.

A variety of systems allow users of the Web to search for particular information among all of the public sites that are part of the Web. Services such as Yahoo, Magellan, Alta Vista, Webcrawler, Lycos and Infoseek provide tools called "search engines." Once a user has accessed the search service she simply types a word or string of words as a search request and the search engine provides a list of matching sites.

Blocking software is configured to hide or prevent access to certain Internet sites. Most blocking software comes packaged in a box and can be purchased at retail computer stores. It is installed on individual and/or networked computers that have access to the Internet, and works in conjunction with a Web browser to block information and sites on the Internet that would otherwise be available.

What Kind of Speech Is Being Blocked?

Most blocking software prevents access to sites based on criteria provided by the vendor. To conduct site-based blocking, a vendor establishes criteria to identify specified categories of speech on the Internet and configures the blocking software to block sites containing those categories of speech. Some Internet blocking software blocks as few as six categories of information, while others block many more.

Blocked categories may include hate speech, criminal activity, sexually explicit speech, "adult" speech, violent speech, religious speech, and even sports and entertainment.

Using its list of criteria, the software vendor compiles and maintains lists of "unacceptable" sites. Some software vendors employ individuals who browse the Internet for sites to block. Others use automated searching tools to identify which sites to block. These methods may be used in combination. (Examples of blocked sites can be found below.) . . .

Typical examples of blocked words and letters include "xxx," which blocks out Superbowl XXX sites; "breast," which blocks website and discussion groups about breast cancer; and the consecutive letters "s," "e" and "x," which block sites containing the words "sexton" and "Mars exploration," among many others. Some software blocks categories of expression along blatantly ideological lines, such as information about feminism or gay and lesbian issues. Yet most websites offering opposing views on these issues are not blocked. For example, the same software does not block sites expressing opposition to homosexuality and women working outside the home.

Clearly, the answer to blocking based on ideological viewpoint is not more blocking, any more than the answer to unpopular speech is to prevent everyone from speaking, because then no viewpoint of any kind will be heard. The American Family Association [AFA], a conservative religious organization, recently learned this lesson when it found that CyberPatrol, a popular brand of blocking software, had placed AFA on its "Cybernot" list because of the group's opposition to homosexuality.

AFA's site was blocked under the category "intolerance," defined as "pictures or text advocating prejudice or discrimination against any race, color, national origin, religion, disability or handicap, gender or sexual orientation. Any picture or text that elevates one group over another. Also includes intolerance jokes or slurs." Other "Cybernot" categories include "violence/profanity," "nudity," "sexual acts," "satanic/cult," and "drugs/drug culture."

In a May 28th [1999] news release excoriating CyberPatrol, AFA said, "CyberPatrol has elected to block the AFA website with their filter because we have simply taken an opposing viewpoint to the political and cultural agenda of the homosexual rights movement." As one AFA spokesman told reporters, "Basically we're being blocked for free speech."

The AFA said they are planning to appeal the blocking decision at a June 9th meeting of CyberPatrol's Cybernot Oversight Committee, but expressed doubt that the decision would be overturned. The conservative Family Research Council also joined in the fight, saying they had "learned that the Gay Lesbian Alliance Against Defamation (GLAAD) is a charter member of CyberPatrol's oversight committee," and that "it was pressure by GLAAD that turned CyberPatrol around."

Until, now, AFA, FRC and similar groups had been strong advocates for filtering software, and AFA has even assisted in the marketing of another product, X-Stop. AFA has said that they still support blocking but believe their group was unfairly singled out.

Indeed, as the AFA and others have learned, there is no avoiding the fact that somebody out there is making judgments about what is offensive and controversial, judgments that may not coincide with their own. The First Amendment exists precisely to protect the most offensive and controversial speech from government suppression. If blocking software is made mandatory in schools and libraries, that "somebody" making the judgments becomes the government.

To Block or Not to Block: You Decide

According to a recent story in The Washington Post, a software vendor's "own test of a sample of Web sites found that the software allowed pornographic sites to get through and blocked 57 sites that did not contain anything objectionable."

And in a current lawsuit in Virginia over the use of blocking software in libraries, the ACLU argues that the software blocks "a wide variety of other Web sites that contain valuable and constitutionally protected speech, such as the entire Web site of Glide Memorial United Methodist Church, located in San Francisco, California, and the entire Web site of The San Francisco Chronicle."

Following are real-world examples of the kind of speech that has been found to be inaccessible in libraries where blocking software is installed. Read through them—or look at them online—and then decide for yourself: Do you want the government telling you whether you can access these sites in the library?

www.afa.net   The American Family is a non-profit group founded in 1977 by the Rev. Donald Wildmon. According to their website, the AFA "stands for traditional family values, focusing primarily on the influence of television and other media—including pornography—on our society."

www.cmu.edu   Banned Books On-Line offers the full text of over thirty books that have been the object of censorship or censorship attempts, from James Joyce's Ulysses to Little Red Riding Hood.

www.quaker.org   The Religious Society of Friends describes itself as "an Alternative Christianity which emphasizes the personal experience of God in one's life." Their site boasts the slogan, "Proud to Be Censored by X-Stop, a popular brand of blocking software."

www.safersex.org   The Safer Sex Page includes brochures about safer sex, HIV transmission, and condoms, as well as resources for health educators and counselors. X-Stop, the software that blocks these pages, does not block the "The Safest Sex Home Page," which promotes abstinence before marriage as the only protection against sexually transmitted diseases.

www.iatnet.com.aauw   The American Association of University Women Maryland provides information about its activities to promote equity for women. The Web site discusses AAUW's leadership role in civil rights issues; work and family issues such as pay equity, family and medical leave, and dependent care; sex discrimination; and reproductive rights.

www.sfgate.com/columnists/morse   Rob Morse, an award-winning columnist for The San Francisco Examiner, has written more than four hundred columns on a variety of issues ranging from national politics, homelessness, urban violence, computer news, and the Superbowl, to human cloning. Because his section is considered off limits, the entire www.sfgate.com site is blocked to viewers.

http://www.youth.org/yao/docs/books.html   Books for Gay and Lesbian Teens/Youth provides information about books of interest to gay and lesbian youth. The site was created by Jeremy Meyers, an 18-year-old senior in high school who lives in New York City. X-Stop, the software that blocks this page, does not block web pages condemning homosexuality....

In addition to these examples, a growing body of research compiled by educators, public interest organizations and other interested groups demonstrates the extent to which this software inappropriately blocks valuable, protected speech, and does not effectively block the sites they claim to block....

Teaching Responsibility: Solutions That Work...

Instead of requiring unconstitutional blocking software, schools and libraries should establish content-neutral rules about when and how young people should use the Internet, and hold educational seminars on responsible use of the Internet.

For instance, schools could request that Internet access be limited to school-related work and develop carefully worded acceptable use policies (AUPs), that provide instructions for parents, teachers, students, librarians and patrons on use of the Internet....

Successful completion of a seminar similar to a driver's education course could be required of minors who seek Internet privileges in the classroom or library. Such seminars could emphasize the dangers of disclosing personally identifiable information such as one's address, communicating with strangers about personal or intimate matters, or relying on inaccurate resources on the Net.

Whether the use of blocking software is mandatory or not, parents should always be informed that blind reliance on blocking programs cannot effectively safeguard children.

Libraries can and should take other actions that are more protective of online free speech principles. For instance, libraries can publicize and provide links to particular sites that have been recommended for children.

Not all solutions are necessarily "high tech." To avoid unwanted viewing by passers-by, for instance, libraries can place privacy screens around Internet access terminals in ways that minimize pubic view. Libraries can also impose content-neutral time limits on Internet use.

These positive approaches work much better than restrictive software that works only when students are using school or library computers, and teaches no critical thinking skills. After all, sooner or later students graduate to the real world, or use a computer without blocking software. An educational program could teach students how to use the technology to find information quickly and efficiently, and how to exercise their own judgment to assess the quality and reliability of information they receive.

. . . and Don't Work

In an effort to avoid installing blocking software, some libraries have instituted a "tap on the shoulder" policy that is, in many ways, more intrusive and un-constitutional than a computer program. This authorizes librarians to peer at the patron's computer screen and tap anyone on the shoulder who is viewing "inappropriate" material.

The ACLU recently contacted a library in Newburgh, New York to advise against a proposed policy that would permit librarians to stop patrons from accessing "offensive" and "racially or sexually inappropriate material." In a let-ter to the Newburgh Board of Education, the ACLU wrote: "The Constitution protects dirty words, racial epithets, and sexually explicit speech, even though that speech may be offensive to some." The letter also noted that the broad lan-guage of the policy would allow a librarian to prevent a patron from viewing on the Internet such classic works of fiction as Chaucer's Canterbury Tales and Mark Twain's Adventures of Huckleberry Finn, and such classic works of art as Manet's Olympia and Michelangelo's David.

"This thrusts the librarian into the role of Big Brother and allows for arbi-trary and discriminatory enforcement since each librarian will have a different opinion about what is offensive," the ACLU said.

The First Amendment prohibits librarians from directly censoring pro-tected speech in the library, just as it prevents indirect censorship through blocking software.

Battling Big Brother in the Library

In Loudoun County, Virginia, the ACLU is currently involved in the first court challenge to the use of blocking software in a library. Recently, the judge in that case forcefully rejected a motion to dismiss the lawsuit, saying that the government had "misconstrued the nature of the Internet" and warning that Internet blocking requires the strictest level of constitutional scrutiny. The case is now set to go to trial. . . .

Earlier this year, the ACLU was involved in a local controversy over the mandatory use of Internet blocking programs in California's public libraries. County officials had decided to use a blocking program called "Bess" on every library Internet terminal, despite an admission by Bess's creators that it was impossible to customize the program to filter only material deemed "harmful to minors" by state law.

After months of negotiation, the ACLU warned the county that it would take legal action if officials did not remove Internet blocking software from public library computers. Ultimately, the library conceded that the filters presented an unconstitutional barrier to patrons seeking access to materials including legal opinions, medical information, political commentary, art, literature, information from women's organizations, and even portions of the ACLU Freedom Network website.

Today, under a new policy, the county provides a choice of an unfiltered or a filtered computer to both adult and minor patrons. No parental consent will be required for minors to access unfiltered computers.

The ACLU has also advocated successfully against mandatory blocking software in libraries in San Jose and in Santa Clara County, California. The ACLU continues to monitor the use of blocking software in many libraries across the nation, including communities in Massachusetts, Texas, Illinois, Ohio and Pennsylvania.

The Fight in Congress: Marshaling the Cyber-Troops Against Censorship

In February of this year, Senator John McCain (R-AZ) introduced the "Internet School Filtering Act," a law that requires all public libraries and schools to use blocking software in order to qualify for "e-rate," a federal funding program to promote universal Internet access. An amendment that would have allowed schools and libraries to qualify by presenting their own plan to regulate Internet access—not necessarily by commercial filter—failed in committee.

Another bill sponsored by Senator Dan Coats (R-IN) was dubbed "Son of CDA," because much of it is identical to the ill-fated Communications Decency Act.

The ACLU and others are lobbying against these bills, which have not yet come up for a vote as of this writing.

Censorship in the States: A Continuing Battle

Federal lawmakers are not the only politicians jumping on the censorship bandwagon. In the last three years, at least 25 states have considered or passed Internet censorship laws. This year, at least seven states are considering bills that require libraries and/or schools to use blocking software.

These censorship laws have not held up to constitutional scrutiny. Federal district courts in New York, Georgia and Virginia have found Internet censorship laws unconstitutional on First Amendment grounds in challenges brought by the ACLU. In April, the ACLU filed a challenge to an Internet censorship law in New Mexico that is remarkably similar to the failed New York law.

Conclusion

The advent of new forms of communication technology is always a cause for public anxiety and unease. This was as true for the printing press and the telephone as it was for the radio and the television. But the constitutional ideal is immutable regardless of the medium: a free society is based on the principle that each and every individual has the right to decide what kind of information he or she wants—or does not want—to receive or create. Once you allow the government to censor material you don't like, you cede to it the power to censor something you do like—even your own speech.

Censorship, like poison gas, can be highly effective when the wind is blowing the right way. But the wind has a way of shifting, and sooner or later, it blows back upon the user. Whether it comes in a box or is accessed online, in the hands of the government, blocking software is toxic to a democratic society.

Questions and Answers About Blocking Software

In the interest of "unblocking" the truth, here are answers to some of the questions the ACLU most often encounters on the issue of blocking software:

Q: Why does it matter whether Internet sites are blocked at the library when people who want to see them can just access them at home?

A: According to a recent Nielsen Survey, 45 percent of Internet users go to public libraries for Internet access. For users seeking controversial or personal information, the library is often their only opportunity for privacy. A Mormon teenager in Utah seeking information about other religions may not want a parent in the home, or a teacher at school, looking over her shoulder as she surfs the web.

Q: What about library policies that allow patrons to request that certain sites be unblocked?

A: The stigma of requesting access to a blocked site deters many people from making that request. Library patrons may be deterred from filling out a form seeking access, because the sites they wish to visit contain sensitive information. For instance, a woman seeking to access the Planned Parenthood website to find out about birth control may feel embarrassed about justifying the request to a librarian.

Q: But as long as a library patron can ask for a site to be unblocked, no one's speech is really being censored, right?

A: Wrong. Web providers who want their speech to reach library patrons have no way to request that their site be unblocked in thousands of libraries around the country. They fear patrons will be stigmatized for requesting that the site be unblocked, or simply won't brother to make the request. If public libraries around the country continue to use blocking software, speakers will be forced to self-censor in order to avoid being blocked in libraries.

Q: Isn't it true that libraries can use blocking software in the same way they select books for circulation?

A: The unique nature of the Internet means that librarians do not to have to consider the limitations of shelf space in providing access to online material. In a recent ruling concerning the use of blocking software in Virginia libraries, a federal judge agreed with the analogy of the Internet as "a collection of encyclopedias from which defendants [the government] have laboriously redacted [or crossed out] portions deemed unfit for library patrons."

Q: Doesn't blocking software help a librarian control what children see online?

A: The ability to choose which software is installed does not empower a school board or librarian to determine what is "inappropriate for minors." Instead, that determination is made by a software vendor who regards the lists of blocked sites as secret, proprietary information.

Q: Why shouldn't librarians be involved in preventing minors from accessing inappropriate material on the Internet?

A: It is the domain of parents, not librarians, to oversee their children's library use. This approach preserves the integrity of the library as a storehouse of ideas available to all regardless of age or income. As stated by the American Library Association's Office of Intellectual Freedom: "Parents and only parents have the right and responsibility to restrict their own children's access—and only their own children's access—to library resources, including the Internet. Librarians do not serve *in loco parentis.*"

Q: What do librarians themselves think about blocking software?

A: The overwhelming majority of librarians are opposed to the mandatory use of blocking software. However some, under pressure from individuals or local officials, have installed blocking software. The ALA has a Library Bill of Rights, which maintains that filters should not be used "to block access to constitutionally protected speech." . . .

Q: Are libraries required to use blocking software in order to avoid criminal liability for providing minors access to speech that may not be protected by the Constitution?

A: No. The First Amendment prohibits imposing criminal or civil liability on librarians merely for providing minors with access to the Internet. The knowledge that some websites on the Internet may contain "harmful" matter is not sufficient grounds for prosecution. In fact, an attempt to avoid any liability by installing blocking software or otherwise limiting minors' access to the Internet would, itself, violate the First Amendment.

Q: Would libraries that do not use blocking software be liable for sexual harassment in the library?

A: No. Workplace sexual harassment laws apply only to employees, not to patrons. The remote possibility that a library employee might inadvertently view an objectionable site does not constitute sexual harassment under current law.

Q: Can't blocking programs be fixed so they block only illegal speech that is not protected by the Constitution?

A: There is simply no way for a computer software program to make distinctions between protected and unprotected speech. This is not a design flaw that may be "fixed" at some future point but a simple human truth. . . .

Q: What if blocking software is only made mandatory for kids?

A: Even if only minors are forced to use blocking programs, constitutional problems remain. The Supreme Court has agreed that minors have rights too, and the fact that a 15-year-old rather than an 18-year-old seeks access online to valuable information on subjects such as religion or gay and lesbian resources does not mean that the First Amendment no longer applies. In any case, it is impossible for a computer program to distinguish what is appropriate for different age levels, or the age of the patron using the computer.

Q: Is using blocking software at schools any different than using it in public libraries?

A: Unlike libraries, schools do act in place of parents, and play a role in teaching civic values. Students do have First Amendment rights, however, and blocking software is inappropriate, especially for junior and high school students.

In addition, because the software often blocks valuable information while allowing access to objectionable material, parents are given a false sense of security about what their children are viewing. A less restrictive—and more effective —alternative is the establishment of content-neutral "Acceptable Use Policies" (AUPs).

Q: Despite all these problems, isn't blocking software worth it if it keeps some pornography from reaching kids?

A: Even though sexually explicit sites only make up a very small percentage of content on the Internet, it is impossible for any one program to block out every conceivable web page with "inappropriate" material.

When blocking software is made mandatory, adults as well as minors are prevented from communicating online, even in schools. According to a recent news story in the Los Angeles Times, a restrictive blocking program at a California school district meant coaches couldn't access the University of Notre Dame's website, and math instructors were cut off from information about Wall Street because of a block on references to money and finance.

POSTSCRIPT

Should Internet Access Be Regulated?

There will probably be many attempts to create some types of controls over content on the Internet, and these attempts will be controversial. While the initial concept of blocking technology was simple, its introduction into the realm of public institutions has raised many troubling questions. Here are a few that have emerged: If information is to be evaluated, who should do the evaluation— the authors/distributors, the public institution, the government, or the public? In a society barraged by information, how feasibly can a ratings system protect vulnerable audiences? Are there information sites that should be exempt from filtering, such as news organizations? What forms of assessment exist to test the effectiveness of such a filter? What should the criteria be for labeling a filtering experience a success or a failure? There is much material on the Internet that most of us would decry. In addition to graphic sexual images, one can find out how to make a bomb or how to join a hate group. In most cases, there are books in the library that contain the same information. It offends many people that individuals can go into a library and find hate groups online. Yet, anyone can check out books with similar information. Of course, the library can control its inventory in a way that cannot be done with unfiltered Internet access.

Extensive writing on this issue can be accessed by any Internet search engine. The ACLU volume from which the No-side selection was obtained can be further researched at the Electronic Privacy Information Center's Internet site: www.epic.org. Parents' organizations and child advocacy groups have argued for some form of protection for children. *Wired* magazine is an excellent resource for a number of perspectives on issues dealing with computers and the Internet. A different perspective is offered by Brian Kahin and James Keller, who have edited *Public Access to the Internet* (MIT Press, 1995), which features articles that focus on the benefits of Internet use.

Undergirding much of this debate is concern about pornography, which is an important topic for thought. How accessible is it, and should it be controlled on the Internet? Some recent publications dealing with this subject include Nicholas Wolfson's *Hate Speech, Sex Speech, Free Speech* (Praeger, 1997) and James M. Ussher's *Fantasies of Feminity: Reframing the Boundaries of Sex* (Rutgers University Press, 1997).

ISSUE 12

Do Ratings Work?

YES: Paul Simon, Sam Brownback, and Joseph Lieberman, from "Three U.S. Senators Speak Out: Why Cleaning up Television Is Important to the Nation," *The American Enterprise* (March/April 1999)

NO: Marjorie Heins, from "Three Questions About Television Ratings," in Monroe E. Price, ed., *The V-Chip Debate: Content Filtering From Television to the Internet* (Lawrence Erlbaum Associates, 1998)

ISSUE SUMMARY

YES: Senators Paul Simon, Sam Brownback, and Joseph Lieberman speak up on why cleaning up television is important to the nation. They detail the frustrating experiences that caused them to support legislation to clean up television.

NO: Marjorie Heins, founding director of the American Civil Liberties Union's Arts Censorship Project, poses three questions about television ratings: First, what is the ratings system meant to accomplish? Second, who will rate programming, and how? Third, what are the likely political and artistic effects of the ratings scheme? The V-chip and television ratings will do nothing, she argues, to solve the problems of American youth and society.

The most obvious consequence of the massive 1996 Telecommunications Act was the extensive restructuring of the industry as corporations took advantage of relaxed ownership regulation to bolster their organizational reach. One other consequence, mysterious to many people, is the ratings that appear in the corner of the television screen at the beginning of programs. Not only did the 1996 Telecommunications Act force the industry to implement a ratings system, it required the installation of a V-chip in television sets, which would "read" violent ratings so families could block violent programming.

Controversy raged over the implementation of the ratings and V-chip system. Are such ratings an infringement of the free speech rights of broadcasters? Government mandated this system; should it be involved in the creation and application of the system? Does this attempt to protect children infringe on the rights of adults? Will it have a chilling effect on production? Will it encourage more explicit programming, with more shows rated "M" for mature audiences? Will ratings create a "forbidden fruit" appeal for some children?

Now a ratings system is in effect. After much controversy over whether ratings should be age- or content-based, most networks are using a combination of age and content systems. The original system had only age guidelines, but extensive debate produced a system that not only provided age guidelines but also descriptive labels upon which parents can base informed decisions. For children's programs the designation TV-Y is for all children, and TV-Y7 indicates a show for older children. TV-G, and TV-PG are easily understood, but TV-14 is used for general programs where parents may find material unsuitable for children under 14. TV-MA programs are designed for adults and are deemed unsuitable for children under 17. Content labels are also attached to many of the age designations: FV for fantasy violence in children's programs, V for violence, S for sexual situations, L for coarse language, and D for suggestive dialogue. Only in the past year have V-chip–equipped sets become widely available. Now parents can program into the set what levels of ratings will be used to block the set. When that is done and a program with an unacceptable rating is scheduled, a blank screen, sometimes with the words "this is a blocked program," will show up on the screen. For the first time, the pieces are in place to implement the 1996 Communications Decency Act. Now is the time to begin assessment. Does the ratings system work?

Paul Simon, Sam Brownback, and Joseph Lieberman each discuss why they are convinced that television can only be cleaned up through legislative action. They outline the frustration of parents and child advocates and the failure of self-regulative efforts. They assert that ratings exist to provide parents with information they need to monitor their children's exposure. Marjorie Heins questions the consequences of the ratings. Will they actually be used? And, if used, what will the consequences be for children and for society? What problems might arise from the fact that the entertainment industry governs the ratings? Finally, Heins fears the artistic and political effects of such regulation on a creative industry.

Paul Simon, Sam Brownback,
and Joseph Lieberman

Three U.S. Senators Speak Out:
Why Cleaning up Television
Is Important to the Nation

*These remarks are from presentations to the conference on TV program-
ming held in Washington, D.C. in December by the Center for Media &
Public Affairs and* The American Enterprise.

Senator Paul Simon
(D-Illinois, Retired)

I got into the effort to clean up TV accidentally. I checked into a motel in Lasalle
County, Illinois, and turned on my television set. All of a sudden there in front
of me in living color someone was being cut in half by a chainsaw. Now, I'm
old enough to know it wasn't real, but it bothered me that night. I thought,
what happens to a ten-year-old who watches this?

So I called my office the next morning and said, "Someone has to have
done research on this; find out what research has taken place." My staff came
back with all kinds of research showing that entertainment violence harms us.

I called a meeting of representatives of the TV industry and said, "I don't
want government censorship, but I think we have to recognize we have a problem, and I'd like you to come up with the answers." One of those present said,
"Violence on television doesn't do any harm." I replied, "You remind me of the
Tobacco Institute people who come into my office saying they have research
that cigarettes don't do any harm." Then they said, "Well, we can't collaborate
on this because it would violate the antitrust laws."

That led me to introduce a bill that included an exemption in the antitrust
laws for television violence, and to give you some sense of the breadth of interest in this, my co-sponsors eventually included Senator Jesse Helms (R-N.C.)
and Senator Howard Metzenbaum (D-Ohio). Now that's a broad philosophical
spectrum.

The industry opposed my bill. The ACLU [the American Civil Liberties
Union] opposed my bill. But we finally got the bill passed. George Bush signed

it. And both broadcasters and cable operators began to adopt standards. I have to say they were fairly anemic, but they were better than nothing.

On the broadcast side, there has been progress. Arthur Nielsen of the Nielsen ratings says there have been significant improvements in terms of violence on the broadcast side—not going as far as needed, but still improvements. On the cable side, improvement is not perceptible.

At a meeting of about 700 TV and movie executives where I spoke, I said,"Many of you disagree with my conclusions. Why don't you do your own analysis of TV violence." And to their credit, both the broadcast and the cable industries authorized three-year studies. That research has recently come back, and I think they got more than they bargained for. The many damaging findings included the fact that three-quarters of all entertainment violence shows no immediate adverse consequences for the person committing the violence. The lessons for children and for adults, but particularly for children, is that violence pays.

The entertainment industry has periodically changed what it does and improved our society. For instance, if you look back at old movies and TV clips, you'll see the heros and heroines smoking and drinking much more heavily than they do today. I think this change is one of the reasons there has been a diminution in smoking and drinking in our society.

When television glamorizes violence, we imitate that. We have the most violent television of any nation on the earth with the possible exception of Japan, and there is one huge difference: In Japan, the people who commit the violence are the bad guys; people one wouldn't want to associate with. In American television, too frequently, those who commit the violence are the good guys.

The V-chip and ratings can offer an assist against objectionable TV content, but they are not a substitute for the industry's being responsible. First of all because children are technologically adept. I can't even program my VCR to tape a program. I have my son-in-law do it for me.

Second, the Nielsen ratings clearly show that in the impoverished areas in our country, which are also the high-crime areas, children watch 50 percent more television than they do in other areas; the TV set becomes a companion and babysitter.

Third, you're an unusual parent if, when Johnny or Jane go next door to play, you say, "Just a second. I want to find out what the neighbors have on television."

Finally, as a recent University of Wisconsin study shows, adult ratings, instead of repelling, frequently have an appeal for TV-watching children.

Another argument favored by the TV industry is, "We're just giving the public what it wants." That's the worst excuse of all. It is the same excuse that people in politics, business, and other fields use to rationalize irresponsible decisions. We ought to expect from the leaders in any field some sense of responsibility, some long-term social outlook.

I am not suggesting there be no violence on television. If you do a story on the Civil War, there's going to be some violence. *Schindler's List,* the most moving film I've ever seen, was on television, but it was on television late at night, when it should have been. And it didn't glorify violence. It associated violence with hurt, people crying. That's truthful.

Senator Sam Brownback (R-Kansas)

TV content has attracted Congress's attention for the past several years because a lot of people across the country are upset.

The main problem with TV is not that a few scenes or even a few shows are horrifically shocking, but rather the near-constant stream of sleaze. Violence, irresponsibility, and vulgarity are staples of prime time. The majority of sexual relationships portrayed are extra-marital or pre-marital, and have no negative consequences. TV scenes of illicit sex rarely include AIDS, unwanted pregnancy, or heartbreak. Television strongly implies that adultery and teen sex are normal, even desirable, when the truth is that such things easily lead to grief, poverty, and shattered lives.

Senator Lieberman and I have co-hosted hearings the past two years on the impact of television sex and violence. We've been struggling with exactly what to do about this problem. I think it's critical that we talk a lot about it, that we put it high on the priority list, and that we look for solutions.

One idea several senators have put forward, so far with little success, is encouraging a voluntary code of conduct within the industry. We'd like to help reinvigorate and bring back the voluntary code that the broadcasting industry abided by until a 1982 ruling by the courts suggested that cooperating on standards might violate antitrust laws. Last year I introduced a bill that would remove this potential violation of antitrust laws and let the industry work together on standards. We're going to try again this year.

Entertainment companies have fought me on this. It's a strange situation for an industry to resist being given new powers, but so far the National Association of Broadcasters [NAB] and others have been uncooperative. They don't want the authority and responsibility to control their programming. But we're not giving up, because this project is very important.

Some people in the industry assert, "We don't make the culture. We just reflect it." But actually, television is a very powerful culture-shaping medium. As a candidate for public office, I've found that TV advertising is the key to transmitting a message today. If I could get by without buying it, I would in a heartbeat. But I can't.

What today's TV programmers are actually holding up is not a mirror but a mirage. The world of TV characters is, thank goodness, far more violent, disturbed, and perverse than typical American life. There are more Amish people in the United States than there are serial murderers. There are far more pastors than prostitutes. But you'd never know it from TV.

Does this matter? Of course. Television is the dominant influence on our culture. It rules the world because of its invasiveness, because of the impact it has on people. We all know by watching our own children watch television that

TV has clear effects, and studies confirm this. Consider just a couple of current examples:

- A recent study by Professor Mark Singer at Case Western University found that sustained TV viewing was linked to aggression, anxiety, and anger and violent behavior in children.
- The American Medical Association recently concluded that "exposure to violence in entertainment increases aggressive behavior ... and contributes to Americans' sense that they live in a 'mean society.'"

These kinds of findings keep building and building.

We have to be much more aggressive in combating this problem. Abraham Lincoln taught that "He who molds public sentiment goes deeper than he who enacts statutes or pronounces decisions." I think what we have to do is mold public sentiment, inform people that television is hurting our children, and start moving to correct that.

My office stands ready and willing to do anything we can to help this effort, but I don't think you can legislate the problem out of existence: The First Amendment's protections on speech are clear and appropriate, and I wouldn't want to try. Instead, we have to change behavior in this area the old-fashioned way, the hard way, where you just continually talk, tell the story, push and encourage.

We need to tell the TV industry, "You are influencing our young and our nation, and it's not for the good. And we can't afford it as a people."

Sen. Joseph Lieberman (D-Connecticut)

We can't expect individual broadcasters to unilaterally institute controls on the kind of material they put out—not with the competitive pressures being what they are. That is why I strongly believe that one of the best things the industry could do to address the concern over exploitative shows would be to bring back a set of basic standards that would insulate programmers from the temptation to be more shocking or titillating than their competitors.

The National Association of Broadcasters maintained such a code for more than three decades and then chose to abandon it after a few of its provisions (restricting advertising only) were struck down by the courts on antitrust grounds. Re-reading the NAB standards today, I am struck by what a powerful statement of citizenship and community responsibility it was, and what a mistake it was to scrap it. America's families have paid the price for that decision, by way of sinking standards and vanishing values.

My argument is the same one made [in 1998] by ABC president Bob Iger, who said in a speech:

> The thing that differentiates television from other businesses is that so many of our program decisions impact the public in a powerful way. I believe there is room on the air for adult-oriented programs, provided they are high in quality. Programs like "Jerry Springer" are another matter. I question the logic of putting him on the air, and I believe the entire industry suffers from the association. Programs that are embarrassments to our business will, in the long run, alienate our viewers. Let's make these improvements—without any government intervention.

Good idea.

Despite the troubling direction the industry has been heading in, I still believe that the lion's share of local broadcasters take seriously their obligation to serve the public interest. And it is in that spirit that we are asking for their help in making television a safer place for children, by beginning to work together to develop a new code of standards for the next century. If help from Capitol Hill is necessary, rest assured such a measure would fly through both houses of Congress.

We are not calling for a return to the 1950s, but simply a respite from the graphic gunplay and foreplay that increasingly dominate the tube and send the worst messages to the public. We don't want to take away broadcaster discretion. We simply want them to take it back and use it responsibly.

NO

Marjorie Heins

Three Questions About Television Ratings

In the 1996 Communications Decency Act [CDA], Congress mandated that all television sets manufactured or distributed in the United States after February 1998 contain "a feature designed to enable viewers to block display of all programs with a common rating"—that is, to have a so-called V-chip.[1] A chip enabling viewers "to block display of all programs with a common rating" is, of course, meaningless without someone to sit down and actually rate programming. Who will rate, how, and with what effect, have thus become critical issues for television producers and artists, for parents, children and teenagers, and for others who may rely upon the ratings. This article poses three questions worth pondering as the United States for the first time embarks upon a massive program of evaluating, labeling, and blocking hundreds of thousands of broadcast and cable television productions.

First, what exactly is the TV rating system that the industry created in response to the CDA[2] meant to accomplish? The answer is not so obvious, and looking beyond the conventional answer ("parental empowerment"), it becomes clear that the congressional purpose was to disfavor, and hopefully chill, broad categories of speech of which Congress disapproved.

Second, who will rate programming, and how will they decide? Unless one believes that the mandated V-chip combined with the industry's rating system will have no effect whatsoever on what is produced or viewed, these procedural questions are critical.

Finally, what are the likely political and artistic effects of the U.S. ratings scheme? The evidence is just beginning to come in, but it tends to confirm that the ratings will indeed be used to censor, chill, and pressure the industry into dropping controversial shows.

I. What Exactly Is the Rating System Meant to Accomplish?

The V-chip law, which forced the TV industry's creation of the rating system, is often touted as a form of parental empowerment; that is, its proponents characterize it as an innocent means of giving information to parents that will enable them to decide for themselves what programs their children should and should not watch. But the law is not quite so benign and noncensorial as its defenders sometimes would have it appear. For the CDA singles out certain categories of television content that Congress disliked (primarily violence and sexuality), and imposes, or at least very strongly encourages, the creation of a rating system to identify, and facilitate the blocking of, programs with just this content. The V-chip law is thus not simply an attempt to inform parents generally about the content of television programming.

Indeed, the "findings" portion of the law is quite explicit on this point. It reads, in pertinent part:

The Congress makes the following findings:

> (1) Television influences children's perception of the values and behavior that are common and acceptable in society....
>
> (4) Studies have shown that children exposed to violent video programming at a young age have a higher tendency for violent and aggressive behavior later in life than children not so exposed, and that children exposed to violent video programing are prone to assume that acts of violence are acceptable behavior....
>
> (6) Studies indicate that children are affected by the pervasiveness and casual treatment of sexual material on television, eroding the ability of parents to develop responsible attitudes and behavior in their children....[3]

These findings make clear that the purpose of the V-chip legislation was to target certain subjects and ideas with plainly stated censorial purposes. Those subjects and ideas, as spelled out in the law, are "sexual, violent, or other indecent material about which parents should be informed before it is displayed to children."[4]

But what is the basis for Congress's conclusions that "children exposed to violent video programming at a young age have a higher tendency for violent and aggressive behavior later in life," or that "casual treatment of sexual material on television [erodes] the ability of parents to develop responsible attitudes and behavior in their children"? Putting aside the constitutional questions raised by a law that imposes congressional value judgments about "responsible attitudes and behavior,"[5] what precisely are the subjects or ideas that Congress thought to be harmful, and what is the nature of the social science evidence that is said to prove the point? The two questions are related, for without defining what we are talking about (*all* violence? only "excessive" or "gratuitous" violence? explicit sex? implied sex? irresponsible attitudes *about* sex?), it is impossible to say whether "violence" or "sex" cause harm, or whether labeling and blocking TV programs is likely to reduce such harm.

One of the weaknesses in the social science literature on minors, television, and violence is precisely the inconsistency among researchers in defining these terms. Some studies attempt to identify the effects of films or TV shows with realistic physical violence; others look at make-believe play or cartoon violence; still others include verbal aggression. Some researchers attempt to distinguish "good" from "bad" violence—that is, they would excuse war movies, educational documentaries, or situations in which the hero uses force in self-defense. As a recent report by the Committee on Communications and Media Law of the Association of the Bar of the City of New York points out,

> The subject of violence and aggression in psychology is vast. These topics are fundamental to the models and theories created in the fields of psychology, biology, ethnology and evolution. One author estimated that there were 20,000 to 30,000 references on the subject of human aggression. What is most striking, even after sampling only a small part of this literature and thought, is how little agreement there is among experts in human behavior about the nature of aggression and violence, and what causes humans to act aggressively or violently. There is even difficulty defining the words "aggression" and "violence."[6]

The report goes on to note that aggression and violence themselves

> are necessarily defined relative to culture, intent, and context. While all societies condemn murder, the same act may be seen as treason or heroism. Physical discipline of a child may be viewed as appropriate or abusive, depending on viewpoint and culture. Physical assault may be viewed as reprehensible conduct or as an appropriate part of a sport or entertainment, like hockey or boxing.[7]

Thus, despite numerous pronouncements over the past decade that a causative link between television violence and social or psychological harm has been definitively proven, the ambiguities in scientists' own use of definitional terms is in itself enough to raise questions about the "findings" that Congress made.

The social science literature is too vast and technical to review in detail here; in any event, excellent critiques have been published elsewhere.[8] The report of the Association of the Bar of the City of New York, however, does provide a useful summary of the types of studies that have been done and of what, if any, political, scientific, and legal conclusions can reasonably be drawn from them. The report notes first that there are many schools of psychology, only one of which considers "social learning" to be the primary cause of aggressive or violent behavior:

> [P]sychologists do not even agree on the basic mechanisms that cause aggression—and therefore on the possible role of stimuli such as media depictions of violence in contributing to it. Some see aggression as innate in human beings, a drive which demands discharge in some form. Evolutionary psychologists see human aggressiveness and destructive violence as a naturally evolved response to particular environments. Violence is simply the route to status in certain social environments. Another psychologist sees human destructiveness and cruelty not as an instinct but as a part of character, as "passions rooted in the total existence of man." For psychologists who emphasize the social needs of humans, violence is a reflection of psychological trauma in establishing relations to others. The failure to develop a mediating conscience because of a deficient family structure may lead to an inability to control aggressive impulses which arise.
>
> Finally, there are psychologists who believe aggressive behavior is learned from the environment. It is primarily these theorists who have

looked particularly at television and violence. But, although it is some-times sweepingly said that television violence causes violence in society, the research of these psychologists by no means supports so broad a state-ment. For over thirty years researchers have been attempting to discern the relationship, if any, between aggressive behavior and viewing television violence. The results remain controversial and skeptics abound.[9]

The report then describes the four basic methodological approaches that have been used by this last category of social scientists, who believe that "ag-gressive behavior is learned from the environment." These four are laboratory experiments, field experiments, quasi or natural experiments, and longitudi-nal studies. After examining the strengths and weaknesses of each method, the report concludes that the results of empirical research

> offer only modest support, and to a greater extent contradict, the legislative findings drawing connections between media violence and violent conduct or predispositions that underlie most of the efforts to regulate violent media content.

This is because, first,

> most psychological studies of the effects of television are studies of ag-gression or aggressive attitudes, not violence. The distinction is significant: many behaviors which few would deem "violent" may be counted and mea-sured by psychologists as aggressive. Yet the purported focus of most legisla-tive efforts is violent behavior caused by media content. It would therefore be erroneous to rely on psychological studies of aggression to justify such regulations.

Second, as the report noted,

> research studies are generally influenced by more fundamental, underlying conceptions of the causes of human social behavior—issues on which there is little agreement. For example, theorists who believe that behavior is learned by children from what they observe are more inclined to construct studies focusing on television or media than theorists who place more weight on the child's family structure or position in a social pecking order.

Finally,

> determining psychological causation is problematic, difficult and the sub-ject of a considerable amount of disagreement. The empirical findings normally speak in terms of correlation of events and not causation; the researchers' findings are usually carefully limited and, in general, do not make broad or definitive assertions about the causes of particular behavior. For many reasons, generalizing from research results to everyday experience can be perilous. It is difficult, for example, for psychologists to duplicate the mix and range of violent and non-violent programming that an individual may choose. There is also great variation in the population viewing violent programming: some persons may be unusually susceptible to imitation of violent media portrayals, and research populations may be skewed by over-representation of such individuals. It is also difficult to isolate ev-eryday viewing of violent media portrayals from other experiences that

psychologists believe may contribute to violent behavior. There is no consensus among even the researchers who have found some correlations that there is any clear causal link between media violence and violent behavior. Many psychologists point to other factors—such as watching television in general, or watching fast-paced programming—as the most likely causes of any aggressiveness associated with television viewing. And no researcher, to our knowledge, purports to demonstrate that eliminating media violence is necessary to reducing violent behavior.[10]

In short, Congress's "findings" about exposure to TV violence and subsequent behavior do not hold up to even the most cursory examination. The effects of art and entertainment on the complex and idiosyncratic human mind are still largely a mystery. The unavoidable conclusion is that Congress seized upon social science literature to cloak what was essentially a political and moral judgment that large, vague categories of television programming are offensive or at least inappropriate for youth.[11]

II. Who Will Rate Programming, and How Will They Decide?

The V-chip puts significant power in the hands of the people who will actually rate TV programming. Those parents who choose to activate the chip will not be evaluating programs themselves to determine if they are consonant with their own values or appropriate for the age and maturity levels of their children. Instead, parents will be blocking programs based on simple, conclusory V, S, L (for language), or D (for dialogue) labels, combined with the industry's originally proposed TV-G, TV-PG, TV-14, and TV-MA age-based recommendations.[12] The system will give no further information about the multitude of shows subject to the rating system—their context, purpose, viewpoint, quality, or educational value.

Those parents who block will thus do so based on *Congress's* determination that it is sex, "indecency," and violence that must be restrained, and the industry's apparent interpretation of "indecent," to the extent it differs from "sexual," to mean primarily "coarse" language (L) or "suggestive dialogue" (D).[13] Other types of content that have occasionally been blamed for juvenile delinquency or other ills—for example, racist speech, discussions of drug use, or paeans to "Satanism" or other disapproved religious beliefs—are not included.

Critics of ratings systems have pointed out the dangers of using broad, conclusory labels as measures of the value of speech, or of the harm it may cause. An often cited, and still powerful, example is Steven Spielberg's film *Schindler's List*, which will presumably receive V, S, L, and D labels because of its violent content (it is, after all, about the Holocaust) and occasional nudity (Schindler has affairs—sexual nudity—and the Jews who are being rounded up for slaughter are frequently deprived of their clothing—nonsexual nudity). Yet *Schindler's List* is probably among the most important and educational of commercial films in recent years. Whatever arguments might be made about the psychological effects on children of *gratuitous* violence, the violence shown in *Schindler's List* can hardly be deemed gratuitous, and indeed the film has been criticized in some quarters for not giving a vivid *enough* depiction of the horrors of the Nazi regime. What then, is the point exactly of shielding minors, particularly teenagers, from the knowledge of human pain and brutality imparted by this and other historical films? How are they to learn about human history without studying the evil that characterized one of its most gruesome episodes? Does it really help educate young people to airbrush the atrocities of history— or, for that matter, to pretend that the powerful force of human sexuality does not exist? Certainly, there is little basis to believe that viewing *Schindler's List* will cause young people to develop greater tolerance for violence, to behave more aggressively, or to acquire irresponsible attitudes about sex.[14]

Eyes on the Prize, to cite an example of a program specifically designed for TV, is a powerful documentary of the American civil rights movement, and contains violence galore—most of it visited by Southern white citizens or law enforcement officers against black protesters. The film would be historically false if it did not. Yet its educational value and dramatic power cannot be doubted. What is the justification for labeling with a V—and therefore suggesting to parents that they block it as unsuitable—this masterwork of documentary filmmaking?

On a more mundane level, the process of deciding whether a program merits a V, D, S, or L—or a TV-14 or TV-MA—will inevitably be subjective, value-laden and time consuming, as a Fox Broadcasting executive noted in September 1997.[15] Ellen DeGeneres, the recently "out" lesbian of the popular eponymous ABC sitcom, discovered in October 1997, that her completely nonviolent and nonsexually explicit show was slated to receive a TV-14, presumably because it deals approvingly with homosexuality. "How can I go forward?" DeGeneres was quoted as asking. "This is blatant discrimination.... This advisory is telling kids something's wrong with being gay."[16]

A December 1993 report from North Dakota Senator Byron Dorgan is pertinent here. The report summarized the results of a one-week survey of violence on prime time television conducted by college students earlier that year. Among the shows found to contain the highest number of violent acts per hours were *The Miracle Worker, Civil War Journal, Star Trek 9, The Untouchables, Murder She Wrote, Back to the Future, Our Century: Combat at Sea, Teenage Mutant Ninja Turtles,* and Alfred Hitchcock's classic *North by Northwest.*[17] Even if a TV ratings system purported to give pejorative V labels to only the programs on this list deemed to contain "bad" violence, which the industry's current plan does not, it would be difficult for a team of raters to make those judgments, expected as they will be to decide upon labels for dozens of programs daily. Indeed, the subjectivity of judgments about "value" or about the meaning or propriety of the messages contained in creative works, as well as long-standing First Amendment rules against "viewpoint discrimination,"[18] are one reason that the ratings, like the Communications Decency Act itself, do not distinguish between "good" and "bad" violence or sex.

But if making value judgments of this type is both difficult and offensive to our anticensorship instincts, a system that fails to do so, and thus encompasses *all* programming bearing on large subjects like sexuality or violence, is hopelessly overbroad. As Professor Burt Neuborne recently pointed out:

> The impossibly broad reach of a literal ban on all speech depicting violence inevitably requires a narrowing set of criteria designed to distinguish *Hamlet* from forbidden speech depicting violence. But any effort by the FCC, or anyone else, to decide when speech depicting violence crosses the line from an acceptable exercise in artistic creation, as in *Hamlet,* or *Oedipus Rex,* or *Antigone,* or *The Crucible,* to a forbidden depiction of "gratuitous" or "excessive" violence must involve purely subjective notions of taste and aesthetic judgment. Indeed, once it is recognized that the ban on violence cannot be applied literally, any effort to apply a narrower ban is utterly without objective guidance. In effect, efforts to ban violent programming would turn the FCC into a drama critic, forced to pass judgment on the artistic merits of any effort to depict a violent act.[19]

The problems Professor Neuborne identifies with respect to a ban are equally present in a ratings system. The American Psychological Association has acknowledged that "[t]elevision violence per se is not the problem; rather, it is the manner in which most violence on television is shown that should concern us."[20] But as Professor Neuborne points out, trying to distinguish between "excessive" or "gratuitous" violence on the one hand, and violent material presented in an instructive or morally approved way, as the APA suggests, would enmesh whoever is responsible for the ratings in a vast process of policing thought and censoring ideas.

Nor are these problems resolved if television companies decide not to assign the task of rating to in-house staff but instead force producers or directors to evaluate and label their own programs. Many of those on the creative side of the industry will object to being compelled to attached pejorative ratings to their works, or will bridle at the constraints of a system that substitutes overgeneralized and fundamentally uninformative labels for real contextual information about programs.[21] If, despite their objections, they are forced to label, the results are likely to be arbitrary and idiosyncratic. For example, the distinction between "strong, coarse language," requiring a TV-14 rating, and "crude indecent language," requiring a TV-MA,[22] is likely to elude many raters and lead to inconsistent results.

On the other end of the television continuum, there are countless programs with no violence, sex, "coarse language," or "suggestive dialogue," and also with little educational or artistic value. Mindless entertainment—the "idiot box" of popular discourse—may be a greater threat to healthy child development, to the nurturing of thoughtful young people who are knowledgeable about and capable of dealing with the complexities and tragedies of human life, than violent or sexual content per se. Justice Brandeis's much-quoted rhetoric about "more speech"[23] is pertinent here: teaching young people about responsible sexuality or other aspects of human behavior requires education and discussion, not censorship.

III. What Are the Likely Political and Artistic Effects of the U.S. Ratings Scheme?

Regardless of its unambiguously stated censorial purposes,[24] the 1996 V-chip law, it is sometimes said, will not have any speech-suppressive effect, or at least none attributable to the government. Parents will make their own decisions based on accurate information about programming—an outcome no more repressive of free speech than the existing operation of market forces as consumers choose some programs and reject others.

Let's examine this seductively simple proposition. First, even in the constitutional sense (as the First Amendment generally applies only to government), the television ratings are not likely to operate wholly in the unregulated sphere of private choice. Some public schools will rely upon the ratings in choosing—or, more accurately, disqualifying—what may be worthy and valuable TV programs for homework assignments or in-class viewing. Indeed, there are school districts that already rely upon the familiar Motion Picture Association of America/Classification and Rating Administration movie ratings in just this fashion,[25] despite the fact that MPAA/CARA raters have no background or expertise in education or child development.[26] Just as numerous students have been deprived of *Schindler's List* as part of their high school history courses because of its R rating from CARA, so *The Accused, The Miracle Worker, The Civil War*, and countless other educationally profitable TV movies or other shows with violent content will receive V ratings and be subject to at least a presumption against curricular use in many public schools.

Second, ratings necessarily imply that certain programs contain themes that are morally disapproved or psychologically harmful to minors. They thus provide an easy set of symbols for "family values" activists in local communities to seize upon. The average public school administration will not be particularly eager to countenance curricular use of S-, V-, L-, or D-rated material in the face of likely protest from such groups. Ratings thus advance censorship by giving private pressure groups easy red flags to wave in the faces of nervous government officials.

Moving from the local to the national government level, it is difficult to imagine that the Federal Communications Commission, which is so enmeshed in the regulation of "indecency" in broadcasting,[27] will not be drawn into disputes over ratings as well. It will no doubt receive complaints from politicians, members of the public, and perhaps rival broadcasters, that some companies are not accurately rating their programming, or are refusing to rate at all. Indeed, one member of Congress has already made such a threat explicitly. In September 1997, Senator John McCain wrote to NBC, which had so far resisted the addition of content-based letter labels to the original age-based industry ratings plan, that if NBC continued to "refuse to join with the rest of the television industry,"

> I will pursue a series of alternative ways of safeguarding, by law and regulation, the interests that NBC refuses to safeguard voluntarily. These will include, but not be limited to, the legislation offered by Senator Hollings to channel violent programming to later hours, as well as urging the Federal

Communications Commission to examine in a full evidentiary hearing the renewal application of any television station not implementing the revised TV ratings system.[28]

Is the FCC to ignore the complaints of Senator McCain and others? It may, to be sure, be wary of initiating formal reviews of allegedly inaccurate or deceptive ratings, for fear of establishing the very "state action," and consequent vulnerability to a First Amendment court challenge, that the authors of the V-chip legislation attempted to avoid. Nevertheless, the agency is charged by law with evaluating a broadcast licensee's record of contribution to the "public interest" when reviewing requests for license renewals, transfers, or acquisitions.[29] Just as the commission has long considered broadcasters' records on community programming and their capacity to disseminate diverse points of view,[30] and just as it has threatened adverse licensing action based on complaints of "indecency,"[31] it is likely to consider allegations that broadcasters have rated programs improperly when it makes licensing decisions. At the very least, the possibility that it may do so, and the power of economic life and death that the FCC holds over broadcasters, will make the television industry cautious about displeasing the agency.

What about private censorship? Putting aside the legal question whether private marketplace choices made as a result of the V-chip law create First Amendment concerns,[32] it cannot be doubted that such private choices do have an effect on artistic freedom. Again, the analogy to movie ratings is instructive. Just as many theaters are reluctant to book NC-17 movies, some advertisers will be reluctant to support V-, S-, L-, or D-rated TV shows. Less advertising means less revenue, which in turn means less likelihood that the show will survive —unless, of course, its content is toned down. In many situations, advertisers' threats of withdrawal will not even be necessary, since for large entertainment companies the mere prospect of pejorative ratings may be daunting enough in terms of public relations to cause them to instruct producers to self-censor their material.

In recent years, the MPAA/CARA film ratings system has had just this effect. Leading directors like the late Louis Malle have been forced to eliminate artistically important scenes from their work because of the studios' insistence on obtaining at least nothing more pejorative and audience-thinning than an R rating.[33] Self-censorship will thus be a predictable and intended effect of the V-chip law.

I have discussed in the previous two sections whether such pressures to self-censor are justifiable, given the ambiguity of the social science literature, the difficulty of defining what it is that is supposed to be harmful, and the dangers of reposing discretionary ratings powers in either program producers themselves or large numbers of industry-employed functionaries. The point here is that, regardless of the strength of the justifications or the fairness of the procedures, the inevitable pressures of the ratings system will in many instances lead to blander, less provocative programming—less coverage of controversial but important issues like sexuality, and less artistic freedom.[34]

V-chips and ratings will do nothing to solve the tough, persistent social problems we associate with youth: poor education, violence, alienation, high teen pregnancy rates. American political leaders, however, seem increasingly devoted to the art of making symbolic gestures while ignoring serious solutions to social problems. V-chips and ratings are such gestures, but they are not entirely empty ones. For although they will do nothing to reduce irresponsible sexual activity or violence, they will restrain artistic freedom. Moreover, they create the illusion that "something is being done," and reinforce the pernicious notion that information about such complex human phenomena as sexuality and aggression is better suppressed than examined.

Notes

1. 47 U.S.C. §303(x), Public Law 104–104, Title V, §551(c). The law only applies to TV sets with screens 13 inches or larger, and allows the FCC to alter the requirement consistent with advances in technology. *Id.*, §551(c)(4).

2. The law provided that if the television industry did not within a year develop a ratings system satisfactory to the Federal Communications Commission, the FCC must "prescribe" one that would identify "sexual, violent, or other indecent material," and then, "in consultation" with the industry, must establish rules requiring programmers to transmit the ratings in a manner allowing parents to block rated shows. 47 U.S.C. §303(w). Despite initial protests, the industry responded promptly by setting up a committee to design a ratings system. See n. 12, *infra*.

3. Section 551(a), Public Law 104–104 (1996), published in the Historical and Statutory Notes to 47 U.S.C. §303(w). Congressional "findings" may or may not be based on accurate empirical evidence, and in any event are not binding on courts, particularly not in First Amendment cases, where the judicial branch must make its own judgment about the facts on which the government relies to justify restrictions on free speech. See, e.g. *Sable Communications, Inc. V. FCC*, 492 U.S. 115, 129 (1989); *Landmark Communications v. Virginia*, 435 U.S. 829, 843 (1978).

4. 47 U.S.C. §303(w). The section goes on to assure that "nothing in this paragraph shall be construed to authorize any rating of video programming on the basis of its political or religious content." *Id.*

5. A fundamental First Amendment principle is that government cannot suppress ideas because it thinks them dangerous. See Marjorie Heins, "Viewpoint Discrimination," 24 *Hastings Con.L.Q.* 99 (1996); *American Booksellers Association v. Hudnut*, 771 F.2d 323 (7th Cir.) aff'd mem., 475 U.S. 1001 (1985).

6. "Violence in the Media: A Position Paper," *The Record of The Association of the Bar of the City of New York*, vol. 52, no. 3 (April 1997), at 283–84 (citations omitted). Reprinted with permission from *The Record of The Association of the Bar of the City of New York*, copyright 1997, 52 *The Record* 273, 283–84.

7. *Id.* at 284.

8. See e.g., Jonathan Freedman, "Television Violence and Aggression: A Rejoinder," *Psychological Bulletin*, Vol. 100(3), 372–78 (1986); Robert Kaplan, "Television Violence and Viewer Aggression: A Reexamination of the Evidence," *Journal of Social Issues*, vol. 32, no. 4, 35–70 (1976); Robert Kaplan, "TV Violence and Aggression Revisited Again," *American Psychologist*, vol. 37, no. 5, 589 (May 1982); O. Wiegman, M. Kuttschreuter & B. Baarda, "A Longitudinal Study of the Effects of Television Viewing on Aggressive and Prosocial Behaviours," *British Journal of Social Psychology*, vol. 31, 147–64 (1992).

9. "Violence in the Media," *Record of The Association of the Bar of the City of New York*, *supra* n. 6, at 286 (citations omitted).

10. *Id.* at 296–97 (citations omitted).

11. Social science studies with respect to sexual situations on television are quite limited compared to the extensive, if inconclusive, literature on violence. The few studies that do exist are at best suggestive of a correlation, not necessarily a causal relation, between viewing habits and sexual behavior. See, e.g., Charles Corder-Bolz, "Television and Adolescents' Sexual Behavior," *Sex Education News,* vol. 3 (Jan. 1981), p. 3 (survey showed that of seventy-five adolescent girls, half of them pregnant, the pregnant ones watched more TV soap operas and were less likely to think that their favorite characters used contraceptives). As the American Academy of Pediatrics, a proponent of more sexually responsible TV programming, acknowledges, "there is no clear documentation that the relationship between television viewing and sexual activity [among teenagers] is causal." American Academy of Pediatrics, "Children, Adolescents, and Television," *Pediatrics,* vol. 96, no. 4 (Oct. 1995), p. 786.

12. The industry's original plan, submitted by the National Association of Broadcasters (NAB), the Motion Picture Association of America (MPAA), and the National Cable Television Association (NCTA) to the FCC for its approval on January 17, 1997, was wholly age-based and gave no information about the content of specific programs. It encountered widespread criticism from politicians and advocacy groups. After a six-month period of negotiations with these groups, the three industry associations agreed to add V, S, L, and D labels to the scheme. See Letter Submission of Jack Valenti, President and CEO of the MPAA, Decker Anstrom, President and CEO of the NCTA, and Eddie Fritts, president and CEO of the NAB, to William Caton, FCC Secretary, Aug. 1, 1997 (hereinafter, "Valenti letter").

13. *Id.,* p. 2. As a legal term "indecency" derives from the Federal Communications Commission's policing of radio and television broadcasting, as approved by the Supreme Court in *FCC v. Pacifica Foundation,* 438 U.S. 726 (1978). The monologue by comedian George Carlin found to be indecent in *Pacifica* consisted of the repetitive use of the so-called seven dirty words, not of any explicit description of sexual activity.

    Under the industry's plan, news and sports are to be exempt from labeling requirements. See Valenti letter, p. 3. Disputes may easily be anticipated about what programming qualifies as "news."

14. Many other examples of fine films with violent content could, of course, be cited: *The Accused, Bonnie and Clyde, The Burning Bed, Psycho,* and almost any war story or Biblical epic.

15. Lawrie Mifflin, "Helping or Confusing, TV Labels are Widening," *New York Times,* Sept. 30, 1997, p. E1 (quoting Roland McFarland, Vice President for Broadcast Standards and Practices at Fox, as stating that "the process had become much more time-consuming now that D, L, S, and V had to be considered." "Is it a punch? A gunshot? A gunshot plus killing? These are all subjective interpretations. The classic discussion here is around shows where there's heavy jeopardy involved, but not real on-screen violence. You might see a body, the aftermath of violence.... Where's the tilt factor, as far as giving it a V?" *Id.,* p. E8.

16. Bill Carter, "Star of 'Ellen' Threatens to Quit Over Advisory," *New York Times,* Oct. 9, 1997, p. E3.

17. Press Release from U.S. Senator Byron L. Dorgan (North Dakota), "Report on Television Violence Shows Fox Network Has the Most Violence Programming," Dec. 16, 1993, and attached report, "Television Violence Demonstration Project Conducted at Concordia College, Moorhead, Minnesota, Sept.–Dec. 1993."

18. See n. 5, *supra.*

19. Television Rating System: Hearings on S.409 Before the Senate Comm. on Commerce, Science and Transp., 105th Cong. (1997) (testimony of Burt Neuborne, Professor of Law, New York University).

20. Comments of the American Psychological Association to the Federal Communications Commission 3 (April 8, 1997) (in the matter of Industry Proposal for Rating Video Programming, No. 97–55).

21. In the analogous context of Internet ratings, producers of online information have loudly objected to proposals that they "self-rate" their sites: as one editor explained, "The rating of content, particularly in the area of violence—to tell people whether they should or shouldn't read about war in Bosnia—takes news and turns it into a form of entertainment." Amy Harmon, "Technology," *New York Times*, Sept. 1, 1997, p. D3.

22. As set out in the Valenti Letter, *supra* n. 12, p. 2.

23. "Those who won our independence . . . believed that freedom to think as you will and to speak as you think are means indispensable to the discovery and spread of political truth; that without free speech and assembly, discussion would be futile; that with them, discussion affords ordinarily adequate protection against the dissemination of noxious doctrine. . . . [T]hey knew that . . . the path of safety lies in the opportunity to discuss freely supposed grievances and proposed remedies; and that the fitting remedy for evil counsels is good ones." *Whitney v. California*, 274 U.S. 357, 375 (1927) (Brandeis, J., concurring).

24. See *supra*, text accompanying notes 2–3.

25. See *Borger v. Bisciglia*, 888 F.Supp. 97 (W.D.Wis. 1995) (rejecting First Amendment challenge to school district's ban on showing any R-rated film as part of curriculum, which resulted in inability of students to see *Schindler's List* as part of their study of the Holocaust); *Desilets v. Clearview Regional Board of Education*, 137 N.J. 584 (1994) (striking down school authorities' refusal to allow student newspaper to review R-rated films, *Rain Man* and *Mississippi Burning*); " 'Schindler' Blacklisted," *New York Times*, March 18, 1994, p. A28 (Letters to the Editor) (describing Plymouth, Massachusetts's school board's decision not to allow high school students to see *Schindler's List* because of R rating); "Twin Falls, Ohio," American Library Association *Newsletter on Intellectual Freedom* (Sept. 1997), p. 127 (describing parent's challenge to use of films *Schindler's List* and *Macbeth* because of their R ratings).

26. See Richard M. Mosk, "Motion Picture Ratings in the United States," in this volume. I do not mean to suggest that a ratings board composed of literary or psychological experts, as is found, for example, in Britain, would necessarily be an improvement.

27. See *FCC v. Pacifica Foundation*, 438 U.S. 726 (1978); *Action for Children's Television v. FCC* ("ACT III"), 58 F.3d 654 (D.C. Cir. 1995), cert. denied, 116 S.Ct. 701 (1996).

28. Letter from Senator John McCain, chairman, Senate Committee on Commerce, Science and Transportation, to Robert Wright, President and CEO, National Broadcasting Company, Sept. 29, 1997. At around the same time, Senator McCain asked each of four new FCC commissioner candidates "to agree to consider a station's use or nonuse of the revised ratings-code as a factor in deciding whether to renew a station's license." Lawrie Mifflin, "Media," *New York Times*, Oct. 6, 1997, p. D11. Although refusing to use the letter labels, NBC was already giving "full-sentence advisories" about violent content at the start of some shows. *Id.*

29. See 47 U.S.C. §§303–309.

30. See *Metro Broadcasting, Inc. v. FCC*, 497 U.S. 547 (1990) (approving FCC's consideration of diversity of viewpoint in awarding licenses), overruled on other grounds in *Adarand Constructors, Inc. v. Peña*, 515 U.S. 200 (1995).

31. See *Action for Children's Television v. FCC* ("ACT IV"), 59 F.3d 1249, 1266 (D.C. Cir 1995), cert. denied, 116 S.Ct. 773 (1996) (Tatel, J., dissenting) (noting FCC use of administrative "indecency" determinations to threaten loss of broadcast licenses).

32. In *Denver Area Educational Telecommunications Consortium v. FCC*, 116 S.Ct. 2374 (1966), Justice Stephen Breyer, writing for a plurality of four members of the Supreme Court, asserted that although a law authorizing private cable companies to censor "indecent" leased access cable programming was clearly "state action," it did not violate the First Amendment because, among other things, the law addressed "an extremely important problem"—"protecting children from exposure to patently offensive depictions of sex"—and it reflected a balancing of cable companies' and leased access programmers' free speech rights. *Id.* at 2385, 2382–88. As to public, educational, and governmental access cable programming, the Court reached the opposite conclusion. *Id.* at 2394–97.

33. See Marjorie Heins, *Sex, Sin and Blasphemy: A Guide to America's Censorship Wars* 58–59 (1993) (describing Malle's cutting, over protest, of his controversial film, *Damage*); Stephen Farber, *The Movie Rating Game* 71 (1972) (recounting how line about pubic hair was cut from *The Reivers* to obtain GP rating and how pot-smoking scene and two short love-making scenes were eliminated from *Alice's Restaurant* for the same reason); see also *Miramax Films Corp. v. Motion Picture Association of America*, 560 N.Y.S. 730, 734 (Supreme Ct., NY County 1990) ("[t]he record also reveals that films are produced and *negotiated* to fit the ratings. After an initial 'X' rating of a film whole scenes or parts thereof are cut in order to fit within the 'R' category. Contrary to our jurisprudence which protects all forms of expression, the rating system censors serious films by the force of economic pressure"). Since the decision in *Miramax*, CARA's dreaded X has been replaced with the almost equally undesirable NC-17.

34. Some critics of ratings claim that the censorial purpose may backfire—that is, the quest for adventuresome (especially teenage) audiences may in some cases cause producers gratuitously to *add* sexual or violent content to their work, for what self-respecting adolescent wants to attend a G-rated movie? Whatever the accuracy of this speculation, it seems evident that television ratings, like movie ratings, will distort artistic judgments and introduce extraneous pressures into the creative process.

POSTSCRIPT

Do Ratings Work?

From the earliest years of television broadcasting, parents and educators have expressed concerns that television is harmful, particularly to such a vulnerable population as children. These concerns have become important public policy issues. Groups, such as Action for Children's Television (ACT), have lobbied the Federal Communications Commission (FCC) for guidelines on appropriate practices for entertaining and advertising to young audiences. In addition to the 1996 Telecommunications Act, the 1990 Children's Television Act imposed an obligation on broadcasters to serve the educational and informational needs of children. Broadcasters are now required to schedule at least three hours of educational and informational (ELI) programming for children per week. And that regulation accounts for another piece of information appearing on television screens at the beginning of programs, often an ELI symbol indicating that the program fulfills the educational or informational needs of children.

A common theme of arguments for and against regulation has to do with the responsibility of parents. To monitor children's viewing, parents have to be full-time television watchdogs, states George Gerbner, head of the Violence Index project. Those on the other side of the argument say that monitoring children is exactly what parents should do; television is not a babysitter. Some worry that concern over ratings will produce homogenous, uninteresting entertainment fare.

The Annenberg Public Policy Center (APPC) has been studying the state of children's television for the past four years. The aims of this research have been to determine the availability of high-quality choices for children of different age groups with different resources, to identify the high-quality programs that exist on broadcast and cable, and to track the impact of government regulation of children's television programs. *The 1998 State of Children's Television Report* notes that many programs do not contain appropriate labels previewing violent content. They particularly argued for the more common use of the FV rating (for fantasy violence) rather than the less informative TV-Y7, which was more commonly used. This report seems to have been heard, as the FV rating is showing up considerably more frequently than it used to in children's programs. The 1999 APPC report notes that 64 percent of parents and 72 percent of children are aware of the existence of a TV ratings system; even fewer know of the ELI designation. Over half of parents indicated that they would use the V-chip system if they had it, but also over half of children have a television in their own bedroom, which presumably limits parental monitoring.

Much has been written on this subject. One place to start is with the volume edited by Monroe E. Price, *The V-chip Debate: Content Filtering From*

Television to the Internet (Lawrence Erlbaum Associates, 1998). The bibliography and appendices are particularly useful. In the debate over the potentials and problems of the V-chip, the Canadian experiment with the technology is frequently mentioned. Two essays, one by Al MacKay and another by Stephen D. McDowell and Carleen Maitland in the Price volume, explore the Canadian experience with the V-chip.

ISSUE 13

Have the Direction and Power of the FCC Changed?

YES: Robert W. McChesney and John Nichols, from "The Making of a Movement: Getting Serious About Media Reform," *The Nation* (January 7/14, 2002)

NO: Brendan I. Koerner, from "Losing Signal," *Mother Jones* (September/October 2001)

ISSUE SUMMARY

YES: Since the passage of the Telecommunications Act of 1996, the Federal Communications Commission (FCC) has undergone several revisions of its mission. Professor Robert W. McChesney and author John Nichols discuss the "media reform movement" and outline the purpose of several interest groups to deal with the FCC's changes. In particular, they critique the current role of the FCC with Commissioner Michael Powell with regard to whether or not the FCC can still claim to operate in the "public interest."

NO: Author Brendan I. Koerner sees any changes under Powell's FCC leadership as more of the same pandering to industry ties that characterized past commissions. While he feels that the direction of the FCC has been driven for some time by the promise of digital technology, he speculates that technology is now leading regulation. In this case, the power of the FCC can be seen to encourage mergers that will ultimately result in greater involvement and control by multimedia corporations.

W hen the Federal Communications Commission (FCC) was officially established in 1934, it served as a government agency to address issues of the relationship among the government, the public, and the companies involved in technology development and content distribution. Throughout the 1980s, deregulation of many important industries in the United States changed the relationship between government and industry and effectively limited the role of government as a "regulator" of business. Instead, "marketplace rules" were allowed to gain preeminence, and expanding the power of business and industry to set their own rules was seen as the most effective means of spurring economic growth and competition. The passage of the Telecommunications Act of 1996 was the culmination of the new relationship between business and government, which fully complied with deregulation and marketplace rules. With less of a need for the government agency of the FCC to monitor and control telecommunications practices, the agency's mission changed.

The FCC under President Bill Clinton, a Democrat, maintained the deregulatory approach, and many critics say that he also enhanced deregulation, mergers, and industry dominance over former practices. Since George W. Bush assumed the presidency, the leadership of the FCC has been Republican under Michael Powell, and the pro-industry approach has continued to foster industry ties. Many find it amazing that in less than 10 years, we have gone from thinking that the FCC still maintained some connection to the mission of the Communications Act of 1934, which mandated that the FCC operate in the "public interest," to recognizing the engine of industry and commerce that it has become.

The following selections assume that the FCC will maintain its pro-industry direction, but the authors of the two selections view the future differently. Robert W. McChesney and John Nichols maintain that there is an opposition to the FCC's direction and that pressure groups demanding media reform must be heard. They believe that public pressure could shape and redirect the FCC's actions if coalitions were to be built. Brendan I. Koerner takes a decidedly more technological determinist view; he states that the technology is now driving the move, whether toward regulation or deregulation, and industry action. Because technology is evolving so rapidly, says Koerner, the regulatory climate can't possibly keep up the pace, and therefore the FCC's decision-making capacity will decrease, while its ability to foster industry interests will continue to grow.

The following selections call our attention to several issues in telecommunications regulation. Has the FCC changed so much that it no longer serves the purpose for which it was created? Can public interest groups effect change? What relationship does the FCC, or any federal agency, have to the political will of Congress and the president? Probably most importantly, the authors ask us to question what type of future the FCC may have, as technological development continues to accelerate.

Equally important is the notion of what action in "the public interest" means. Does this phrase provide a mission? If so, how can an agency know and understand what the public interest really means? In what ways can the phrase be interpreted?

Robert W. McChesney and
John Nichols

 **YES**

The Making of a Movement:
Getting Serious About Media Reform

No one should be surprised by the polls showing that close to 90 percent of Americans are satisfied with the performance of their selected President, or that close to 80 percent of the citizenry applaud his Administration's seat-of-the-pants management of an undeclared war. After all, most Americans get their information from media that have pledged to give the American people only the President's side of the story. CNN chief Walter Isaacson distributed a memo effectively instructing the network's domestic newscasts to be sugarcoated in order to maintain popular support for the President and his war. Fox News anchors got into a surreal competition to see who could wear the largest American flag lapel pin. Dan Rather, the man who occupies the seat Walter Cronkite once used to tell Lyndon Johnson the Vietnam War was unwinnable, now says, "George Bush is the President.... he wants me to line up, just tell me where."

No, we should not be surprised that a "just tell me where" press has managed to undermine debate at precisely the time America needs it most—but we should be angry. The role that US newsmedia have played in narrowing and warping the public discourse since September 11 provides dramatic evidence of the severe limitations of contemporary American journalism, and this nation's media system, when it comes to nurturing a viable democratic and humane society. It is now time to act upon that anger to forge a broader, bolder and more politically engaged movement to reform American media.

The base from which such a movement could spring has already been built. Indeed, the current crisis comes at a critical moment for media reform politics. Since the middle 1980s, when inept and disingenuous reporting on US interventions in Central America provoked tens of thousands of Americans to question the role media were playing in manufacturing consent, media activism has had a small but respectable place on the progressive agenda. The critique has gone well beyond complaints about shoddy journalism to broad expressions of concern about hypercommercial, corporate-directed culture and the corruption of communications policy-making by special-interest lobbies and pliable legislators.

Crucial organizations such as Fairness & Accuracy In Reporting (FAIR), the Institute for Public Accuracy, the MediaChannel, Media Alliance and the Media Education Foundation have emerged over the past two decades. Acting as mainstream media watchdogs while pointing engaged Americans toward valuable alternative fare, these groups have raised awareness that any democratic reform in the United States must include media reform. Although it is hardly universal even among progressives, there is increasing recognition that media reform can no longer be dismissed as a "dependent variable" that will fall into place once the more important struggles have been won. People are beginning to understand that unless we make headway with the media, the more important struggles will never be won.

On the advocacy front, Citizens for Independent Public Broadcasting and People for Better TV are pushing to improve public broadcasting and to tighten regulation of commercial broadcasting. Commercial Alert organizes campaigns against the commercialization of culture, from sports and museums to literature and media. The Center for Digital Democracy and the Media Access Project both work the corridors of power in Washington to win recognition of public-interest values under extremely difficult circumstances. These groups have won some important battles, particularly on Internet privacy issues.

In addition, local media watch groups have surfaced across the nation. Citizens' organizations do battle to limit billboards in public places and to combat the rise of advertising in schools—fighting often successfully to keep Channel One ads, corporate-sponsored texts and fast-food promotions out of classrooms and cafeterias. Innovative lawsuits challenging the worst excesses of media monopoly are being developed by regional groups such as Rocky Mountain Media Watch and a national consortium of civic organizations, lawyers and academics that has drawn support from Unitarian Universalist organizations. Media activists in Honolulu and San Francisco have joined with unions and community groups to prevent the closure of daily newspapers that provided a measure of competition and debate in those cities.

⋘◉⋙

Despite all these achievements, however, the media reform movement remains at something of a standstill. The sheer corruption of US politics is itself a daunting obstacle. The Center for Public Integrity in 2000 issued "Off the Record: What Media Corporations Don't Tell You About Their Legislative Agendas"— an alarming exposé of the huge lobbying machines employed by the largest communications corporations and their trade associations, as well as the considerable campaign contributions they make. According to the center, the fifty largest media companies and four of their trade associations spent $111.3 million between 1996 and mid-2000 to lobby Congress and the executive branch. Between 1993 and mid-2000, the center determined, media corporations and their employees have given $75 million in campaign contributions to candidates for federal office and to the two major political parties. Regulators and politicians tend therefore to be in the pockets of big-spending corporate communications lobbies, and—surprise, surprise—the corporate newsmedia rarely cover media policy debates. Notwithstanding all the good work by media activists, the "range" of communications policy debate in Washington still tends to run all the way from GE to GM, to borrow a line from FAIR's Jeff Cohen.

At this very moment, for example, the FCC is considering the elimination of the remaining restrictions on media consolidation, including bans on cross-ownership by a single firm of TV stations and newspapers in the same community, and limits on the number of TV stations and cable TV systems a single corporation may own nationwide. The corporate media lobbying superstars are putting a full-court press on the FCC—which, with George W. Bush's imprint now firmly on its membership, is now even more pro-corporate than during the Clinton years. The proposed scrapping of these regulations will increase the shareholder value of numerous media firms dramatically, and will undoubtedly inspire a massive wave of mergers and acquisitions. If the lessons of past ownership deregulation—particularly the 1996 relaxation of radio ownership rules—are any guide, we can expect even less funding for journalism and more commercialism. All of this takes place without scrutiny from major media, and therefore is unknown to all but a handful of Americans.

◦◦◉◦◦

The immensity of the economic and political barriers to democratic action has contributed to demoralization about the prospects for structural media reform and an understandable turn to that which progressives can hope to control: their own media. So it has been that much energy has gone into the struggle over the future of the Pacifica radio chain, which looks at long last to be heading toward a viable resolution. The Independent Press Association has grown dramatically to nurture scores of usually small, struggling nonprofit periodicals, which are mostly progressive in orientation. And dozens of local Independent Media Centers [IMC] have mushroomed on the Internet over the past two years. These Indy Media Centers take advantage of new technology to provide dissident and alternative news stories and commentary; some, by focusing on local issues, have become a genuine alternative to established media at a level where that alternative can and does shift the dialogue. We have seen the positive impact of the IMC movement firsthand—in Seattle, in Washington, at the 2000 Democratic and Republican national conventions, at the three lamentable presidential debates later that year, during the Florida recount and in the aftermath of September 11 in New York and other cities. It is vital that this and other alternative media movements grow in scope and professionalism.

Yet, as important as this work is, there are inherent limits to what can be done with independent media, even with access to the Internet. Too often, the alternative media remain on the margins, seeming to confirm that the dominant structures are the natural domain of the massive media conglomerates that supposedly "give the people what they want."

The trouble with this disconnect between an engaged and vital alternative media and a disengaged and stenographic dominant media is that it suggests a natural order in which corporate media have mastered the marketplace on the basis of their wit and wisdom. In fact, our media system is not predominantly the result of free-market competition. Huge promotional budgets and continual rehashing of tried and true formulas play their role in drawing viewers, listeners and readers to dominant print and broadcast media. But their dominance is still made possible, in large part, by explicit government policies and subsidies that permit the creation of large and profitable conglomerates. When the government grants free monopoly rights to TV spectrum, for example, it is not setting the terms of competition; it is picking the winner of the competition. Such policies amount to an annual grant of corporate welfare that economist Dean Baker values in the tens of billions of dollars. These decisions have been made in the public's name, but without the public's informed consent. We must not accept such massive subsidies for wealthy corporations, nor should we content ourselves with the "freedom" to forge an alternative that occupies the margins. Our task is to return "informed consent" to media policy-making and to generate a diverse media system that serves our democratic needs.

In our view, what's needed to begin the job is now crystal clear—a national media reform coalition that can play quarterback for the media reform movement. The necessity argument takes two forms.

First, the immense job of organizing media reform requires that our scarce resources be used efficiently, and that the various components of a media reform movement cooperate strategically. The problem is that the whole of the current media reform movement is significantly less than the sum of its parts. Isolated and impoverished, groups are forced to defend against new corporate initiatives rather than advance positive reform proposals. When they do get around to proposing reforms, activists have occasionally worked on competing agendas; such schisms dissipate energy, squander resources and guarantee defeat. More important, they are avoidable. Organizers of this new coalition could begin by convening a gathering of all the groups now struggling for reform, as well as the foundations and nonprofits willing to support their work. "All the issues we talk about are interlinked. We are fighting against a lot of the same corporations. The corporations, while they supposedly compete with one another, actually work together very well when it comes to lobbying," explains Jeffrey Chester of the Center for Digital Democracy. "We need to link up the activists and start to work together as well as the corporations do for the other side." Will every possible member organization get on the same media reform page? No. But after years of working with these groups in various settings, we have no doubt that most will.

⋯◉⋯

Second, a coherent, focused and well-coordinated movement will be needed to launch a massive outreach effort to popularize the issue. That outreach can, and should, be guided by Saul Alinsky's maxim that the only way to beat organized money is with organized people. If the media reform movement stays within the Beltway, we know that we will always lose. Yet, so far, outreach beyond the core community of media activists has been done on a piecemeal basis by various reform groups and critics with very limited budgets. The results have, by and large, been predictably disappointing. As a result, says Representative

Jesse Jackson Jr., "the case for media reform is not being heard in Washington now. It is not easy to make the case heard for any reform these days. That's why we need to do more. I hear people everywhere around the country complaining about the media, but we have yet to figure out how to translate those complaints into some kind of activist agenda that can begin to move Congress. There has to be more pressure from outside Washington for specific reforms. Members have to start hearing in their home districts that people want specific reforms of the media."

That will only happen if a concerted campaign organized around core democratic values takes the message of media reform to every college and university, every union hall, every convention and every church, synagogue and mosque in the land. To build a mass movement, the new coalition must link up with organized groups that currently engage in little activity in the way of media reform but that are seriously hampered by the current media system. Organized labor, educators, progressive religious groups, journalists, artists, feminists, environmental organizations and civil rights groups are obvious candidates.

These groups will not simply fall into place as coalition partners, however. Media corporations do not just lobby Congress; they lobby a lot of the groups that suffer under the current system. Some of those groups have been bought off by contributions from foundations associated with AOL, Verizon and other communications conglomerates; others—particularly large sections of organized labor—have been convinced that they have a vested interest in maintaining a status quo that consistently kicks them in the teeth. Building a broad coalition will require a tremendous amount of education and old-fashioned organizing that will inevitably involve pressure from the grassroots on major institutions and unions in order to get the national leadership of those organizations to engage. Movement-building will require that able organizers like Chester, Cohen, FAIR's Janine Jackson and Media Alliance executive director Jeff Perlstein—who have already been engaged in the struggle—be provided with the resources to travel, organize and educate.

All the organizing in the world won't amount to a hill of beans, however, unless there is something tangible to fight for, and to win. That's why we need reform proposals that can be advocated, promoted and discussed. Media reform needs its equivalent of the Voting Rights Act or the Equal Rights Amendment—simple, basic reforms that grassroots activists can understand, embrace and advocate in union halls, church basements and school assemblies. And there has to be legislation to give the activism a sense of focus and possibility.

Fortunately, there are several members of Congress who are already engaged on these issues: Senator Fritz Hollings has emerged as a thoughtful critic of many of the excesses of media monopolies; Senator John McCain has questioned the giveaway of public airwaves to communications conglomerates; Representative John Conyers Jr., the ranking Democrat on the House Judiciary Committee, has been outspoken in criticizing the loss of diversity in media

ownership and the failure of the FCC to battle monopolization and homogenization; Representative Louise Slaughter has introduced legislation mandating
free airtime for political candidates; Senator Paul Wellstone has expressed an
interest in legislation that would reassert standards for children's programming
and perhaps adopt the approaches of other countries that regulate advertising
directed at young children; and Jesse Jackson Jr. has expressed a willingness
to introduce legislation aimed at broadening access to diverse media, along
with a wide range of other media reform proposals. If an organized movement
demands it, there are people in Congress with the courage and the awareness to
provide it with a legislative focus.

Ultimately, we believe, the movement's legislative agenda must include
proposals to:

- Apply existing antimonopoly laws to the media and, where necessary,
  expand the reach of those laws to restrict ownership of radio stations to
  one or two per owner. Legislators should also consider steps to address
  monopolization of TV-station ownership and move to break the lock
  of newspaper chains on entire regions.
- Initiate a formal, federally funded study and hearings to identify reasonable media ownership regulations across all sectors.
- Establish a full tier of low-power, noncommercial radio and television
  stations across the nation.
- Revamp and invest in public broadcasting to eliminate commercial
  pressures, reduce immediate political pressures and serve communities
  without significant disposable incomes.
- Allow every taxpayer a $200 tax credit to apply to any nonprofit
  medium, as long as it meets IRS criteria.
- Lower mailing costs for nonprofit and significantly noncommercial
  publications.
- Eliminate political candidate advertising as a condition of a broadcast
  license, or require that if a station runs a paid political ad by a candidate
  it must run free ads of similar length from all the other candidates on
  the ballot immediately afterward.
- Reduce or eliminate TV advertising directed at children under 12.
- Decommercialize local TV news with regulations that require stations
  to grant journalists an hour daily of commercial-free news time, and
  set budget guidelines for those newscasts based on a percentage of the
  station's revenues.

We know from experience that many of these ideas are popular with Americans—when they get a chance to hear about them. Moreover, the enthusiasm
tends to cross the political spectrum. Much of our optimism regarding a media
reform movement is based on our research that shows how assiduously the corporate media lobbies work to keep their operations in Washington out of public
view. They suspect the same thing we do: When people hear about the corruption of communications policy-making, they will be appalled. When people

understand that it is their democratic right to reform this system, millions of them will be inclined to exercise that right.

What media policy-making needs is to be bathed in democracy. The coalition we envision will have its similarities to the civil rights movement or the women's movement—as it should, since access to information ought to be seen as a fundamental human right. It will stand outside political parties and encourage all of them to take up the mantle of democratic media reform, much as Britain's impressive Campaign for Press and Broadcasting Freedom has done. Although its initial funding may well come from large grants, this reform coalition ultimately must be broad-based and member-funded, like Greenpeace or, dare we say it, the National Rifle Association. Activists must feel a sense of ownership and attachment to a citizen lobby if it is to have real impact. We understand that success will depend, over the long term, upon a rejuvenation of popular politics and, accordingly, a decrease in corporate political and economic power. At the same time, we are certain that a movement that expands the range of legitimate debate will ultimately change not just the debate but the current system. "I am convinced that when people start talking about these big issues, these fundamental issues, when they start to understand that they have the power as citizens in a democracy to take on the powers that be and change how things are done, then change becomes inevitable," says Jackson. "The challenge, of course, is to get people to recognize that they have that power."

Even before it gets down to the serious business of reforming existing media systems, the coalition we propose can lead an organized resistance to corporate welfare schemes like the proposed FCC deregulation. And it might even be able to prevent the complete corporatization of the Internet [see Jeffrey Chester and Gary O. Larson, "Something Old, Something New," page 12]. The key is to have a network of informed organizations and individuals who are already up to speed on media issues and can swing into action on short notice. Currently that network does not exist. The heroic public-interest groups that now lead the fight to oppose corporate domination of FCC policies find themselves without sufficient popular awareness or support, and therefore without the leverage they need to prevail. The movement we propose will be all about increasing leverage over the FCC and Congress in the near term, with an eye toward structural reform down the road.

But is it really possible that such a coalition can take shape in the months and years to come and begin to shift the debate? History tells us that the possibility is real. At times of popular political resurgence throughout the twentieth century, media activism surfaced as a significant force. It was most intense in the Progressive Era, when the rise of the modern capitalist media system was met with sustained Progressive and radical criticism from the likes of Upton Sinclair, Eugene Victor Debs and Robert La Follette. In the 1930s a heterogeneous movement arose to battle commercial broadcasting, and a feisty consumer movement organized to limit advertising in our society. In the post-war years, the Congress of Industrial Organizations attempted to establish a national FM radio network, one of the first casualties of the war on independent labor and the left that marked that period. In the 1960s and '70s the underground press provided vital underpinning for the civil rights, antiwar and feminist movements.

◆

In short, we are building on a long tradition. And there is considerable momentum at present to coalesce. In November some thirty-five media activists from all over the nation met for a day in New York to begin coordinating some of their activities on a range of issues, from local and national policy matters to creating alternative media. Leading media scholars and educators are forming a new national progressive media literacy organization, one that will remain independent of the media conglomerates that bankroll existing groups. We are excited by speculation that Bill Moyers, who has done so much to drum up funding for reform initiatives, will in 2002 use his considerable influence to convince progressive foundations to make a genuine commitment to this fundamental democratic initiative.

The bottom line is clear. Until reformers come together, until we create a formal campaign to democratize our communications policy-making and to blast open our media system, we will continue to see special issues of *The Nation* like this one lamenting our situation. We need no more proof than the current moment to tell us that the time to build a broad coalition for media reform has arrived.

Brendan I. Koerner

 **NO**

Losing Signal

Early [in] December [2000] as the postelection fracas neared its end, the conservative Progress and Freedom Foundation hosted a one-day Washington conference on the future of communications. The event drew a Who's Who of telecom lobbyists, elite members of prestigious K Street firms that represent companies like Verizon, AT&T, and Viacom. The top draw was a keynote speech by Michael K. Powell, a member of the Federal Communications Commission [FCC] who was widely expected to become the agency's next chairman.

The high-powered audience was eager to learn how Powell, son of Secretary of State Colin Powell, would steer the FCC through the second digital revolution—a time when multimedia corporations are establishing unprecedented control over the nation's airwaves, wires, and cables. The crowd was not disappointed. Powell bookended his speech with Dr. Seuss-style couplets comparing the FCC to the Grinch, a regulatory spoilsport that could impede what he termed a historic transformation akin to the opening of the West. "The oppressor here is regulation," declared the man George W. Bush would soon appoint his top telecommunications watchdog, prompting a round of enthusiastic applause.

Not long ago, it would have been unlikely that an FCC official could so delight a roomful of industry emissaries—or, for that matter, generate much Washington buzz at all. Before TV cables carried Internet access, before media conglomerates' revenues shot into the billions and cell phones became middle-class accessories, the FCC was a bureaucratic backwater. Its chief tasks included doling out broadcast licenses to radio stations and keeping the airwaves free of "indecent" language like comedian George Carlin's "Seven Dirty Words" routine. In *The Politics of Regulation*, James Q. Wilson's authoritative 1980 treatise on the Washington bureaucracy, the FCC merited just a single, passing mention; the Federal Maritime Commission got its own chapter.

But the advent of the information economy has turned the FCC from a minor D.C. player into one of the government's most powerful agencies. As the de facto czar of the nation's communications infrastructure, the commission now makes daily decisions affecting America's technological destiny—reviewing megamergers like the AOL Time Warner union, evaluating the Baby Bells' expansion plans, determining whether cable companies should decide what Web content their Internet customers can view. And no one appreciates the FCC's newfound authority better than the communications industry, whose lobbying expenses now stand at roughly $125 million, more than twice the amount spent by defense firms.

Most observers agree that the $950-billion telecom industry is headed for seismic change over the coming years, even the next few months. According to a recent study by the financial research firm Legg Mason, the Bush-era FCC, along with Congress and the courts, is "poised to unleash sweeping consolidation" across the broadcast and telecommunications sectors. Much of the wireless spectrum—a priceless public commodity and the key to the mobile communications boom—could fall into fewer than half a dozen corporate hands, the report noted. And if the merger craze persists, most of the nation's cable lines could soon be controlled by just two corporations, Comcast and AOL Time Warner.

Meanwhile, companies are scrambling to secure control over what Powell's speech extolled as "the great digital broadband migration." As the nation gets wired for high-speed Internet access, multimedia giants are positioning themselves to sell online news, movies, and digital music over the same connections—and, if the FCC allows it, to restrict customers' access to anyone else's news, movies, or music. Privacy debates are heating up as companies develop the power to gather data on everything from consumers' tastes in late-night TV to online buying habits and even—thanks to new tracking devices—the physical movements of cell-phone users.

With regulation lagging far behind technology, the only check on many of these developments is the FCC's power to block practices it deems contrary to the public's "best interest." But just as the stakes are rising, the commission has been adopting a hands-off approach. Hear the same DJ whether you're driving through Arizona or Minnesota? The radio industry, with FCC approval, has consolidated into four companies that control 90 percent of the advertising revenue and beam their programs nationwide. Wish you could ditch your sluggish phone company? Fewer than 10 percent of Americans have any meaningful choice of local telephone service, according to Consumers Union, while the four Bells—down from seven a decade ago, via FCC-blessed mergers—rake in upward of $60 billion per year. Meanwhile, basic cable rates have risen 33 percent since 1996, almost three times the rate of inflation; the typical monthly charge for high-speed Internet access is $49.95, up $10 from a year ago; and phone bills have crept up due to increases in voice-mail charges and basic hardware fees.

But none of these developments rivals the changes in store as the FCC's new Bush-appointed majority—led by Republican loyalist Powell and former US West lobbyist Kathleen Abernathy—redefines the agency's role. Among the Powell commission's first actions was an April decision to relax a decades-old rule prohibiting companies from owning multiple broadcast networks. The move allowed Viacom, which merged with CBS [in 2000], to hold on to UPN. A few weeks earlier, Powell had expedited the approval of 32 radio-station mergers. And in the coming months, the commission is slated to discuss whether to lift anti-concentration rules designed to prevent media monopolies, whether to permit broadcasters to sell billions of dollars' worth of publicly owned spectrum, and whether to allow wireless companies to gather data on their customers' every move.

On these and other far-reaching questions, the agency's positions are shaping up to be virtually identical to the ones being drawn up in corporate boardrooms. In April, during a panel discussion conducted by the American Bar Association, Powell dismissed the FCC's historic mandate to evaluate corporate actions based on the public interest. That standard, he said, "is about as empty a vessel as you can accord a regulatory agency." In other comments, Powell has signaled what kind of philosophy he prefers to the outdated concept of public interest: During his first visit to Capitol Hill as chairman, Powell referred to corporations simply as "our clients."

◆

When the FCC was created in 1934, New Deal politicians considered the nation's communications infrastructure a vital public asset, akin to the railroads. As that asset's trustee, the commission was charged with protecting consumers from industry monopolies and price gouging. An appointed body, the theory went, would be insulated from influence peddling, and thus better equipped than politicians to safeguard the public.

Those Roosevelt-era idealists would be stunned at the scale of corporate solicitation directed at today's FCC. "There's a song called 'Pressure Drop' by The Specials—that ought to be your theme song if you're chairman of the FCC," says Reed Hundt, the commission's head from 1993 to 1997. "You're really struck by the pressure of the lobbying. It just stuns you—it's ubiquitous, it's personal, it's hard-edged. It's also seductive."

Representatives from SBC Communications ($9.5 million in lobbying expenditures for 1999), AT&T ($8.56 million), and the National Association of Broadcasters ($4.9 million) have long been omnipresent on Capitol Hill; now they're regulars at the commission, too. In a memoir of his FCC tenure, *You Say You Want a Revolution*, Hundt recalls his surprise at the lobbyists' tenacity: "On questions like the price paid by long-distance companies for connecting to the local telephone system, as many as 50 different teams of lobbyists pounded the linoleum halls of the commission building for not hours, but weeks, sometimes months. A single company might send soldiers from its regiments to the commission as many as 100 times [on a single issue], visit or phone the chairman on a dozen occasions, call the chairman's staff perhaps daily."

The FCC press office did not return phone calls seeking interviews with Powell or other commissioners. But disclosure filings confirm that commissioners and their staff spend a large chunk of each day listening to corporate representatives in meetings known as ex parte proceedings. *Mother Jones* reviewed the records for 43 such meetings reported from June 4 to June 7, a typical stretch. At least 38 of those sessions were with lobbyists from SBC, AT&T, WorldCom, and other corporate interests.

Public-interest advocates, by contrast, rarely have enough time or staff to make their presence felt. "It's a real problem for us—we only have the capacity to go in there every couple of weeks," says Christopher R. Day of Georgetown

University's Institute for Public Representation, which has fought the sale of 10 TV stations owned by Chris-Craft Industries to Rupert Murdoch's Fox. "Fox has, for one particular commissioner, sent in attorneys and lobbyists from three different law firms."

Among the Fox lawyers' victories during the ex parte meetings was an FCC decision to seal Murdoch's and Chris-Craft's financial records—a move that hampered critics' ability to pull together a counterargument. In other cases, public-interest advocates only learn of FCC decisions after the fact: The sole public notice of a recent radio-station merger in Montana, Day notes, was a line on the agency's lengthy list of "broadcast applications received."

Much more far-reaching decisions are sometimes made behind closed doors. Last year, the FCC reviewed AT&T's $54-billion purchase of cable giant MediaOne, which stood to give the company control of 42 percent of the nation's cable market. Citing a rule limiting a single firm's share to 30 percent, the commission allowed the merger to proceed, but ordered AT&T to sell some of its holdings. . . .

⚜

The FCC has long enjoyed a cozy relationship with the industry it regulates —not surprisingly, given that commissioners and their staff frequently come from corporate backgrounds or move on to lucrative posts in the private sector. One former chairman, Dennis Patrick, is now president of AOL Wireless; Powell's immediate predecessor, William Kennard, came to the FCC from the powerful law and lobbying firm Verner Liipfert, known for its influential communications practice. Powell's chief of staff, Marsha McBride, formerly lobbied for Disney, and Powell's only post-law school job in the private sector was as an attorney at a D.C. law firm where his clients included GTE. (Now 38, Powell joined the commission in 1997, after a brief stint at the Justice Department.)

But the Bush-era FCC is diverging from its predecessors in one key respect. While Powell wants to step up enforcement of specific rules (the FCC has recently revived the indecency debate, fining a Colorado station for playing a sanitized version of Eminem's "The Real Slim Shady"), he seeks to eliminate many of the commission's broader regulations, including antimonopoly rules he considers "artificial." In addition to the ban on corporate ownership of multiple broadcast networks, the chairman has vowed to review the "cross-ownership" rule, which forbids companies from owning a newspaper and a TV station in the same region. And he has expressed doubts about rules that limit how much wireless spectrum a company can own in any one market.

On other issues, the future may be determined by the Powell commission's deliberate inaction. One hot-button topic is open access—the question of whether owners of broadband lines, specifically TV cables used for high-speed Web connections, should be compelled to give customers a choice of Internet service providers (ISPs). Phone lines, the Internet's original highway, have always operated under open-access conditions; a Verizon or SBC customer can choose from thousands of independent ISPs. But telecom companies argue that the same doesn't have to be true for broadband. AT&T, for instance, could limit cable-modem customers to its own ISP, much as it now decides which cable channels subscribers can watch.

Open access is especially relevant to the rollout of interactive television. In the telecom world, the personal computer is seen as a dinosaur, its presence having plateaued at about 50 percent of American households; the future lies in all-in-one boxes that offer both standard TV and Web access. AOL Time Warner, for example, is preparing AOLTV, a $200 set-top box that will be sold primarily to its subscribers, some 20 percent of the nation's cable households. Without an open-access rule, the company could use its device to discriminate, Microsoft-style, against competitors' programs—by, say, making it easier to view AOL Time Warner's CNN/SI than a regional sports channel, or by offering "bonus" interactive content only for AOL Time Warner shows.

Telecom firms have strenuously argued that the First Amendment prohibits open-access rules. But during the past year, two federal appeals courts have indicated that the FCC does have the power to regulate broadband. Still, the commission—which has been working on a study of the issue for at least 18 months—seems disinclined to act. Last June, when asked about open access in interactive television, Powell suggested that he didn't think the agency should get involved. "To me, that's when government is often at its worst—when it's trying to regulate phantoms, you know, straw men. What might happen as opposed to what's happening."

Industry representatives hope that Powell's hands-off philosophy will also apply to privacy issues. State and federal lawmakers are mulling hundreds of bills that could, for example, force companies to ask consumers' permission before sharing data with third parties, or require Web sites to lock away personal information in ultrasecure databases. Industry studies warn that such rules could wreak havoc for online commerce; one Microsoft-funded report claims that the proposed privacy laws would cost U.S. companies up to $36 billion.

Most privacy matters are the domain of Congress and state legislators, rather than the FCC. But one big issue on the commission's agenda is the controversy over location-based services (LBS), technology that lets companies track the movements of mobile-phone users. Phone manufacturers have developed microchips that can pinpoint a user's position and feed the information back to a central server. The FCC has mandated that all new phones feature such chips after October 1 to help emergency workers locate 911 callers.

But marketers envision more commercial uses for LBS, which, according to most estimates, could generate $6 billion in annual sales by 2005. Walking by a donut store? A corporate server can detect your proximity and immediately zap a "10 percent off!" coupon to your Palm Pilot. Delinquent on your bills? A collector can determine your location and send you a message like "You're in luck! There's a mailbox just around the corner where you can drop off your check!" Companies are also eager to use the technology to control employee behavior; in April, the *New York Times* reported that one trucking company put LBS in place after hearing that its drivers were visiting strip clubs during work hours.

The FCC is conducting a long-term study to decide whether it should issue privacy rules for location-based services. Consumer groups want the agency to require explicit ("opt-in") permission from customers before location data can be used; industry, meanwhile, is touting the virtues of self-regulation. A group called the Location Privacy Association argued in an April FCC filing that the commission should go ahead and discuss opt-in rules but should not interfere with the technology in the meantime. The otherwise obscure organization—there is no record of its activities besides that filing—seeks, according to the mission statement it supplied to the FCC, to educate the public about "the privacy and public safety benefits of... location technologies." As its founders, the association listed two of the nation's leading wireless companies, Airbiquity and Qualcomm.

<hr>

With its innocent-sounding name and barely concealed pro-industry agenda, the Location Privacy Association is a classic example of an "Astroturf" group, Beltway slang for pseudo-grassroots organizations. Though telecom issues have yet to generate much public debate, companies are sponsoring a variety of groups to suggest that Americans are clamoring for deregulation. One of the most visible is the Alliance for Public Technology, whose board members are frequently quoted in the media as crusaders for the public interest, especially for rural and minority consumers. According to the group's 1989 application for nonprofit status, its mission is to "educate the general public about new technology" and "bridge the gap between technology providers and special-need consumers."

Other filings, however, reveal that the alliance operates out of the offices of Issue Dynamics, a consulting firm often hired by the Bells; in 1999, the group paid Issue Dynamics $140,000 in "management fees." On its Web site the alliance lists four corporate sponsors—AOL Time Warner, BellSouth, SBC, and the U.S. Telecom Association—and it regularly provides press statements and congressional testimony in support of its backers' goals. When a broadband deregulation bill co-sponsored by Rep. W.J. "Billy" Tauzin (R-La.) and Rep. John Dingell (D-Mich.) came under fire from consumer advocates, alliance representative Don Vial emerged to praise the measure before the House Commerce Committee: "There can never be enough broadband to serve the increasing needs of our technology-driven economy and society."

To mobilize, or at least imply, real public support, corporations have used massive ad campaigns, often targeted at the Washington media market. The Tauzin-Dingell bill, for example, has spurred a flood of commercials from Keep America Connected, a Bell-funded group that says it represents "older Americans, people with disabilities, rural and inner-city residents, people of color, low-income citizens, labor and local telephone companies." The organization lists a bevy of affiliates, including the American Beekeeping Federation, the Delta Waterfowl Foundation—and the Alliance for Public Technology. Another Bell lobbying group, Connect USA, has been saturating the D.C. airwaves with ads assuring viewers that Tauzin-Dingell "guarantees high-speed access to inner cities and small towns, making sure that no one is left behind."

As the broadband controversy shows, corporations aren't shy about asking Congress to get involved in FCC matters. Big Media's influence on Capitol Hill is legendary—the National Association of Broadcasters once moved Newt Gingrich to declare, "The practical fact is, nobody's going to take on the broadcasters." Along with the standard millions in campaign spoils, the communications industry offers some of Washington's most enticing perks, including events that a House telecom aide who has attended one of them describes as "professional bribery sessions.... You go down to Palm Springs where [an industry group] is having a convention, or SBC takes you to the Gulf of Mexico. They wine and dine you. It's ridiculous. Everyone goes."

The industry also wields what Jeff Chester of the Center for Digital Democracy, a telecommunications watchdog, calls "a silent campaign contribution"—access to the media. "Congressmen perceive that if one takes on these concerns in a meaningful way, they may no longer be invited to be interviewed on the local TV station, or the kind of coverage they get online will no longer be the same." Regardless of whether such retribution ever occurs, Chester argues, the prospect alone helps keep lawmakers in line.

When industry feels threatened by the FCC, senators and representatives are all too happy to remind the commission that it's a "creature of Congress" dependent on lawmakers for its budget. In 1998, then-FCC Chairman William Kennard proposed a study of whether the networks could provide free airtime to political candidates. Members of the Senate Appropriations Committee killed the idea by ordering that no FCC funds be spent on the effort, to the relief of broadcasters who were apoplectic over the potential loss of revenue from political advertising.

Individual members also frequently intercede in FCC matters of interest to their contributors. When the agency announced plans to give the AT&T-MediaOne union "very careful scrutiny," Senator John McCain—then chair of the Senate Commerce Committee, which reviews FCC nominations—threatened to revoke its authority over such mergers. He also publicly criticized the commission's go-slow attitude, scolding the panel as "unable to lead or unwilling to follow." According to the Center for Public Integrity, McCain's presidential campaign received $10,000 from AT&T two weeks later. AT&T has been McCain's third most generous donor over the course of his career, just ahead of Viacom.

An even more dependable friend to the industry has been Tauzin, chairman of the House Commerce Committee and the chief sponsor of Powell's elevation to the FCC chairmanship. Tauzin is a regular beneficiary of telecom firms' largesse. At [the 2000] GOP Convention, he was feted with a $400,000 Mardi Gras-themed bash underwritten by SBC, BellSouth, and Comsat. The previous December, Tauzin and his wife took a seven-day, $19,000 trip to Paris, courtesy of Time Warner and the online brokerage Instinet. His son, Billy III, is a BellSouth lobbyist; his daughter, Kimberly, is a former government-relations official with the National Association of Broadcasters.

Tauzin frequently attacks the FCC for heel-dragging. In December, the congressman blamed the commission for causing [the recent] meltdown of telecom stocks with its "stupid micromanagement and insidious inclination to hold things up." One of his top legislative priorities is the Tauzin-Dingell bill, which would lift a requirement that phone companies relinquish their local monopolies before gaining access to the national broadband market.

Another telecom ally is Senate Minority Leader Trent Lott (R-Miss.), a key player in convincing the FCC to go along with what critics call the biggest corporate welfare scheme in American history—the spectrum giveaway. In 1995, broadcasters began contending that digital television was the wave of the future and that they required additional transmission licenses to broadcast the new clearer signals. And they wanted the spectrum for free, despite its estimated $70-billion value on the open market.

Bob Dole, then Senate majority leader, vehemently opposed the giveaway, which was nonetheless written into the Telecommunications Act of 1996. He convinced then-FCC Chairman Hundt to withhold the gift, at least until the Senate had a chance to look into auctioning off the spectrum instead. But when Dole abruptly left the Senate to pursue his bid for the presidency, congressional leaders including Lott (who was a college roommate of National Association of Broadcasters president Eddie Fritts) asked Hundt to "proceed with bringing this exciting new technology to the American people without further delay."

The FCC complied and issued the licenses, with only one condition: that the broadcasters give back their old analog spectrum once digital TV reaches 85 percent of the national market. At the current rate of deployment (less than 1 percent of the country has all-digital TV), that could take decades.

In the meantime, the broadcasters have come up with another idea. The boom in demand for mobile phones, Palm Pilots, and the like has made the airwaves a truly precious commodity, and the value of the new spectrum has ballooned to $180 billion, more than all the nation's TV stations combined. To cash in on the appreciation, some companies are offering to switch to digital now—if the FCC will let them sell their analog spectrum, technically a public asset on loan, to the highest bidder. Broadcasters claim that, aside from enriching station owners, such a move would benefit consumers anxious for digital TV. Now it's up to the FCC to determine whether corporate profit equals public good.

"Based on four years of experience, I would say the public interest is not the same thing as private interests," says Hundt. "You know, roughly speaking, it's just the opposite. If [the FCC] looks at the opposite direction from where the private interests are pointing, it'll probably see the public interest." Which, of course, is its job.

POSTSCRIPT

Have the Direction and Power of the FCC Changed?

The FCC is somewhat unique in its capacity to effect change in communications technologies and practices. It was established to provide guidance to Congress to enact socially responsible policies and procedures, but because it cannot legislate change itself, it has remained a relatively weak federal agency. When the critical decision was made to auction off portions of the electromagnetic spectrum—the airspace in which telecommunications signals travel —a major refocusing of the FCC's agenda turned the FCC into more of an investment broker than a regulator.

In many other countries, the same regulatory role is often given to organizations that have more power to safeguard the public interest or to be accountable to government. For example, in some countries, the minister of information or head of the post, telegraph, and telecommunications (PTT) organization functions similar to the way a cabinet post would in America's presidential power hierarchy. In the United States and other nations, the officials of the agency are often appointed by the head of the government (in the case of the United States, the president), but serve different constituencies.

Many of the publications of the FCC are available on the Web site (http://www.FCC.gov), or through the Government Printing Office (GPO). The Telecommunications Act of 1996 is rather cumbersome, but it does constitute the present rules for telecommunications operation. Additionally, the July 10, 1995 House of Representatives publication, "Media Mergers and Takeovers: The FCC and the Public Interest: Hearing Before the Subcommittee on Telecommunications Protection and Finance of the Committee on Energy and Commerce" (GPO, 1996), has many important points to make with regard to how the FCC envisions its own role as an arbiter of the current flurry of megamergers in U.S. media businesses.

The philosophical problems of media mergers are discussed in Nancy J. Woodhull and Robert W. Snyder, eds., *Media Mergers* (Transaction Publications, 1998). This collection of essays provides excellent contrasting views on whether mergers are good or bad for business and the consumer.

On the Internet ...

National Association of Broadcasters

The National Association of Broadcasters (NAB) is dedicated to promoting the interests of broadcasters. Some of the pages found at this site include information on television parental guidelines, laws and regulations, and research on current issues.

http://www.nab.org

The National Cable Television Association

The National Cable Television Association (NCTA) is dedicated to promoting the interests of the cable television industry. This site contains discussions of current issues and updates on issues of importance to the NCTA.

http://www.ncta.com

Telecom Information Resources

This Telecom Information Resources site has over 7,000 links to telecommunication resources throughout the world. At this site you will find information on service providers, government agencies, government policies, economic policies, and much more.

http://china.si.umich.edu/telecom/telecom-info.html

Television Bureau of Advertising

The Television Bureau of Advertising is a nonprofit trade association of the broadcast television industry. This Web site provides a diverse variety of resources to help advertisers make the best use of local television. Go to the "television facts" section for useful information.

http://www.tvb.org

PART 5

Media Business

*F*reedom *of speech and the press makes producing news and enter-tainment content somewhat different from manufacturing toasters. It is important to realize that media industries are businesses and that they must be profitable to be able to thrive. However, are there special stan-dards to which we should hold media industries? Are the structures of media industries responsive to the public's interest? How do monopolies affect media content? What is the primary function of advertising?*

- Media Monopolies: Does Concentration of Ownership Jeopardize Media Content?

- Is Civic Journalism Good Journalism?

- Have the News Media Improved Since 9/11?

ISSUE 14

Media Monopolies: Does Concentration of Ownership Jeopardize Media Content?

YES: Ben H. Bagdikian, from *The Media Monopoly,* 6th ed. (Beacon Press, 2000)

NO: Michael Curtin, from "Feminine Desire in the Age of Satellite Television," *Journal of Communication* (Spring 1999)

ISSUE SUMMARY

YES: Ben H. Bagdikian, a Pulitzer Prize–winning journalist, argues that the public must be aware of the control that international conglomerates have over the media. He contends that despite hopes that new technologies would control giant corporations, these corporations have wrested control of the production and distribution of most of the media content in the world. Conglomerate domination remains, concludes Bagdikian.

NO: Professor Michael Curtin questions whether or not concentration of media ownership leads to a conservative, homogenous flow of popular imagery. For example, television contexts around the world are increasingly featuring female characters who resist conventional gender roles. This happens because media firms benefit from transnational circulation of multiple and alternative representations of feminine desire.

Since the 1980s the U.S. media industries have undergone simultaneous shifts —in the economy within which the media industry functions, the technology through which media are distributed, and the regulatory philosophy through which media are viewed by government and the public. Since its inception, U.S. media have been based on the dual principles of private ownership and freedom from government interference with content. This libertarian philosophy was imported from Britain and was enshrined in the First Amendment to the Constitution. Freedom of the press and the public service expectations it engendered include serving as a watchdog of the government, providing fair and balanced coverage of political issues, and refraining from content that would harm children, inflame public passions, or increase social divisions. In the last quarter of the twentieth century, theories about the public service responsibilities of the media began to change. Federal Communications Commission (FCC) chairman Mark Fowler famously remarked that television was no different from any other household appliance, "a toaster with pictures." The public interest began to be defined as what the public was interested in. Public "good" was increasingly defined as that which promoted the economic vitality and global competitiveness of the industry, including its ability to provide jobs, create wealth, and compete successfully in global markets.

At the same time, changing national and global economies were offering their own challenges. Even while media corporations were subjected to extreme pressures for financial performance, they were also losing substantial portions of their markets to increased competition. A decline in viewer loyalty and increased sources of media led to market fragmentation. Pressure to create larger corporate entities and changes in the ownership rules made by the Telecommunications Act of 1996 opened the market for substantial restructuring. Although the restructuring of the U.S. media industry is still very much under way, one effect is clear: the U.S. media are much more consolidated. The rapid transformation of the U.S. media industry over the last two decades of the twentieth century makes it difficult to predict long-term trends. Further consolidation is probably the most easily predicted factor, although there is not sufficient evidence to indicate whether or not the media industries in their current form will meet financial performance demands. Nonetheless, it is easy to expect that the industry will continue to respond to financial performance demands by continuing efforts to consolidate, cluster properties, gain market power within local and regional operational areas, and capture synergies through vertical and horizontal integration.

Ben H. Bagdikian, in the sixth edition of *Media Monopoly*, restates his concern with the consequences of consolidation of media industries for political and social life. Six firms dominate all American mass media, and, in fact, much of the world. These dominant corporations, through control of news and other public information, can censor public awareness of the dangers of information control by the corporate elite. When the central interests of controlling corporations are at stake, Bagdikian argues, news becomes weighted toward what serves the economic and political interests of the corporations that own the media, not the public interest. The concept of media as a public trust seems to be lost in the new era of corporate restructuring.

Michael Curtin contends that the consequences of consolidation are not necessarily the homogenization of content. He points to, as a case study, the representations of feminine desire in multiple contexts as an example of how the issue of content production is much more simple than control of information by a corporate elite. Although not dismissive of the dangers of consolidation, Curtin explores the opportunities that internationalization and integration can provide.

Ben H. Bagdikian

The Media Monopoly

As the United States enters the twenty-first century, power over the American mass media is flowing to the top with such devouring speed that it exceeds even the accelerated consolidations of the last twenty years. For the first time in U.S. history, the country's most widespread news, commentary, and daily entertainment are controlled by six firms that are among the world's largest corporations, two of them foreign.

Even with the dramatic entry of the Internet and the cyber world with their uncounted hundreds of new firms, the controlling handful of American and foreign corporations now exceed in their size and communications power anything the world has seen before. Their intricate global interlocks create the force of an international cartel.

There are pernicious consequences. While excessive bigness itself is cause for economic anxieties, the worst problems are political and social. The country's largest media giants have achieved alarming success in writing the media laws and regulations in favor of their own corporations and against the interests of the general public. Their concentrated power permits them to become a larger factor than ever before in socializing each generation with entertainment models of behavior and personal values.

The impact on the national political agenda has been devastating. For years, the mainstream news has overdramatized its reporting of congressional and White House debate on the national debt and deficit beyond their intrinsic importance. Politicians raised the issue, but it was seized upon and overblown by the major media—media that politicians use as a bellwether on what issues will get them the most public attention and partisan advantage. During these crucial years, the American economy was undergoing an astonishing phenomenon that the mainstream news left largely unreported or actually glamorized in its infrequent references: the largest transfer of the national wealth in American history from a majority of the population to a small percentage of the country's wealthiest families.

The handful of dominant corporations have pursued quick, ever-higher profits, mainly by producing more trivialized and self-serving commercialized news. Their entertainment, with its powerful impact on the popular culture, has become further coarsened and brutalized. As each use of shock-as-attention-getter becomes bolder, more barriers have fallen.

Main media talk shows and entertainment have vulgarized language as a ratings technique, introducing changes that go beyond the inevitable evolution of all language in modern societies. New terms have always emerged for new phenomena and experiences. The cyber world, for example, has invented words because the Internet and its offshoots need new words to describe what never existed before. Advertisers and adolescents have always invented their own novel jargon. But today that normal process is artificially escalated. In the race for ever-higher profits, each of the dominant media owners tries to outdo competitors in the once-private language of barroom fights and locker-room sexual boasts.

Fortunately, not everything in the new mass media is dismal. There are positive changes. In mainstream news, the general level of reporters' education and writing has risen, and there are more stories reported with appreciation of context and supportive factual data. The *New York Times*, for one, has looked at some social phenomena it had ignored in the past. In both television and movies there are admirable and sometimes even stunning presentations of drama and history, as well as agreeable entertainment. When the Internet is added, those with the technical equipment and motivation have gained unprecedented and growing access to information and self-expression.

Nevertheless, the money rewards for advertising's drive for mass audiences have escalated so sharply that the repeated use of stereotyped trivial and brutal material has overwhelmed what is positive in printed and electronic mass media. The unprecedented billions to be made by the commercial media themselves and the resulting revenues for their sponsors have made both resistant to growing pleas by parents, educators, and social scientists to lower the level of demeaning and violent content.

The Internet, with its chaotic vastness, has brought sweeping changes for industry and individuals, from selling books to midnight stock market trading at home. It is an effective instrument for personal expression, a formidable source of information and entertainment, and of instant electronic mail for the minority currently equipped to use it. But it has been overblown as the final liberation of the individual from "the system." Advertising and other corporate promotion on the Internet seem to grow exponentially, with "the system" becoming more fully embedded in the cyber world each day.

The American population is remarkably diverse in background, politics, geography, and tastes, and has always needed this variety reflected in a parallel diversity in its public information and entertainment. But more than ever, the major media have treated the public as a homogeneous mass with low taste and limited intelligence. With the country's widest disseminators of news, commentary, and ideas firmly entrenched among a small number of the world's wealthiest corporations, it may not be surprising that their news and commentary is limited to an unrepresentative narrow spectrum of politics.

The Intertwined Six

Six firms dominate all American mass media. Each is a subsidiary of a larger parent firm, some of them basically operating in other industries. The six parent firms are General Electric, Viacom, Disney, Bertelsmann, Time Warner, and Murdoch's News Corp. Bertelsmann is based in Germany and News Corp in Australia, the other four in the United States. All the parent firms are listed in *Fortune* Magazine's 1999 Global 500 of the largest corporations in the world. Other giant firms in other industries clearly were on the prowl for new mass media in order to join the Big Six—like Sony, a Japanese hardware firm; Seagram's, a Canadian liquor firm; and AT&T, a telephone company traditionally providing one-to-one (not mass) communication.[1]

The top six firms, ordered solely on their annual media revenues, are Time Warner, Disney, Viacom (an amalgam of CBS and Westinghouse), News Corp, Bertelsmann, and General Electric. These six have more annual media revenues than the next twenty firms combined.[2]

The number of dominant firms remains six, even with an announcement in early 2000 that stunned the country's businesses and all computer-users—the world's largest Internet service provider, America Online, Inc., said it would acquire the world's largest media company, Time Warner, to form AOL Time Warner, Inc. Consequently, while six firms still dominate all mass media, the largest of those six would become a corporation valued at $350 billion. It would be history's largest merger, in the media or in any other enterprise.

(If the new merger prevails, references elsewhere [written as] "Time Warner" should be read as "AOL Time Warner.")

Barring government anti-trust intervention or other unforeseen events, the new company, like all mammoth players in a field, is likely to force other giant media firms, like Disney, Viacom, and News Corp, to make similar mergers with Internet and communication giants like Microsoft, AT&T, and MCI World, affecting commonly known cyber operations like Yahoo, Amazon.com, and eBay. The prospect is for a giantism and concentrated power beyond anything ever seen. Advertising becomes even more dominant and inescapable in the human landscape. AOL Time Warner becomes what the computerized news service MSNBC described on January 10, 2000, as "the most powerful global advertising force across all media, including Internet, publishing, television and music."

What was clearly the focus of the top executives of AOL and Time Warner in their joint announcement of the merger was a shopping mall of global dimensions in which media and other products could be promoted, displayed, and ordered instantly with a click of the computer mouse or interactive television set. In the midst of the executives' expected rhetoric about the wonders of their joined enterprises, the two leaders' stress was on instant merchandizing. AOL, for example, already owns Compuserve and Netscape and has a strategic alliance with Sun Microsystems that gives it enhanced entry into the burgeoning e-commerce.

The merged firms will have more than 100 million global subscribers, 20 million cable homes, AOL access to Time Warner's 30 magazines and 75 million homes that receive the cable networks CNN, TBS, and TNT. Expected annual revenues are $40 billion. Given Time Warner's vast holdings in all media, the ordinary citizen, whether a reader, TV viewer, movie-goer, or Internet user, would be forced to deal with a communications cartel of a magnitude and power the world has never seen before.

The lasting social and political implications are sobering. Mergers of this size further dwarfs news as merely another industrial byproduct. As dramatized by the case of the *Los Angeles Times*, the new mergers deepen the dangers of more deterioration of news as a handmaiden of its owners' corporate ambitions, endangering the future of the independent and diverse public information on which democracy depends.

The immense size of the parent firms means that some of their crucial media subsidiaries, like news, have become remote within their complex tables of organization. That remoteness has contributed to the unprecedented degree to which the parent firms have pressed their news subsidiaries to cross ethical lines by selecting news that will promote the needs of the owning corporation rather than serve the traditional ethical striving of journalism.

Symbolically, *the* largest corporation in the world, General Motors, has now entered the mass media field. GM has acquired the three largest satellite TV broadcasting companies and has received $1.5 billion from the Internet's America Online, Inc., in a joint race for high-capacity speed in the expanding cyber world.[3]

The power and influence of the dominant companies are understated by counting them as "six." They are intertwined: they own stock in each other, they cooperate in joint media ventures, and among themselves they divide profits from some of the most widely viewed programs on television, cable, and movies.[4]

News reporting and commentary controlled by mainstream media companies are the most politically narrow in the democratic world. Their presentations and analyses are limited to the center-right, ignoring political views held by almost a third of American voters. In 1999, the Roper Center for Public Opinion Research surveyed the political ideologies of Americans, offering the choices "very liberal," "somewhat liberal," "lean liberal," "moderate," "lean conservative," "somewhat conservative," and "very conservative." The first three choices received a combined 31 percent self-identification. Thus, almost a third of the respondents seldom see news and commentary selected to meet their political interests and concerns.[5]

Political narrowness in the media reportage and commentary inevitably leads to a narrow range of genuine choices at elections, and since meaningful voter choice is vital to sustain any democracy, to that extent, the contemporary mass media's constricted politics weaken the foundation of the democratic process.

Major industries, including those controlling the media, have always been more comfortable with conservative politics. Now that these industries own the country's daily printed and broadcast news, it is not surprising that their newly acquired staffs have come to understand that they remain in their employers' good graces by downplaying or keeping unwanted ideas out of the printed and broadcast news. With time, this shrunken social-political range becomes the accepted definition of what is news. The emerging picture has overtones, subtle or otherwise, of an Orwellian Big Brother, Incorporated.

Such concentrated private power is not what the creators of the American democracy had in mind when they created the First Amendment guaranteeing free speech and free press. They could not foresee that two hundred years later, by the twenty-first century, the sacred First Amendment guaranteeing every citizen free speech would, to an appalling degree, become dependent upon the "speaker's" wealth.

Enter: The Internet

In the beginning, the Internet was celebrated as a welcome liberation of the individual from powerful mass media systems. Anyone with a computer and a modem connection to the outside electronic world has access to the growing vastness of the new medium. Individuals expressing themselves on the Internet are provided gratification of being one voice among thousands. Civic bodies and an unlimited variety of propagandistic groups and individuals can display their goals and values at less expense than ever before and have a potentially large—if mostly anonymous and uncertain—audience. Internet's e-mail, with its own cyber address system for each participant, permits private messages that are close to instantaneous and permits replies at the same speed.

But with each passing month, the balance in favor of the individual looks less reassuring. Thanks to the Internet's heavy presence of corporations, intrusive advertising, and other highly orchestrated business displays designed to be seen by millions, the individual's private Internet space is continually invaded by electronic sales pitches. And on-line commerce has its share of fraudulent or ludicrous ads, like ads for the nonexistent vitamins F, P, T, and U, presented as cures for everything from sexual dysfunction to leg cramps.[6]

Internet capabilities have also raised serious problems of copyright protection, since any anonymous person can place copyrighted articles, book chapters, photographs, recordings, and other intellectual property on the Internet that other anonymous users can copy and reissue.[7]

Whatever its final form, the present and future power of the Internet remains formidable. Though by century's end, only a minority had home modems, it most certainly will become a future large majority. Except for television fifty years ago, few technological devices have acculturated society as rapidly as the computer-plus-Internet.

The Internet's growth and versatility—10,000 new sites every day—have created anxieties among the older media. Printed news media, with their complex production and manual distribution on daily, weekly, or monthly schedules, fear the Internet's immediacy and twenty-four-hour operations. They fear that an on-line source might possibly contain a news break that has not been verified by good journalistic standards. As a result, most metropolitan and smaller printed newspapers also place their dailies on the Internet.[8]

At the same time, the Internet has created its own version of the older printed forms, like its family of magazines designed solely for the Internet, called "zines." Unlike their slower, hierarchically organized, printed grandparent, the zines can change content at any time. They can be started without buying press time, distributors, or mailed delivery, and can be created by anyone with the urge, either with or without training in traditional disciplines. Many zines are private gossip and rumor fountains. Their lack of concern with accuracy periodically creates mischief and injustice for individuals and groups. Consequently, along with new content that is broadening, practical, and beneficial, the zines also spread messages that are hateful, socially destructive, and plainly psychotic, and all directed at the same potential large audience.

Nevertheless, despite their awareness of capricious Internet standards, printed papers, fearful of electronic scoops, have become Internet-watchers. An Internet gossipmonger, Matt Drudge, who admits he isn't worried about accuracy, was the first to hint at the Clinton sex scandal. Drudge's account caused a *Newsweek* reporter to rush his story onto the Internet, even though his print editors wanted another week to verify facts. Clearly, the competition to sell news has encouraged print sources to lower their standards of what is fit to print....[9]

Can It Be Changed?

For the last thirty years, government agencies and the Congress have been wedded to the "free market," an oxymoron when it describes political and corporate tolerance of conglomeration and monopoly. In past decades, the most common remedy for excessive market domination has been the Anti-Trust Act, which is supposed to break up alliances and mergers that reduce competition.

Contrary to the present conventional wisdom that antitrust law cannot work, when it became an almost established fact that the big bookseller Barnes & Noble would merge with Ingram, the country's largest supplier of books to bookstores, an intense campaign by independent booksellers caused lawyers in the Federal Trade Commission to murmur that they were considering legal action to block the merger. The two corporate parties abandoned their plan. But it was a rare murmur and a rare victory.[10]

The most effective remedies require congressional and White House approval, and most fail because the telecommunications industry is the fourth largest contributor to political campaigns. The recent Gore Commission on the future of broadcasting entered the field like a lion. But after the head of CBS threatened a "declaration of war" if Gore recommended specifics for "serving the public interest," Gore's report emerged like a lamb. The problem is money. Viacom's CBS and its allies in broadcasting have a great deal of money....[11]

Government indifference to the immense and still growing power of major media corporations has left the task of protecting consumers from exploitative prices and harmful media content to individual and citizen action groups. These groups have done and continue to do vital service to keep the public informed and to keep alive the struggle for a better media world.[12]

But no citizen action group has the money to match the private corporate funds that flood the American political system. On lobbying alone, more than $1.4 billion a year is spent in Washington. This breaks down to $2.7 million and

38 lobbyists for each of the 535 members of Congress. By far, most of the money comes from corporations; most of the lobbyists work for corporate interests.

Consequently, there is a fundamental need for basic and sweeping campaign reform and drastic curtailment of money used for lobbying. That happens to be an issue that major newspapers editorially support, and one in which they can play a dramatic role, if in their coverage of crucial issues with wide public consequences they would list by name each member of Congress with an influential role in the fate of the measure and every source and amount of financial contributions from any entity with a clear stake in the outcome. This would make it explicit if private money is in danger of prevailing and help illuminate the insidious, behind-the-scenes buying of the country's laws.

There is convincing evidence that the relationship between big money and political votes already angers most voters. An aroused public can make a difference. The environmental movement that transformed the legislative and natural landscape began as a grassroots movement without initiative from the standard political parties and with powerful opposition from industry. When conservatives in Congress moved to abolish public broadcasting, House and Senate members were stunned and retreated when citizens, Republicans and Democrats alike, rose in unison in anger against the move.

Voters are rebelling. As public complaints escalate, more of the public expresses open disgust. New parties slowly gather strength. The general public is more vocal than ever about irresponsible mass media. The two standard parties are hemorrhaging votes to a vague and growing category entitled "Independent." Many voters have stopped voting or are electing candidates formerly considered unelectable, or others that are bizarre nonentities. These changes reflect growing voter rejection of contemporary politics, the same kind of dismissal as implied by Ralph Nader's proposal of a ballot line that offers "None of the above."

The power of corporate money to stop reforms cannot continue without further erosion of the relevant and responsible public information needed to sustain the American democracy.

It is true that corporate money in politics acts with swift and arrogant certitude. An informed public responds more slowly, but it does make the final decisions on election day.

In the fabled race between the swift-and-overconfident hare and the slow-but-steady tortoise, it helps to remember who crossed the finish line first.

The race is not always to the swift.

Notes

The *New York Times* was used extensively as a source because it is regarded as the country's most authoritative and widespread source of foreign and domestic news and because hundreds of client papers throughout the country use its news service. Spot checks of other papers showed that most did far less than the *Times*. So major media failures or inadequacies in reporting public information needed for properly informed voters throughout the country is, if anything, understated. Important lapses or inadequate accounts frequently are attributed to the *Times* for the same reason, though such negative judgments are by no means limited to the *Times*. Note: earlier editions of *The Statistical Abstract of the United States* indexed data by page number, but more recent editions index by table number.

1. `http://cgi.pathfinder.com/fortune/global500/500list2.html` and `http://www.forbes.com/tool/toolbox/privateasp/rankindex.asp?index=500`.

2. `wysiwyg://428/http://www.cjr.org/owners/` (Cjr=*Columbia Journalism Review*); *New York Times*, 8 September 1999, 1.

3. `http:/cgi.pathfinder.com/fortune/global500/500list2.html` and *New York Times*, 16 July 1999, 1.

4. *New York Times*. 29 February 1996, 3.

5. 1999 Roper Center for Public Opinion Research, Question ID: USMS. 99 Feb R20.022; *EXTRA!*, July/August 1997, 24.

6. *University of California Berkeley Wellness Letter*, June 1999, 8.

7. *College English*. May 1999, 532; *National Writers Union Hearsay*, November 1998, 4.

8. *Business Week*, 17 May 1999, 108.

9. *New York Times*, 9 July 1999, 13; *American Journalism Review*, March 1999, 28; and "Death of Print," *Columbia Journalism Review*, January/February 1999, 56.

10. *New York Times*, 3 June 1999, C–1.

11. *COUNTDOWN*, Center for Media Education, 20 November 1998; Civil Rights Forum and Project on Media Ownership, 18 December 1998, 2.

12. Center for Responsive Politics, 29 July 1999, 1.

Michael Curtin

 **NO**

Feminine Desire in the Age
of Satellite Television

Television texts around the world increasingly feature female characters who resist or reformulate conventional gender roles. This trend
seems to defy expectations that the concentration of media ownership leads to a conservative, homogeneous flow of popular imagery.
Such an apparent contradiction can be explained by close analysis of
the strategies, operations, and discourse of culture industries in the
neo-network era of satellite and cable media. This era is paradoxically characterized by corporate conglomeration and by strategies
of flexibility and decentralization. Consequently, media firms actually
benefit from the transnational circulation of multiple and alternative
representations of feminine desire. Although this does not necessarily democratize media, in most societies it significantly expands the
range of feminine imagery available in popular culture.

The original version of *Macarena*, the transnational popular music hit, was released in April 1993 by a couple of flamenco singers, Antonio Romero and Rafael
Ruiz, who perform under the name Los del Rio.... Because flamenco is a rather
localized genre, they are by no means major pop icons. Indeed, legend has it
that the origins of *Macarena* were rather modest. The song was written one night
by Romero after he and his partner had performed with a flamenco dancer
named Diana Patricia Cubillan, a good friend of theirs, at a Caracas hotel in
1992.

The song is a tribute to Cubillan and briefly became a modest hit in Spain
during the summer of 1993. This original version was especially popular with
older listeners, who tend to appreciate the traditional music of Andalusia, but it
failed to capture the attention of younger mainstream audiences. Nevertheless,
several remixes of *Macarena* were commissioned by the Zafiro label based on the
song's limited success, and it slowly began to migrate to dance clubs throughout
Europe and Latin America. In 1994, Zafiro was bought by Bertelsmann, the
German media conglomerate that also owns BMG and RCA records. A young
BMG executive in Paris reportedly took notice of the song's popularity on the
European disco scene and decided to escalate the international marketing of
Macarena by ordering the production of a music video and by commissioning

From Michael Curtin, "Feminine Desire in the Age of Satellite Television," *Journal of Communication*, vol. 49, no. 2 (Spring 1999). Copyright © 1999 by The International Communication
Association. Reprinted by permission of Oxford University Press. References omitted.

a dance instructor to choreograph a set of moves that could easily be learned by viewers of all ages.

In an explicit attempt to crack the U.S. market, BMG then hired a Miami hip-hop group, the Bayside Boys, to do an English-language remix of the song, hoping to attract a crossover audience. *Macarena* hit number one on the U.S. music charts in the summer of 1996 and was played in heavy rotation on radio and music television for the next few months.... It also generated perhaps the biggest dance craze since John Travolta's disco film, *Stayin' Alive*. Ultimately, *Macarena* enjoyed extensive transnational circulation, traveling to the top of the world where it was featured in the nightclubs of Lhasa and Tibet, and in the schoolyards in Australia, where children methodically practiced and performed the dance steps in synchrony (DuLac & Smith, 1996; Hinckley, 1996; Lannert, 1995; Llewellyn, 1996; Navarro, 1995; Smith, 1996).

The global success of *Macarena* owes much to the video and to the Bayside Boys's remix, featuring a techno beat with a heavy bass line and synthesizer accompaniment, which moves the song close to the *MTV* mainstream. Although the remix was obviously targeted at the music television market, the beat was intentionally made slower than the average techno hit to make it danceable for a broad audience. The lyrics were also retooled to blend the original Spanish text with a new set of English-language lyrics that bring the song closer to a Madonnaesque version of femininity. According to the remixed version, Macarena likes to shop and she likes to chase boys, regardless of what her absent lover, Vitorino, might think. Indeed, Macarena seems to exercise power both in her relationship with Vitorino and in her relationships with young men whom she invites to dance. "Move with me, chant with me," she sings in English, "and if you're good, I'll take you home with me." To this, Ruiz and Romero respond, "Dale a tu cuerpo alegria Macarena" (give your body pleasure, Macarena).

This mixture of fantasy, desire, and feminine power is, of course, open to other interpretations. The video is liberally sprinkled with what male executives in the entertainment industry often refer to as "eye candy," in this case, a dance troupe of suggestively dressed young women from a range of racial and ethnic backgrounds, wearing trendy street fashions that appropriate design elements from a range of ethnic apparel. Looking somewhat like a Benetton ad, the video is both a United Nations of hip hop and a masculine fantasy of scantily clad young women gyrating around two middle-aged White men (Romero and Ruiz) in three-piece suits who applaud the lascivious sensibilities of their female collaborators.

Macarena seemingly has a little something for everyone and represents a very calculated effort to move a product through the elaborate circuits of global popular culture. In the parlance of the industry, *Macarena* was "leveraged every which way imaginable" to wring out every ounce of profitability by thoroughly exploiting it throughout the value chain of the Zafiro-Ariola-BMG-RCA-Bertelsmann music empire.

This example raises several significant issues for media critics. First, *Macarena* unambiguously directs our attention to media representations of feminine desire. Throughout this century, as capitalist economies around the world have entered a consumerist phase, marketing strategies increasingly focus their attention on women as the key arbiters of family purchasing decisions. What is more, as disposable income rises among the general population, hygiene and beauty products industries become especially conscious of the role that feminine desire plays in promoting their products. Consequently, radio, television, and print media are important sites where codings of woman as homemaker and romantic partner have been produced, circulated, and conventionalized. As many scholars have demonstrated, however, alternative and even subversive images of women's desires have become more widespread recently, with the literature on Madonna generating perhaps the greatest amount of attention (Bradby, 1992; Brown & Campbell, 1986; Curry, 1990; Fiske, 1992; Kaplan, 1987; Leung, 1997; Lewis, 1990; Miller 1991; Schwichtenberg, 1992; Watts, 1996; Wilson & Markle, 1992; Young, 1991).

Why and how have these transgressive images of feminine desire emerged? Certainly one can tie them to feminist struggles since the early 1970s to challenge dominant assumptions about women's roles in society. But how and why do images of feminine power and desire become marketable products in the increasingly globalized culture industries? In this essay I show how the changing discourse and structure of the culture industries accommodate, nurture, and even benefit from the circulation of transgressive images of feminine desire.

Second, *Macarena* is an important departure point for analysis, because it seems to represent much of what is feared about global media conglomerates. It serves as an example of a song that expresses local cultural tastes and values, but which takes on another life as it is repackaged and endlessly exploited in a seemingly cynical and calculated fashion. Rather than celebrating or promoting a distinctive genre of music, the Bertelsmann media conglomerate apparently dipped into its semiotic toolbox to refashion the product for mass, transnational consumption. The implication is that all culture is headed the way of *Macarena*, that there is little room for authentic difference or alternative cultural forms of expression. The homogenizing power of media conglomerates seems insurmountable, as they tighten the bolts on a well-oiled system of production, circulation, and exchange.

Curiously, we find this characterization of transnational media in the work of postmodern and postcolonial scholars such as Frederic Jameson (1991), Masao Miyoshi (1996), Arif Dirlik (1996), and Edward Said (1994), as well as in the scholarly writings of political economists such as Herbert Schiller (1992), Nicholas Garnham (1990), and Ben Bagdikian (1992). All these critics focus their attention on a supposed correlation between the emergence of huge media conglomerates and what they take to be a homogenization of public culture. In their eyes, ownership is the crucial concern. The actual operation of media industries is treated as epiphenomenal. Ownership is equated with control, and control is maintained by forging ever larger markets for particular cultural forms through a process of homogenization.

In this essay I first argue that these assumptions about the homogenizing power of huge media conglomerates are based on residual concepts from the classical or high network era of television. Such an approach fosters a misrecognition of the actual forces at work in the contemporary culture industries and obscures the ways in which popular culture serves as a site for reimaging social relations during periods of cultural and political change. A better way to understand the actual operations of media conglomerates is to delineate the corporate logic of what I refer to as the neo-network era, which most prominently features decentralizing strategies via multiple circuits of production, distribution, and consumption. The emerging principles of this new era also help to explain contradictory tendencies toward conglomeration and specialization, toward globalization and fragmentation.

In the second part of this essay I examine a cult television hit, *Absolutely Fabulous*, which provides an example of an unruly text that never would have been produced or distributed during the high network era but has proven extremely lucrative during the neo-network era. This example not only suggests a new textual and corporate logic to television programming practices, it reveals the relative immaturity and incoherence of corporate responses to the new media environment.

In the final section I explore the political implications of the neo-network era on the Indian subcontinent, where huge media conglomerates are wrestling with local music, television, and film producers for the attention of hundreds of millions of viewers. If *Macarena* shows us a very calculated effort to leverage profitably a local cultural form into a transnational phenomenon, then Alisha Chinai's gender-bending pop music shows the reverse: the opportunity for local producers to appropriate elements of cosmopolitan media in ways that produce distinctive and alternative forms of cultural expression in national and local contexts.

The Neo-Network Era

In many ways television, more than any other popular form of communication, seems to embody the defining features of a mass medium. During its first 3 decades in the United States, for example, television stood at the intersection of entertainment and information, of imagination and consumption, and of private leisure and public life. Huge mass audiences engaged it on a daily, simultaneous basis, making it arguably the most central cultural institution in U.S. history.[1] Even though the audience has been splintering for close to 20 years, the heyday of network television continues to shape much of our thinking about the culture industries. The "classical" or "high network" era of television emerged during the early 1950s and lasted roughly until the early 1980s, when cable and satellite television began to siphon off significant portions of the audience. During this time, television seemed to represent both everything that was good and bad about a mass medium. It was widely available, relatively inexpensive, and offered a showcase for some of the best talent in the history of modern entertainment. It also "brought us together" for some of the most densely textured moments of political and cultural exchange.

Nevertheless, it is difficult for those who have lived through these moments not to see the television industry as controlled by a small coterie of White males who have the ability to shape popular consciousness in profound ways. Our imagination of how the industry operates is still influenced by the imposing shadows cast by the likes of Sarnoff, Paley, and Goldenson. Yet, despite the supposed power of these media moguls, the high network era also seemed to be governed by the inexorable logic of a mass medium, premised upon an interlocking system of mass production, mass marketing, mass consumption, and national regulation (Curtin, 1996). The "shared sense of experience" that television seemed to provide during the high network era was less a matter of consensus than it was a manifestation of a particular set of capitalist relations of production and exchange. Such relations have been described by scholars under the rubric of Fordism.

This era was also dominated by the belief that huge, integrated enterprises could serve the needs of vast national and international markets. Even though television audiences of this period were fragmented along many axes, network executives aspired to represent their audiences as a unified entity in ratings, marketing reports, and promotions. Moreover, they characterized their over-arching mission as integrative (i.e., pulling people together, uniting various regions, forging ever larger markets). Of course, niche markets existed then as now, but they were not celebrated in trade discourse among the major corporate players who controlled the medium.

The operative principles of the high network era still exercise a powerful hold on our imaginations. As we have witnessed the merging of gigantic media firms into huge conglomerates over the past decade, many scholarly and popular critics seem to have assumed that this concentration of ownership means greater control at the top of the corporate pyramid and an increasing homogenization of cultural products. They revert to past stereotypes of media moguldom to convey a sense of the organizing intentions behind firms like News Corporation, Disney, and Viacom. Each conglomerate is represented as an institutional extension of the personality of its chief corporate officer (e.g., Rupert Murdoch, Michael Eisner, Sumner Redstone).

As conglomeration has intensified over the past couple decades, the power of these moguls has supposedly assumed transnational proportions, reaching into virtually every culture and society. Critics like Bagdikian (1989) have suggested that what we are witnessing is the continuation of a trend toward concentration that began earlier in this century. Whereas media moguls once controlled popular culture and public opinion on a national scale, they now control it on a global scale. This presumption is also widely featured in popular narratives, like the ... James Bond film, *Tomorrow Never Dies*.

Despite frightening apparitions of gigantic media octopuses, Fordist principles seem to be undergoing a period of significant transformation. Changes in national and global economies over the past 2 decades have fragmented the marketplace and pressured the culture industries to reorganize and restrategize. As opposed to the relative stability of huge, nationally based media corporations during much of this century, the current period of transition is paradoxically characterized by both transnationalization and fragmentation. New technologies, deregulation, and relentless competition have undermined national frameworks and are reconfiguring the cultural landscape.

Although mass markets continue to attract corporate attention, industry discourse about the mass audience no longer refers to one simultaneous experience so much as a shared, asynchronous cultural milieu. In part, this is because the culture industries exercise less control over the daily scheduling of popular entertainment. Audiences time-shift and channel surf, or they pursue a myriad of other entertainment options. Consequently, trends and ideas now achieve prominence in often circuitous and unanticipated ways.

Media executives therefore strive for broad exposure of their products through multiple circuits of information and expression. They also seek less to homogenize popular culture than to organize and exploit diverse forms of creativity toward profitable ends. Besides their heavily promoted mass products, media corporations cultivate a broad range of products intended for more specific audiences. Flexible corporate frameworks connect mass market operations with more localized initiatives.

Therefore, two strategies are now at work in the culture industries. One focuses on mass cultural forms aimed at broad national or global markets that demand low involvement and are relatively apolitical (e.g., Hollywood films or broadcast television). Media operations that deal in this arena are cautious about the prospect of intense audience responses either for or against the product they are marketing. By comparison, those products targeted at niche audiences actively pursue intensity. They seek out audiences that are more likely to be highly invested in a particular form of cultural expression. These firms do not aim to change niche groups. They aim instead to situate their products within them. Among industry executives, these are referred to as products with "edge." They received little attention 30 years ago, but today product development meetings are peppered with references to attitude and edge, that is, references to products that sharply define the boundaries of their intended audience.

We are therefore witnessing the organization of huge media conglomerates around the so-called synergies that exploit these two movements. This is what I refer to as the neo-network era, an era characterized by the multiple and asynchronous distribution of cultural forms. It is an era that operates according to neo-Fordist principles, what Harvey (1989) referred to as a flexible regime of accumulation. Rather than a network structure anchored by highly centralized systems of national finance, production, and regulation, the neo-network era features elaborate circuits of cultural production, distribution, and reception.

This transformation is not a radical break with the past. Rather, it is a transitional phase in which Fordist and neo-Fordist principles exist side-by-side. Blockbuster films that appeal to a transnational audience are still the desideratum of major Hollywood studios, but the same conglomerate that may own a studio may also own a cable service, a specialty music label, and a collection of magazines that target very specific market niches.[2] ... The key to success is no longer the ownership and control of a centralized and highly integrated media empire, but the management of a conglomerate structured around a variety of firms with different audiences and different objectives. According to media executives, these firms are simply following a marketing strategy that is strictly capitalistic and generally disinterested in content issues.

Ideally, this neo-network strategy will present opportunities whereby a micromarket phenomenon crosses over into a mainstream phenomenon, making it potentially exploitable through a greater number of circuits within the media conglomerate. Some rap artists' careers obviously followed this trajectory. This may be best represented by the success of a performer like Will Smith, who has scored hits in both Hollywood film and broadcast television. The converse is also true, however. A product that was originally a mass phenomenon can be spun out through myriad niche venues, which has been Viacom's strategy behind *Star Trek*, one of its most profitable brands.[3] In an interview while he was in charge of the Turner Entertainment Group, Scott Sassa elaborated on this approach and pointed out that his job was to exploit the profitability of copyrighted material throughout the so-called value chain of the conglomerate. Sassa said that, "Every copyright that starts out anywhere in the system gets leveraged every which way imaginable" (quoted in Kline, 1995, p. 112). The key to profitability in the neo-network era is still distribution, but the distribution system is more diverse and decentered. It also remains highly volatile, given the unpredictable nature of popular responses to new cultural forms.

An Era of Indeterminacy

These corporate strategies help to explain the seemingly contradictory impulses toward globalization and fragmentation. They suggest how a niche product like *Macarena* might be leveraged into a mass global phenomenon. However, they also show how a television program like *Absolutely Fabulous* might never become a mass phenomenon, but could nevertheless prove enormously profitable if it were cleverly managed within the multiple and asynchronous circuits of global distribution. Another reason to turn our attention to *Absolutely Fabulous* is that this example reminds us that the seemingly tidy logic of the neo-network era, so elegantly laid out by executives like Sassa, is still at a very formative stage. We need to recognize that gaps, contradictions, and inconsistencies are much more characteristic of this era than what might be suggested by more common representations of highly integrated media juggernauts run by powerful moguls like Rupert Murdoch.

Interestingly, this era of indeterminancy also engenders unexpected opportunities to explore, criticize, and undermine dominant representations of feminine desire. It is therefore instructive to examine carefully the production, circulation, and textual logic of television programs like *Absolutely Fabulous*. The series features the omniholic Patsy Stone and Edina Monsoon—two aging flower children cum fashion divas with enormous appetites—who are bent on consuming every trendy drug, garment, and comestible on which they can lay their hands. This campy, ironic, and some argue queer take on contemporary consumer society had a bit too much edge for broadcast television executives when it was first pitched to them, but, then, that was exactly the point.

Absolutely Fabulous was designed from the outset to represent feminine desire as so voracious and uncontrollable that it was unlike most anything that has ever graced the airwaves of popular television. Conventional television texts, like the *Macarena* music video, will usually contain feminine desire or transform it into a mirror image of masculine fantasies, a tendency that has prevailed from the very earliest years of the medium (Doty, 1990; Mellencamp, 1991; Ritrosky-Winslow, 1998; Rowe, 1995; Spigel, 1992). *Absolutely Fabulous* not only resisted these conventions, it directly assaulted them, savaging the tidy little bows and wrappers of mass television on its way to ripping open a Pandora's box of kinky feminine desire

Edina and Patsy, the lead characters, represent the exact opposite of everything the domestic comedy has ever imagined for adult women. They are neither nurturing nor self-sacrificing. Rather than mediating conflicts among the characters, they incite sensational confrontations. Edina is not a good mother to her daughter Saffy. Instead, she is manipulative, self-indulgent, and appallingly neglectful. Instead of guiding her adolescent daughter along the path to adulthood, Edina is racing backwards in a frantic attempt to recover her own youth. Her vodka-swilling best friend, Patsy, chain-smokes her way through the series with only occasional interruptions to pursue cynically her seemingly insatiable sexual desires. These are not nice people, and their physical appearance is not conventionally pretty.

Indeed, the series was developed from the outset as a hyperparodic niche product that would invite intense reactions from viewers. Only with the greatest reluctance did the BBC produce the series for a limited run of 18 episodes. ABC was so skittish about a U.S. prime-time adaptation of *Absolutely Fabulous* that the network declined to pick it up, despite considerable pressure from ABC's then comedy superstar, Roseanne, a strong supporter of the series (Bellafante, 1995; Jacobs & Nashawaty, 1996).

Absolutely Fabulous clearly is not a mass product. Unlike *Macarena*, in which feminine desire is represented through fairly conventional images of a "liberated" woman whose licentious behavior also appeals to masculine fantasies of the naughty temptress, *Absolutely Fabulous* makes few concessions aimed at broadening its appeal. In addition to the intriguingly repulsive gender, generational, and family dynamics, the dialogue is laden with in-jokes about everything from high fashion to tabloid celebrity gossip to New Age health practices. It seems to beg viewers, who are not on the inside, to stay away. Of course, this strategy makes the programs even more attractive to those who appreciate the jokes. However, these very qualities limit the ways that media executives might market the series. Attempts to reconstitute it as a mass product for U.S. network television failed, and one could imagine that such a program would never have been considered, much less broadcast, 30 years ago at the height of the classical network era.

Absolutely Fabulous proved to be a cult favorite that BBC's niche marketing operation successfully hawked in more than 20 countries around the globe.... Videotape episodes of the show were among the top three sellers at Virgin Megastores in 1995, and they made the *Billboard* sales charts for more than 40 weeks. At the Comedy Central cable network in the U.S., a joint venture of Time-Warner and Viacom, *Absolutely Fabulous* was far and away the ratings leader during its three-season run (BBC Programme Purchases, 1996; Berger, 1995; King, 1996).

The series seems to demonstrate a cultural shift in representations of feminine desire facilitated by a transformation in the strategies and operations of the culture industries. Yet, before we begin to write paeans to the corporate geniuses of the neo-network era who exploited this trend, a couple of observations highlight the messiness of this current moment of transformation in the culture industries. First, although *Absolutely Fabulous* was marketed successfully by the sales division of the BBC, the series almost failed to make it into production because of reservations expressed by male network executives who found it difficult to reconcile the program's imagery with their own notions of femininity and with industry conventions for representing feminine desire. They worried the program had too much edge for a prime-time audience. The series ultimately was approved only because it was coded as an "alternative" offering on the noncommercial, highly regulated airwaves of Great Britain (Bellafante, 1995). Thus, the series was not initially conceived and developed with a commercial, neo-network strategy in mind.

The marketing phase was not a clearly organized campaign either. In the United States, Comedy Central almost passed on the series because executives at the newly established cable network imagined their target demographic as a niche audience of young men. They believed that women simply would not find the series among the clutter of cable offerings, and that their target audience of young male viewers would fail to appreciate the humor. Although the latter proved true, female viewers flocked to the series in droves, a response that ran contrary to the market research done in preparation for launching the new network.... During the early years of Comedy Central, *Absolutely Fabulous* was without a doubt the network's breakthrough success. Yet executives failed to recognize the potential value of the show when it was first offered to them (Bellafante, 1995; Berger, 1995).

Consequently, one must be careful not to characterize the neo-network culture industries as well-oiled corporate machines operating according to a coherent, mature logic. The popularity of specific products is still notoriously unpredictable, and the content is often unruly and even subversive.... The landscape has changed, but popular culture remains an active site of social and political contest. In fact, the media industries may be more open to alternative forms of cultural expression today, simply because executives are not certain from where the next hit will come (Curtin, in press). Unlike the high network era in which executives exercised some control over product popularity because of their monopoly control of limited distribution channels, this new era is characterized by a cluttered marketplace of niche offerings and the constant fragmentation of audiences. By jettisoning a narrowly defined approach to political economy that primarily focuses on ownership issues, a more specific analysis of the operations and strategies of neo-network media firms reveals the existence of opportunities that are not readily apparent.

One could argue, however, that the social significance of programs like *Absolutely Fabulous* is relatively modest. Even if it does in fact undermine prevailing representations of gender relations, it nevertheless appeals primarily to middle-class women in advanced industrial and postindustrial societies. On a global scale, these are television's most privileged viewers. One might wonder if the logic of the neo-network era is likewise affecting popular images of feminine desire in other parts of the world.

Subcontinental Implications

In April 1995, Alisha Chinai's music video *Made in India*, rocketed to the top of the national charts soon after it premiered across the subcontinent on the Hong Kong-based STAR TV satellite network. Credited with sparking the current Indo-Pop craze, this video foregrounded a young Indian woman's desires in ways that are both global and local and both subversive and traditional. The success of the video and the rapidly growing popularity of satellite television has been discussed more thoroughly in other research (Kumar & Curtin, 1997). In this section I briefly sketch our critique of the video and connect it with the foregoing analysis of the neo-network era.

Since the beginning of the decade, Indian television has changed from a government media monopoly to a rapidly expanding selection of satellite services that now draws large audiences in major cities and most large towns across the country. In 1991, satellite or cable services were available to 330,000 Indian homes. According to recent estimates, the number has grown to 15 million, with an average of 5 viewers to each household (Duncan, 1995; Popham, 1997).... With an estimated 40 million television households nationwide, the market is considered large enough to invite fierce competition between regional, national, and transnational program providers. This means that Indian television has changed from an educational, public service medium to a panoply of services that includes the same range of program genres available in most industrialized societies.

According to Emma Duncan (1995), South Asia editor of the *Economist*, the rise of satellite television "gets the blame (or the credit)" for all the changes taking place in India over the past few years, especially changes in gender relations. Many young women are now wearing "western, not Indian, clothes" and "some advanced cosmopolitan couples" are now living together before they are married because "it's easier to explain it to a mother who has seen *The Bold and The Beautiful*" on satellite TV (Duncan, 1995, p. 3). According to Dhillon (1996),

> No one has remained unaffected by the transformation brought about by satellite TV.... For the first time, viewers [are seeing] the kind of scenes that westerners consider tame—kissing, love-making, nudity, homosexuality —but that are shocking in India. Consider that this is a nation where celluloid kisses were banned until three years ago, where most women feel uncomfortable in sleeveless tops and few know the Hindi word for sex. (p. A7)

Without a doubt, the growth of satellite television has played a role in the naked display of bodies and commodities in India. Yet, to describe these changes solely as a response to satellite television would be a gross simplification. For several decades, well before the advent of satellite television, Indian cinema—primarily based in Bombay and, therefore, commonly referred to as Bollywood—provided desiring audiences many avenues of exposure, in all senses of the term. Indian cinema was, and continues to remain, the most popular mass medium. It has always thrived on fantastic displays of luxury, wealth, and consumption, as well as the blatant exploitation of women as titillating objects of sexual desire. The predominant Bollywood genre is the film musical in which romantic complications are ultimately resolved in a series of lavish song and dance numbers.

By comparison, Indian pop music, especially a single album like *Made in India*, is a very recent phenomenon, emerging only in the last few years. Despite the rapid rise of this new genre, what some refer to as Indo-Pop, the music industry continues to be dominated by the sale of songs from film musicals, accounting for about 70% of all sales, compared to Indo-Pop's much more modest share of 7%. Nevertheless Indo-Pop is the fastest growing part of the market, jumping 25% to 30% annually (Dua & Bhat, 1997). BMG-Crescendo, one of the largest films in the Indian music business, estimates that Indian pop music should push past a 20% share of the $572 million music market by the year 2000 (Fernandes, 1996).

The rapid growth of this new musical genre can be tied directly to the rise of satellite television services, like MTV and STAR. In 1991, when Hong Kong-based STAR TV started its pan-Asian broadcasts, it tapped the resources of MTV with its familiar line-up of Beavis and Butthead, Nirvana, Madonna, and other Generation-X icons. Three years later, when MTV and STAR TV announced their parting of the ways, STAR TV decided to launch its own music service called Channel V. Initially, Channel V seemed content playing an MTV clone. However, it soon became clear that the STAR-based service was charting a new course as part of an effort to distinguish itself from its competition. Claire Marshall, Channel V manager in Hong Kong, contended,

> MTV's philosophy is international programming. It has a very Westernized... very American image. They pick up Western youth trends and establish those as the norm in their programming. But a lot of what they produce has no relation to the Asian context. It is a copycat culture for Asian youth. So we had to go Asian; we had to localize. (quoted in Bavadam, 1995, p. 69)

... Channel V saw its mandate as creating a local channel with an international flavor, a clear contrast to MTV's approach of being an international channel with a local flavor. In its efforts to localize, Channel V established production facilities in Delhi and Bombay. It also appropriated MTV's verité camera work, cacophonous editing style, provocative animation, and Top 40 song rotation, which Channel V then infused with iconographic elements of the Bollywood musical and the self-deprecating humor and slapstick comedy that are hallmarks of Indian cinema. Channel V thus promoted the rise of a new hybrid satellite channel, casually mixing elements from East and West. Channel V then pushed the market even further by nurturing its own pop music stars outside the circuits of the Bollywood film musical. Alisha Chinai's *Made in India*, the first big hit of the Indo-Pop genre, sold 2 million albums, plus an estimated 6 million pirated copies. The phenomenal success of Alisha's album was primarily ascribed to the popularity of the Channel V-produced video ("Channel V," 1997; Fernandes, 1996; "Synergy," 1997).

The video begins in ornate palatial surroundings similar to those commonly found in Bollywood films. Princess Alisha is watching an elaborate performance by dancers and musicians at the royal court, yet she seems distracted and indifferent. Ultimately, she breaks into song, lamenting a boredom that springs from the fact that, despite her travels around the world, the princess has yet to find one true love. In desperation, she summons a sorcerer, whose fervent incantations over a boiling cauldron conjure up steamy apparitions of the handsome young man of Alisha's dreams. A montage of shots that most prominently feature erotic poses of his naked torso startle and titillate the desirous princess, who orders her minions to bring her the man at once. Her wish is fulfilled when a wooden shipping crate—prominently emblazoned *Made in India*—is portered to Alisha's lair containing the cargo of her desire. Out of the crate springs the muscular, forthright man of her dreams, naked to the waist, who literally sweeps Alisha off her feet. At this moment of closure, she playfully turns to the camera and offers a knowing smile to the audience as the image cuts to a closing shot of the final page of a storybook that reads, "and the handsome prince carried the princess away and they lived happily ever after. The End."

At this point of narrative closure, the video seems a rather conventional text by the standards of Bollywood musical. Yet, *Made in India* inverts dominant representations of desire in rather profound ways. Traditionally, in Bollywood musicals, dream sequences are used to foreground transgressive masculine desire featuring spectacular displays of the female body. A powerful masculine gaze encourages the viewer to accept a hierarchy of gender relations that indulges male fantasies while effectively silencing feminine desire. *Made in India* inverts these conventions by transforming the male body into the sight of spectacle, so as to fix the attention of the viewer on questions of feminine desire: What does an Indian woman want, need, and deserve?

These are not inconsequential issues in a society where most women exercise few choices about labor and family relations. In such a context, the very act of fantasizing about feminine desire has such subversive implications that the narrative must recuperate this moment of textual transgression by literally sweeping the protagonist off her feet and restoring some semblance of masculine dominance to this counterhegemonic fantasy. Yet, even this moment of recuperation is undermined when Alisha, swaddled in the arms of her prince, playfully acknowledges the camera as if to say it is she who ultimately controls the trajectory of the narrative.

In short, the subversive possibilities of this text and their implications for women across India are in large part a product of the intersecting forces at work in Asian television. As such, the new worldliness of Indian media imagery that has been sparked by the invasion of transnational media firms need not be reductively interpreted as homogenizing nor as constraining popular modes of expression. Indeed, the transformation of India's media economy created the very opportunities from which Indo-Pop emerged and thereby created a context in which young women might fantasize about their futures outside the patriarchal representational norms of traditional religion, Bollywood film, and government television.

Conclusion

This analysis does not attempt to project a particular politics onto alternative images of feminine desire. Rather my aim is to understand the growing circulation of such images and the political potential that they may present. If our attention remains primarily fixed on the global march of gigantic media conglomerates like News Corporation—the parent company of STAR TV—then we will fail to recognize the potential spaces in which alternative gender politics might be constructed. If one wants to comprehend the dynamic interactions between global and local forces, and if one wants to locate the fleeting but significant cultural spaces in which women might imagine a more liberated future, then one would do well to explore the specific operations of neo-network media industries and the textual possibilities they present.

The growing prominence of huge media conglomerates does not automatically herald the homogenization of culture, the death of free expression, or the end of public life. Ownership does not necessarily equal control. As suggested earlier, cultural conditions are always shifting and uncertain. Even though media conglomerates have fashioned their strategies to accommodate these uncertainties, the second section of this essay reminds us that these strategies are in many ways immature and incoherent if not inadequate. The final part of this paper suggests how one local artist has embraced the opportunities of this era to fashion a sly challenge to the masculine conventions of Indian popular culture.

At the same time, we should take care to recognize this moment of opportunity for what it is: fleeting, contingent, and indeterminate. History reminds us that the public sphere, which has received such conspicuous attention in recent scholarly discussions, was not an intentional outcome of the transition to capitalism, and it did not become a stable feature that would endure for centuries. Instead, it was an opening that was exploited by an emergent class at a specific historical moment (Habermas, 1962/1989).

Likewise, the current reorganization of the culture industries provides fluid and ephemeral spaces in which to imagine new gender roles, political affinities, and sexual orientations. An understanding of the neo-network era asks us to rethink our assumptions about the homogenizing power of global media conglomerates, pressing us instead to explore this terrain as a site of contest, and a productive space within civil society. Such an approach neither denies corporate power nor uncritically celebrates popular culture. Instead it suggests how scholarly criticism might help us identify locations in which to construct alternative images of feminine desire.

Notes

1. By comparison, the film studies dealt only with entertainment. Although widely popular, films were not enjoyed as a simultaneous mass experience. Radio in many ways anticipated the television era by generating huge national audiences, yet most stations remained independent and programming was primarily in the hands of sponsors and ad agencies, not the networks. Neither the newspaper nor music industries have been as centralized as television, and their audiences have been

subdivided by geography or taste. As for the general circulation magazine, it has been national in scope, but its audience skewed more toward the educated and affluent.

2. For example, Interscope, an "independent" music company formerly owned by Time-Warner, became very controversial because one of its niche labels, Death Row Records, prominently featured "gangster rap" artists like Snoop Doggy Dog and the late Tupac Shakur. After intense public pressure, Time-Warner put Interscope up for sale. This quickly attracted the attention of Sony and MCA/Universal, with the latter taking control after a high-stakes bidding war. Rather than actually going independent, Interscope is now racking up record-breaking sales in new niche markets that include punk-ska and Gospel music (Sandler, 1996; Thigpen, 1997).

3. Smith starred in the NBC prime-time series, *Fresh Prince of Bel Air*, and the Sony Pictures blockbuster, *Men in Black*, which earned over $500 million in global box office revenues 4 months after its premier, making it the 10th highest grossing film in Hollywood history ("Box Office," 1997; Klady, 1997). The aim behind new corporate strategies is for a star like Smith to score his various successes under a single corporate umbrella. Regarding Viacom's strategy for the exploitation of product brands like *Star Trek*, see Batelle, 1995.

POSTSCRIPT

Media Monopolies: Does Concentration of Ownership Jeopardize Media Content?

What are the consequences of media consolidation for the role and responsibilities of media in society? Unfortunately, there is little research on the effects of media restructuring. Is media concentration a problem? We may not think so if economies of scale reduce the prices we pay for our media. We may, however, have problems if most of the media outlets in our community are owned by the same corporation. For example, is a chain owner more likely to impose a one-size-fits-all perspective on its coverage of local events, thus reducing diversity? The Telecommunications Act of 1996 has unleashed a torrent of mergers and acquisitions. Is the promise of erasing traditional monopolies, which will reduce prices for services, being realized? Or, has the law opened the door for new forms of monopoly?

What is certain is that the media industry in the United States is still in the midst of a period of rapid, transformational change, the outcome of which has significant implications for civic society and the global media economy. The realization of synergy from consolidation is elusive, which is why, in general across all industries, approximately half of all mergers are undone within a decade.

The issues of corporate restructuring are being played out daily in the pages of the business press and media trade publications. See, for example, the *Wall Street Journal, Broadcasting/Cable* magazine, and *Electronic Media* for discussions of the successes and failures in this realm. Recent national scandals involving corporate financial irregularities may have an impact on the financial performance pressures brought to bear on corporations. *The Business of Media: Corporate Media and the Public Interest,* by David Croteau and William Hoynes (Pine Forge Press, 2001), is an excellent exploration of the tensions between corporate ownership and traditional obligations of the press. See also *Conglomerates and the Media,* Patricia Aufderheide, ed. (New Press, 1997). For an overview of the issues of media and the economy, see *Media Economics: Theory and Practice* (Erlbaum, 1998).

ISSUE 15

Is Civic Journalism Good Journalism?

YES: Chuck Clark, from "In Favor of Civic Journalism," *Harvard International Journal of Press/Politics* (Summer 1997)

NO: William E. Jackson, Jr., from "Save Democracy From Civic Journalism: North Carolina's Odd Experiment," *Harvard International Journal of Press/Politics* (Summer 1997)

ISSUE SUMMARY

YES: Chuck Clark, government editor of the *Charlotte Observer*, defends the use of civic journalism by the *Observer* in covering election campaigns in North Carolina. He describes the publication's goal: to provide the readers of the newspaper with enough relevant information to make decisions concerning the elections.

NO: William E. Jackson, Jr., professor and U.S. House candidate in 1996, criticizes the use of civic journalism. He charges that coverage was narrowly focused on only a few issues, evolving issues were ignored, and important other races were not covered. According to Jackson, political coverage and the people of North Carolina suffered because of this experiment in civic journalism.

T he focus of this interchange is the "Your Voice, Your Vote" campaign, an experiment in civic (sometimes called public) journalism launched by a consortium of six newspapers and nine public and commercial television stations in the 1996 North Carolina election contests—the races for governor and for the U.S. Senate. The project began with a poll of the audience, asking them to identify the issues that they cared about. They selected four of the top five issues (crime and drugs, health care, taxes and spending, and education), interviewed the candidates, put together issue packages, and continued to pursue information and comments from the candidates about these issues throughout the campaign.

Where did this plan come from, and how did such an innocuous-sounding project become the object of national debate? First, what is civic journalism? Jay Rosen is an advocate for public, or civic, journalism, which he says is journalism designed to bring a genuine public alive. Since the Hutchins Commission of the 1940s challenged the press to focus on "social responsibility," critics have argued that the press should be committed to improving public discourse. According to Rosen, the press can identify issues of public concern through direct interaction with the public and report on those issues in such a way that individuals are empowered to become more connected with public life and with other interested citizens. Rather than focus solely on the "horse race" aspects of electoral races, journalists began to consider changing their practices. Starting with the public concerns and connecting these concerns to the candidates' platforms and interview responses was a key element of what was seen as problem-solving process. Or, more eloquently, the goal was to make good journalism operate in service to democracy and be of use to citizens.

But the reality was somewhat different. National media attacked the way the project partners went about the process. These national press writers contended that journalists were pandering to readers, abdicating their own professional responsibility to assess the news, and undermining the candidates' own political judgments about the important issues for the campaign.

Chuck Clark defends the use of civic journalism in covering the election campaigns in North Carolina. He describes the approach journalists used and their goal of providing readers with the relevant information they needed to make decisions concerning the election. He offers an analysis of what went well and what went wrong, and he reflects on some aspects of the election that were beyond anyone's control.

William E. Jackson, Jr. offers a spirited attack on the civic journalism project. He notes that important issues of race and health were ignored, as were other important races. Jackson argues that too great a focus on the civic journalism project undercut other significant aspects of the electoral race and hurt certain candidates' chances with the voters. Candidates could not get their own agendas in the press and so were denied the opportunity to present their own visions of what was important and necessary for public knowledge and debate.

Chuck Clark

 **YES**

In Favor of Civic Journalism

Sometimes in the world of journalism, you go out on a limb. Sometimes people try to chop that limb off while you're out there.

The *Charlotte Observer* has been out on something of a limb since 1992, when we launched "Your Vote," our first public journalism elections project. In 1996, with our participation in North Carolina's "Your Voice, Your Vote" partnership, we attempted to use a slice of our election coverage to see that people across North Carolina got a side-by-side comparison of candidates for president, U.S. Senate, and governor on the major issues that citizens identified as important.

The "Your Voice, Your Vote" partnership was misunderstood, misinterpreted—and, in our opinion, wrongly maligned. Let me qualify that: The only people who did not understand it, or who got it outright wrong, were other journalists and political insiders. The readers? The voters? They got it, they liked it, and that's what is important.

One of the first people to wield a hatchet at *The Charlotte Observer*'s election coverage in 1996 was Bill Jackson, an adjunct college professor from Iredell County in suburban Charlotte.... Jackson was soon joined by columnists and reporters from *The Washington Post*, *The Boston Globe*, *The Wall Street Journal*, and *The New Yorker*—all of whom seized onto an error-riddled op-ed piece in *The New York Times* by Jackson. They all decried the *Observer*'s citizen-based approach to political journalism as no less than the death knell for democracy. Jackson, who ran a distant second in the Democratic primary for North Carolina's Republican-voting Ninth Congressional District, was outspoken among the critics. He blamed the media for his loss, criticized us for not covering every incremental development in his campaign, and chalked it up to "Your Voice, Your Vote." He characterized his congressional primary as the only one in the *Observer*'s "prime circulation area."

In fact, there are four congressional districts winding their way through the *Observer*'s territory—three of them in our home country of Mecklenburg. Both the Eighth and Ninth Districts had primaries, though only the Eighth District Republican primary was truly competitive. Though Jackson asserts coverage of his race was part of "Your Voice, Your Vote," it was not; "Your Voice, Your Vote" focused only on specific issues in the races for governor, U.S. Senate

From Chuck Clark, "In Favor of Civic Journalism," *Harvard International Journal of Press/Politics*, vol. 2, no. 3 (Summer 1997). Copyright © 1997 by The President and Fellows of Harvard College. Reprinted by permission of Sage Publications, Inc.

and president. The *Observer* covered all congressional races as part of its regular political coverage in 1996.

The Citizen Approach

So what did *The Charlotte Observer* do in 1996? We watched the issues the people raised and relayed what the candidates said. We also explored issues that the candidates raised. We crisscrossed our state with candidates in traditional campaign-trail coverage. We reported on the crucial TV campaigns and "truth-squadded" the barrage of advertising in regular ad-watch features. We followed the record amounts of money pouring into the campaigns. We honed in on issues ranging from the broad basics of education and taxes to the complex, like values, corporate welfare, affirmative action and foreign policy for the twenty-first century. We tried new techniques, from the Internet to the telephone to a sophisticated new graphic style. We presented the news in a variety of ways voters could find useful. Bottom line: We tried to equip Carolinians with the information they needed to make decisions on Election Day. Most important, while we covered the candidates, we kept a strong focus on the voters—their issues and their concerns.

Therein lies the controversy. An important part of our focus on voters in 1996 was our work with the "Your Voice, Your Vote" project. Through that effort, the *Observer* joined hands with five other North Carolina newspapers, five commercial television stations, our statewide public television network, and three public radio stations to cover citizen issues in the races for U.S. Senate, North Carolina governor, and president.

Why did the *Observer* do it? To understand our approach, we need to begin in 1992, with the *Observer's* original "Your Vote" project. That effort, which has been copied and adapted across the country since, launched us toward political journalism that focuses on the people and their issues in addition to our traditional coverage. For the first time in North Carolina's modern history, candidates were being pushed by our reporters to answer the questions on citizens' minds. Instead of the press-conference stenography that so much political journalism had become, we set out to explore what mattered to people in the Carolinas and to ask the candidates about those issues. We let our readers help set our reporting agenda. We probed their issues. We brought them together with candidates. When that was not possible, we often asked the candidates reader questions in addition to our own.

Why the shift in our approach? Carolinians, like so many of their American brothers and sisters, had grown increasingly disconnected and uninterested in public life and the democratic process. We believe that irrelevant reporting—obsessed with campaign strategy and "horse-race" politics rather than how our public officials would solve our problems—was, and is, part of the problem. So we set out to tailor our election coverage around citizen concerns.

Reading Statewide

In the middle of 1995, some of us at the *Observer* wondered, if it was good that politicians were being asked about citizen concerns in the Southern Piedmont —and there was no question that readers liked that coverage—would it be good for citizens across the state to get the same benefits?

We sat down with the state's second-largest newspaper, *The News & Observer* of Raleigh, to discuss whether editors and reporters there were interested in "an experiment" in political journalism. We outlined a proposal for a very limited project, focusing on citizen issues as a supplement to each newspaper's regular election coverage. Though the two papers had never considered cooperating before, we agreed to give it a try, hoping this effort would be good for North Carolina voters. Both newspapers then agreed to broaden the partnership to include newspaper and broadcast partners in Asheville, Chapel Hill, Durham, Fayetteville, Greensboro, and Wilmington. In November 1995, the entire partnership assembled—fifteen organizations in all—in the board room of *The News & Observer* and gave birth to what would become "Your Voice, Your Vote."

As a model, we looked to the 1994 "Voices of Florida" project, involving the *St. Petersburg Times, The Miami Herald, The Florida Times-Union, The Tallahassee Democrat,* and some smaller Florida dailies. Pete Weitzel of the Poynter Institute, and former managing editor of *The Miami Herald*, coached us from his experiences in Florida.

The "Your Voice, Your Vote" partnership polled our state twice—once in January, again in July, 2,001 people in all—to determine what North Carolinians wanted politicians to address. The partnership focused on the races for U.S. senator and North Carolina governor. Then the partnership reported on the voter concerns, sharing stories, graphics, and photos for two series of issue-driven articles—one series of seven packages before the spring primary and another series of five packages before the fall election.

Everyday Worries

To nobody's surprise, North Carolinians expressed concern about the core issues they live with every day—things like taxes, educating their children, being able to get and afford health care, jobs and economic security, crime and drugs, the state of American values. The politicians were already talking about some of those issues; others they were not. Nevertheless, they were on the voters' minds, so the partnership set about seeing that the politicians answered the questions.

Our partnership interviewed every candidate whose name appeared on the ballots for senator and governor, except one. Each was interviewed for three hours in the spring, talking about the six big issues on Carolinians' minds, at length and in depth. The partners interviewed those candidates who survived the primary process again in the late summer.

The only candidate who refused to participate was Jesse Helms, North Carolina's long-time senior senator. Reporters from *The Charlotte Observer* tracked him down wherever he went and got him to answer citizen-based questions so the partners could show voters where he stood too. True, Senator Helms's answers were not as complete as those from the six hours of interviews with his Democratic opponent, Harvey Gantt, but each partner newspaper was careful to explain the circumstances to its readers.

Each "Your Voice, Your Vote" package consisted of in-depth articles exploring the candidates' proposals and records on particular issues as well as a full-page graphic comparing the major candidates' answers to citizen questions about that issue. Reporters from different papers worked together on these packages. Their copy was edited by yet other partner papers. Each partner did its own final edit, layout, and headlines, often customizing the stories or supplementing them with local sidebars. Our broadcast members largely worked with their local newspaper partners to forge their coverage. Jointly, all fifteen partners produced three citizen forums, where voters posed their own questions to the major candidates for governor and senator in the spring primaries, and the major candidates for governor in the fall.

Praise and Criticism

The candidates for governor—even the loser—praised "Your Voice, Your Vote" for honing in on what North Carolinians think is important. Through most of the campaign, even Harvey Gantt said he liked it, though he did say Senator Helms's refusal to participate compromised the project.

The political strategists—including Gantt's campaign manager—hated it. It wasn't nearly as easy for them to steer and manipulate the coverage. The pundits and political science professors found citizens' voices filling the space where they had traditionally been quoted. Some were critical. The critics said we didn't go out on the trail, didn't write about what the candidates were saying, didn't write about important issues unless prompted by a poll—all false charges as any review of coverage in *The Charlotte Observer* shows. Perhaps the most invective opinion came from columnist Jonathan Yardley of *The Washington Post*. He called the project "insidious" and "dangerous." He published those remarks without ever talking to any journalist involved in the project and without ever reading the first word any of the partners published. Perhaps that's insidious and dangerous.

Throughout all the criticism of "Your Voice, Your Vote" one assessment is conspicuously missing: that of the voters. Frederick Schneiders Research of Washington, D.C., polled six hundred registered voters statewide in North Carolina, between November 11 and 13. The poll found that "Your Voice, Your Vote" coverage caught the attention of 25 percent of North Carolina's registered voters. Of those, 82 percent viewed it "favorably" or "very favorably." A majority (56 percent) of all voters surveyed felt that media coverage of the Helms-Gantt race was balanced and fair. Those aware of the project said they felt better informed about issues in the Helms-Gantt race than those who weren't exposed to "Your Voice, Your Vote."

We're pleased with those numbers, particularly with the indication that 1 million North Carolina voters were aware of a project that appeared just twelve times over a year in newspapers that reach about 850,000 subscribers in a state with 7 million residents. The survey was conducted a month after the last "Your Voice, Your Vote" installment was published.[1] Anecdotally, all the partners heard the same thing. Compliments far outweighed complaints, particularly in the communities where the citizen-based approach to political journalism was a completely new concept.

What Worked, What Didn't

Several things worked well in the partnership, most notably the statewide polling, the in-depth candidate interviews, the televised forums in which citizens posed questions, and the synergy of three media that reach different audiences.

What didn't work so well? Sharing stories and graphics was difficult because each paper uses a different editing, photo, and graphics systems, and the lead time to get each package to each paper hampered last-minute creativity. The partnership went down the road toward team writing and presentation somewhat out of necessity; *The Observer* was the only partner paper to have tackled citizen-based political journalism before, so there was an instructive nature to sharing the stories. While this approach produced sound journalism, it was a cumbersome process.

The Partnership and the Observer

Was "Your Voice, Your Vote" all the *Observer* did in 1996? Not even close.

We're in the process of a detailed analysis of all the *Observer's* locally produced political coverage in 1996, so we don't have final numbers yet. However, our estimates are that "Your Voice, Your Vote" accounted for no more than 20 percent of our coverage of the races for North Carolina governor and U.S. Senate, and about 10 percent of our overall locally produced political journalism for the year. The rest was from the trail, from the news of the day, from other issues raised by voters, from other issues raised by the candidates, from other races—and from issues our own journalistic instincts told us were important.

At the *Observer*, in addition to political news we put in our run-of-day normal space, we published about 700 columns of extra space—that's roughly 117 newspaper pages—of locally produced political coverage through the election. We covered every race, from the presidency to the soil and water conservation district supervisor—albeit some more than others. More than 120 races appeared on the ballot in our home Mecklenburg County in the November general election, including a dozen referendums to change the state constitution or borrow money for state and local projects.

No Surprises

Our goal was that the astute reader of the *Observer* would have enough relevant information to make decisions in each contest and would encounter no unfamiliar race, name, or ballot question at the polls.

The Ninth District primary in which Bill Jackson was a candidate was slated for a moderate level of coverage—meaning that the reporter assigned to it needed to monitor the race closely, report on newsworthy candidate appearances (particularly joint appearances), and file appropriate dispatches on news and campaign events.

Why not all-out coverage of the Ninth District primary? First, because there were very close contests for the Democratic nomination for U.S. Senate (in which one of the candidates was a former Charlotte mayor) and for the Republican nomination for governor (again, one a former Charlotte mayor and another a millionaire businessman from Charlotte's suburban Cabarrus County). We directed the largest share of our resources to these high-profile races. Second, because the Democratic primary in the Ninth District, which regularly sends Republicans to Congress, simply wasn't as hotly contested as some others.

The race for the Republican nomination in the politically tight Eighth District, which includes portions of our home Mecklenburg County and all of suburban Cabarrus and Union counties, was close and hotly contested. Two prominent candidates and a third political newcomer were embroiled in a race that captured national attention, with visits from prominent GOP leaders. The newcomer won, though he eventually lost a close race to incumbent Democrat Bill Hefner. That wasn't the case in the traditionally Republican Ninth District, where Jackson gathered 29 percent of the vote to Democratic nominee Michel Daisley's 49 percent in a three-way race. (Republican incumbent Sue Myrick beat Daisley in the general election by a 2:1 margin.)

The campaign for the Ninth District's Democratic nomination was low-key. Daisley spoke to Democratic groups here and there. Jackson did a handful of radio interviews and flooded the fax machines. The third candidate did make news—for owing $40,000 in child support to his ex-wife and three children. Jackson raised $3,442 and spent $3,251 on his campaign, according to Federal Election Commission [FEC] records, which list five contributions. Only one major-party candidate seeking a North Carolina seat in Congress in 1996 raised and spent less, FEC records indicate. Of course, all candidates tend to want more coverage, but we have to set limits because our resources have limits.

Assessing the Work

We feel good about our coverage in 1996. It was thorough, focused, and well executed. Was it perfect? No. We missed some stories, did too much on some subjects, not enough on others. We'll do some things differently next time. On the balance, however, our readers seem to feel we gave them useful and unbiased information to help them make decisions.

Michael Kelly from *The New Yorker* was one of the journalists who wrote extensively about "Your Voice, Your Vote" and *The Charlotte Observer*. He scanned volumes of our daily and special coverage. He called the project, and the *Observer's* participation, a "fraud" because of "the notion that a self-selected group of reporters and editors somehow could or should determine the fit subjects for debate in an election." That's a misconception of what we did.

We used a variety of approaches to guide our coverage: what candidates were saying on the trail and in their ads; what we, as journalists, felt we needed to cover; and what people in the Carolinas were telling us. And, yes, we did use polling to help inform us about what's important to our readers. But we're not slaves to polling. As Jennie Buckner, editor of the *Observer* often says: Ignorance about what's important to citizens isn't bliss; it's simply ignorance.

In the end, even Michael Kelly had to admit one thing in his article. The journalism that the *Observer* published on the '96 elections was, he wrote, "notably superior."

Note

1. The survey was commissioned by the Pew Center for Civic Journalism. It was designed and analyzed by Greg Schneiders, a Democratic pollster, and Dan Casey, former director of research for the Republican National Committee. It has a margin of error of ± 4 percentage points.

NO

William E. Jackson, Jr.

Save Democracy From Civic Journalism: North Carolina's Odd Experiment

In early February of 1996, I journeyed to the state capital to file for the U.S. House in the Ninth Congressional District of North Carolina. As the state's largest and richest newspaper in the biggest city, the *Charlotte Observer* dominates the district. Therefore I was puzzled when reporters for the paper in Raleigh and Charlotte indicated no interest in an early interview, despite the fact that the Democratic primary race was the only congressional contest that had shaped up in the heart of the paper's prime circulation area. I soon learned that the *Observer*—a leading evangelist for so-called civic journalism—had already decided that its resources would be directed toward covering the races for governor and the U.S. Senate[1]. House races did not figure in its plans for in-depth election coverage.

In 1996, in both the primary and general elections, the whole state of North Carolina was subjected to public journalism by consortium under the rubic of "Your Voice, Your Vote." The stated purpose was to help voters to understand issues they had identified as "very important" in polls and to know where the candidates stood on their chief concerns. In the words of *Charlotte Observer* editor Jennie Buckner—less space would be devoted to the day-to-day activities of the candidates "that appear to be designed more to manipulate voters than to enlighten them." She added, "We'll also report about matters candidates think are important regardless of whether they surface in our polls and discussions with voters. It certainly would be wrong to ignore the messages of candidates with leadership vision that rises above conventional wisdom."[2]

Led by Knight-Ridder's *Observer* and the McClatchy Newspapers' *News & Observer* recently purchased from the Daniels family, a partnership was formed to do what was "best for the voters of North Carolina." Six of the major metropolitan dailies—stretching from the mountains to the sea—five TV stations, three public radio stations, and UNC-PBS television statewide came to a consensus on what the most important issues were for citizens.

The top four issues selected by consortium editors and reporters were crime and drugs, taxes and spending, health care, and education. "Families and values" actually ranked above "taxes and spending" in consortium polling.

From William E. Jackson, Jr., "Save Democracy From Civic Journalism: North Carolina's Odd Experiment," *Harvard International Journal of Press/Politics*, vol. 2, no. 3 (Summer 1997). Copyright © 1997 by The President and Fellows of Harvard College. Reprinted by permission of Sage Publications, Inc.

However, according to the Charlotte paper's explanation, the journalists involved "felt strongly that we could not produce a sound project without dealing in depth with the most basic relationship government has with people —collecting and spending money" (" 'Your Voice, Your Vote' . . ." 1996). Whew!

One way or the other, the cartel was determined to force candidates for governor and the U.S. Senate to address these issues. (It failed in the case of incumbent Senator Jesse Helms.) The coordination to steer the debate was so tight that the papers ran almost identical articles (larded with quotes from citizens who participated in the surveys) by the same reporters, with the same headlines, Sunday after Sunday from mid-September to mid-October—even though each partner was free to edit as it saw fit. There was a consortium commitment to publish each "package" on a given date. The *Observer* also offered "Families and Values" as an optional package to the other partners. Formulaic journalism took on a new meaning for daily newspapers.

The Charlotte paper's Weltanschauung shaped the whole undertaking. The *Observer* explained its approach in " 'Your Voice, Your Vote' and *The Charlotte Observer*," a defensive tract issued in October after the project came under heavy fire:[3]

> Our philosophy began to emerge in 1992 when we concluded that much of what we had been doing was not connecting with readers and citizens. . . . Most people involved with political campaigns—candidates, strategists, and often journalists—view those campaigns as a horse race with the finish line being election day. Much "traditional coverage" in papers today focuses on the strategy of getting a particular candidate across that finish line. We at *The Observer* . . . believe coverage of issues and ideas, as well as strategy, is crucial to strong and meaningful political journalism. (" *'Your Voice, Your Vote'* . . .")

One can almost hear the sound of organ music from the Pew Foundation's Center for Civic Journalism accompanying this somewhat trite revelation! The *News & Observer*, the state's premier paper for political reporting, converted to the Zeitgeist after the 1994 election. However, the Raleigh paper could claim with greater credibility than the Charlotte paper that its 1996 participation in "Your Voice, Your Vote" was a supplement to—not a substitute for—traditional coverage. After the election, according to its assistant managing editor for special projects: "We're reviewing our experiences with the media partnership, both from our perspectives and from readers."[4]

Polls Reveal the Obvious

An introductory article on September 15 read, "North Carolinians agree on one thing this election year. It's not just 'the economy stupid.' They also care strongly about education, crime, health care, families and taxes" according to a new poll. The "Your Voice, Your Vote" partnership would use the July poll for a series of reports on where top statewide candidates stood on the issues.[5]

The poll of one thousand state residents in mid-July built on a similar survey of one thousand in January—both conducted by Knight Publishing's KPC Research subsidiary in Charlotte.[6] The polls showed "general agreement . . . on which problems are important," regardless of party affiliation. Note that the prioritized concerns from the poll conducted before the party conventions were not written about until September and October. Argued the *Observer*, a "well-crafted issues poll has a long and stable shelf life. These are (four) core issues that rank high through years of polling" ("'Your Voice, Your Vote'..." 1996).

Indeed. Does it take a big poll to know that general concerns like crime and education and health and taxes are always out there, and the views of candidates on them are thought to be "very important" by the public? Of course, there was a broad consensus. Imagine a serious candidate for governor or senator who did not address these issues! As Jennie Buckner admitted in the *Washington Post*, "The results were not surprising."[7]

In general, there was a strong bias against coverage of the ebb and flow— or the dynamics—of the chosen campaigns. There was not a good balance between the space allotted to the well-researched issue packages and to reporting on campaign developments—labeled as the "horse race." "Enterprise" political journalism was no match for "explanatory" journalism. The *Observer* estimated that the "Your Voice, Your Vote" project accounted for "no more than 20–30% of our overall election coverage." Yet, in the same defensive brief, the paper claimed that "this type of [public] journalism is costly, consuming far more manpower and news hole than campaign trail coverage" ("'Your Voice, Your Vote'..." 1996).[8]

Justifications

Noble motives for civic journalism were offered by principals in the cartel. State editor Steve Riley of the *News & Observer* told the *New York Times*, "I don't want it to seem like ['Your Voice, Your Vote'] is a power play on the part of the media. It's a power play on behalf of the voters." Yet he also noted that the united media consortium gave each news organization more resources and more leverage. Without the alliance, some candidates could say, "the heck with it, it is just the *News & Observer*."[9] Still the Charlotte paper claimed, "we're not trying to force or limit the political debate in any way" ("'Your Voice, Your Vote'..." 1996).

Ed Williams, editorial paper editor of the *Charlotte Observer*, offered this justification: It is "journalism that helps public life go well," parroting public journalism's guru, New York University professor Jay Rosen, who was echoing Harvard philosopher Michael Sandel. Rosen, whose research on journalism and public life is generously funded by the Knight Foundation, visited the Charlotte daily on a mission "to help journalists realize there is more to our craft—more public benefit, more satisfaction—than we imagine."[10] According to Rosen, "public journalists want public life to work. In order to make it work they are willing to declare an end to their neutrality on certain questions." Does the end to neutrality mean an end to objectivity (Hoyt 1995)?

Bill Kovach, director of the Nieman Foundation for Journalism at Harvard, has commented, "An awful lot of [public journalism] is pseudo journalism. If there's a kind of 'celebratory tinge' to your journalism, it's easy to overlook things that don't fit into your mold."[11] A case of the tinge: Based on skimpy results from a postelection survey funded by the Pew Center for Civic Journalism, the Charlotte paper editorialized, "The big-city political journalists who knew about the project disliked it; the voters who knew about it liked it. A message there, perhaps?"[12]

There is a fine line to be walked. It is in the newspaper's interest to portray its efforts as helpful, perhaps even when they are not. "With a twist of semantic dials, public journalism can become public posturing" (Hoyt 1995). Is it just the latest substitute for a healthy newsroom budget and sold journalistic instincts? Is civic journalism essentially a rationalization—a cover of respectability—for newspapers to pursue bigger financial returns?[13]

The rhetoric of public journalism makes an excellent "cover" for pandering. "Reader interaction can easily become a slavish effort to sell ourselves to our 'customers' "—warned a 1995 memorandum sent by reporters to the editors of the *Minneapolis Star Tribune* (Hoyt 1995). There is a multi-faceted corporation to keep afloat. Therefore, profits and "community" purpose are melded. What is good for Charlotte is good for the *Observer*, and vice versa? Conflicts of interest, abuses of power, corruption—to report on these is to alienate some powers in the community.

The Question of Power

Skepticism is in order about this heralded effort to reduce cynicism in the body politic. There *is* the question of power and influence. When local publishers and editors buy into public journalism—in the name of "the people"[14]—an uneasy suspicion arises that they are pursuing their own version of "buckraking" as part and parcel of a "customer-friendly" approach that downplays tough reporting on the established order. To quote editor Williams,

> How many significant problems in Charlotte [Rosen asked] do you think are the result of corruption or wrongdoing? My answer: very few. Problems in public life... result mostly from the disparity of citizen involvement and influence. Some people are heard, some aren't.... Promoters of shopping centers, stadiums and highways are [heard]—and not because of corruption.[15]

This is an approach the local power structure is bound to appreciate, as sanitized "soft" coverage may result—a point of criticism that has been aimed at Knight-Ridder's *Wichita Eagle* in recent years (Hoyt 1995). The perceived need to "connect" with readers becomes entwined with the fear of offending them. The ethic evolves into one of shying away from an adversarial role and embracing a kind of journalism that advocates "solutions," as practices in the *Observer's* 1994–1995 "Taking Back Our Neighborhoods" series, the most celebrated experiment in public journalism—funded by the Pew Foundation's Center for Civic Journalism.[16]

No Skunks Covering the Senate Race

There needs to be a skunk at the garden party in reporting on—not necessarily "perfuming" or nurturing—public life. If not the "extinct stained wretches" who write for newspapers, then who?[17]

The problem is illustrated by one story that broke during the Senate campaign between Republican incumbent Jesse Helms and Harvey Gantt, his Democratic challenger. The *Washington Post* reported on October 26 that a foundation holding Helms's papers had received solicited donations in the hundreds of thousands of dollars from the governments of Kuwait and Taiwan.[18] Even though the issue of foreign contributions to campaigns was national news at the time, both the *Observer* and the *News & Observer* ran the *Post* story on their inside pages and did no follow-up investigation using their own reporters. It was treated as a tit-for-tat matter. Local television effectively ignored the story. The Helms Center would not release its list of contributors for the last two years; and the Senator stated that he knew nothing about the center's donors and had no role in the foundation.[19]

A newspaper exposé could have become an important new factor in the flow of the tight campaign. Had other foreign governments been solicited and contributions made to the Senate Foreign Relations Committee chairman's "education foundation"? What if the statewide consortium had done a late poll on the issue of foreign contributions designed to buy influence in the U.S. Congress? To pursue the story with investigative reporters would have created conflict with the incumbent and alienated readers, not to mention broadcasters crossing viewers. It was not far-fetched for University of North Carolina Professor Thad Beyle to suggest that "some reporters have been intimidated by Jesse Helms, and it is a strategy that seems to be working."[20]

Rick Thames—the "public editor" at the *Observer* and "partnership coordinator"—revealed that the decision not to follow up immediately on foreign contributions was based on an "editorial decision" unrelated to public journalism.[21] Better to let the despised national media deal with the matter than to dig around in the *Observer's* own backyard? This left it to Gantt to buy last-minute television advertising time to be heard on the issue. Helms deflected Gantt's exaggerated populist charge—"Now we learn Helms got millions in secret donations from foreign governments and multinational corporations" —with a typical injection of homophobia and hyperbole into his own ads: Gantt had "raised millions from gay activists from New York to San Francisco."[22]

To follow the public's lead in determining which broad issues are the most important may lead to coverage that plays down other issues that have yet to crystallize or surface. However, several issues given a lower profile by the consortium were already firmly entrenched in public consciousness. What about jobs and the condition of the national economy in 1996? The *Observer* reported in mid-September that "North Carolinians still worry about the economy" and that more than six in ten in the July poll thought it "very important" to know where the candidates stood on issues affecting their financial security. This issue, and that of the environment, did not get top billing in the consortium's Sunday feature presentations.[23]

Quite different and significant issues can and do arise in senatorial as distinguished from gubernatorial campaigns—donations from foreign governments being a case in point—and not necessarily the same "big four" issues of crime and drugs, taxes and spending, health care, and education. Yet Gantt and Helms and the two candidates for governor were squeezed like toothpaste into the tubes of mind-numbing generic question matrixes, along with the two presidential candidates—who were allowed to submit their answers in writing. All six were asked, "What should government do to keep children from getting into trouble?" in the "Violent Crime" grid. They were asked, "What role, if any, should government institutions play in promoting positive values?" as part of the "Families and Values" grid.

Race and Health

What about race, in a year when Jesse Helms sought reelection against a black opponent and raised—over a period of weeks—the issue in numerous negative television ads? He linked Harvey Gantt to support for elimination of the death penalty and to the use of his minority status to gain preferential treatment in the award of a television station license. Incidentally, six out of ten survey respondents had said it was "very important for them to understand what a candidate would do to improve race relations." Seven in ten were "very supportive of ensuring that minorities have equal job opportunities."[24]

It defies rational explanation as to how the *Observer*, three days before the election, could run a headline entitled "Race Emerges as Issue Late in Senate Battle."[25] Just because race was not on the consortium's chosen list did not mean it was relatively unimportant out on the hustings. The North Carolina Republican party mailed out hundreds of thousands of fliers with pictures of Gantt and selected Democratic members of the House. One version featured a picture of Gantt and Representative Mel Watt of Charlotte, both African-Americans, with the headline, "Mel's bad enough. Do you want Harvey, too?" On the fliers, the pictures of Gantt were darker than in most photos.[26]

Anybody who knew anything about Helms's past four Senate campaigns, especially the previous campaign against Gantt in 1990, would know that race was bound to be a major issue from the beginning and would not just "surface with the flow of the campaign" (" 'Your Voice, Your Vote' ..." 1996). However, reporters and editors in the consortium seemed to have convinced themselves early on that there was a "new Jesse" in 1996, despite his noncooperation, and that there was a softer, more moderate tone to his campaign.[27] There was an unmistakable bias against covering the dark side of the campaign.

The media also decided not to focus on the seventy-five-year-old incumbent's health—in sharp contrast with the damaging attention given to Terry Sanford's health lapses in the very close 1992 Senate contest. Senator Helms had had a quadruple heart bypass and had suffered from prostate cancer and a debilitating bone disease in recent years. He frequently moved about on the arms of aides. In some respects, he displayed less robustness in public than Strom Thurmond, the ninety-four-year-old senator from South Carolina.[28] During the short period in which Jesse campaigned in the state before the November election, his press secretary sometimes would not inform the major media as to where he was.

One late-October event in particular was conspicuously underplayed. At a Republican fund-raiser in Raleigh featuring former President George Bush—the only campaign appearance by Helms in his home town—the senator spoke briefly and disappeared from the stage. Even though it was announced he would return, he never came back. Was he ill? This was an important unanswered question, but there was no mention of it in either the Raleigh or Charlotte newspapers the next day.[29]

Consequences

Were there possible political consequences—one campaign hurt, the other helped—from the consortium's decision to emphasize some issues over others? Michael Kelly has criticized the cartel, in its emphasis on four "very important" concerns, for lowering the profile of the "Families and Values" cluster of issues —"It was pretty much a coin toss," Kelly was told by the *Observer's* "public editor"—when the senator might have been more exposed for his extreme stands on them among centrist voters (Kelly 1996).[30] Of course, Gantt could have been more exposed politically as well, depending on the facets highlighted. Nevertheless, the incumbent was able to finesse a softening of his image by the brief suggestion that he could now appreciate the fact that "people are sincere on both sides" of the abortion issue.[31]

It is quite possible that self-described moderates and the hundreds of thousands of potential voters who had moved into the state since 1990—Gantt won a majority of these "swing voters" who went to the polls—would have turned out in heavier numbers for Gantt if they had been more sensitized to the senator's views on the "hot button" issues that the media partners were determined to play down.[32] The "Christian right" turned out a much higher rate—providing about 40 percent of Helms's total. More than half of those who voted for Helms said they had reservations about voting for him, according to an exit poll.[33]

There were more fundamental, systemic consequences of civic journalism's approach as represented by the North Carolina cartel. A kind of statewide "group-think" was encouraged when newspapers from Asheville to Wilmington tried to control the debate over public policy. What is the role of the candidate with ideas or solutions that speak to concerns not anticipated in the consortium survey? It is extremely audacious for the media to—in a real sense—supplant the role of the candidate, editor Buckner's pledge to report on "matters candidates think are important regardless of polls" notwithstanding. Putting up a large filter dam between candidates and voters is troublesome. How would the public know if the newspaper was ignoring "messages of candidates with leadership vision that rises above conventional wisdom"?[34]

Rob Christensen, the chief political reporter of the *News & Observer*, admitted to the *New York Times* in September, "We're not writing about the issues that [the candidates] want to talk about."[35] This is to play "Election God" (Kelly

1996). The concept of the public interest becomes even more of a bobbing cork in a sea of confusion....

Connecting With the Voters?

There is something perversely circular about the North Carolina media's "bottom-up" approach to political campaigns. The will of the press is the will of the people, and the will of the people is the will of the press. If readers cannot fill the need for reasonably thorough and objective coverage—an anchor that only regional newspapers can provide for the average voter—then of what value are their opinions? They normally do not read the *New York Times* or the *Wall Street Journal* or watch *Lehrer* on PBS. The surveys become snapshots of predominantly uninformed opinion, eliciting time-gap responses on a few broad issues. This does not facilitate a promising dialogue between voters and candidates.

Whatever the "reconnect" benefits between the media and the public, voter turnout reached a modern low in the spring primary election—about 20 percent of age-eligible citizens—despite hotly contested races for the Democratic Senate nomination and the Republican gubernatorial nomination. Turnout in November was the lowest for a presidential election in North Carolina since at least 1972. This, after more than five months—three in the spring, two in the fall—of being deluged with "Your Voice, Your Vote" by the state's major dailies.

One wonders how voters reacted to being informed so often and at such length as to what their chief concerns were. Perhaps greater campaign excitement would have been generated by a relatively more traditional approach. A survey commissioned by the Pew Center found that "Your Voice, Your Vote" reached about 25 percent of voters and helped inform many of them.[36] However, there is nothing much to compare the numbers to; they are out there in a vacuum. Harrison Hickman, a political consultant who helped reelect Governor Jim Hunt, maintained that the project did not influence the public one way or the other. In thirty focus groups during the fall campaign, Hickman reports that "maybe two people even mentioned having read any of the stuff or exhibited any sense of having read it. And the two people who did, both said the same thing: it was confusing" (Effron 1997).

Conclusion

Market research is the basis for advertising. The consortium polling operation —conducted by KPC Research—was meant to find out on which issues citizens most wanted to know the candidates' stands, so that the campaign coverage could then focus on the chosen four or five issues and force the politicians to address them. In this way, the imperatives of "Your Voice, Your Vote" restricted coverage and encouraged candidates to cope by telling the voters what they wanted to hear. There was little incentive to talk to them about things they did not seem to care about as much (and therefore the press did not care about as much).

The most serious flaw in this new approach to covering campaigns is that it claims to help citizens "connect" with candidates and the political system through market-research-type surveys. The problem is not one of consumer marketing in a plebiscitary democracy—that is, identifying the concern (or design or flavor) voters care most about, then matching that concern with the right candidates. Public journalism is a misguided effort to cast a kind of bogus rationality and efficiency over campaign coverage. Citizen-oriented campaign coverage is only as good as the vitality of the information available to the voters —in print—as they proceed to choose their representatives.

If some journalists are so unhappy or cynical in their own views of government and politics, let them quit. Or they can resort to "just good journalism" that collects, delivers, and analyzes information, and makes news judgments about priorities—but does not attempt to promote worthy policies and well-motivated politicians in their news coverage. As Walter Lippmann once believed, in 1920, the job of the press is to provide "trustworthy news, unadulterated data, fair reporting, disinterested fact" so that the public can form intelligent decisions. (Steel 1980:172). The "proposition that the media are complicit in the public's disenchantment with politics and its cynicism about democratic government" (Hume 1996, quoting E. J. Dionne) should not be allowed to disembowel the fourth estate. If the uniqueness of the product is destroyed, the investment *will* be destroyed (Jones 1996). If newspapers abandon their traditional identity, they *will* disappear (Cf. Fallows 1996).[37]

The "Your Voice, Your Vote" exercise was not an aberration. The new journalism claims to be the agent for the reader-voter. *Who will be the agent to protect democracy from civic journalism?*

Notes

1. In November 1996, Democratic Gov. Jim Hunt won his fourth term (1977–85, 1993–) by 56 to 43 percent and Republican Sen. Jesse Helms won his fifth term (1973–) by 53 to 46 percent.

2. Jennie Buckner, letter to the author, Jan. 19, 1996.

3. James Bennet, "North Carolina Media Try to Lead Politics to Issues," *New York Times*, Sept. 24, 1996; Jennie Buckner, "*Charlotte Observer* did Candidate No Injustice," letter to the editor, *New York Times*, Oct. 15, 1996; William E. Jackson, Jr., "The Press Cops Out," op-ed, *New York Times*, Oct. 7, 1996; and Jonathan Yardley, "Let Politics Be Politics," column, *Washington Post*, Sept. 30, 1996.

4. Anders Gyllenhaal, "Look for New Approaches in *N & O* Election Coverage," *News & Observer*, Jan. 7, 1996; Melanie Sill, "The *N & O* Responds," *The Independent Weekly* 14(48):7.

5. Jim Morrill and Lorraine Ahern, "Economy Not Only Issue That Stirs N.C. Voters," *Charlotte Observer*, Sept. 15, 1996.

6. Knight Publishing publishes the *Charlotte Observer*, KPC Research is a local market research firm.

7. Buckner, "Assault on 'Public Journalism,'" op-ed, *Washington Post*, Oct. 31, 1996. In this version of her response to columnist Jonathan Yardley's critique of public journalism, she left out a complaint that she had written in her own newspaper: Critics of public journalism in "the American journalism establishment" were practicing the "ethic of the Grand Inquisition." Incidentally, after a "values clash"

with her subordinate editors, Buckner restored objectionable paragraphs she had cut from Yardley's column when it was originally reprinted in the *Observer* (Buckner, "Public Journalism: Good or Bad News," op-ed. *Charlotte Observer*, October 19, 1996; Buckner, " 'Without Fear or Favor' to Any Institution or Individual," op-ed., *Charlotte Observer*, October 26, 1996). Associate Editor Jack Betts would appear to be one of the dissenters. He later saluted "a generation of journalists who believed it was important to put in the newspaper what they thought people needed to know—not what the pollsters and marketing staff believed people wanted to read about. There are fewer and fewer places where you can practice that kind of journalism anymore." (Betts, "N.C. Press Loses Two Old Pros," *Charlotte Observer*, March 16, 1997.) As a protégé of James K. Batten—a reporter who became a corporate chief committed to forging stronger bonds between newspapers and their communities—Buckner felt that Yardley had smeared the deceased chairman and CEO of Knight-Ridder. He had been a patron of public journalism (Batten 1989; Batten 1990; Villano 1996). (Batten was a college classmate and friend of the author.)

8. No fewer than six issue "packages" plus one poll report were published by the consortium partners during the spring primary season, compared to four packages and one poll in the fall. Each one took up more than two pages—including two separate thirty-five to forty-inch stories contrasting the views of the major candidates for governor and senator on the given issue, accompanied by a full-page grid outlining the positions of the major party candidates on questions central to the issue. The grid included vignettes of people who were affected by the issue to give "context" to the questions—not to mention "pull-out" boxes discussing "options" on a particular issue, and graphics explaining the background on the issue. Some "enhancements" to supplement normal campaign coverage! Outside of the partnership, the *Observer* produced its own issue packages on foreign policy, the deficit, corporate welfare, and other issues (" 'Your Voice, Your Vote' . . .").

9. Bennet, "North Carolina Media."

10. Ed Williams, "Journalism and Public Life," column, *Charlotte Observer*, Sept. 22, 1996. Was morale so low that *Observer* editors and reporters needed a pep talk in the midst of "Your Voice, Your Vote" coverage of the fall election campaign? Howard Kurtz reported in 1995 that "morale is particularly low at two of the industry's most prominent chains": Knight-Ridder and Times Mirror ("The Bad News Starts at Work in Nation's Newsrooms," *Washington Post*, Oct. 30, 1995).

11. James Bennet, "PBS Breaks Further Ground with Debate of Congressional Leaders," *New York Times*, Sept. 27, 1996.

12. " 'Your Voice, Your Vote': Voters Liked It, Press Didn't," editorial, *Charlotte Observer*, Dec. 10, 1996.

13. Gene Miller, a veteran of the *Miami Herald*, told one critic that "Knight-Ridder's terribly schizophrenic—they speak of quality and they talk of profits." Said Jeff Gottlieb, a reporter for the *San Jose Mercury News:* "We aren't practicing journalism. We are practicing capitalism" (Thomas Rosenstiel, "Hi-tech Media: Blessing and Curse," *Charlotte Observer*, Oct. 2, 1994 [reprinted from the *Los Angeles Times*]). "Bottom-line values degrade journalistic values" (Oberdorfer 1996). Gene Roberts, now managing editor of the *New York Times*, objected to Knight-Ridder squeezing his editorial budget at the *Philadelphia Inquirer:* "If I'd wanted to be an accountant, I'd have been one" (Todd Gitlin, *"NY Times* Executive Sounds Alarm," *Creative Loafing* 10(43):14 [reprinted from the *New York Observer*]).

14. In 1997, the *Charlotte Observer* is reporting on state government, using the logos of "The People's Business" and "Citizens' Agenda"—complete with a state flag.

15. Williams, "Journalism and Public Life."

16. Pew's money continued to flow into the *Observer* newsroom in 1996, with $50,000 going toward projects to integrate the civic journalism approach into day-to-day coverage. Buckner asserted in a rebuttal to a *Wall Street Journal* story, "There is no evidence that Pew funding has undermined any newspaper's independence. She was joined in her benign assessment by Ellen Hume of PBS's "Democracy Project." Since 1994, Pew has funded projects that benefit more than thirty American newspapers from Norfolk to Miami to San Jose. (Bruce Knecht, "Why a Big Foundation Gives Newspapers Cash to Change Their Ways," *Wall Street Journal*, 17 October 1996; Jennie Buckner, "Free from Ideological Bias," letter to the editor, *Wall Street Journal*, Nov. 8, 1996.)

17. Richard Harwood, "Extinct Stained Wretches," *Washington Post*, Nov. 2, 1995.

18. The "Jesse Helms Center" is attached to Wingate University. Several prominent North Carolinians sit on the board, along with Helms' wife, daughter, and the Foreign Relations Committee's chief of staff, Adm. "Bud" Nance.

19. Ruth Marcus, "Donations to Helms Center Aren't Covered by Limits," *Charlotte Observer*, Oct. 26, 1996, p. 6. This was a strange headline for the *Washington Post* story. The *News & Observers's* headline read: "Foreign Nations Gave Cash to Helms Center," Oct. 26, 1996, p. 4. Also, see Curtis Wilkie, " 'Public Journalism' Plays Out in N.C.," *Boston Globe*, Oct. 30, 1996.

20. James Perry, "GOP's Helms Follows Unusual Tactic: Low Visibility," *Wall Street Journal*, Oct. 29, 1996.

21. Wilkie, " 'Public Journalism' Plays Out in N.C."

22. Jim Morrill, "The Last Days," *Charlotte Observer*, Nov. 2, 1996; and Rob Christensen and James Rosen, "Helms, Gantt Slug and Plug," *News & Observer*, Nov. 3, 1996.

23. Asked to prioritize issues on a scale of 1 to 10, 40 percent of survey respondents gave "preserving lakes, rivers and the coastline" a 9 or 10. The *Observer* must have thought environmental issues were more important in 1992. Editor Rich Opel threatened to run blank spaces under Senator Terry Sanford's name, indicating a refusal to answer the questions, unless he produced his views on the environment in the spring primary season. Sanford had preferred to discuss the issue opposite his Republican challenger (Lauch Faircloth) later in the fall election campaign—when he would have a real opponent. Of course, Sanford was voting on environmental matters in the Senate (Fallows 1996:256).

  In the premier "Your Voice, Your Vote" report outlining the findings of the July poll, financial security and the environment were grouped with race relations and families and values as "other issues." The first and the last of these four had received the "package" treatment leading up to the May primary election. There was little rhyme or reason to the consortium reporters' explanations of the method used in choosing and ranking the issues. Grids and graphs can cloak sloppy polling analysis. (Morrill and Ahern, "Economy Not Only Issue.")

24. Morrill and Ahearn.

25. Jim Morrill, "Race Emerges as Issue Late in Senate Battle," *Charlotte Observer*, Nov. 2, 1996.

26. Exit polls of November 5 showed that Helms received nearly two out of three votes cast by whites, whereas substantially less than 10 percent of black voters supported him. African-Americans constitute 19 percent of registered voters in North Carolina.

27. John Monk, "Campaign's Theme: 'Helms the Statesman,' " *Charlotte Observer*, July 28, 1996; Jim Morrill, " '96 Gantt, Helms Race Takes on Softer Tone," *Charlotte Observer*, Sept. 17, 1996; and Morrill, "Helms Stance [on Social Security] a Switch?" *Charlotte Observer*, Sept. 10, 1996.

28. John Monk and Henry Eichel, "Old South Senators Prosper in the New," *Charlotte Observer*, Nov. 10, 1996.

29. Bob Geary, "Your Voice, Your Vote, Our Loss," *Independent Weekly*, Nov. 13, 1996; and Rob Christensen and Joe Dew, "Big Political Guns Take Aim at N.C.," *News & Observer*, Nov. 1, 1996.

30. Kelly argued that high-minded civic journalism "blew" the North Carolina Senate contest by "fudging the most clear-cut race in the country." The "Your Voice, Your Vote" approach was exposed as a "fraud" by "the collision between the theory of civic journalism and Jesse Helms."

31. Associated Press, "Helms Shifts on Abortion," *Charlotte Observer*, Aug. 6, 1996.

32. Buckner, "Public Journalism: Good or Bad News."

33. Associated Press, "Half of Those Voting for Helms Had Reservations about Decision," *Charlotte Observer*, Nov. 7, 1996.

34. Buckner, letter to the author.

35. Bennet, "North Carolina Media."

36. Tinker Ready, Media's Election Project Draws Mixed Reaction," *News & Observer*, Dec. 9, 1996.

37. James Fallows spoke in May 1996 at the first "James K. Batten Symposium and Award for Excellence in Civic Journalism"–sponsored by the Pew Charitable Trusts.

References

Batten, James K. 1989. "America's Newspapers: What Are Our Prospects?" Press-Enterprise lecture series, University of California, Riverside, Apr. 3.

Batten, James K. 1990. "Newspapers and Communities: The Vital Link." Forty-first Annual William Allen White Speech, William Allen White School of Journalism, University of Kansas, Feb. 8.

Effron, Seth. 1997. "Civic Journalism: The North Carolina Experiment." *Columbia Journalism Review* 35(5):12–14.

Fallows, James. 1996. *Breaking the News: How the Media Undermines American Democracy.* New York: Pantheon.

Hoyt, Mike. 1995. "Are You Now, Or Will You Ever Be, A Civic Journalist?" *Columbia Journalism Review* 34(3):27–33.

Hoyt, Mike. 1996. "Can James Fallows Practice What He Preaches?" *Columbia Journalism Review* 35(4):27–30.

Hume, Ellen. 1996. "Why Americans Hate the Press." *Columbia Journalism Review* 34(6):49–52.

Jones, Tim. 1996. "The Day of the Analysts: Wall Street and the Future of Newspapers," *Columbia Journalism Review* 35(4):42–44.

Kelly, Michael. 1996. "Media Culpa." *New Yorker*, Nov. 4:45–49.

Oberdorfer, Don. 1996. "A Journalist to His Profession: 'I Am Deeply Worried.' " *Press/Politics* 1(4):147–51.

Steel, Ronald. 1980. *Walter Lippmann and the American Century.* Boston: Little Brown.

Villano, David. 1996. "Has Knight-Ridder's Flagship Gone Adrift? Trouble at the *Miami Herald*" *Columbia Journalism Review* 34(5):29–33.

" 'Your Voice, Your Vote' and The *Charlotte Observer*." 1996. Monograph. Charlotte: Knight Publishing Co.

POSTSCRIPT

Is Civic Journalism Good Journalism?

Neither Clark nor Jackson comments on another reason why civic journalism has been widely embraced: newspapers are suffering a significant loss of readership and television news is overwhelmed with the local and national competition for viewers. Projects that link the interests and needs of the public with the stories covered may attract readers or viewers. In a tight market, all news organizations are looking to brand themselves—to be seen as providing stories that display their involvement and mesh with local interests is a "brand" to be desired. Look at your own local news shows. How do they promote themselves within the market? There are very real business issues that are at work in the acceptance of this reform movement.

Nonetheless, most of the pro and con arguments have to do with the realization of the ideal and the threats that it might impose on traditional journalistic judgment. Seth Effron, in the *Columbia Journalism Review* (February 1997), notes that the major national papers weighed in and were not happy. By relying on polls journalists were accused of pandering to the public and abdicating their professional judgment. Critics also charged that the journalists ignored equally important public issues and undermined the candidates' own attempts to assert a platform for debate.

In *Journalism Studies* (vol. 1, no. 4, 2000), Steve Davis comments on the problems working journalists face as they try to integrate the tenets of civic journalism into the practices of the newsroom. Too often, he asserts, well-intentioned editors have rushed to implement projects that are not well thought out, nor well planned. Journalists have concerns that they are being asked to give up their news judgments to the vagaries of public opinion. And some simply resist change that they do not understand and that they feel is being forced upon them.

The Pew Center for Civic Journalism is a foundation that has taken on civic journalism as a project. Check http://www.pewcenter.org for information on their awards for civic journalism, publications in the area, and other useful information. There are many other organizations that hold discussions on the actions of the press. Many provide useful Internet sites for analysis and discussion of the performance of the press. These include the Joan Shorenstein Center for Press, Politics and Public Policy at http://www.ksg.harvard.edu/presspol/index.htm, the Project for Excellence in Journalism at http://www.journalism.org, and the Committee to Protect Journalists at http://www.cpj.org.

ISSUE 16

Have the News Media Improved Since 9/11?

YES: Ken Auletta, from "Battle Stations," *The New Yorker* (December 10, 2001)

NO: Michael Parks, from "Foreign News: What's Next?" *Columbia Journalism Review* (January/February 2002)

ISSUE SUMMARY

YES: Media critic Ken Auletta discusses how the events of September 11, 2001, refocused news journalism toward foreign news and an explanation of world events. He discusses the industry's decisions about news, and the motivation of journalists who want to cover issues in greater depth.

NO: Michael Parks, director of the School of Journalism at the University of Southern California, warns that as the terrorist events recede in our memories, print and broadcast journalists will return to the same tactics they used prior to September 11th. These include less of an interest in foreign news, primarily because of the financial costs borne by the media industries.

W hen the shocking events of September 11, 2001, were covered by the media, we witnessed the most heavily documented tragedy in history. Along with live coverage of stationery cameras in New York, the cameras of filmmakers in the area, and amateur videographers and photographers, when the human tragedy of the collapse of the World Trade Towers and the attack on the Pentagon occurred, broadcast and print media chronicled the on-going events for the world.

Once again, television and radio functioned as monitors of our environment. Many people watched and listened in groups, hoping to find some answers or some assurance that the attacks had stopped. The event marked another day in our lives in which we will all remember what we were doing when we heard the news.

As Americans struggled to make sense of these events, how much they did not know about other cultures became a common theme. Suddenly, people began to openly discuss the way in which news media had systematically cut news from foreign locations and about other cultures. The ethnocentrism of Americans became a topic for general discussion.

Subsequent discussions arose about the quality of news and the role of America in the world. One important question many Americans asked was, Why do people in other countries hate us? Through debates on American foreign policy, general questions about religions they knew little about, and the growing importance of geographic areas about which many Americans had no knowledge, Americans were humbled by the realization of how little they knew or understood.

The press has often functioned as a monitor of the surveillance of our environment. Suddenly, many people were questioning what had happened to that press function. Ken Auletta and Michael Parks discuss the realities of how much foreign news we actually had available to us and why the amount and quality had diminished over the years.

As you read the following selections, keep in mind that the topic of news—what it does, and how it functions in our lives—has been a major topic of debate for some time and promises to remain a very important topic for the future.

Ken Auletta

 **YES**

Battle Stations

Like so much else, television news changed on the morning of September 11th. Six weeks later, as Aaron Brown, CNN's new anchorman, shifted from a Pentagon briefing to the ruins of the World Trade Center and then to a dissection of the latest anthrax scare, a familiar figure appeared in a box in the right half of the screen: O.J. Simpson on the witness stand. He was testifying in a Florida court, accused of road rage. Brown peered earnestly into the camera and said of the latest Simpson travail, "It is inconceivable to me that seven weeks ago, or six weeks ago, this would not have been carried live." It wasn't now, he said, because "it doesn't matter a whole lot. And here's why it doesn't." The screen filled with rescue workers pulling a body from the rubble of the World Trade towers.

Before September 11th, the evening news, to say nothing of the morning programs and the magazine shows, paid scant attention to foreign news. Instead, the networks filled the air with "weather events," Viagra breakthroughs, reports on various ailments, the murder of Jon Benet Ramsey, the trials of O.J., the death of Princess Diana, the sagas of Monica and Chandra. The networks delivered the headlines of the day, and the dismissive characterization once applied to local television news—"If it bleeds, it leads"—increasingly applied to network news as well. Stories that once might have been noted in passing, if at all, on the half-hour nightly newscasts were now reported endlessly on the nine-o'clock and ten-o'clock magazine shows, which long ago displaced documentaries.

After September 11th, journalists who had grown accustomed to feeling slightly embarrassed by what they did for a living began to look at their jobs with a renewed sense of pride. Even their bosses, who had slashed budgets and trivialized the news in the name of higher ratings and sound business practice, seemed like earnest preachers spreading the gospel of serious journalism. "Over the past ten weeks, we've been reminded why we do what we do," Mel Karmazin, who is the president and C.O.O. of Viacom, the parent company of CBS, said [recently]. Karmazin was speaking at a lunch given in his honor by the Center for Communication, at the Plaza Hotel. He has a fearsome reputation, based in no small part on the demands he makes of his employees. When an executive on the sales force is exhausted and claims that, in the midst of a recession, he cannot sell more ads, Karmazin has been known to reply, "I haven't heard of anyone having a heart attack yet!" But now, at the Plaza, Karmazin aligned himself with a different set of standards. He invoked Edward R. Murrow and quoted Martin Luther King, Jr., on character. Karmazin said, "We want it said of us that when it mattered most we measured up." His peers at NBC, ABC, Fox, and CNN in the audience rose and applauded—both for Karmazin and, it seemed, themselves.

And yet by mid-November news ratings were slipping. Anxiety has spread at the networks as journalists worry that their born-again bosses will start leaning on them to cut costs and produce more fluff. Is the revival of serious news and foreign reporting going to vanish as quickly as it occurred?

⚫

"I'm probably the only person in the world who has watched every network newscast since 1988," Andrew Tyndall says. Tyndall produces the Tyndall Report, an analysis of what appears each night on the three network news broadcasts. In 1988, he calculates, the networks generated about two thousand minutes of international news each. Since then, foreign-news coverage—with a few exceptions, such as the Gulf War, in 1991—has plunged. [In 2000], ABC and CBS offered roughly twelve hundred minutes of international news each, and NBC, the ratings leader, provided about eleven hundred. All three networks have slashed their foreign bureaus and correspondents during the last decade, and before September 11th only about nine per cent of an average nineteen-minute-long broadcast was devoted to foreign news.

Tyndall's methodology can be disputed. For example, when a report on terrorism comes out of Washington, Neal Shapiro, the president of NBC News, argues, "it may count as a Washington story," not as an international story. But neither Shapiro nor his counterparts at ABC, CBS, CNN, Fox, and MSNBC dispute Tyndall's conclusion about the over-all trend. Asked about [summer 2001's] "news"—the Congressman and the Missing Intern—NBC's president, Andrew Lack, said, "Are there things we should have done differently? Yes. I don't want to be defensive about that. That's a fair criticism. But I am pretty proud of our work. For some people, dwelling on child care is a 'soft news' story— frivolous. As opposed to what Arafat said to Madeleine Albright as she passed through the West Bank!" But he added, "Do I wish that we had spent a little more time probing around corners in the Middle East? Absolutely."

CBS, which once referred to itself as "the Tiffany network," and in June of 1981 replaced its prime-time programming with a brilliant, week-long five-part documentary, "The Defense of the United States," was covering Asia with a single correspondent, based in Tokyo, and the rest of the non–North American world with seven correspondents. Fox News, which has been less reliant on original reporting than on opinion, had only four overseas correspondents. "We basically sent hit teams overseas from out of here," Roger Ailes, the chairman of Fox news, said. CNN had about the same number of overseas bureaus—thirty —as the five other networks combined. But when Walter Isaacson, the former managing editor of *Time*, was appointed CNN's chairman and C.E.O., ... to revive a tired-looking network, there was talk about moving more toward the raucous formula of Fox, which was climbing in the ratings. At *Time*, circulation rose as Isaacson shifted the balance of the magazine's covers and content away from traditional politics and foreign news. At CNN, he led discussions about cutting foreign correspondents and changing the emphasis of the network's non-crisis coverage. There were also talks about creating a less serious morning show to try to win younger viewers. Isaacson acknowledges, "I was pushing for more technology and life-style reporting." There was even talk of hiring the popular right-wing radio talk-show host Rush Limbaugh.

With some notable exceptions—the *Times*, for example, maintains twenty-six bureaus overseas; the Washington *Post* has twenty-two—many newspapers and news magazines also have cut back on resources devoted to foreign news. As early as 1992, only twenty-five of the top hundred American newspapers had at least one full-time overseas correspondent, according to "International News & Foreign Correspondents," a book by Stephen Hess, of the Brookings Institution. Before accepting a recent buyout offer, *Time's* Paris bureau chief, Tom Sanction, told me of his frustration with the magazine, which had "reduced international coverage to periodic stories on the Middle East and Russia, unavoidable breaking news like the Kosovo war, and occasional touchy-feely features on AIDS in Africa, et cetera."

Still, the sharpest change was in television. For a man rewarded with, reportedly, a seven-million-dollar salary, Dan Rather, the CBS anchor, betrays deep anger. At his office one afternoon, he told me that he blames warped values for the drop in international-news coverage—"the Hollywoodization and 'frivolization' of the news"—and he blames the networks, including his own: "Entertainment values began to overwhelm news values." Rather recalled that, during debates within CBS over what stories to feature on the nightly news, some executives would say, "Don't do two and a half minutes on the crushing of dissent in China. Do it on how to prevent snoring. 'If snoring is a big problem, here's what you can do about it.' " CBS's producers were driven by the conviction, Rather said, that in order to catch NBC in the ratings they needed to create "a modern broadcast," which meant more "news-you-can-use." Of course, Rather disdained—but nevertheless delivered—the news about snoring.

Of ABC's eight overseas correspondents before September 11th, five were in London and the others were in Jerusalem, Hong Kong, and Nairobi. Earlier . . . , to save money, ABC forced out Sheila MacVicar, a correspondent with extensive experience. (She was then hired by CNN.) Costs sometimes also determine whether a network will cover an important story with its own people. James Wooten, ABC's senior correspondent based in London, recalls that if he wanted to go to Africa he would be told, "We're not going to spend forty thousand dollars on that story." The budget for sending a team to Africa would include airfare for a correspondent, a producer, a cameraman, a sound technician, and perhaps even an editor, if the piece was to be cut and fed to the network from the field; steep charges to cover transporting equipment that was over the plane's weight limit per passenger; the daily cost for a fixer on the ground to translate and arrange transportation; hotels, meals, phones, travel. Networks increasingly came to the conclusion that it was often far less expensive to "cover" a story by buying footage from a service like ITN and having a correspondent in London or Washington supply a voiceover narration. Along the way, such techniques for transmitting basic information became confused, at least in the minds of some executives, with actual reporting.

Even CNN, with its enormous foreign staff, was giving less airtime to its overseas bureaus and was imitating the cheaper-to-produce shout-fests on Fox and MSNBC. During the week of July 16th, Larry King devoted five straight nights to the Chandra Levy case; Greta van Susteren's legal program, "The Point," featured it on four of five nights; and "Crossfire" featured it on three of five nights. Many of the newscasts also led with the names Levy and Condit. In August, I asked Gerald Levin, the C.E.O. of CNN's parent corporation, AOL Time Warner, how he squared the ubiquitous Condit coverage with his frequent declarations of loyalty to high-minded journalism. "The reason I don't have a problem with that—obviously, I'm not the news editor—is that it's a story about character," he replied. "It's not a tabloid story. It's about the character of the people who are running our government." . . .

◦◦◉◦◦

Andrew Lack was the president of NBC News for eight years, and near the end of his stint, he says, he would "complain all the time" to Tom Brokaw and others that his tenure spanned Presidential elections and the war in Kosovo but never a really "big story." His "big" stories were the tabloid narratives: O.J., Diana, Monica, Condit. Like other news executives, he aggressively, and sometimes mindlessly, pursued these stories. That all changed, of course, when the planes crashed into the World Trade Center towers and the Pentagon. The networks suspended their regular programming and substituted news for the first ninety-plus hours of this new war, exceeding the continuous airtime they had devoted to the assassination of John F. Kennedy or to the start of Operation Desert Storm.

The experience of covering the war on terrorism, with its various tributaries at home and abroad, has reignited a professional pride that had been, for numerous journalists, badly diminished or lost. "I can't tell you how many people at the networks used to call us and say they wanted to marry money and meaning," Danny Schechter, of Globalvision, says. Because of the light news and the hyped "crises" they often chased, he says, "they hated themselves."

Few moments have demonstrated the sudden prestige of the serious journalist and the eclipse of the bogus better than an improvised Thanksgiving lunch for forty foreign correspondents in Jalalabad. Geraldo Rivera, a tabloid warrior who jumped from CNBC to Fox, crashed the feast just as the reporters were sitting down to eat a turkey that they'd found in the market, one participant recalled. The guests ignored Rivera, and his crew had to pull up an extra table for their star. . . .

In the wake of September 11th, television news divisions were working with budgets that had been imposed with no such epochal story in mind. Unlike CNN, with its vast international apparatus, the other networks had to rush to send depleted cadres of correspondents first to Pakistan and then to Afghanistan, leaving them short-handed on other stories: the antiterrorism effort in Europe, the fissures in the NATO [North Atlantic Treaty Organization] alliance, Turkey's decision to offer troops to battle fellow-Muslims in Afghanistan. "I don't feel too much was missed," Leslie Moonves, the president of CBS, said, but that view is not widely shared at his network, or at others.

Nevertheless, perhaps for the first time since the early eighties, corporate bosses stopped complaining about "waste." The additional cost of covering this war at home and in Afghanistan, according to Andrew Lack, will be about fifty million dollars a year. Each network news division spends roughly four to five hundred million dollars, and the war is expected to add a minimum of a million dollars per week to the budget. This does not include the extra expenditures undertaken by the parent company's other news divisions, including local TV and radio stations. Nor does it include lost advertising dollars or spiralling costs should the war effort against terrorism expand to, say, Iraq. Mel Karmazin estimated that by the end of the year the war effort's cost to his company could reach five hundred million dollars. AOL Time Warner says that it does not compute the additional costs to CNN, and Gerald Levin says that he will pay any price: "Whatever it takes, particularly as it relates to news gathering." Reflecting a common, if perhaps temporary, sentiment about his corporate superiors, Dan Rather told me, "From Sumner Redstone to Mel Karmazin to Les Moonves, everything we needed we got. They've been marvellously supportive at a cost to the corporation. Supportive to a degree I would not have thought possible."

Optimists believe that the tragedy of September 11th could give a lasting sense of purpose to a diminished profession. Even such critics as Rory O'Connor, who says he decided to leave CBS after he was asked to produce a "48 Hours" on the subject of fat, agree. "The worm has turned," O'Connor, who co-founded Globalvision with [former ABC and CNN producer Danny] Schechter, says now. "The audience wants more information." O'Connor's optimism is echoed by Tom Brokaw, who believes that the press will expand America's appetite for international news; he hopes that, since news is cheaper to produce than entertainment, perhaps the networks will make more time for serious news programming. Peter Jennings says, "The country's definition of foreign news has changed forever. What we learned from this crisis—from the airplanes that crashed on September 11th to the potential horror of a smallpox scare—is that everything about this story is about globalization." The events of September 11th have prompted NBC to "hire more people overseas," Neal Shapiro says, and he believes that NBC's being part of a large, rich company like General Electric will be advantageous.

But many of these people are not wholly convinced that the networks' approach to foreign news has changed fundamentally. "It's still a work in progress," Brokaw said.

"Nobody wants to say that television is going to return to its usual ways," Jennings said. "But there is some anxiety that, without assertive leadership at the top of the company, it will." CNN's Aaron Brown, asked if he thought the crisis would permanently bolster the amount of international news on the air, said, "My head doesn't know, and my gut says yes." Dan Rather, aware that foreign coverage is costlier and that management will continue to try to make news "a profit center," says, "I'm hopeful, but I'm not optimistic." . . .

"The larger the entities that own and control the news operations, the more distant they become," Dan Rather says. He knew William Paley well when Paley ran the network, through the early eighties, but he barely knows the current C.E.O., Sumner Redstone. "At one time, news was an integral part of the corporation," Rather explains. "The person who ran the corporation was intimate with the people in news and had a dialogue with them that provided a little check and balance to the drive for profits and ratings."

The picture may become even bleaker when the three main network anchormen, Rather, Brokaw, and Jennings, retire. Rather turned seventy on October 31st, and although he says, "My plan is to keep on as long as I can do it," he has already held the job five years longer than his predecessor, Walter Cronkite. Jennings is sixty-three and his contract expires [soon]; for years, he has professed a desire to go back to reporting. Brokaw will be sixty-two in February, and had considered retiring in 2002, in order to spend more time writing. All three have a kind of vestigial authority within their networks—they are links to a different and better era—but when they are gone the executives may well feel liberated to cut costs even more. Brokaw, for example, has been hammered by critics like David Halberstam for preaching the value of foreign news while presiding over a program that has cut it to the bone; and yet Brokaw argues, in his own defense, that he has resisted still deeper cuts.

Already there is evidence that executives are getting anxious about the ratings decline and the cost of covering the war. One network-news president told me that by November a quiet backlash had begun. Only ABC broke into its prime-time schedule at 8 P.M. on Thursday, November 8th, to carry an address by President Bush, a decision that was perhaps influenced by its own weak offering that night, "Whose Line Is It Anyway?" No doubt, NBC and CBS declined to preëmpt their programs because they had two of the top-rated prime-time shows ("Friends" and "Survivor"); Fox was counter-programming with a cartoon show ("Family Guy"). One ABC correspondent says that network executives and senior producers are pressing the prime-time magazine shows to return to softer stories and to relegate war-related magazine pieces to a projected 8 P.M. Friday slot. Although NBC's "Today" show still leads the ratings, it is slumping; the network's news president, Neal Shapiro, told the *Times*, "We stayed in the war game too long." To compensate for the escalation in news costs, the Walt Disney Corporation, which owns ABC, has ordered other ABC divisions to reduce spending. NBC's president, Andrew Lack, says that the network will offset any news cost increases with compensating budget reductions or revenue increases elsewhere.

At CBS, Leslie Moonves says that he is turning his attention back to the financial ledger. With the budget at CBS News having grown considerably since September 11th, he will have to find compensating cuts elsewhere in order to meet his projected profit numbers. "60 Minutes" has been asked to pare five or six associate producers. "Earnings is what I'm judged on," Moonves said. He foresees a future that resembles nothing so much as the recent past, the days before the horror at the southern end of Manhattan. "We're in a competitive business," he says, "and ratings will be important for the news magazines and for the news telecasts. As you get further away from September 11th, that will revert back to normal."

NO

Michael Parks

Foreign News: What's Next?

American newspapers have carried more stories about Afghanistan on page one in the four months since the September 11 attacks than in the previous four decades. Network news programs that examined, almost nightly, a California congressman's relationship with a missing female intern were now offering hour-long specials on Osama bin Laden. Newsmagazines that for years had hesitated to put a foreign story on the cover, knowing that it would likely mean a drop of 25 percent or more in newsstand sales, ran cover stories week after week on the attacks, the hunt for bin Laden, the threat of biological terrorism, and the U.S. counterattack in Afghanistan. What had seemed foreign and far away was suddenly frightening, and of intense interest to readers.

Much of the coverage of the terrorist attacks and the U.S. response has been American journalism at its best. But many news organizations were playing catch-up. The terrorist threat from radical Islamic fundamentalists had been clear for years—attacks on the World Trade Center in 1993, on apartments housing U.S. Air Force personnel in Saudi Arabia in 1996, on the U.S. embassies in Kenya and Tanzania in 1998, and on the U.S.S. *Cole* in the Yemeni port of Aden in 2000. Coverage of these attacks was largely episodic with limited investigative reporting and few follow-up stories even when participants were brought to trial.

The failure was sweeping. "We did not examine the country's antiterrorism efforts adequately, our intelligence capabilities, our immigration policies, or the reasons for anti-Americanism," says Edward Seaton, editor-in-chief of the *Manhattan* (Kansas) *Mercury*, former president of the American Society of Newspaper Editors, and an ardent advocate of more international coverage. "While we can debate whether this failure played a role in our national lack of preparedness, there is no question that we failed our readers."

Bill Wheatley, vice president of NBC News, is also self-critical. "We all have done a good job since September 11," he says, "but I and a lot of others wish we had done more to help the public understand the intensity of feelings, the anger, among the radical Islamic fundamentalists."

News executives were significantly out of touch with their communities. Most Americans, even before the attacks, had concluded that global terrorism was the country's greatest international concern. In a 2001 study by the

Pew Research Center and the Council on Foreign Relations conducted before September 11, the public ranked protecting the United States from terrorist attacks as the country's top foreign policy priority. In 1999, a similar survey by The Gallup Organization for the Chicago Council on Foreign Relations found that more Americans (53 percent to 40 percent) thought that the twenty-first century would be even bloodier than the twentieth. When the U.S. Commission on National Security, chaired by former Senators Gary Hart and Warren Rudman, reported [recently] that international terrorism threatened the United States directly and that "Americans will likely die on American soil, possibly in large numbers," few news organizations covered it (CJR, November/December 2001).

Even with the surge of coverage over the past four months, many stories have remained thinly reported. "Few of us understand, for example," says Robert Rivard, editor of the *San Antonio Express-News*, "how it is that our intelligence agencies have maintained ties with Pakistani intelligence agencies at the same time those same Pakistani agencies helped the Taliban consolidate power and build an alliance with Al Qaeda."

Levels of Interest

Simply put, most news organizations failed to cover what a substantial number of their readers and viewers believed was vitally important—the danger posed to the United States by global terrorism. News organizations were guilty of the same lack of judgment and neglect of duty for which editorial writers have rebuked the Central Intelligence Agency and other government institutions.

The question now is whether the news organizations will change, whether they will respond to what the *Mercury*'s Seaton describes as "a wake-up call" or revert to the patterns of localism and cost-cutting that came in the decade after the gulf war in 1991 and left much of the world uncovered by U.S. media.

"The test is not what we or *The New York Times* or *The Wall Street Journal* or the *Los Angeles Times* does," says Leonard Downie, executive editor of *The Washington Post*. "We are committed to national and foreign coverage and will remain so. The big question is what the large ownerships will do—the networks and the chains—and I'm skeptical they will change. They put foreign news at the bottom of their priorities. They thought it turned audiences off and drove readers away. Will they now put public service ahead of profits?"

The first measurements of this commitment are newshole and airtime. For most U.S. newspapers, the issue is not sending correspondents overseas but committing space to international news and hiring editors knowledgeable about the world to pull together packages from news services. For most television stations, the question will be giving up a crime story or two on the evening news to make room for a longer foreign story. For the networks, it is committing correspondents, producers, crews, and time on their main news programs.

"We will be covering this story for a considerable period of time," NBC's Wheatley says. "Will there, for example, be another terrorist attack in the U.S.?

We've been told this war will be long, not just against the Taliban, but against terrorists wherever they are. That will take sizable resources."

The huge costs of covering the conflict will continue, but the real financial problem for most news organizations is the decline in advertising revenues resulting from the economic downturn. "It's a tough time, but this is what we do," says Eason Jordan, chief news executive of the CNN News Group. "Our new leadership [at AOL Time Warner] fully understands and supports world coverage. We have been told we will have all the resources we need."

Paul Friedman, executive vice president of ABC News, argues that the larger issue is one of audience interest. "Coverage will in time sink down to the previous levels—as little or as much as before," he says. "I don't share the cockeyed optimism that we have all learned our lesson and will now rededicate ourselves to foreign news. The interest simply isn't there, and when the impact subsides so will the interest. It's the nature of the beast."

Many news executives see the question of the public's level of interest as a test of the journalistic craft, of persuading readers and viewers to read and watch what they need to know and understand. "This is about telling important stories in interesting ways, about why the world matters," Jordan says. "It's not fair to put the onus on the people. News organizations have to take responsibility for coverage."

Local vs. Global

But study after study has shown declining space and airtime devoted to international news. One recent analysis by the Newspaper Advertising Bureau estimated that, before September 11, foreign stories accounted for 2 percent or less of the average daily paper's newshole, down from 10 percent in 1971 during the Vietnam War; another estimated that the proportion of international news in the major newsweeklies had declined to 13 percent from 22 percent between 1985 and 1995. Before September 11, network newscasts on some nights had no international stories at all, though a generation ago foreign reports constituted an average of 45 percent of the newscasts.

The reduction in international coverage has brought complaints from policy analysts, who argue that the decline fueled a new isolationism in the United States and that, as a result, the country might fail to exercise appropriate leadership in the world. Celinda Lake, a Democratic pollster, told a 1997 conference on the issue: "The media cover violence, conflict, and instability abroad and little else, and have made international involvement look very undesirable." Those who described themselves to Gallup as "hardly interested" in international affairs jumped from 3 percent to 22 percent, between the Chicago Council on Foreign Relations studies in 1990 and 1998.

Ever since the collapse of the Soviet Union and with it, the cold war, Americans have felt safe within their borders. "For fifty years, Americans had been on the edge, worried about nuclear confrontation," says Kevin Klose, the chief executive of National Public Radio. "Suddenly, we felt blessed with peace. We are being very rough on ourselves when we say we just lost interest in international news."

Foreign coverage was easier during the cold war, says NBC's Wheatley, "because there were good guys and bad guys and if the bad guys got out of control there would be nuclear holocaust. Then, it got a lot more complex, and the public was less certain where American interest lay in, say, Bosnia. We did hundreds of stories on Bosnia, but few Americans are able to find it on a map or tell you what went on there."

While some news organizations were doing a commendable job reporting on global terrorism, Islamic fundamentalism, and the dangers of biological warfare, others were trimming the staffs that reported and produced such stories. After covering the cold war for half a century, the emphasis was on local news, life-style stories—and on higher rates of return for shareholders in capital markets made fiercely competitive by high-tech companies and dot-com start-ups.

"You can almost hear the discussion between the business side and the news department," says Klose. " 'The cold war's over,' the business side was saying. 'Why do you need a bureau in Moscow? Why can't we centralize European coverage in London? Wouldn't you like to trade a Moscow correspondent for five more local reporters?' "

Even news organizations where the commitment to international coverage is strong were caught by the September attacks. CNN was in the midst of laying off 400 staffers, Reuters was cutting more than 1,500 positions worldwide, *The Boston Globe* was going through a round of buyouts, and departing Knight Ridder executives were sharply criticizing cutbacks at the San Jose *Mercury News, Philadelphia Inquirer,* and other papers in the chain.

Over the years, newspaper executives had seized on market surveys to put new emphasis on local coverage and, they hoped, to halt declining readership, particularly among youth. The same surveys that indicate deep concern about international terrorism as a foreign policy issue also show twice as many people (generally about 60 percent) interested in local news as in foreign coverage.

POSTSCRIPT

Have the News Media Improved Since 9/11?

The selections by Auletta and Parks were written at a very specific time in history. As you reflect on the authors' positions now, consider whether or not anything has changed since each wrote his article. You may want to question how much you know about other countries, the genesis of that type of terrorist activity, and the role of the United States in the world.

This issue reminds us that our world is far larger than we may think it is and that the values we hold may not be universally shared. It is sometimes humbling to think that many of the images we may have of the United States as a world leader, or world power, are not universally held.

This issue also reminds us that as citizens we have a responsibility to understand our role in the world and our obligation toward working for peace and a sustainable political environment. After September 11th, many students' interests began to broaden. Interest in foreign affairs, political science, and other cultures appeared to grow on college campuses across the country. Has this remained so? How did the events of September 11th change your life and the lives of others around you?

In addition to memorial tributes to those who died in the September 11th tragedy, an emerging body of written work has prompted us to think through the issues discussed in the selections by Auletta and Parks. Two particularly insightful books are James W. Cortada and Edward Waku's *Betting on America: Why the U.S. Can Be Stronger After September 11* (Financial Times/Prentice Hall, 2002) and Noam Chomsky's thoughtful collection of essays on events leading up to September 11th, in *9-11* (Seven Stories Press, 2001). Since the event, Don Hazen, Tate Hauseman, Tamara Straus, and Michele Chihara have collected and edited *After 9/11: Solutions for a Saner World* (The Independent Media Institute, 2002), which includes articles written prior to and after September 11th by many noted experts and pundits, like Barbara Kingsolver, Robert Reich, Edward Said, and Barbara Ehrenreich.

On the Internet ...

Educause

The Educause Web site contains summaries of new technology news from various publications as well as links to many other resources. This site is designed to facilitate the use of technology in teaching, research, and learning.

http://www.educause.edu

The Electronic Frontier Foundation

The Electronic Frontier Foundation (EFF) is a nonprofit civil liberties organization that is working to protect free expression and access to public resources and information online. It also works to promote responsibility in the news media.

http://www.eff.org

The Journal of Computer-Mediated Communication

The Journal of Computer-Mediated Communication Web site has been maintained by the Annenberg School for Communication at the University of Southern California since 1995. Many issues are discussed in this electronic journal, including electronic commerce, law and the electronic frontier, Netplay, and designing presence in virtual environments.

http://www.ascusc.org/jcmc/

Yahoo International

This Yahoo International service contains resources on different countries, providing information about media systems and media programming available around the world.

http://dir.yahoo.com/regional/countries/index.html

Citizens Internet Empowerment Coalition

The Citizens Internet Empowerment Coalition (CIEC) is a broad group of Internet users, library groups, publishers, online service providers, and civil liberties groups working to preserve the First Amendment and to ensure the future of free expression. You will find discussions of the Communications Decency Act and Internet-related topics on this site.

http://www.ciec.org

PART 6

The Information Society

*P*redictions *of a world that is increasingly reliant upon media and communication technologies have generally provided either utopian or dystopian visions about what our lives will be like in the future. But now the ability to communicate instantly around the world has become a reality. New media distribution technologies present new options for traditional ways of doing things. Not too many years ago, people were talking about the possibility of an information superhighway. Today, surfing the World Wide Web is common. Although we are still learning how electronic communication may change our lives and the ways we work and communicate, many questions have not changed. Will new ways of communication change the way individuals interact? Will the decision making of citizens change? Will everyone have access to the services and technologies that enable more immediate information exchange? What will new technologies mean to us as individuals as we enter the information age?*

- Can Privacy Be Protected in the Information Age?

- Will Technology Change Social Interaction?

ISSUE 17

Can Privacy Be Protected in the Information Age?

YES: Simson Garfinkel, from "Privacy and the New Technology," *The Nation* (February 28, 2000)

NO: Adam L. Penenberg, from "The End of Privacy," *Forbes* (November 29, 1999)

ISSUE SUMMARY

YES: Journalist Simson Garfinkel discusses how today's technology has the potential to destroy our privacy. He makes the case that the government and individuals could take steps to protect themselves against privacy abuse, particularly by returning to the groundwork set by the government in the 1970s and by educating people on how to avoid privacy traps.

NO: *Forbes* reporter Adam L. Penenberg discusses his own experiences with an Internet detective agency, and he explains how easy it is for companies to get unauthorized access to personal information. He specifically describes how much, and where, personal information is kept and the lack of safeguards in our current system.

P rivacy, or the legal right "to be left alone," is something we often take for granted until we feel that our privacy has been violated. In the following selections, Simon Garfinkel and Adam L. Penenberg discuss the range of privacy issues with which we now are faced, due to the computer's ability to store and match records for virtually any transaction we make using a computer. Data companies are emerging that have various standards about seeking the permission to save and sell personal information. While Garfinkel discusses how we could protect our privacy by drawing from already existing laws and statutes, Penenberg explains that many companies have avoided any prior legislation or standards to become information brokers.

This issue brings up questions of what privacy is, and what it means to us, but it also reminds us that as we use newer technologies, there are often unavoidable problems caused by and related to their use. The "transparency," or lack of obvious technological control, is apparent in uses of the Internet and in the ability of high-speed computers to match check numbers, driver's license numbers, and other identifying bits of information. For those who wonder why their names appear on certain mailings, why they are contacted by telemarketers, or how secure their personal information is, this issue will bring up questions and uncover some of the answers.

Survey research reveals that many people feel that their privacy has been invaded at some time and that concerns about privacy are growing. But there are also some disturbing studies to indicate that young people are far less concerned about privacy issues than their parents. Could it be that younger people have not yet experienced the potential situations for privacy invasion, or, are we seeing a social value, in this case the right to privacy, in some type of transition?

Garfinkel advocates a position on privacy protection that would return us to a time in history when government was much more proactive in protecting the rights of citizens and residents. If his theory is correct, many agree that it would not be very expensive for the government to ensure safeguards about this basic right. However, trends in government involvement in businesses seem to be leading away from government oversight and toward giving greater control to businesses to monitor their own actions. Many of the companies discussed by Penenberg operate with few standards or guidelines at all. When the government itself is one of the primary repositories for personal information, could it, or should it, take the lead in defining certain standards and criteria for the protection of the innocent? Furthermore, if control should be exercised, would it be best left to the federal government, state, or local legislators?

Perhaps one of the key issues behind the privacy dilemma is the question of how and what people can do if they find that their privacy is invaded. With so many laws and statutes on the books, the legal wrangling over questions of privacy can be expensive and difficult to challenge. Many times people do not know how much information has been gathered about them until they find that the information is wrong, and it causes a problem. Consider the person who knows that he or she always pays bills on time, but for some reason, a credit reporting agency finds him or her negligent. Consequently, his or her new car loan or credit card application is denied because of the incorrect records. What recourse should that person have, and how long would it take to correct any misinformation? How could that person find out what other records might be inaccurate?

One of the growing areas of privacy concern is the collection and appropriate distribution of medical information about a person. Is it right to let others know the status of someone's confidential medical records? Should the results of voluntary or required drug testing, pregnancy tests, or AIDS tests be available to employers or anyone else without written authorization of the person being tested? Can those confidential records be used to prevent someone from buying insurance, getting a job, or getting a driver's license?

There are many questions related to issues of privacy, and we will undoubtedly see the courts debating exact parameters of privacy and information control in the near future. For now, we all need to think of the related issues of privacy and keep searching for answers to these important questions.

Simson Garfinkel

Privacy and the New Technology

You wake to the sound of a ringing telephone—but how could that happen? Several months ago, you reprogrammed your home telephone system so it would never ring before the civilized hour of 8 AM. But it's barely 6:45. Who was able to bypass your phone's programming?

You pick up the receiver, then slam it down a moment later. It's one of those marketing machines playing a recorded message. What's troubling you now is how this call got past the filters you set up. Later on you'll discover how: The company that sold you the phone created an undocumented "back door"; last week, the phone codes were sold in an online auction.

Now that you're awake, you decide to go through yesterday's mail. There's a letter from the neighborhood hospital you visited last month. "We're pleased that our emergency room could serve you in your time of need," the letter begins. "As you know, our fees (based on our agreement with your HMO) do not cover the cost of treatment. To make up the difference, a number of hospitals have started selling patient records to medical researchers and consumer-marketing firms. Rather than mimic this distasteful behavior, we have decided to ask you to help us make up the difference. We are recommending a tax-deductible contribution of $275 to help defray the cost of your visit."

The veiled threat isn't empty, but you decide you don't really care who finds out about your sprained wrist. You fold the letter in half and drop it into your shredder. Also into the shredder goes a trio of low-interest credit-card offers. Why a shredder? A few years ago you would never have thought of shredding your junk mail—until a friend in your apartment complex had his identity "stolen" by the building's superintendent. As best as anybody can figure out, the super picked one of those preapproved credit-card applications out of the trash; called the toll-free number and picked up the card when it

From Simson Garfinkel, "Privacy and the New Technology," *The Nation* (February 28, 2000). Adapted from Simson Garfinkel, *Database Nation: The Death of Privacy in the 21st Century* (O'Reilly, 2000). Copyright © 2000 by Simson Garfinkel. Reprinted by permission of O'Reilly & Associates, Inc. and the author.

was delivered. He's in Mexico now, with a lot of expensive clothing and electronics, all at your friend's expense.

On that cheery note, you grab your bag and head out the door, which automatically locks behind you.

This is the future—not a far-off future but one that's just around the corner. It's a future in which what little privacy we now have will be gone. Some people call this loss of privacy "Orwellian," harking back to *1984*, George Orwell's classic work on privacy and autonomy. In that book, Orwell imagined a future in which a totalitarian state used spies, video surveillance, historical revisionism and control over the media to maintain its power. But the age of monolithic state control is over. The future we're rushing toward isn't one in which our every move is watched and recorded by some all-knowing Big Brother. It is instead a future of a hundred kid brothers who constantly watch and interrupt our daily lives. Orwell thought the Communist system represented the ultimate threat to individual liberty. Over the next fifty years, we will see new kinds of threats to privacy that find their roots not in Communism but in capitalism, the free market, advanced technology and the unbridled exchange of electronic information.

The problem with this word "privacy" is that it falls short of conveying the really big picture. Privacy isn't just about hiding things. It's about self-possession, autonomy and integrity. As we move into the computerized world of the twenty-first century, privacy will be one of our most important civil rights. But this right of privacy isn't the right of people to close their doors and pull down their window shades—perhaps because they want to engage in some sort of illicit or illegal activity. It's the right of people to control what details about their lives stay inside their own houses and what leaks to the outside.

Most of us recognize that our privacy is at risk. According to a 1996 nationwide poll conducted by Louis Harris & Associates, 24 percent of Americans have "personally experienced a privacy invasion." In 1995 the same survey found that 80 percent felt that "consumers have lost all control over how personal information about them is circulated and used by companies." Ironically, both the 1995 and 1996 surveys were paid for by Equifax, a company that earns nearly $2 billion each year from collecting and distributing personal information.

Today the Internet is compounding our privacy conundrum—largely because the voluntary approach to privacy protection advocated by the Clinton Administration doesn't work in the rough and tumble world of real business. For example, a study just released by the California HealthCare Foundation found that nineteen of the top twenty-one health websites have privacy policies, but most sites fail to follow them. Not surprisingly, 17 percent of Americans questioned in a poll said they do not go online for health information because of privacy concerns.

✦❦✦

But privacy threats are not limited to the Internet: Data from all walks of life are now being captured, compiled, indexed and stored. For example, New York City has now deployed the Metrocard system, which allows subway and bus riders to pay their fares by simply swiping a magnetic-strip card. But the system also records the serial number of each card and the time and location of every swipe. New York police have used this vast database to crack crimes and disprove alibis. Although law enforcement is a reasonable use of this database, it is also a use that was adopted without any significant public debate. Furthermore, additional controls may be necessary: It is not clear who has access to the database, under what circumstances that access is given and what provisions are being taken to prevent the introduction of false data into it. It would be terrible if the subway's database were used by an employee to stalk an ex-lover or frame an innocent person for a heinous crime.

"New technology has brought extraordinary benefits to society, but it also has placed all of us in an electronic fishbowl in which our habits, tastes and activities are watched and recorded," New York State Attorney General Eliot Spitzer said in late January [2000], in announcing that Chase Manhattan had agreed to stop selling depositor information without clear permission from customers. "Personal information thought to be confidential is routinely shared with others without our consent."

Today's war on privacy is intimately related to the recent dramatic advances in technology. Many people today say that in order to enjoy the benefits of modern society, we must necessarily relinquish some degree of privacy. If we want the convenience of paying for a meal by credit card or paying for a toll with an electronic tag mounted on our rearview mirror, then we must accept the routine collection of our purchases and driving habits in a large database over which we have no control. It's a simple bargain, albeit a Faustian one.

This trade-off is both unnecessary and wrong. It reminds me of another crisis our society faced back in the fifties and sixties—the environmental crisis. Then, advocates of big business said that poisoned rivers and lakes were the necessary costs of economic development, jobs and an improved standard of living. Poison was progress: Anybody who argued otherwise simply didn't understand the facts.

Today we know better. Today we know that sustainable economic development depends on preserving the environment. Indeed, preserving the environment is a prerequisite to the survival of the human race. Without clean air to breathe and clean water to drink, we will all die. Similarly, in order to reap the benefits of technology, it is more important than ever for us to use technology to protect personal freedom.

Blaming technology for the death of privacy isn't new. In 1890 two Boston lawyers, Samuel Warren and Louis Brandeis, argued in the *Harvard Law Review* that privacy was under attack by "recent inventions and business methods." They contended that the pressures of modern society required the creation of a "right of privacy," which would help protect what they called "the right to be let alone." Warren and Brandeis refused to believe that privacy had to die for technology to flourish. Today, the Warren/Brandeis article is regarded as one of the most influential law review articles ever published.

Privacy-invasive technology does not exist in a vacuum, of course. That's because technology itself exists at a junction between science, the market and society. People create technology to fill specific needs and desires. And technology is regulated, or not, as people and society see fit. Few engineers set out to build systems designed to crush privacy and autonomy, and few businesses or consumers would willingly use or purchase these systems if they understood the consequences.

⋅⟨⦿⟩⋅

How can we keep technology and the free market from killing our privacy? One way is by being careful and informed consumers. Some people have begun taking simple measures to protect their privacy, measures like making purchases with cash and refusing to provide their Social Security numbers—or providing fake ones. And a small but growing number of people are speaking out for technology with privacy. In 1990 Lotus and Equifax teamed up to create a CD-ROM product called "Lotus Marketplace: Households," which would have included names, addresses and demographic information on every household in the United States, so small businesses could do the same kind of target marketing that big businesses have been doing since the sixties. The project was canceled when more than 30,000 people wrote to Lotus demanding that their names be taken out of the database.

Similarly, in 1997 the press informed taxpayers that the Social Security Administration was making detailed tax-history information about them available over the Internet. The SSA argued that its security provisions—requiring that taxpayers enter their name, date of birth, state of birth and mother's maiden name—were sufficient to prevent fraud. But tens of thousands of Americans disagreed, several US senators investigated the agency and the service was promptly shut down. When the service was reactivitated some months later, the detailed financial information in the SSA's computers could not be downloaded over the Internet.

But individual actions are not enough. We need to involve government itself in the privacy fight. The biggest privacy failure of the US government has been its failure to carry through with the impressive privacy groundwork that was laid in the Nixon, Ford and Carter administrations. It's worth taking a look back at that groundwork and considering how it may serve us today.

The seventies were a good decade for privacy protection and consumer rights. In 1970 Congress passed the Fair Credit Reporting Act, which gave Americans the previously denied right to see their own credit reports and demand the removal of erroneous information. Elliot Richardson, who at the time was President Nixon's Secretary of Health, Education and Welfare, created a commission in 1972 to study the impact of computers on privacy. After years of testimony in Congress, the commission found all the more reason for alarm and issued a landmark report in 1973.

The most important contribution of the Richardson report was a bill of rights for the computer age, which it called the Code of Fair Information Practices. The code is based on five principles:

- There must be no personal-data record-keeping system whose very existence is secret.
- There must be a way for a person to find out what information about the person is in a record and how it is used.
- There must be a way for a person to prevent information about the person that was obtained for one purpose from being used or made available for other purposes without the person's consent.
- There must be a way for a person to correct or amend a record of identifiable information about the person.
- Any organization creating, maintaining, using or disseminating records of identifiable personal data must assure the reliability of the data for their intended use and must take precautions to prevent misuse of the data.

⁕

The biggest impact of the Richardson report wasn't in the United States but in Europe. In the years after the report was published, practically every European country passed laws based on these principles. Many created data-protection commissions and commissioners to enforce the laws. Some believe that one reason for Europe's interest in electronic privacy was its experience with Nazi Germany in the thirties and forties. Hitler's secret police used the records of governments and private organizations in the countries he invaded to round up people who posed the greatest threat to German occupation; postwar Europe realized the danger of allowing potentially threatening private information to be collected, even by democratic governments that might be responsive to public opinion.

But here in the United States, the idea of institutionalized data protection faltered. President Jimmy Carter showed interest in improving medical privacy, but he was quickly overtaken by economic and political events. Carter lost the election of 1980 to Ronald Reagan, whose aides saw privacy protection as yet another failed Carter initiative. Although several privacy-protection laws were signed during the Reagan/Bush era, the leadership for these bills came from Congress, not the White House. The lack of leadership stifled any chance of passing a nationwide data-protection act. Such an act would give people the right to know if their name and personal information is stored in a database, to see the information and to demand that incorrect information be removed.

In fact, while most people in the federal government were ignoring the cause of privacy, some were actually pursuing an antiprivacy agenda. In the early eighties, the government initiated numerous "computer matching" programs designed to catch fraud and abuse. Unfortunately, because of erroneous data these programs often penalized innocent people. In 1994 Congress passed the Communications Assistance to Law Enforcement Act, which gave the government dramatic new powers for wiretapping digital communications. In 1996 Congress passed two laws, one requiring states to display Social Security numbers on driver's licenses and another requiring that all medical patients in the United States be issued unique numerical identifiers, even if they pay their own bills. Fortunately, the implementation of those 1996 laws has been delayed, thanks largely to a citizen backlash and the resulting inaction by Congress and the executive branch.

Continuing the assault, both the Bush and Clinton administrations waged an all-out war against the rights of computer users to engage in private and secure communications. Starting in 1991, both administrations floated proposals for use of "Clipper" encryption systems that would have given the government access to encrypted personal communications. Only recently did the Clinton Administration finally relent in its seven-year war against computer privacy. President Clinton also backed the Communications Decency Act (CDA), which made it a crime to transmit sexually explicit information to minors—and, as a result, might have required Internet providers to deploy far-reaching monitoring and censorship systems. When a court in Philadelphia found the CDA unconstitutional, the Clinton Administration appealed the decision all the way to the Supreme Court—and lost.

One important step toward reversing the current direction of government would be to create a permanent federal oversight agency charged with protecting privacy. Such an agency would:

- Watch over the government's tendency to sacrifice people's privacy for other goals and perform governmentwide reviews of new federal programs for privacy violations before they're launched.
- Enforce the government's few existing privacy laws.
- Be a guardian for individual privacy and liberty in the business world, showing businesses how they can protect privacy and profits at the same time.
- Be an ombudsman for the American public and rein in the worst excesses that our society has created.

Evan Hendricks, editor of the Washington-based newsletter *Privacy Times*, estimates that a fifty-person privacy-protection agency could be created with an annual budget of less than $5 million—a tiny drop in the federal budget.

Some privacy activists scoff at the idea of using government to assure our privacy. Governments, they say, are responsible for some of the greatest privacy violations of all time. This is true, but the US government was also one of the greatest polluters of all time. Today the government is the nation's environmental police force, equally scrutinizing the actions of private business and the government itself.

At the very least, governments can alter the development of technology that affects privacy. They have done so in Europe. Consider this: A growing number of businesses in Europe are offering free telephone calls—provided that the caller first listens to a brief advertisement. The service saves consumers money, even if it does expose them to a subtle form of brainwashing. But not all these services are equal. In Sweden both the caller and the person being called are forced to listen to the advertisement, and the new advertisements are played during the phone call itself. But Italy's privacy ombudsman ruled that the person being called could not be forced to listen to the ads.

There is also considerable public support for governmental controls within the United States itself—especially on key issues, such as the protection of medical records. For example, a 1993 Harris-Equifax survey on medical privacy issues found that 56 percent of the American public favored "comprehensive federal legislation that spells out rules for confidentiality of individual medical records" as part of national healthcare reform legislation. Yet Congress failed to act on the public's wishes.

The Fair Credit Reporting Act [FCRA] was a good law in its day, but it should be upgraded into a Data Protection Act. Unfortunately, the Federal Trade Commission and the courts have narrowly interpreted the FCRA. The first thing that is needed is legislation that expands it into new areas. Specifically, consumer-reporting firms should be barred from reporting arrests unless those arrests result in convictions. Likewise, consumer-reporting firms should not be allowed to report evictions unless they result in court judgments in favor of the landlord or a settlement in which both the landlord and tenant agree that the eviction can be reported. Companies should be barred from exchanging medical information about individuals or furnishing medical information as part of a patient's report without the patient's explicit consent.

●◆●

We also need new legislation that expands the fundamental rights offered to consumers under the FCRA. When negative information is reported to a credit bureau, the business making that report should be required to notify the subject of the report—the consumer—in writing. Laws should be clarified so that if a consumer-reporting company does not correct erroneous data in its reports, consumers can sue for real damages, punitive damages and legal fees. People should have the right to correct any false information in their files, and if the consumer and the business disagree about the truth, then the consumer should have a right to place a *detailed* explanation into his or her record. And people should have a right to see all the information that has been collected on them; these reports should be furnished for free, at least once every six months.

We need to rethink consent, a bedrock of modern law. Consent is a great idea, but the laws that govern consent need to be rewritten to limit what kinds of agreements can be made with consumers. Blanket, perpetual consent should be outlawed.

Further, we need laws that require improved computer security. In the eighties the United States aggressively deployed cellular-telephone and alphanumeric-pager networks, even though both systems were fundamentally unsecure. Instead of deploying secure systems, manufacturers lobbied for laws that would make it illegal to listen to the broadcasts. The results were predictable: dozens of cases in which radio transmissions were eavesdropped. We are now making similar mistakes in the prosecution of many Internet crimes, going after the perpetrator while refusing to acknowledge the liabilities of businesses that do not even take the most basic security precautions.

We should also bring back the Office of Technology Assessment, set up under a bill passed in 1972. The OTA didn't have the power to make laws or issue regulations, but it could publish reports on topics Congress asked it to study. Among other things, the OTA considered at length the trade-offs between law enforcement and civil liberties, and it also looked closely at issues of worker monitoring. In total, the OTA published 741 reports, 175 of which dealt directly with privacy issues, before it was killed in 1995 by the newly elected Republican-majority Congress.

Nearly forty years ago, Rachel Carson's book *Silent Spring* helped seed the US environmental movement. And to our credit, the silent spring that Carson foretold never came to be. *Silent Spring* was successful because it helped people to understand the insidious damage that pesticides were wreaking on the environment, and it helped our society and our planet to plot a course to a better future.

Today, technology is killing one of our most cherished freedoms. Whether you call this freedom the right to digital self-determination, the right to informational autonomy or simply the right to privacy, the shape of our future will be determined in large part by how we understand, and ultimately how we control or regulate, the threats to this freedom that we face today.

The End of Privacy

T he phone rang and a stranger cracked sing-songy at the other end of the line: *"Happy Birthday."* That was spooky—the next day I would turn 37. "Your full name is Adam Landis Penenberg," the caller continued. "Landis?" My mother's maiden name. "I'm touched," he said. Then Daniel Cohn, Web detective, reeled off the rest of my "base identifiers"—my birth date, address in New York, Social Security number. Just two days earlier I had issued Cohn a challenge: Starting with my byline, dig up as much information about me as you can. "That didn't take long," I said.

"It took about five minutes," Cohn said, cackling back in Boca Raton, Fla. "I'll have the rest within a week." And the line went dead.

In all of six days Dan Cohn and his Web detective agency, Docusearch. com, shattered every notion I had about privacy in this country (or whatever remains of it). Using only a keyboard and the phone, he was able to uncover the innermost details of my life—whom I call late at night; how much money I have in the bank; my salary and rent. He even got my unlisted phone numbers, both of them. Okay, so you've heard it before: America, the country that made "right to privacy" a credo, has lost its privacy to the computer. But it's far worse than you think. Advances in smart data-sifting techniques and the rise of the massive databases have conspired to strip you naked. The spread of the Web is the final step. It will make most of the secrets you have more instantly available than ever before, ready to reveal themselves in a few taps on the keyboard.

For decades this information rested in remote mainframes that were difficult to access, even for the techies who put it there. The move to desktop PCs and local servers in the 1990s has distributed these data far and wide. Computers now hold half a billion bank accounts, half a billion credit card accounts, hundreds of millions of mortgages and retirement funds and medical claims and more. The Web seamlessly links it all together. As e-commerce grows, marketers and busybodies will crack open a cache of new consumer data more revealing than ever before.

It will be a salesman's dream—and a paranoid's nightmare. Adding to the paranoia: Hundreds of data sleuths like Dan Cohn of Docusearch have opened up shop on the Web to sell precious pieces of these data. Some are ethical; some aren't. They mine celebrity secrets, spy on business rivals and track down hidden assets, secret lovers and deadbeat dads. They include Strategic Data Service (at datahawk.com) and Infoseekers.com and Dig Dirt Inc. (both at the PI Mall, www.pimall.com).

Cohn's firm will get a client your unlisted number for $49, your Social Security number for $49 and your bank balances for $45. Your driving record goes for $35; tracing a cell phone number costs $84. Cohn will even tell someone what stocks, bonds and securities you own (for $209). As with computers, the price of information has plunged.

You may well ask: What's the big deal? We consumers are as much to blame as marketers for all these loose data. At every turn we have willingly given up a layer of privacy in exchange for convenience; it is why we use a credit card to shop, enduring a barrage of junk mail. Why should we care if our personal information isn't so personal anymore?

Well, take this test: Next time you are at a party, tell a stranger your salary, checking account balance, mortgage payment and Social Security number. If this makes you uneasy, you have your answer.

"If the post office said we have to use transparent envelopes, people would go crazy, because the fact is we all have something to hide," says Edward Wade, a privacy advocate who wrote *Identity Theft: The Cybercrime of the Millennium* (Loompanics Unlimited, 1999) under the pseudonym John Q. Newman.

You can do a few things about it. Give your business to the companies that take extra steps to safeguard your data and will guarantee it. Refuse to reveal your Social Security number—the key for decrypting your privacy—to all but the financial institutions required by law to record it.

Do something, because many banks, brokerages, credit card issuers and others are lax, even careless, about locking away your records. They take varied steps in trying to protect your privacy. Some sell information to other marketers, and many let hundreds of employees access your data. Some workers, aiming to please, blithely hand out your account number, balance and more whenever someone calls and asks for it. That's how Cohn pierced my privacy.

"You call up a company and make it seem like you're a spy on a covert mission, and only they can help you," he says. "It works every time. All day long I deal with spy wannabes."

I'm not the paranoid type; I don't see a huddle on TV and think that 11 football players are talking about me. But things have gone too far. A stalker would kill for the wealth of information Cohn was able to dig up. A crook could parlay the data into credit card scams and "identity theft," pilfering my good credit rating and using it to pull more ripoffs.

Cohn operates in this netherworld of private eyes, ex-spooks and ex-cops, retired military men, accountants and research librarians. Now 39, he grew up in the Philadelphia suburb of Bryn Mawr, attended Penn State and joined the Navy in 1980 for a three-year stint. In 1987 Cohn formed his own agency to investigate insurance fraud and set up shop in Florida. "There was no shortage of work," he says. He invented a "video periscope" that could rise up through the roof of a van to record a target's scam.

In 1995 he founded Docusearch with childhood pal Kenneth Zeiss. They fill up to 100 orders a day on the Web, and expect $1 million in business this year. Their clients include lawyers, insurers, private eyes; the Los Angeles Pension Union is a customer, and Citibank's legal recovery department uses Docusearch to find debtors on the run.

Cohn, Zeiss and 13 researchers (6 of them licensed P.I.s work out of the top floor of a dull, five-story office building in Boca Raton, Fla., sitting in cubicles under a flourescent glare and taking orders from 9 a.m. to 4 p.m. Their Web site is open 24 hours a day, 365 days a year. You click through it and load up an online shopping cart as casually as if you were at Amazon.com.

The researchers use sharp sifting methods, but Cohn also admits to misrepresenting who he is and what he is after. He says the law lets licensed investigators use such tricks as "pretext calling," fooling company employees into divulging customer data over the phone (legal in all but a few states). He even claims to have a government source who provides unpublished numbers for a fee, "and you'll never figure out how he is paid because there's no paper trail."

Yet Cohn claims to be more scrupulous than rivals. "Unlike an information broker, I won't break the law. I turn down jobs, like if a jealous boyfriend wants to find out where his ex is living." He also says he won't resell the information to anyone else.

Let's hope not. Cohn's first step into my digital domain was to plug my name into the credit bureaus—Transunion, Equifax, Experian. In minutes he had my Social Security number, address and birth date. Credit agencies are supposed to ensure that their subscribers (retailers, auto dealers, banks, mortgage companies) have a legitimate need to check credit.

"We physically visit applicants to make sure they live up to our service agreement," says David Mooney of Equifax, which keeps records on 200 million Americans and shares them with 114,000 clients. He says resellers of the data must do the same. "It's rare that anyone abuses the system." But Cohn says he gets his data from a reseller, and no one has ever checked up on him.

Armed with my credit header, Dan Cohn tapped other sites. A week after my birthday, true to his word, he faxed me a three-page summary of my life. He had pulled up my utility bills, my two unlisted phone numbers and my finances.

This gave him the ability to map my routines, if he had chosen to do so: how much cash I burn in a week ($400), how much I deposit twice a month ($3,061), my favorite neighborhood bistro (the Flea Market Cafe), the $720 monthly checks I write out to one Judith Pekowsky: my psychotherapist. (When you live in New York, you see a shrink; it's the law.) If I had an incurable disease, Cohn could probably find that out, too.

He had my latest phone bill ($108) and a list of long distance calls made from home—including late-night fiber-optic dalliances (which soon ended) with a woman who traveled a lot. Cohn also divined the phone numbers of a few of my sources, underground computer hackers who aren't wanted by the police—but probably should be.

Knowing my Social Security number and other personal details helped Cohn get access to a Federal Reserve database that told him where I had deposits.

Cohn found accounts I had forgotten long ago: $503 at Apple Bank for Savings in an account held by a long-ago landlord as a security deposit; $7 in a dormant savings account at Chase Manhattan Bank; $1,000 in another Chase account.

A few days later Cohn struck the mother lode. He located my cash management account, opened a few months earlier at Merrill Lynch & Co. That gave him a peek at my balance, direct deposits from work, withdrawals, ATM visits, check numbers with dates and amounts, and the name of my broker.

That's too much for some privacy hawks. "If someone can call your bank and get them to release account information without your consent, it means you have no privacy," says Russell Smith, director of Consumer.net in Alexandria, Va., who has won more than $40,000 suing telemarketers for bothering him. "The two issues are knowledge and control: You should know what information about you is out there, and you should be able to control who gets it."

How did Cohn get hold of my Merrill Lynch secrets? Directly from the source. Cohn says he phoned Merrill Lynch and talked to one of 500 employees who can tap into my data. "Hi, I'm Dan Cohn, a licensed state investigator conducting an investigation of an Adam Penenberg," he told the staffer, knowing the words "licensed" and "state" make it sound like he works for law enforcement.

Then he recited my Social Security, birth date and address, "and before I could get out anything more he spat out your account number." Cohn told the helpful worker: "I talked to Penenberg's broker, um, I can't remember his name...."

"Dan Dunn?" the Merrill Lynch guy asked. "Yeah, Dan Dunn," Cohn said. The staffer then read Cohn my complete history—balance, deposits, withdrawals, check numbers and amounts. "You have to talk in the lingo the bank people talk so they don't even know they are being taken," he says.

Merrill's response: It couldn't have happened this way—and if it did, it's partly my fault. Merrill staff answers phoned-in questions only when the caller provides the full account number or personal details, Merrill spokesperson Bobbie Collins says. She adds that I could have insisted on an "additional telephonic security code" the caller would have to punch in before getting information, and that this option was disclosed when I opened my CMA [cash management account]. Guess I didn't read the fine print, not that it mattered: Cohn says he got my account number from the Merrill rep.

Sprint, my long distance carrier, investigated how my account was breached and found that a Mr. Penenberg had called to inquire about my most recent bill. Cohn says only that he called his government contact. Whoever made the call, "he posed as you and had enough information to convince our customer service representative that he was you," says Russ R. Robinson, a Sprint spokesman. "We want to make it easy for our customers to do business with us over the phone, so you are darned if you do and darned if you don't."

Bell Atlantic, my local phone company, told me a similar tale, only it was a Mrs. Penenberg who called in on behalf of her husband. I recently attended a conference in Las Vegas but don't remember having tied the knot.

For the most part Cohn's methods fly below the radar of the law. "There is no general law that protects consumers' privacy in the U.S.," says David Banisar, a Washington lawyer who helped found the Electronic Privacy Information Center (www.epic.org). In Europe companies classified as "data controllers" can't hand out your personal details without your permission, but the U.S. has as little protection as China, he contends.

The "credit header"—name, address, birth date, Social Security—used to be kept confidential under the Fair Credit Reporting Act. But in 1989 the Federal Trade Commission exempted it from such protection, bowing to the credit bureaus, bail bondsmen and private eyes.

Some piecemeal protections are in place: a 1984 act protecting cable TV bills; the 1988 Video Privacy Protection Act, passed after a newspaper published the video rental records of Supreme Court nominee Robert Bork. "It's crazy, but your movie rental history is more protected under the law than your credit history is," says Wade, the author.

Colorado is one of the few states that prohibit "pretext calling" by someone pretending to be someone else. In July James Rapp, 39, and wife Regana, 29, who ran info-broker Touch Tone Information out of a strip mall in Aurora, Colo., were charged with impersonating the Ramseys—of the JonBenet child murder case—to get hold of banking records that might be related to the case.

Congress may get into the act with bills to outlaw pretext calling. But lawyer Banisar says more than 100 privacy bills filed in the past two years have gone nowhere. He blames "an unholy alliance between marketers and government agencies that want access" to their data.

Indeed, government agencies are some of the worst offenders in selling your data. In many states the Department of Motor Vehicles was a major peddler of personal data until Congress passed the Driver's Privacy Protection Act of 1994, pushing states to enact laws that let drivers block distribution of their names and addresses. Some states, such as Georgia, take it seriously, but South Carolina has challenged it all the way up to the U.S. Supreme Court. Oral arguments are scheduled. . . .

As originally conceived, Social Security numbers weren't to be used for identification purposes. But nowadays you are compelled by law to give an accurate number to a bank or other institution that pays you interest or dividends; thank you, Internal Revenue Service. The bank, in turn, just might trade that number away to a credit bureau—even if you aren't applying for credit. That's how snoops can tap so many databases.

Here's a theoretical way to stop this linking process without compromising the IRS' ability to track unreported income: Suppose that, instead of issuing you a single 9-digit number, the IRS gave you a dozen 11-digit numbers and let you report income under any of them. You could release one to your employer, another to your broker, a third to your health insurer, a fourth to the firms that need to know your credit history. It would be hard for a sleuth to know that William H. Smith 001–24–7829–33 was the same as 350–68–4561–49. Your digital personas would converge at only one point in cyberspace, inside the extremely well guarded computers of the IRS.

But for now, you have to fend for yourself by being picky about which firms you do business with and how much you tell them. If you are opening a bank account with no credit attached to it, ask the bank to withhold your Social

Security number from credit bureaus. Make sure your broker gives you, as Merrill Lynch does, the option of restricting telephone access to your account, and use it. If a business without a legitimate need for the Social Security number asks for it, leave the space blank—or fill it with an incorrect number. (Hint: To make it look legitimate, use an even number between 10 and 90 for the middle two digits.)

Daniel Cohn makes no apologies for how he earns a living. He sees himself as a data-robbing Robin Hood. "The problem isn't the amount of information available, it's the fact that until recently only the wealthy could afford it. That's where we come in."

In the meantime, until a better solution emerges, I'm starting over: I will change all of my bank, utility and credit-card account numbers and apply for new unlisted phone numbers. That should keep the info-brokers at bay for a while—at least for the next week or two.

POSTSCRIPT

Can Privacy Be Protected in the Information Age?

Without a doubt, different cultures have various attitudes, laws, and values with regard to issues of personal privacy. In the United States, the definition of privacy has been handed down from the Supreme Court. Challenges to privacy often are debated in our highest court, and therefore, are influenced by legal precedent. New technology challenges the court to examine those precedents and see if a balance among the right to know, the right to privacy, and the technological capability to share information can coexist.

In many other countries, however, there are different cultural attitudes and concepts of what is "private" and what is not. Both the UN Declaration of Human Rights and the World International Property Organization (WIPO) have considered the right to privacy as a basic human need for all people. It is the role of governments then, to come up with national and regional policies to enforce these various beliefs with regard to their specific cultures. An excellent collection of issues such as these can be found in James R. Michael's *Privacy and Human Rights: An International and Comparative Study With Special Reference to Development in Information Technology* (UNESCO, 1994).

A number of studies further illuminate how broad a concept privacy may be for individuals. Ann Cavoukian's *Who Knows: Safeguarding Your Privacy in a Networked World* (McGraw-Hill, 1997) takes a practical approach toward understanding how we can control information about ourselves.

ISSUE 18

Will Technology Change Social Interaction?

YES: Matt Goldberg, from "Generation IM," *Yahoo! Internet Life* (April 2002)

NO: Peter F. Drucker, from "Beyond the Information Revolution," *The Atlantic Monthly* (October 1999)

ISSUE SUMMARY

YES: Author Matt Goldberg discusses the way in which the estimated 150 million people around the world are changing their social interaction habits and expectations, thanks to the ability to use instant messaging (IM). By focusing on this one particular application of technology, he offers specific behavioral changes and attitudes observed in some of the IM users and then speculates as to what the eventual outcome will be as more people use IM for a broader range of purposes.

NO: Professor Peter F. Drucker, a noted expert on technological change, outlines a history of social organization in relation to technology in order to put the "information revolution" into perspective. He compares the changes in our present and future lives to the introduction of the Industrial Revolution and reminds us that while social change often takes much longer than the term *revolution* suggests, the real impact of social change is often accompanied by more subtle shifts in our institutions.

The speed of change is critical to understanding the positions of both Matt Goldberg and Peter F. Drucker. Goldberg focuses on a particular application, and therefore, by narrowing his subject, has some specific positions to relate. On the other hand, Drucker paints a broader picture for us to understand how long change, in its greater sense, actually takes. While Goldberg primarily looks at early adopters, such as young people and people in a business setting, Drucker is more concerned with major societal changes that take longer but infiltrate our social institutions.

Goldberg and Drucker's selections demonstrate clearly how the issue can change when different types of evidence are used to support one's theories and how the phrasing of a question forces one to look at the quality of the evidence one accumulates. While Goldberg uses personal interviews and creates generalities based upon specific examples, Drucker looks at the broader field of history to see how trends repeat themselves over a longer period of time.

We are all concerned with changing behaviors and would like to accurately predict the success of various technologies and software, but the following selections remind us that while the phrase "information revolution" *suggests* rapid change, it may take a considerable amount of time to see whether something new is a fad or whether it will create lasting change.

Goldberg and Drucker raise a fundamental question for the study of any form of media: is anything ever really new? Is instant messaging just an alternative to the way we have communicated in the past? What considerations might there be for the way IM could change our communication patterns in the future, and what other parts of our lives might change because of the ability to send messages instantly?

New applications of technology seem to proliferate so quickly that we do not often have the time to evaluate their potential for change or form judgments as to whether such changes might be good, bad, or possibly neutral in society. The issue here reminds us how easy it is for us to think that change is imminent —but the real effects of change take far longer to see clearly.

Matt Goldberg

 **YES**

Generation IM

Y o, what's your SN? "

Freddy, a smooth-talking college freshman in New York City, is starting to put the moves on Sarah, one of his new classmates. If you're not a teenager, you may have no idea what he's talking about. But Sarah knows exactly what he wants. He's asking for her screen name so he can keep chatting her up after school via instant messaging. To Sarah, the thought of Freddy (or anyone else, for that matter) asking for her phone number is laughably antiquated. "No one asks for telephone numbers anymore," she says. "IM is for me what the phone is to most other people."

Eric Heckler (not quite his real name), a 32-year-old lawyer in Manhattan, uses IM all day, every day, to maintain the rapport he once enjoyed with his college buddies. Many of his friends now live in California, but by exchanging in excess of 100 instant messages on any given day, they manage to stay as tight as ever. "It's definitely like we're sitting around on the couch, channel surfing and having a beer," he says. "We surf the Web together, sending each other links, and chat about sports." Although they used to speak on the phone regularly, IM allows them to recapture the sort of constant contact they had in school. "I used to stay informed about the important news in their lives by speaking on the phone every week or so," Heckler says. "But with IM, I know the minutiae of their lives, every little thing that happens to them."

Teens like Sarah and adults like Heckler—and the majority of their friends—are card-carrying members of Generation IM, a rapidly emerging world where real-time text messaging over the Net is rewriting the rules of human communication. According to the Pew Internet & American Life Project (June 2001), 44 percent of all online adults have used instant messaging. IM has revolutionized the way companies do business and the way far-flung friends and family members keep in touch. During the events surrounding September 11, IM proved itself an indispensable communications tool for the modern world. When long-distance phone lines and cell phones quickly became overloaded, instant messaging served as many people's only connection to coworkers, friends, and loved ones. And IM is having such a dramatic impact on the millions of people around the world who use it every day that the pace of the technology's evolution is speeding up. In fact, it's on the cusp of metamorphosing into a bona fide computing platform in its own right: It may very well signal the arrival of what might be called a post-Web world.

Because an estimated 150 million people around the globe use IM—that's about one-third of all people who use the Net in any capacity—it has become a battlefield for the world's biggest media and technology companies. For the likes of AOL Time Warner and Microsoft, IM is the future: more urgent than the Web, more immediate than interactive television. Meanwhile, many other enterprising people are working to make IM useful for the sorts of online tasks that most of us associate with the Web: searching for content, checking the news, booking travel tickets, swapping songs, trading stocks, and fetching sports scores, to name just a few of the basics. The continued development of IM technology will likely be what gives us those oft-discussed but, so far, not-ready-for-prime-time intelligent agents that live out there on the Net, doing our bidding minute by minute, representing us to other people and their attendant agents.

Already, IM has grown considerably beyond its initial uses. In the wake of the implosion of the original Napster, an IM-based successor called Aimster provided millions of users with a new way to share files—and cause headaches for the recording industry. [Recently], Yahoo! announced a video-capable version of its IM software, allowing intrepid IMers with Web cams to experience real-time videoconferencing. IM is becoming a de facto part of the online gaming experience and an increasingly common way for people to learn if they've received new e-mail. But perhaps the most dynamic area of IM growth is the wireless world. AOL and Voice-Stream run ads on prime-time TV touting their IM-on-your-cell-phone service; and those PDA-toters among us who are lucky enough to have wireless. Net connections have begun tapping out IMs as we walk down the street, ride the bus, or sit on a park bench.

To understand this IM gold rush, one need only look at just how ubiquitous and essential IM has become in the daily lives of its users. The more that people use IM, particularly teenagers and people in the workplace, the less they can imagine life before—or without—it.

Take teens, the mainstream of the future and the first group to come of age in an IM-enabled world. According to a report released [in 2001] by Pew, nearly three-fourths of all online teens between the ages of 12 and 17 use IM, a number the report places at nearly 13 million. Of these, 44 percent use IM every time they go online and nearly 20 percent claim that IM is their primary mode of communication with their peers. As Amanda Lenhart, a research specialist with Pew and a coauthor of the report, declares: "This is definitely the instant-messaging generation."

❧

Sarah, 18, started using IM three years ago as a sophomore in high school. Her friends were all online, but she didn't have a computer. She'd use her friends' computers for IM, sometimes overstaying her welcome by instant messaging until 2 in the morning. Finally, under the pretense of needing it for schoolwork, she persuaded her parents to buy her a PC. Soon enough, Sarah became, to put it mildly, a prolific IM user. "On school days, I'd IM from the minute I got home until 2:30 in the morning," she says, "and on weekends I'd be on until 4."

Sarah may be a typical teen, yet she's unusual in the dramatic way IM has influenced her life—how radically IM has altered her interpersonal relationships and family dynamics. Sarah is a first-generation Asian American whose very traditionally minded parents have always set extraordinarily strict limits on the parameters of her social life. This is especially hard for an outgoing young woman who is typically dressed in low-slung, flared jeans and a favored cropped baby tee emblazoned with a big red Superman S.

For as long as she can remember, Sarah's use of the phone at home has been severely curtailed. "I'm not allowed to get any calls after 7 at night, but if a boy calls, no matter what time it is, my dad goes absolutely psychotic," she says. IM became her savior, her lifeline to the outside world, and the key to having what she considered a normal social life. Sarah was lucky in that for the most part her parents—who thought their sincerely held beliefs about the right way to raise their daughter were being successfully carried out—were not what you'd call computer literate. Initially her parents had no way of knowing that she wasn't doing homework or research when she was in reality instant messaging. "But the more they'd hear me laughing at the computer," she says, "as if I were somehow talking to friends, the more suspicious they'd get. Then, one time, my dad went over to the computer when I was out of the room and clicked on a blinking message. Unfortunately, it was obvious from the SN that it was from a boy and so I got busted." The punishment was having the computer taken away for a week, a fate that Sarah compares, without a trace of irony, to "having my leg cut off."

Though Sarah's use of IM to thwart what she saw as egregiously backward-looking parenting techniques took place in a context with more than the average amount of teen angst, Pew's Lenhart says that this sort of battle is not at all uncommon, with some 40 percent of parents surveyed reporting that they've had arguments with their kids about Internet use. The teens and parents agreed that the teens are much more savvy when it comes to IM and related technologies. "And in the age-old battle between them," Lenhart says, "the teens will use what's available to win."

Use of IM is not always a win-win situation for teens. The Pew report reveals that 37 percent of them have written something that they would not have said face-to-face. While Lenhart points out that this can sometimes be "liberating," all this disembodied communication can also complicate social situations.

Scott Siegel, an enterprising 15-year-old who manages two IM-oriented clubs on Yahoo!, explains via IM that he often spends as many as eight hours at a time instant messaging. Asked if he IMs more frequently with boys or with girls, he responds, "Girls." Girls he knows from school? "Most are girls I met on the Net," he wrote. How many of those has he ever met, seen, or spoken to? "Well, none."

Lenhart suggests that "it can be really hard in the offline world to talk to members of the opposite sex" and that experiences such as Scott's can be "very refreshing"—educational even, in terms of gaining confidence and learning how to talk to people. But she admits, "You have to wonder how many of those girls are actually teenage girls and how many are people pretending to be teenage girls. When you think about it, it's kind of scary."

RETHINK EVERYTHING: AS IM MOVES TOWARD THE MAINSTREAM, NEW HABITS EMERGE

DIFFICULT CONVERSATIONS   Asking out, breaking up? Someone needs to use mouthwash? A recent Pew study of online teens found out that 17 percent of IM users have used the medium to ask someone out on a date. Thirteen percent have used IM to break off a relationship. When the going gets tough, the tough go IM. Note: This also works for thirtysomethings whose dates have bad breath.

SMOOTH SHOPPING   Shopping online cries out for the human touch. Some online shops are using IM systems to provide it. Describe your mom to **MSN eShop: Gift Concierge [eshop.msn.com]**, and the site will make your Mother's Day selections.

SMART STUDIES   Kids in the know use IM as a study tool. Quiz a buddy on upcoming exams. Trade a few notes from class. One person can be the quiz-master as the others hunt for answers.

HOME INTERCOM SYSTEM   Instant messaging from room to room? You bet—whether it's a crossword puzzle answer, a "when is dinner ready?" query, or "lights out." It's a surprisingly effective—and quieter—form of modern family communications.

SONG SWAPPING   Sending a song or a photo worthy of checking out is de rigueur in many IM circles. Voice IM is still a bit funky and so is video, but the capabilities are there. It won't be long before IM is truly a multimedia telephone.

REAL-TIME REUNIONS   Connected families and friends instant message to meet at predetermined times—and then export the whole shebang to an impromptu chatroom for a group session.

—Robin Raskin

Or, think about what happened to Sarah once she caved in to Freddy's advances and handed over her SN. They wound up having an hourlong IM session, their first real interaction other than the assorted nods and "heys" exchanged on campus. Unlike what you might expect from an introductory conversation in person or on the phone, this initial IM exchange got very intense, very quickly. "Half the stuff I said I would never have said on the phone," Sarah, recalls. "On IM you're just so much less self-conscious. You don't see the other person's face or reactions." By the time this IM chat was over, Sarah and Freddy had discussed extremely intimate details, such as whether Sarah was still a virgin (she was) and whether Freddy, like Sarah, had ever tried the drug Ecstasy (he hadn't). Because IM is, as Lenhart describes it, a "mediated communication," it fails to provide "the same information feedback as face-to-face communication. There's no tone, no body language." After some reflection, Sarah became increasingly worried that this first hang with Freddy had progressed way too fast and that seeing him at school would now be awkward. "After that one hour," she says, "everything was just totally different."

⁂

Although 25-year-old Jessica Bodie is past the social hyperactivity of the teen years, she, too, is a member of the IM generation. Like millions of Americans, Bodie's experience in the workplace has been irrevocably altered by IM, affecting not only the relationships she has with coworkers but also the way she does her job. A project manager for a New York City–based publishing company, Bodie was introduced to instant messaging at her last job, where she was a Web producer for college-oriented marketing firm Student Advantage. "I didn't start using IM at work until everyone else around me did," she says. "It became a necessity from a work perspective, as essential as an e-mail address, if not more so. If you weren't on IM, you were definitely out of the loop."

Increasingly, employees are already experiencing—or soon will experience —a similar imperative to get on IM. Gartner Inc. reports that workers at nearly 50 percent of North American corporations use IM for business or personal use, and it projects that this will grow to 90 percent within two years. Research firm Jupiter Media Metrix placed the number of at-work IMers in the U.S. at 13.4 million for September 2001, a 34 percent increase over the figure for that month a year before. These folks spent a collective total of 4.9 billion minutes —or nearly 82 million hours—instant messaging at work in September.

"Instant messaging is almost entirely replacing the telephone at work," says Gartner research director Rob Batchelder. "Because of the prevalence of voice mail in the office, the phone is becoming more of a store-and-forward method of communication like e-mail. IM is the best way to facilitate more fluid connections among employees." As Batchelder points out, e-mail is an asynchronous mode of communication. You send a question to a coworker on the West Coast via e-mail at 7 in the morning from your East Coast office; your colleague reads and replies to it while you're in an afternoonlong meeting; later that evening you finally check your e-mail again and get your answer. But the telephone, which had always been the definitive tool for real-time communication, is becoming more and more like e-mail, with people making calls expecting (if not also hoping) to leave a message instead of actually speaking to the person. Which leaves IM for all those tasks that require immediate (or close to it) responses from your coworkers. In this way, Batchelder says, "IM is the anti—e-mail; it liberates workers. Stuff starts getting done faster."

Stuff certainly started getting done faster for Bodie. "Using IM, five days of work seemed to get condensed into one," she says. "It definitely increased productivity, though it also made work a lot more intense." She became adept at using IM for a variety of tasks that required what AT&T Labs researcher Steve

Whittaker calls rapid exchanges of information—things such as "asking quick questions and organizing impromptu meetings." . . .

IM can facilitate these preternaturally social ways of reaching out to coworkers because of something called *presence*. Presence is arguably the most critical feature of instant messaging both in its capacity as a communications tool and as a platform for real-time, post-Web computing. To understand presence, one need only think of the contact list. Introduced to the Web in 1996 by four Israeli entrepreneurs as part of ICQ—one of the first IM powerhouses—the contact list added an entirely new dimension to online interaction. You could finally see if the people you knew and wanted to talk to were online, if they were available to chat, or if they were too busy or away from their computers. AOL, which would eventually buy the parent company of ICQ for $400 million, soon followed suit with the 1996 release of its own presence-oriented IM client, AIM. Presence is the special sauce of IM, or as Clay Shirky, a senior analyst for O'Reilly & Associates, says, "Presence is the thing that gives you *the vibe*—and as of now is not really possible with the Web alone."

Using a Buddy List—type contact-manager capable of conveying presence information has changed the way a great many of us think about the Internet, offering a people-centered, real-time, social interface to the online world. Teens like Sarah and Scott have 81 and 141 names, respectively, on their Buddy Lists —exact numbers they can rattle off without even thinking about it. AT&T Labs found that the average Buddy List of the employees they studied weighed in at a much lighter 22 contacts, though anecdotal evidence suggests that many people using IM extensively at work have much bigger contact lists.

Largely because of presence, Shirky says, "IM has changed the way people work in really extraordinary ways." To help illustrate the power of presence in the workplace, Shirky tells the story of a major investment bank that had offices at 7 World Trade Center until the building collapsed in the wake of the September 11 attack on the Twin Towers. "The bank had occupied a huge floor and after they'd evacuated, they couldn't find office space in which to recapture the rapid, face-to-face communication that had characterized their interaction," he says. "So the company adopted IM to preserve that all-important, cubicle-to-cubicle kind of dynamic. The IT department had agreed to implement IM only temporarily, but after only two weeks they realized it would be a permanent change. The lesson they learned is that once you introduce IM into an organization, you cannot remove it. Because it maps so well to human behavior, it becomes a permanent part of the landscape."

According to AT&T's Whittaker, "Presence gives users the sense of knowing other people's comings and goings." When IM use starts to permeate an organization, he says, "distributed work groups form, keeping people in close proximity even if they work on different coasts, allowing people to feel closer to their coworkers simply because they can see when someone signs on in the morning or shuts down at the end of the day." . . .

It turns out that IM is helping to reverse a trend in American life many of us have experienced or lamented: the relentless encroachment of our work into our personal lives. Or, if not reverse it exactly, then at least start tipping the scales in the opposite direction. "There's been a lot of research over the years suggesting how people, especially Americans, are working harder and harder," says Whittaker, "a lot of which is associated with taking work home." Now, he says, IM is doing just the opposite, "making the personal a part of everyday office life."

The social connectedness that IM fosters does have its downside. Bodie finds that there's little privacy at work now. "You can't slink into the office unnoticed. When you're a user of IM, just coming into work is a declaration that you are there and ready to go. For that reason, I would love IM use at work if I were a CEO, but for the peons of the world it can create serious issues."

While Heckler's relationships with his friends and his sister have clearly benefited from IM, he has found it necessary to be selective when it comes to initiating IM bonds. Take his mom, for example. "My sister and I have a pact not to tell our mom about our IM relationship," he says. "My mom just moved to New Mexico from New York and is understandably needier in terms of social contact with her kids. She calls all the time and e-mails all the time, which is fine, but adding that next layer of intensity with IM is the last thing I need." He feels the same way about instant messaging with his boss, something he's studiously avoided even though he instant messages friends and family almost exclusively from work. "Until two months ago, I worked at a law firm run by a very hands-on partner who kept asking me to download AIM," Heckler says. "I kept telling him I would download it right away, but never did. The last thing I wanted was an IM relationship with my boss."

NO

Peter F. Drucker

Beyond the Information Revolution

The truly revolutionary impact of the Information Revolution is just beginning to be felt. But it is not "information" that fuels this impact. It is not "artificial intelligence." It is not the effect of computers and data processing on decision-making, policymaking, or strategy. It is something that practically no one foresaw or, indeed, even talked about ten or fifteen years ago: *e-commerce* —that is, the explosive emergence of the Internet as a major, perhaps eventually *the* major, worldwide distribution channel for goods, for services, and, surprisingly, for managerial and professional jobs. This is profoundly changing economies, markets, and industry structures; products and services and their flow; consumer segmentation, consumer values, and consumer behavior; jobs and labor markets. But the impact may be even greater on societies and politics and, above all, on the way we see the world and ourselves in it.

At the same time, new and unexpected industries will no doubt emerge, and fast. One is already here: biotechnology. And another: fish farming. Within the next fifty years fish farming may change us from hunters and gatherers on the seas into "marine pastoralists"—just as a similar innovation some 10,000 years ago changed our ancestors from hunters and gatherers on the land into agriculturalists and pastoralists.

It is likely that other new technologies will appear suddenly, leading to major new industries. What they may be is impossible even to guess at. But it is highly probable—indeed, nearly certain—that they will emerge, and fairly soon. And it is nearly certain that few of them—and few industries based on them—will come out of computer and information technology. Like biotechnology and fish farming, each will emerge from its own unique and unexpected technology.

Of course, these are only predictions. But they are made on the assumption that the Information Revolution will evolve as several earlier technology-based "revolutions" have evolved over the past 500 years, since Gutenberg's printing revolution, around 1455. In particular the assumption is that the Information Revolution will be like the Industrial Revolution of the late eighteenth and early nineteenth centuries. And that is indeed exactly how the Information Revolution has been during its first fifty years.

The Railroad

The Information Revolution is now at the point at which the Industrial Revolution was in the early 1820s, about forty years after James Watt's improved steam engine (first installed in 1776) was first applied, in 1785, to an industrial operation—the spinning of cotton. And the steam engine was to the first Industrial Revolution what the computer has been to the Information Revolution—its trigger, but above all its symbol. Almost everybody today believes that nothing in economic history has ever moved as fast as, or had a greater impact than, the Information Revolution. But the Industrial Revolution moved at least as fast in the same time span, and had probably an equal impact if not a greater one. In short order it mechanized the great majority of manufacturing processes, beginning with the production of the most important industrial commodity of the eighteenth and early nineteenth centuries: textiles. Moore's Law asserts that the price of the Information Revolution's basic element, the microchip, drops by 50 percent every eighteen months. The same was true of the products whose manufacture was mechanized by the First Industrial Revolution. The price of cotton textiles fell by 90 percent in the fifty years spanning the start of the eighteenth century. The production of cotton textiles increased at least 150-fold in Britain alone in the same period. And although textiles were the most visible product of its early years, the Industrial Revolution mechanized the production of practically all other major goods, such as paper, glass, leather, and bricks. Its impact was by no means confined to consumer goods. The production of iron and ironware—for example, wire—became mechanized and steam-driven as fast as did that of textiles, with the same effects on cost, price, and output. By the end of the Napoleonic Wars the making of guns was steam-driven throughout Europe; cannons were made ten to twenty times as fast as before, and their cost dropped by more than two thirds. By that time Eli Whitney had similarly mechanized the manufacture of muskets in America and had created the first mass-production industry.

These forty or fifty years gave rise to the factory and the "working class." Both were still so few in number in the mid-1820s, even in England, as to be statistically insignificant. But psychologically they had come to dominate (and soon would politically also). Before there were factories in America, Alexander Hamilton foresaw an industrialized country in his 1791 *Report on Manufactures*. A decade later, in 1803, a French economist, Jean-Baptiste Say, saw that the Industrial Revolution had changed economics by creating the "entrepreneur."

The social consequences went far beyond factory and working class. As the historian Paul Johnson has pointed out, in *A History of the American People* (1997), it was the explosive growth of the steam-engine-based textile industry that revived slavery. Considered to be practically dead by the Founders of the American Republic, slavery roared back to life as the cotton gin—soon steam-driven—created a huge demand for low-cost labor and made breeding slaves America's most profitable industry for some decades.

The Industrial Revolution also had a great impact on the family. The nuclear family had long been the unit of production. On the farm and in the artisan's workshop husband, wife, and children worked together. The factory, almost for the first time in history, took worker and work out of the home and moved them into the workplace, leaving family members behind—whether spouses of adult factory workers or, especially in the early stages, parents of child factory workers.

Indeed, the "crisis of the family" did not begin after the Second World War. It began with the Industrial Revolution—and was in fact a stock concern of those who opposed the Industrial Revolution and the factory system. (The best description of the divorce of work and family, and of its effect on both, is probably Charles Dickens's 1854 novel *Hard Times*.)

But despite all these effects, the Industrial Revolution in its first half century only mechanized the production of goods that had been in existence all along. It tremendously increased output and tremendously decreased cost. It created both consumers and consumer products. But the products themselves had been around all along. And products made in the new factories differed from traditional products only in that they were uniform, with fewer defects than existed in products made by any but the top craftsmen of earlier periods.

There was only one important exception, one new product, in those first fifty years: the steamboat, first made practical by Robert Fulton in 1807. It had little impact until thirty or forty years later. In fact, until almost the end of the nineteenth century more freight was carried on the world's oceans by sailing vessels than by steamships.

Then, in 1829, came the railroad, a product truly without precedent, and it forever changed economy, society, and politics.

In retrospect it is difficult to imagine why the invention of the railroad took so long. Rails to move carts had been around in coal mines for a very long time. What could be more obvious than to put a steam engine on a cart to drive it, rather than have it pushed by people or pulled by horses? But the railroad did not emerge from the cart in the mines. It was developed quite independently. And it was not intended to carry freight. On the contrary, for a long time it was seen only as a way to carry people. Railroads became freight carriers thirty years later, in America. (In fact, as late as the 1870s and 1880s the British engineers who were hired to build the railroads of newly Westernized Japan designed them to carry passengers—and to this day Japanese railroads are not equipped to carry freight.) But until the first railroad actually began to operate, it was virtually unanticipated.

Within five years, however, the Western world was engulfed by the biggest boom history had ever seen—the railroad boom. Punctuated by the most spectacular busts in economic history, the boom continued in Europe for thirty years, until the late 1850s, by which time most of today's major railroads had been built. In the United States it continued for another thirty years, and in outlying areas—Argentina, Brazil, Asian Russia, China—until the First World War.

The railroad was the truly revolutionary element of the Industrial Revolution, for not only did it create a new economic dimension but also it rapidly changed what I would call the *mental geography*. For the first time in history human beings had true mobility. For the first time the horizons of ordinary people expanded. Contemporaries immediately realized that a fundamental change in mentality had occurred. (A good account of this can be found in what is surely the best portrayal of the Industrial Revolution's society in transition, George Eliot's 1871 novel *Middlemarch*.) As the great French historian Fernand Braudel pointed out in his last major work, *The Identity of France* (1986), it was the railroad that made France into one nation and one culture. It had previously been a congeries of self-contained regions, held together only politically. And the role of the railroad in creating the American West is, of course, a commonplace in U.S. history.

Routinization

Like the Industrial Revolution two centuries ago, the Information Revolution so far—that is, since the first computers, in the mid-1940s—has only transformed processes that were here all along. In fact, the real impact of the Information Revolution has not been in the form of "information" at all. Almost none of the effects of information envisaged forty years ago have actually happened. For instance, there has been practically no change in the way major decisions are made in business or government. But the Information Revolution has routinized traditional *processes* in an untold number of areas.

The software for tuning a piano converts a process that traditionally took three hours into one that takes twenty minutes. There is software for payrolls, for inventory control, for delivery schedules, and for all the other routine processes of a business. Drawing the inside arrangements of a major building (heating, water supply, sewerage, and so on) such as a prison or a hospital formerly took, say, twenty-five highly skilled draftsmen up to fifty days; now there is a program that enables one draftsman to do the job in a couple of days, at a tiny fraction of the cost. There is software to help people do their tax returns and software that teaches hospital residents how to take out a gall bladder. The people who now speculate in the stock market online do exactly what their predecessors in the 1920s did while spending hours each day in a brokerage office. The processes have not been changed at all. They have been routinized, step by step, with a tremendous saving in time and, often, in cost.

The psychological impact of the Information Revolution, like that of the Industrial Revolution, has been enormous. It has perhaps been greatest on the way in which young children learn. Beginning at age four (and often earlier), children now rapidly develop computer skills, soon surpassing their elders; computers are their toys and their learning tools. Fifty years hence we may well conclude that there was no "crisis of American education" in the closing years of the twentieth century—there was only a growing incongruence between the way twentieth-century schools taught and the way late-twentieth-century children learned. Something similar happened in the sixteenth-century university, a hundred years after the invention of the printing press and movable type.

But as to the way we work, the Information Revolution has so far simply routinized what was done all along. The only exception is the CD-ROM, invented around twenty years ago to present operas, university courses, a writer's oeuvre, in an entirely new way. Like the steamboat, the CD-ROM has not immediately caught on.

The Meaning of E-commerce

E-commerce is to the Information Revolution what the railroad was to the Industrial Revolution—a totally new, totally unprecedented, totally unexpected development. And like the railroad 170 years ago, e-commerce is creating a new and distinct boom, rapidly changing the economy, society, and politics.

One example: A mid-sized company in America's industrial Midwest, founded in the 1920s and now run by the grandchildren of the founder, used to have some 60 percent of the market in inexpensive dinnerware for fast-food eateries, school and office cafeterias, and hospitals within a hundred-mile radius of its factory. China is heavy and breaks easily, so cheap china is traditionally sold within a small area. Almost overnight this company lost more than half of its market. One of its customers, a hospital cafeteria where someone went "surfing" on the Internet, discovered a European manufacturer that offered china of apparently better quality at a lower price and shipped cheaply by air. Within a few months the main customers in the area shifted to the European supplier. Few of them, it seems, realize—let alone care—that the stuff comes from Europe.

In the new mental geography created by the railroad, humanity mastered distance. In the mental geography of e-commerce, distance has been eliminated. There is only one economy and only one market.

One consequence of this is that every business must become globally competitive, even if it manufacturers or sells only within a local or regional market. The competition is not local anymore—in fact, it knows no boundaries. Every company has to become transnational in the way it is run. Yet the traditional multinational may well become obsolete. It manufacturers and distributes in a number of distinct geographies, in which it is a *local* company. But in e-commerce there are neither local companies nor distinct geographies. Where to manufacture, where to sell, and how to sell will remain important business decisions. But in another twenty years they may no longer determine what a company does, how it does it, and where it does it.

At the same time, it is not yet clear what kinds of goods and services will be bought and sold through e-commerce and what kinds will turn out to be unsuitable for it. This has been true whenever a new distribution channel has arisen. Why, for instance, did the railroad change both the mental and economic geography of the West, whereas the steamboat—with its equal impact on world trade and passenger traffic—did neither? Why was there no "steamboat boom"?

Equally unclear has been the impact of more-recent changes in distribution channels—in the shift, for instance, from the local grocery store to the supermarket, from the individual supermarket to the supermarket chain, and from the supermarket chain to Wal-Mart and other discount chains. It is already clear that the shift to e-commerce will be just as eclectic and unexpected.

Here are a few examples. Twenty-five years ago it was generally believed that within a few decades the printed word would be dispatched electronically to individual subscribers' computer screens. Subscribers would then either read text on their computer screens or download it and print it out. This was the assumption that underlay the CD-ROM. Thus any number of newspapers and magazines, by no means only in the United States, established themselves online; few, so far, have become gold mines. But anyone who twenty years ago predicted the business of Amazon.com and barnesandnoble.com—that is, that books would be sold on the Internet but delivered in their heavy, printed form —would have been laughed off the podium. Yet Amazon.com and barnesandnoble.com are in exactly that business, and they are in it worldwide. The first order for the U.S. edition of my most recent book, *Management Challenges for the 21st Century* (1999), came to Amazon.com, and it came from Argentina.

Another example: Ten years ago one of the world's leading automobile companies made a thorough study of the expected impact on automobile sales of the then emerging Internet. It concluded that the Internet would become a major distribution channel for used cars, but that customers would still want to see new cars, to touch them, to test-drive them. In actuality, at least so far, most used cars are still being bought not over the Internet but in a dealer's lot. However, as many as half of all new cars sold (excluding luxury cars) may now actually be "bought" over the Internet. Dealers only deliver cars that customers have chosen well before they enter the dealership. What does this mean for the future of the local automobile dealership, the twentieth century's most profitable small business?

Another example: Traders in the American stock-market boom of 1998 and 1999 increasingly buy and sell online. But investors seem to be shifting away from buying electronically. The major U.S. investment vehicle is mutual funds. And whereas almost half of all mutual funds a few years ago were bought electronically, it is estimated that the figure will drop to 35 percent next year and to 20 percent by 2005. This is the opposite of what "everybody expected" ten or fifteen years ago.

The fastest-growing e-commerce in the United States is in an area where there was no "commerce" until now—in jobs for professionals and managers. Almost half of the world's largest companies now recruit through Web sites, and some two and a half million managerial and professional people (two thirds of them not even engineers or computer professionals) have their résumés on the Internet and solicit job offers over it. The result is a completely new labor market.

This illustrates another important effect of e-commerce. New distribution channels change who the customers are. They change not only *how* customers buy but also *what* they buy. They change consumer behavior, savings patterns, industry structure—in short, the entire economy. This is what is now happening, and not only in the United States but increasingly in the rest of the developed world, and in a good many emerging countries, including mainland China.

Luther, Machiavelli, and the Salmon

The railroad made the Industrial Revolution accomplished fact. What had been revolution became establishment. And the boom it triggered lasted almost a hundred years. The technology of the steam engine did not end with the railroad. It led in the 1880s and 1890s to the steam turbine, and in the 1920s and 1930s to the last magnificent American steam locomotives, so beloved by railroad buffs. But the technology centered on the steam engine and in manufacturing operations ceased to be central. Instead the dynamics of the technology shifted to totally new industries that emerged almost immediately after the railroad was invented, not one of which had anything to do with steam or steam engines. The electric telegraph and photography were first, in the 1830s, followed soon thereafter by optics and farm equipment. The new and different fertilizer industry, which began in the late 1830s, in short order transformed agriculture. Public health became a major and central growth industry, with quarantine, vaccination, the supply of pure water, and sewers, which for the first time in history made the city a more healthful habitat than the countryside. At the same time came the first anesthetics.

With these major new technologies came major new social institutions: the modern postal service, the daily paper, investment banking, and commercial banking, to name just a few. Not one of them had much to do with the steam engine or with the technology of the Industrial Revolution in general. It was these new industries and institutions that by 1850 had come to dominate the industrial and economic landscape of the developed countries.

This is very similar to what happened in the printing revolution—the first of the technological revolutions that created the modern world. In the fifty years after 1455, when Gutenberg had perfected the printing press and movable type he had been working on for years, the printing revolution swept Europe and completely changed its economy and its psychology. But the books printed during the first fifty years, the ones called incunabula, contained largely the same texts that monks, in their scriptoria, had for centuries laboriously copied by hand: religious tracts and whatever remained of the writings of antiquity. Some 7,000 titles were published in those first fifty years, in 35,000 editions. At least 6,700 of these were traditional titles. In other words, in its first fifty years printing made available—and increasingly cheap—traditional information and communication products. But then, some sixty years after Gutenberg, came Luther's German Bible—thousands and thousands of copies sold almost immediately at an unbelievably low price. With Luther's Bible the new printing technology ushered in a new society. It ushered in Protestantism, which conquered half of Europe and, within another twenty years, forced the Catholic Church to reform itself in the other half. Luther used the new medium of print deliberately to restore religion to the center of individual life and of society. And this unleashed a century and a half of religious reform, religious revolt, religious wars.

At the very same time, however, that Luther used print with the avowed intention of restoring Christianity, Machiavelli wrote and published *The Prince* (1513), the first Western book in more than a thousand years that contained not one biblical quotation and no reference to the writers of antiquity. In no time at all *The Prince* became the "other best seller" of the sixteenth century, and its most notorious but also most influential book. In short order there was a wealth of purely secular works, what we today call literature: novels and books in science, history, politics, and, soon, economics. It was not long before the first purely secular art form arose, in England—the modern theater. Brand-new social institutions also arose: the Jesuit order, the Spanish infantry, the first modern navy, and, finally, the sovereign national state. In other words, the printing revolution followed the same trajectory as did the Industrial Revolution, which began 300 years later, and as does the Information Revolution today.

What the new industries and institutions will be, no one can say yet. No one in the 1520s anticipated secular literature, let alone the secular theater. No one in the 1820s anticipated the electric telegraph, or public health, or photography.

The one thing (to say it again) that is highly probable, if not nearly certain, is that the next twenty years will see the emergence of a number of new industries. At the same time, it is nearly certain that few of them will come out of information technology, the computer, data processing, or the Internet. This is indicated by all historical precedents. But it is true also of the new industries that are already rapidly emerging. Biotechnology, as mentioned, is already here. So is fish farming.

Twenty-five years ago salmon was a delicacy. The typical convention dinner gave a choice between chicken and beef. Today salmon is a commodity, and is the other choice on the convention menu. Most salmon today is not caught at sea or in a river but grown on a fish farm. The same is increasingly true of trout. Soon, apparently, it will be true of a number of other fish. Flounder, for instance, which is to seafood what pork is to meat, is just going into oceanic mass production. This will no doubt lead to the genetic development of new and different fish, just as the domestication of sheep, cows, and chickens led to the development of new breeds among them.

But probably a dozen or so technologies are at the stage where biotechnology was twenty-five years ago—that is, ready to emerge.

There is also a *service* waiting to be born: insurance against the risks of foreign-exchange exposure. Now that every business is part of the global economy, such insurance is as badly needed as was insurance against physical risks (fire, flood) in the early stages of the Industrial Revolution, when traditional insurance emerged. All the knowledge needed for foreign-exchange insurance is available; only the institution itself is still lacking.

The next two or three decades are likely to see even greater technological change than has occurred in the decades since the emergence of the computer, and also even greater change in industry structures, in the economic landscape, and probably in the social landscape as well.

The Gentleman Versus the Technologist

The new industries that emerged after the railroad owed little technologically to the steam engine or to the Industrial Revolution in general. They were not its "children after the flesh"—but they were its "children after the spirit." They were possible only because of the mind-set that the Industrial Revolution had created and the skills it had developed. This was a mind-set that accepted— indeed, eagerly welcomed—invention and innovation. It was a mind-set that accepted, and eagerly welcomed, new products and new services.

It also created the social values that made possible the new industries. Above all, it created the "technologist." Social and financial success long eluded the first major American technologist, Eli Whitney, whose cotton gin, in 1793, was as central to the triumph of the Industrial Revolution as was the steam engine. But a generation later the technologist—still self-taught—had become the American folk hero and was both socially accepted and financially rewarded. Samuel Morse, the inventor of the telegraph, may have been the first example; Thomas Edison became the most prominent. In Europe the "businessman" long remained a social inferior, but the university-trained engineer had by 1830 or 1840 become a respected "professional."

By the 1850s England was losing its predominance and beginning to be overtaken as an industrial economy, first by the United States and then by Germany. It is generally accepted that neither economics nor technology was the major reason. The main cause was social. Economically, and especially financially, England remained the great power until the First World War. Technologically it held its own throughout the nineteenth century. Synthetic dyestuffs, the first products of the modern chemical industry, were invented in England, and so was the steam turbine. But England did not accept the technologist socially. He never became a "gentleman." The English built first-rate engineering schools in India but almost none at home. No other country so honored the "scientist"—and, indeed, Britain retained leadership in physics throughout the nineteenth century, from James Clerk Maxwell and Michael Faraday all the way to Ernest Rutherford. But the technologist remained a "tradesman." (Dickens, for instance, showed open contempt for the upstart ironmaster in his 1853 novel *Bleak House*.)

Nor did England develop the venture capitalist, who has the means and the mentality to finance the unexpected and unproved. A French invention, first portrayed in Balzac's monumental *La Comédie humaine*, in the 1840s, the venture capitalist was institutionalized in the United States by J. P. Morgan and, simultaneously, in Germany and Japan by the universal bank. But England, although it invented and developed the commercial bank to finance trade, had no institution to finance industry until two German refugees, S. G. Warburg and Henry Grunfeld, started an entrepreneurial bank in London, just before the Second World War.

Bribing the Knowledge Worker

What might be needed to prevent the United States from becoming the England of the twenty-first century? I am convinced that a drastic change in the social mind-set is required—just as leadership in the industrial economy after the railroad required the drastic change from "tradesman" to "technologist" or "engineer."

What we call the Information Revolution is actually a Knowledge Revolution. What has made it possible to routinize processes is not machinery; the computer is only the trigger. Software is the reorganization of traditional work, based on centuries of experience, through the application of knowledge and especially of systematic, logical analysis. The key is not electronics; it is cognitive science. This means that the key to maintaining leadership in the economy and the technology that are about to emerge is likely to be the social position of knowledge professionals and social acceptance of their values. For them to remain traditional "employees" and be treated as such would be tantamount to England's treating its technologists as tradesmen—and likely to have similar consequences.

Today, however, we are trying to straddle the fence—to maintain the traditional mind-set, in which capital is the key resource and the financier is the boss, while bribing knowledge workers to be content to remain employees by giving them bonuses and stock options. But this, if it can work at all, can work only as long as the emerging industries enjoy a stock-market boom, as the Internet companies have been doing. The next major industries are likely to behave far more like traditional industries—that is, to grow slowly, painfully, laboriously.

The early industries of the Industrial Revolution—cotton textiles, iron, the railroads—were boom industries that created millionaires overnight, like Balzac's venture bankers and like Dickens's ironmaster, who in a few years grew from a lowly domestic servant into a "captain of industry." The industries that emerged after 1830 also created millionaires. But they took twenty years to do so, and it was twenty years of hard work, of struggle, of disappointments and failures, of thrift. This is likely to be true of the industries that will emerge from now on. It is already true of biotechnology.

Bribing the knowledge workers on whom these industries depend will therefore simply not work. The key knowledge workers in these businesses will surely continue to expect to share financially in the fruits of their labor. But the financial fruits are likely to take much longer to ripen, if they ripen at all. And then, probably within ten years or so, running a business with (short-term) "shareholder value" as its first—if not its only—goal and justification will have become counterproductive. Increasingly, performance in these new knowledge-based industries will come to depend on running the institution so as to attract, hold, and motivate knowledge workers. When this can no longer be done by satisfying knowledge workers' greed, as we are now trying to do, it will have to be done by satisfying their values, and by giving them social recognition and social power. It will have to be done by turning them from subordinates into fellow executives, and from employees, however well paid, into partners.

POSTSCRIPT

Will Technology Change Social Interaction?

This type of debate results from a long list of research on the impact of social change due to technology. Authors like Lewis Mumford, Harold Innis, Marshall McLuhan, Neil Postman, Joel Meyerowitz, and Jeremy Rifkin, as well as many others have written about the relationship between technological change and everyday experience. We often do not take much time to think about the consequences of the new piece of technology that just became available or the possibility that it might not work without a battery—or a place to recharge it!

We also tend to feel that technological change is inherently good, that it is a product of scientific achievements that will better society; but while this initial desire to want to consume may actually fade in time, is a better question to consider the social impact of changing behavior due to technology? How available is the technology? Is it only available to the rich or to people in certain countries? How might it change and evolve over the years?

The type of technological change brought about by computers and systems like IM shows us that there are consequences for changing practices. But as Drucker reminds us, the consequences may take years to appear, and in the process, can change the way we think of values, laws, and institutions. Take, for example, the issue of privacy. How private are instant messages when they can be stored in files, forwarded elsewhere, or sent to the wrong recipient? While the system promises some control over the message, the end result may be that there are changing expectations, attitudes, and beliefs about the nature of messaging.

Two suggestions for additional readings are Sheldon Charrett's *Identity, Privacy, and Personal Freedom: Big Brother vs. the New Resistence* (Paladin Press, 1999) and Kristina Bergesson's *Into the Buzzsaw: Leading Journalists Expose the Myth of a Free Press* (Prometheus, 2002). Both of these books take extreme measures to make their points, but they are insightful examinations of many examples of how our privacy is sacrificed in the name of different policies and practices. One of the best books to date on how the Internet is changing our way of doing things is *Culture of the Internet*, edited by Sara Kiesler (Lawrence Erlbaum Associates, 1997), which is still as relevant today as the day it was published.

Contributors to This Volume

EDITORS

ALISON ALEXANDER is professor and head of the Department of Telecommunications in the Grady College of Journalism and Mass Communication at the University of Georgia. Prior to becoming department head, she was a faculty member for 11 years at the University of Massachusetts. She received her Ph.D. from Ohio State University, her M.A. from the University of Kentucky, and her B.A. from Marshall University. She was editor of *The Journal of Broadcasting & Electronic Media* from 1989–1991. She is past president of both the Association for Communication Administration and the Eastern Communication Association. She has served on the board of directors of the Broadcast Education Association. Dr. Alexander's research examines audiences and media content, with a focus on media and the family. She is the author of over 40 book chapters, reviews, and journal articles. She is coeditor of *Media Economics: Theory and Practice*, 2d ed. (Lawrence Erlbaum, 1997) and *How to Publish Your Communication Research* (Sage Publications, 2001).

JARICE HANSON is dean of the School of Communication at Quinnipiac University in Hamden, Connecticut. She received a B.A. in speech and performing arts and a B.A. in English at Northeastern Illinois University in 1976, and she received an M.A. and a Ph.D. from the Department of Radio-Television-Film at Northwestern University in 1977 and 1979, respectively. She is the author of *Connections: Technologies of Communication* (HarperCollins, 1994) and coauthor, with Dr. Uma Narula, of *New Communication Technologies in Developing Countries* (Lawrence Erlbaum, 1990). Her research focuses on technology, policy, and media images.

STAFF

Theodore Knight   List Manager
David Brackley   Senior Developmental Editor
Juliana Gribbins   Developmental Editor
Rose Gleich   Administrative Assistant
Brenda S. Filley   Director of Production/Design
Juliana Arbo   Typesetting Supervisor
Diane Barker   Proofreader
Richard Tietjen   Publishing Systems Manager
Larry Killian   Copier Coordinator

AUTHORS

THE AMERICAN CIVIL LIBERTIES UNION (ACLU) is an advocacy organization dedicated to the preservation of individual rights as outlined in the Bill of Rights. It is involved in litigating, legislating, and educating the public on a broad array of issues affecting individual freedom in the United States.

GEORGE J. ANNAS is the Edward R. Utley Professor of Law and Medicine at Boston University's Schools of Medicine and Public Health in Boston, Massachusetts. He is also director of Boston University's Law, Medicine, and Ethics Program and chair of the Department of Health Law. His publications include *Judging Medicine* (Humana Press, 1988) and *Standard of Care: The Law of American Bioethics* (Oxford University Press, 1993).

KEN AULETTA is a media critic who often writes for *The New Yorker*. Auletta has authored many books related to media, the most recent of which is *The Highwaymen: Warriors of the Information Superhighway* (Random House, 1977).

BEN H. BAGDIKIAN is a media critic, former newspaperman, and former dean of the Graduate School of Journalism at the University of California, Berkeley. He played a role in obtaining and publishing portions of the Pentagon Papers.

RUSS BAKER is a freelance writer based in New York City who often writes on issues of media and press policy.

J. M. BALKIN is Knight Professor of Constitutional Law and the First Amendment at Yale Law School. He is founder and director of Yale's Information Society Project, a center devoted to the study of law and new technology. He is the author of *Cultural Software: A Theory of Ideology* (Yale University Press, 1998).

MICHAEL A. BANKS is the author of 40 books, including *The Internet Unplugged: Utilities and Techniques for Internet Productivity... Online and Off* (Information Today, 1997) and many magazine articles for the general and computer press. He writes about Internet criminals and privacy threats and how to protect against them.

DONALD BOGLE is an author and professor at the University of Pennsylvania and at New York University. The author of *Toms, Coons, Mulattoes, Mammies, and Bucks: An Interpretive History of Blacks in American Films* (Continuum International Publishing Group, 2001), Bogle is also the author of numerous other books on blacks and the media.

SAM BROWNBACK (R-Kansas) is active in a number of legislative areas, including music violence and its impact.

JOHN E. CALFEE is a resident scholar at the American Enterprise Institute in Washington, D.C. He is a former Federal Trade Commission economist, and he is the author of *Fear of Persuasion: A New Perspective on Advertising and Regulation* (Agora, 1997).

CHUCK CLARK is government editor of the *Charlotte Observer*. He co-chaired the newspaper partners in "Your Voice, Your Vote" in North Carolina in 1996.

ROGER COTTERRELL is professor of legal theory at the University of London. He is the author of *The Sociology of Law* (LEXIS Publishing, 1992) and *Law's Community* (Oxford University Press, 1997).

MICHELLE COTTLE is a staff editor for *The Washington Monthly*, for which she occasionally writes key features.

MICHAEL CURTIN is a professor of communication arts at the University of Wisconsin–Madison. He writes about the intersections of the media industries and popular culture.

JOSEPH R. DiFRANZA is an M.D. in the Department of Family Practice at the University of Massachusetts Medical School in Fitchburg, Massachusetts. He and his colleagues have written several articles on the effects of tobacco advertising on children.

PETER F. DRUCKER is a professor at the Claremont Graduate School who has authored over 30 books on management and social change. His most recent book is *Management Challenges for the 21st Century* (HarperInformation, 1999).

JIB FOWLES is professor of communication at the University of Houston–Clear Lake. His previous books include *Why Viewers Watch* (Sage Publications, 1992) and *Advertising and Popular Culture* (Sage Publications, 1996). His articles have also appeared in many popular magazines.

SIMSON GARFINKEL is a columnist for the *Boston Globe* and fellow at the Berkman Center for Internet and Society at Harvard Law School. He is author of *Database Nation: The Death of Privacy in the 21st Century* (O'Reilly & Associates, 2000).

MICHAEL GARTNER, former president of NBC News, is editor of the *Ames Daily Tribune*, a daily newspaper near Des Moines, Iowa. His 36-year-long career in print journalism includes 14 years with the *Wall Street Journal*. He received a J.D. degree from New York University and is a member of the bar associations in New York and Iowa.

JAMES W. GENTRY is a professor in the Department of Marketing, College of Business Administration, at the University of Nebraska–Lincoln. He received his Ph.D. from Indiana University.

TODD GITLIN is a professor of journalism and sociology at Columbia University. He is the author of numerous books, including the recent *Media Unlimited: How the Torrent of Images and Sounds Overwhelms Our Lives* (Metropolitan Books, 2001). His commentaries on media and politics appear in the national press and on National Public Radio.

BERNARD GOLDBERG was a CBS newsman for 30 years during which he won seven Emmy Awards. He now reports on HBO's *Real Sports* and writes for the *New York Times* and the *Wall Street Journal*.

MATT GOLDBERG is a regular contributor to *Yahoo! Internet Life*.

MARJORIE HEINS is the former director and staff counsel to the American Civil Liberties Union Arts Censorship Project. She is the author of *Sex, Sins, and Blasphemy: A Guide to American Censorship*, 2d ed. (New Press, 1998) and *Not in Front of the Children: "Indecency" in History, Politics, and Law* (Hill and Wang, 2001).

PAUL M. HIRSCH is a professor at the Kellogg School of Management at Northwestern University. He is the author of many articles on management practices and mass media organizations. His research interests include organization theory and media industries.

WILLIAM E. JACKSON, JR. was a candidate for U.S. House in the Ninth Congressional District of North Carolina in 1996. He was chief legislative assistant to the Senate Democratic Whip and director of President Carter's General Advisory Committees on Arms Control. Jackson is a professor of political science at Davidson College.

BRENDAN I. KOERNER occasionally writes for the *Washington Monthly*. He is a Markle Fellow at the New America Foundation.

S. ROBERT LICHTER is president of the Center for Media and Public Affairs in Washington, D.C., and editor of the online magazine *Newswatch*. His books include *The Media Elite* (Hastings House, 1990) and *Good Intentions Make Bad News: Why Americans Hate Campaign Journalism* (Rowman & Littlefield, 1996).

JOSEPH LIEBERMAN, is a senator (D) from Connecticut and a vice-presidential candidate in 2000.

MARY C. MARTIN is an assistant professor in the Department of Marketing, Belk College of Business Administration, at the University of North Carolina at Charlotte. She received her Ph.D. from the University of Nebraska–Lincoln.

WILLIAM G. MAYER is assistant professor of political science at Northeastern University and was a fellow of the Harvard Center for Ethics and the Profession in 1995–1996. His most recent book is *In Pursuit of the White House 2000: How We Choose Our Presidential Nominees* (Seven Bridges Press, 2000).

ROBERT W. McCHESNEY is a professor at the University of Illinois at Urbana-Champaign, and has authored *Rich Media, Poor Democracy: Communication Politics in Dubious Times* (The New Press, 2000).

JOHN McWHORTER teaches linguistics at the University of California at Berkeley and is the author of *Losing the Race: Self-Sabotage in Black America* (Free Press, 2001).

HORACE NEWCOMB is director of the Peabody Awards and Lambdin Kay Professor at the Grady College of the University of Georgia. He is the editor of *Museum of Broadcast Communications Encyclopedia of Television* (Fitzroy Dearborn Publishers, 1997).

JOHN NICHOLS is a Washington correspondent for *The Nation* and has authored *Jews for Buchanan: Did You Hear the One About the Theft of the American Presidency?* (The New Press, 2001).

MICHAEL PARKS is a former editor for the *Los Angeles Times* and now directs the School of Journalism at the University of Southern California.

ADAM L. PENENBERG writes for *Forbes*. He is a journalist who writes on issues of privacy and security.

KATHA POLLITT, a poet and an essayist, is associate editor for *The Nation*. Best known for her book of poetry, *Antarctic Traveller* (Alfred A. Knopf, 1982), she has also written about the legal and moral ramifications of important social practices and decisions.

W. JAMES POTTER is a professor of communication at Florida State University. He has conducted research on media violence and has served as one of the investigators on the National Television Violence Study. Recent books include *Media Literacy* (Sage Publications, 1998) and *An Analysis of Thinking and Research About Qualitative Methods* (Lawrence Erlbaum, 1996).

LARRY J. SABATO is director of the Center for Governmental Studies at the University of Virginia in Charlottesville and author of numerous books, including *Feeding Frenzy: How Attack Journalism Has Transformed American Politics* (The Free Press, 1993).

PAUL SIMON (D-Illinois, retired) is currently director of the Public Policy Institute and faculty member at Southern Illinois University. As senator, he spearheaded the drive to curb television violence.

MARK STENCEL is politics editor for Washingtonpost.com and coauthor, with CNN's Larry King, of *On the Line: The New Road to the White House* (Harcourt Trade Publishers, 1993).

JAMES WOLCOTT regularly contributes to *Vanity Fair* and other publications dealing with issues of the media and media content.

Index